Transfiguring Capitalism

Transfiguring Capitalism

An Enquiry into Religion and Global Change

John Atherton

scm press

© John Atherton 2008

British Library Cataloguing in Publication data

A catalogue record for this book is available
from the British Library

978 0 334 02831 4

First published in 2008 by SCM Press
13–17 Long Lane,
London EC1A 9PN

www.scm-canterburypress.co.uk

SCM Press is a division of
SCM-Canterbury Press Ltd

Typeset by Regent Typesetting, London

Printed in the UK by CPI William Clowes Beccles NR34 7TL

Contents

To the Faculty of Theology,
University of Uppsala, Sweden
and the William Temple Foundation, Manchester

Acknowledgements

The inspiration for, and development of, this hypothesis has emerged from a number of sources, institutional and personal. I will illustrate them in a little more detail than normal to record how such research develops. It reveals a profoundly collaborative character which very tangibly informs both process and results. For example, my work with the Universities of Manchester and Uppsala in the field of Christian social ethics has focused increasingly on religion and political economy in terms of teaching and research. Manchester classes and research supervision in Christian social ethics have provided a constant arena for testing ideas and findings. Manchester's conference on *Re-moralising Britain* in May 2007, allowed me to develop ideas on happiness and Gordon Brown's economic policies. In Sweden, my Uppsala lecture commemorating the award of Doctor of Sacred Theology Honoris Causae in January 2004 first explored the contemporary link between religion and capitalism. My contact with Professor Grenholm's long and distinguished research involvement in ethics and economics has continued to provide a fruitful source of inspiration. That lecture was significantly expanded in the Edinburgh University John Baillie Memorial Lecture also celebrating the twentieth anniversary of the Centre for Theology and Public Issues in Autumn 2004. The Industrial Christian Fellowship's Annual Lecture in Autumn 2006 provided an opportunity to link this religion and capitalism material to the happiness hypothesis. To all these institutions, I am most grateful for their invitations and kindness.

It is difficult to describe my links to the William Temple Foundation as institutional. It has been a foundational resource for and influence on my practice and theory since 1974, beginning as research officer and director until 1984, and continuing as Company Secretary and Council member to the present. It has inspired my involvement in poverty, then the focusing on political economy and finally the interest in religious capital and well-being. This current project and book bear such marks very precisely.

Woven into these institutions is the contribution of people and networks to my work. Many of my key friendships are part and parcel of institutional life. These include the William Temple Foundation and Chris Baker and John Reader, the University of Manchester and Elaine Graham (succeeding Ronald Preston), and the links this provides to my membership of the University's Research Institute for Religion and Civil Society – here I particularly count Stephen Lowe as friend and colleague, including in his new post as Bishop for Urban Life and Faith, and new chair of the William Temple Foundation; in Uppsala, Professor Carl-Henric Grenholm and Dr Normunds Kamergrauzis, and Professor Will Storrar, then in Edinburgh, have all provided important stimuli. But the centrality of relationships to such a project also cascades out to projects which I have promoted not least because of their contribution to this research. For example, I was centrally involved with an interfaith group in Manchester of Christians and Muslims, which worked patiently and carefully for two years, resulting in the publication *Faiths and Finance: A Place for Faith-Based Economics* (November 2006). The friendships formed with Zahid Hussain and Ajmal Ramzan taught me much about the riches of Islam. Here I need to mention, too, the important contribution of my friend Ian Steedman, now retired Research Professor in Economics at Manchester Metropolitan University. He has been a constant inspiration and necessary check on my wanderings into the field of economics. Dr Wilf Wilde has played a similar role and friendship, but from the quite different perspective of neo-Marxist economics. Another research project powerfully feeding into my work was the two-year process (2005–2007) that produced the book *Through the Eye of a Needle: Theological Conversations on Political Economy* (2007). This arose out of the British and Irish ecumenical movement (CTBI), and the partnership between the William Temple Foundation and the Church of England's Mission and Public Affairs Council. It was a very creative journey with 11 other scholars from different disciplines, and particularly with my joint editor, Hannah Skinner, then William Temple Research Officer in Economic Affairs. My joint editorship, with Dr Peter Sedgwick, of *Crucible*, a journal in Christian social ethics, has also been particularly fruitful in feeding quite directly into my work.

All these friendships and collaborations, and so much more, have sustained me and generated new thinking and practice. Finally, my thanks yet again to Joanne Hooper, a treasure beyond compare, who has typed this and other books. The support she provides, through Manchester Cathedral, my home since 1984, has been irreplaceable. As for my then editor, Barbara Laing, she both supported the project and patiently agreed to defer it for a year so I could complete other complementary research work. I am most grateful for that commitment.

John Atherton

6 August 2007, Feast of the Transfiguration

Introduction

The Nature of an Enquiry into Religious and Global Change

The Thesis

This book tests out a hypothesis – that religion has a necessary if not essential place in our world, historically, contemporarily and in the future, in terms of contributing to the necessary maintenance and transformation of our world. If our concern is promoting human well-being in an environmentally sustainable way, and there are increasing pressures from a variety of sources that this should be so, then it is likely that profound changes in human behaviour and social arrangements will be required.

Of course, this is not to argue that such transformations can be achieved only by religion, or even more so by only one religion. It can only be by involving a variety of contributions from faiths, governments and civil societies. Yet religion is a quite necessary part of that conglomerate even if it is not sufficient.

The thesis will therefore recognize the plural character of that process, including its religious dimensions. As an enquiry into the nature of that religious contribution, which it will be argued offers a paradigm for engaging that process of transformation, it also learns from other experiences and disciplines. Equally, of course, they have much to learn from religion.

As a research project, it did not begin with such a hypothesis. It sought rather to develop the historic debate in British Christian social ethics over the changing nature of the relationship between religion and capitalism into a new stage, religion and the transcendence of capitalism. That remains integral to the present argument but there have been subtle and yet also decisive changes in terms of what has now become an enquiry into religion and global change. In other words, I did not prejudge the outcomes. I say subtle changes, because capitalism and religion are still central to the new enquiry. Yet that concern has been recast in the language, practices and theories of human well-being, including as happiness. It is still powerfully addressing capitals, whether economic or social, but now also engaging religious capital, as a more empirically accurate account of the contemporary scene and as offering a more feasible way of overhauling the present defective system. In that, it represents a decisive change from the original hypothesis, even though I conclude by bringing the argument back to that relationship between capitalism and religion. As the transfiguring of capitalism, it therefore represents continuity with the original hypothesis, but reformulated in a very different way. And that makes all the difference between a rather predictable reworking of an old theme, and a new reformulation using new languages, theories and practices.

Getting Lost on St Cuthbert's Way

As I reflected on how the argument of this book has changed it seemed to me that story-telling would add a rich dimension to the account.

In the summer of 2003, I walked with my dear friend Fred Taylor, now sadly departed and with God, what was for us the final section of the St Cuthbert's Way in the Scottish–English borders. In total, it links various parts of St Cuthbert's life in the seventh century, from Melrose where he began his monastic life to Lindisfarne or Holy Island where he spent his most formative years. Connected with the Way is the account of the monks of Lindisfarne carrying his body around Northern England for over a generation to escape the depredations of the Vikings at the end of the eighth and into the ninth centuries. The first stage of that journey was reputedly from Lindisfarne to Wooler, a small market town in the north of Northumberland. Fred and I walked that route in reverse, leaving Wooler, climbing up to a ridge to St Cuthbert's Cave where the monks rested with their holy burden. From there we passed over the ridge and went almost straight into a great forest. We had a clear picture and sign of our route and destination, Holy Island, but we had not allowed for recently planted conifers, densely packed together on highly uneven ground. In other words, we were soon hopelessly lost and increasingly desperate. After struggling for some time, Fred noticed a small rise with a deciduous tree on it. When we eventually reached it, we found a track alongside it, and with the aid of our Ordnance Survey map, we found our way out of the forest. In other words, we started off confidently with a clear picture of our route, but when we actually did it, it turned out to be very different in very important respects.

Expanding the Thesis

So it was with this research. It began with a clear objective, but once the research was under way, it encountered obstacles which changed the character of the research even though the objective remained very similar. For example, capitalism alone came to provide an inadequate description of the global context, influenced as it is by political structures and globalization processes. Along with the infusion into that context of a heady mixture of globally furious religions and domestic religious capital, that contemporary context was transformed into realities quite inadequately summarized by the traditional religion and capitalism debate.

As I moved deeper into this agenda, just as we had penetrated deeper into the Northumbrian forest, the predicted boundaries were not as predicted, and at first confusing. But then I discovered what became a way forward in the research through encountering a whole series of literatures from different disciplines clustering around, but cascading from the well-being and happiness agendas. Significantly these interacted strongly with all my other more familiar material relating to economics, economic development, poverty reduction, environment, participation, ethics and theology. In other words the new literatures provided a way of organizing the evidence which was both faithful to it and generated credible ways of transforming it. A feasible and creative route through problems had emerged. By using disciplines and languages different from the traditional relations of capitalism, globalization and religion, yet which were clearly connected to them, it became possible to develop a more fruitful linkage between religion and global change.

What the developing hypothesis has revealed is the discovery and presence of a number of building blocks which I have found to be central to this research task, essentially now shaping the enquiry. These include the commitment to exploring the importance of political economy for human well-being; how this is necessarily extended and enlarged in critical conversation with the literatures associated with well-being and happiness, and which essentially became a catalyst running through arguments of the research: how all this material was the basis for what is my main disciplinary perspective, an exercise in Christian social ethics and its development as interfaith ethics and global ethics. Yet putting all that together is about far more than assembling outputs. It is also profoundly concerned with *process* in terms both of multidisciplinary ways of working and of the way the argument itself is organized.

Let me briefly elaborate these features.

As enquiry

As the research began to evolve, I became clear that it was now best described as an enquiry into the contributions of religion to global change. For what emerged was a complexity of secular and religious realities and their historical and contemporary interactions. What was needed, to try to make sense of this, was a map of the terrain, offering possibilities of ways forward to the destination of well-being for all, and which needed testing out in strong and critical conversation with emerging new research material drawn from a variety of secular and faith experiences.

In other words, I began to develop 'simplified paradigms or maps' which both 'portrays reality and simplifies reality in a way that best serves our purposes'.[1] Inevitably, this is a risky strategy because of the breadth and complexity of the exercise and material. It inevitably involves a degree of speculation, it invariably reveals great gaps and inconsistencies in the author's knowledge, yet the challenge of increasingly global problems from inequalities and security to environment, requires, I believe, no less. In this regard, I have some sympathy and respect for the astonishing and creative work of say Livi-Bacci on demography and Diamond on human history[2] with their ability to make fruitful connections across many disciplines and experiences. With them, I can argue that 'Now and then it is worth making an attempt at reconstruction',[3] in my case, of the relationship between religion and social change.

The concept of an enquiry, is of course, very resonant with Adam Smith's *An Inquiry into the Nature and Causes of the Wealth of Nations* (1776), or *Wealth of Nations* for short. With its careful study of political economy in the mid eighteenth century, in assumed dialogue with his earlier *Theory of Moral Sentiments* (1759),[4] the complex whole provides a study of both engineering (or positive, technical) economics and ethical (or normative) economics.[5] Yet its credibility relates equally to its firm grounding in carefully assembled evidence, reflecting a profound indicative and inductive way of working, rather than the increasingly deductive character of what later became a more restricted economics aspiring to value-free science. It is Smith's mixture of disciplines and experiences, surveyed with a purpose (in his case, to suggest ways for poorer nations to become prosperous for the sake of human equity and liberty), which attracts me to the concept. The task of an enquiry therefore becomes both survey and apologetic, in my case a survey of religion and global change for the sake of human well-being.

Introduction

Political economy

The enquiry is conducted in strong conversation with political economy. By this I mean the wider and original concept of what was later narrowed into economics from the end of the nineteenth century. For example, one of the first early political economists, Sir James Steuart, published his *Inquiry into the Principles of Political Oeconomy* (1767) giving a new name and a method to 'a new technique of examining modern commercial society'.[6] In case you doubt the political character of his work, it is worth noting he was exiled as a Jacobite for his role in the disastrous 1745 rebellion. Political economy therefore addresses 'the functioning of entire socio-economic systems',[7] or the 'interrelationships between political and economic institutions and processes'.[8] This broader understanding of economics has increasingly become the focus of my work in Christian social ethics, not least because of my growing awareness, from the mid 1980s, of its increasing centrality to human well-being in modern urban-industrial societies. It is a recognition whose interest now goes back deep into the earliest stage of modern society and modern Christian social ethics. So, the Revd Richard Whately in 1830, as one of the founders of what Waterman[9] has described as Christian political economy, and close associate of other founding economists like Malthus and Ricardo, declared that: 'Religious truth . . . appears to me to be intimately connected, at this time especially, with (political economy). For it seems to me that before long, political economists, of some sort or other, must govern the world.'[10] And, of course, that prophetic hunch came true. The contextual interactions which play such a prominent part in the first part of this book are powerfully influenced by political economy both as capitalism and as empires, and increasingly informed by, and informing, a globalized context. Again, that influence of political economy was central to my more recent engagement with the well-being literatures because it began with the work of such economists, in their chronological order, as Easterlin, Oswald and Layard,[11] even though it necessarily and rightly quickly developed into much wider conversations with a wealth of other disciplines.

And that continuing and evolving focus as political economy provides a connection with hard social science, which is a useful corrective to the economic illiteracy of many theologians and moralists who too easily depend on the softer social sciences for economic knowledge. Of course, the conversation does flow in both directions, for example as the critical analysis of neoclassical economics which is strongly present in the well-being literatures, and in the work of theological partners.

5

Well-being and happiness

As I moved deeper into this enquiry, I began to come across a whole series of what turned out to be overlapping literatures working with and around the theme of well-being in general, and happiness in particular. An important part of the happiness hypothesis, for example, is that increasing income and material well-being is not commensurate at all with increasing happiness once a modest level of income has been achieved. The literatures which both reflect this hypothesis and engage constructively, and sometimes critically, with it, came from a wide spectrum of disciplines, moving in my case, from economics to economic history, psychology, sociology, epidemiology, philosophy and theology. Gradually, it became clear that these literatures could be regarded as an entry point or archaeological trench into a whole series of contemporary secular complexities which both engage with capitalism, empires and globalization in terms of identifying their strengths and limitations, and also recognize the significant role of ethics and religion in well-being. They therefore act as a catalyst across all three parts of the book, but will be expounded in detail in the second and third parts. They are profoundly multidisciplinary, not least because they deal with a whole series of capitals, from economic and financial through social to religious. They are a means to interpret these realities and have the potential to model feasible alternatives to the current global systems. I shall therefore use this tool to help me to unlock the actual realities and potential for change which the commitment to transfiguring capitalism requires.

Christian social ethics

My craft is best described as Christian social ethics, that is, the interaction between Christian beliefs and traditions of thought and practice, and contemporary social realities for, among other things, their mutual benefit. It is therefore ideally placed to be a central part of any serious religious engagement with contemporary social change and particularly with global problems with their intrinsic ethical dimensions in terms of their analysis and, most importantly, for their solutions. Can you really think of environment and poverty reduction without that perspective? That ethical preference is strongly confirmed by the well-being literatures with their recognition of the importance of ethics and religion in human formation and fulfilment. It powerfully resonates, too, with the resurgence of interest in ethical economics and faith-based initiatives nationally and globally. It's just a pity that the theological academy has never really taken Christian social ethics seriously as a relatively autonomous discipline within that theological faculty. But the times will change that. And this book is a contribution to, among other things, establishing that repositioning of Christian social ethics in relation to both secular and religious worlds.

In terms of some of the key elements of this discipline, there is considerable agreement, in the sources I have used, including Catholic, Protestant and liberationist, and confirmed by the wider literatures of the discipline, that Christian social ethics recognizes a number of key features in its basic constitution. First, *personal agency* as foundational in terms of how to make value decisions in accordance with those moral norms arising from Christian beliefs and traditions. That agency, although pre-eminently personal, is always also understood as foundationally *relational*. In addition, there is much contemporary resurgence of interest in the classic recognition that such moral agency is significantly (although not exclusively, given the influence of other social arrangements and relationships) *formed* as character through participation in traditioning communities, pre-eminently the Church. It is that character which generates and nurtures virtues, reversing the recent emphasis in ethics, including Christian social ethics, on the development of moral understandings through addressing social quandaries. Importantly, this development is influencing both Christian opinion, through the work of MacIntyre and Hauerwas,[12] but *also* the secular well-being literatures (Haidt and Kenny).[13]

A second feature of Christian social ethics is the requirement of a *telos* or goal in life, which invariably connects human purposes to God's purposes. Ethics provides both motivational inspiration and resources for the journey from what happens to be, to what it would be if our essential nature in God were more fully realized. This strongly resonates with the happiness literatures' recognition of the need for a philosophy of life as purpose and goals, and the integral contribution of ethics to that. For the radical feminist theologian Rebecca Peters, that agency and telos relate directly to my well-being literatures since 'From the perspective of Christian ethics, a vision of the good life that does *not* adequately account for the well-being of all God's creation is not morally tenable.'[14] Unlike Peters, in some regards, however, most of my sources recognize that Christian social ethics, in terms of its practical proposals, must be more persuasive than declaratory, particularly building bridges with other faiths and a wide variety of disciplines through constructive conversations. It is not the case, as some argue like Hauerwas, that Christian social ethical insights cannot be shared with others except with those who participate in the faith from which they come.[15] Of course, this in no way impinges on the distinctive integrity of Christian social ethics as strongly tradition-related, including delivering faith-based critiques of and alternatives to mainstream economics and politics. Yet it does recognize that the deep Christian concern for human fulfilment is central to God's purposes. Indeed, in terms of religious practices in the evolutionary history of the human, human concerns pre-date the emergence of the formal religious field.

Third, Christian social ethics, in terms of consistency between theory and output, necessarily generates a *logic of practice* as the embodiment of ethical norms. In contemporary theological literature this is increasingly conceptualized as *praxis* or theory (secular and religious) embedded practice. Christian social ethics is both theory and practice of theorizing and practising. For Christian social ethics that therefore relates profoundly to the Christian engagement with social affairs and arrangements, in my case, in the arena of political economy. Increasingly that has required a central commitment to justice, including as the embodiment of love, in complex social structures, and particularly in relation to the most deprived and marginalized in societies. This means that Christian social ethics is increasingly regarded as a performative discipline,[16] guided, for example, by the biblical injunction 'by their fruits ye shall know them', a key understanding in Reinhold Niebuhr's ethics. Chris Baker has interestingly reformulated this, in relation to contemporary analysis, into 'the best fruits and opportunities for delivering the fruits'.[17] Equally, this praxis and its related assessments reinforces the contribution of Christian social ethics to and as a public theology. For Baker, this is defined as 'the sharing of insights, concerns and good practice in the social and political spaces that remain within postmodern society, for the sake of public (or common) goods'.[18] Perhaps the most useful survey of the variety of ways in which Christianity has so related to society, still remains Richard Niebuhr's classic typological study, *Christ and Culture*,[19] both because it is inclusive of Christian stances against culture as well as various forms of engagement with it. Such a survey will be reinforced throughout this book, in terms, for example, of the place of globally furious religion in part one, a spectrum of faith involvements in society in Part 2, and a reformulated typology for Christian social ethics in Part 3.

Fourth, as this enquiry unfolded, it also became increasingly clear that the right and proper development of denominational Christian social ethics has increasingly fed into the development of ecumenical social ethics through the twentieth century. That corpus of traditions is now beginning to also engage with other faiths. It represents a historic evolution from intra-faith Christian social ethics to interfaith social ethics as essentially an agenda for the early twenty-first century. Importantly, this development does not remove the continuing significance of denominational and ecumenical social ethics. It rather represents an enlargement of that total corpus of ethical knowledge.[20] The stages of this evolution have been usefully linked to major upheavals, the growth of the ecumenical movement to the two World Wars of the twentieth century and the beginning of serious interfaith ethical dialogue to the end of that century and the emergence of the threats of globalization.[21] This connection between ethics and continuing turbulence is also strongly present in the post-modernist work of Derrida – *so* 'it is to the extent that stability is not natural, essential or substantial that politics exists and ethics is possible. Chaos is at once a risk and a chance.'[22]

Both ecumenical and interfaith ethics represent, most powerfully, the contemporary engagement with the Other as Other, as equally an integral part of secular and religious thought and practice. For Levinas, out of a Jewish tradition, this encounter with the Other must occur 'without the attempt to convert or transform'. This does not necessarily lead to a process of syncretizing. In recent work in ecumenical social ethics on social issues, while there is clearly a 'concern for and commitment to the world, and that insists on openness to the other', this does not lead to a redefining of 'ecumenism to include "other religious and cultural traditions beyond the Christian community"'.[23] Yet it clearly also encourages interfaith dialogue, which both respects the integrity of the Other and seeks to engage in fruitful dialogue and practical cooperation.

This is acknowledgement that 'At the global level, there is an increasing recognition that the world's problems are not Christian problems requiring Christian answers, but human problems that must be addressed together by all human beings.'[24] In this connection, the various approaches to developing a shared global ethic or ethics is particularly important, reflecting the continuing struggle to hold together singularity and commonality (or contextual and universal) without collapsing the one into the other.[25] Indeed, it is that concern for human well-being as inclusive of a foundational ethical basis, including religious, as an integral part of that recognition of what we share and what is different, which pervades so much of my literatures. It is particularly well summarized by Elaine Graham when she writes of the human task as building moral as well as material worlds of values, 'worlds which take account of human existence in wider contexts of responsibility and mutuality with one another, with animals, with the environment and other living organisms'.[26] That insight is powerfully confirmed across different faith literatures, and relates centrally to the well-being theme of this enquiry.

It's how you do it, stupid: the importance of process

Infilling the nature of this enquiry in terms of important features is clearly a preliminary necessity for understanding what is to be attempted in this book. Yet what has become increasingly clear is that the way things are done is equally important. For example, the realities of capitalism, empires, globalization and religion are important in their own right. Yet what is also of profound significance is both the connections *and* interactions between them. In turn, their linkages with the well-being literatures, and then with other agendas, is also of high importance and profoundly creative and stimulating.

One of the skills I think I have is the ability to make connections across subjects and disciplines, and then to generate hypotheses which in turn can and should be tested empirically.[27] In his summary of a very useful conference on economics and Christianity, John Pisciotta rightly uses a subtitle, 'Connections and Continued Progress' to illustrate this role of connectivity in Christian social ethics.[28] The nature of these connections can clearly be very complex, including the development from correlative to causal (so important in the link between inequality and ill-health, a key part of well-being studies),[29] but also including feedback processes, particularly evident in Part 1 of this enquiry, for example, in examining the relation between population and economic growth, or as autocatalytic processes as 'the positive feedback cycle, going faster and faster'[30] – say population rise, leading to the demand for more food, to the demand for farming and therefore for more people. The constant tendency to reduce analysis to 'chicken and egg' understandings is therefore highly suspect: 'Posing the question in that either-or form misses the point. Intensified food production and societal complexity stimulate each other by autocatalysis.'[31] Interactive processes are similarly complex, and much influenced by the study of the relations between religious and social change, essentially two-way street relationships, the one influencing the other, as my early study of the changing nature of that relationship from 1750 to 2000 revealed.[32]

What has also interested me in this regard, is the influence of these relationships on how I actually structure this book. Traditionally, it would be divided into three parts, each with two chapters. So the first part on context would contain a secular chapter, and then a religious chapter. Yet as the work began to evolve I became increasingly dissatisfied with this way of working – essentially not because it supported what is essentially inseparable, because clearly religion and the secular are separable, but because in doing so it did not convey the ways that religion and the secular continually interact. For example, religion is inextricably bound up with the development of empires and capitalism. I have therefore decided to try to overcome these problems of separation by dividing the enquiry into three parts, each of which reflects, in different ways, this process. (The use of chapters is, therefore, an editorial device to make each part more accessible.) So Part 1 addresses contextual interactions as a series of contested areas, from capitalism, empires and globalization to globally furious religion and social/religious capital. Each argument is in itself multifaceted, and includes frequent resonances and indeed interaction with the other contested fields of influence or power. Part 2 represents more of a spectrum, a mapping of clusters of different ways in which faiths contribute to social change. These move *from* partnerships between faiths and secular agencies addressing the marginalization of people and environment, *to* more distinctively faith-based contributions. Part 3 is a collection of clusterings of key matters emerging from the interaction within and between Parts 1 and 2, and which inform the co-ordinating concept of transfiguration as the most appropriate way to address global capitalism.

Clearly, such a new way of organizing such a complex of materials, in this case secular and religious, is risky. Yet it seemed a worthwhile venture in terms of experimenting with new ways of interpreting the evolving contemporary context, and engaging it in terms of transfiguring it for the better. That is what an enquiry into religion and contemporary global change is concerned with. And, given its emerging nature, it seemed important to reflect that in both the outputs of the enquiry and in the ways they are formulated.

Part I

Competing Perspectives:
A Global Context of Interacting Fields

Introduction

In advanced economies, the development of a more consumption-oriented society has reflected the growing importance of choice between different and often competing options. When linked to the development of post-modernity that difference and plurality become relativized, with no choice being dominant or recognized as a universal grand narrative. Locating such processes in an increasingly globalized context, particularly when it is informed by technologies generating them, then the realities of difference become even more accessible and authenticated, reaching into many areas of thought and practice. We have already seen how that concept of difference, manifested in a respect for Other, has influenced Christian social ethics. In other words, we inhabit an increasingly multi-world, characterized by the growing significance (for this and other enquiries) of the multi-disciplinary, the multidimensional, the multicausal, the multilayered and so on.

I have become more and more aware of plurality and difference every time I sit in my lounge and look at two sets of pictures on my walls. The first set are paintings of Pendle Hill, which dominates north-east Lancashire. It's a place of important histories and stories, from the Pendle Witches, cruelly done to death in the name of religion in the early seventeenth century, the seminal memory for the Quakers of their founder George Fox climbing the Hill's summit and having a greater vision of the heavenly host, to the growth of the industrial revolution and urban living in the city and towns of North East Lancashire, now home to large immigrant populations, sign of the impact on British society of world faiths like Islam, and symbol of global flows par excellence. It is that multidimensional history, it is that profound plurality, which is so tangibly confirmed and exhibited by the four pictures on my wall representing very different perspectives on the same Pendle Hill across very different seasons.

The second set of pictures are linocuts from the Scottish borders, again of hills, this time the three Eildons near Melrose. Again, they tell of a rich history from the site of early British settlements on one summit, and a Roman signalling post on another with a large fort at the bottom, both symbols of the conflicts of a Roman Empire way beyond Hadrian's Wall. It was from their peaks in around 1800 that Sir Walter Scott gained some inspiration for his formative contribution to the romantic movement and Scottish identity. That is a reminder that the dominant position of the Enlightenment, including Adam Smith, in our perceptions of Scotland, particularly when reinforced by inabilities to get beyond Edinburgh as the Athens of the North, has to be complemented by other traditions. I have a print of an astonishing meeting between Rabbie Burns, Scottish poet of the common life, and Adam Smith, epitome of the rationality of the new political economy, with the very young Walter Scott lecturing a galaxy of stars on old Scottish poetry. But it's the technique of the linocuts that interests me most. For I have a picture of the Eildon Hills that brings together, under one glass, the three stages as prints, illustrating how the fourth and final picture was constructed. It is a vivid demonstration of three layers of single basic colours brought together in a final picture of a multilayered complexity.

It is not difficult to actually see how both sets of pictures embody the multinatured character of the contemporary context. As long as we remember how each set also has an interlinking coherence as well. But that's why this is an enquiry engaging with both singularity including as differences and commonality as certain coherencies.

That journey through pictures as a movement from a single subject to a variety of perspectives reflects the way this enquiry's understanding of context emerged. For I began with a view of that context as a coherent whole whether capitalism, globalization or empire. Indeed Hardt and Negri linked these realities into one coherent complex whole, as the empire of global capitalism.[1] This focus on one co-ordinating whole is very persuasively argued, particularly in the work of more radical or neo-Marxist scholars, and particularly from fields like sociology, geography and town planning. Their work on flows, spaces, capitalism, globalization and empires, when linked to French post-modernist philosophers, is both imaginative and persuasive. Their influence certainly impacted on my *Marginalization* (2003).[2] Yet as I began to read for this research, I gradually became aware of other perspectives, particularly from the harder social sciences, including economics, neuroscience and psychology. That core of disciplines, when joined to the growth of understandings of history as a hard social science when interacting with other disciplines like evolutionary biology and physiology, began to reveal a series of arenas which certainly interacted but equally certainly could not be collapsed into one or the other whether capitalism or globalization (each regularly used in more radical literature as a synonym for the other). What emerged was rather a series of arenas of influence, or relatively autonomous *fields* as networks and structures of relationships, including as the distribution of power. These fields focused particularly and initially on capitalism and globalization, but also on a political arena which I have titled empires. Each has a firm identity, and, interestingly, each attracted in my work roughly the same amount of research notes. As important, there were clear and substantial interactions between them. To clarify them, I have been much assisted by the concept of fields, as used by Bourdieu,[3] who usefully as a sociologist-philosopher engages in conversation with economics. Importantly it is a tool used, in my literatures, by political scientists and theologians because it respects the relative autonomy of fields of influence and power, and the relations between them and within them, including as the relationship of power and dominance. An emerging likely modification of this interpretation relates to the interactions between the fields, which can themselves generate hybrid forms, which in turn could evolve as a new field. What the concept of fields also suggests, and indeed requires, is equal recognition of the status and nature of religion as an equal relatively autonomous field, relating to the other fields in a process of interaction.[4] Bourdieu's work is creatively employed by the theologian Tanner in her conversation with economics.[5] Its use by political scientists like Bobbitt,[6] for example, confirms my focus on the political field as empires, as does the field of social capital.

Initially, I focused on the three fields (in order of attention), of empires (Chapter 1), capitalism (Chapter 2) and globalization (Chapter 3). I begin with empires for two reasons, both of which figure prominently in the literatures. First, because the role of the state, governance, politics and military strategies has a formative influence on economic development, including the market economy or capitalism, on poverty reduction and on the promotion of well-being. Second, empires are profoundly historical events and processes.[7] This emphasis on particular histories and contexts has regularly been overtaken by more universalist theorizing and grand narratives, which often dominate the discourses of proponents and opponents of capitalism and globalization. What the literatures have revealed is a remarkable convergence across protagonists of a strong emphasis on historical contexts as key dimensions of empires, capitalism and globalization. Although those concentrate on the fifteenth century to the present, three analysts (a demographer, an economist and a historian-physiologist) locate their studies in much longer time frames, including one beginning 13,000 years ago.[8] As important, in this dimension, is the recurring emphasis on the post-1945 era for all fields from empire and capitalism, through religion as globally furious, to social capital. As a period of immense and continuing change, the conceptualizing of it as the Great Disruption in social and religious capital reminds us of the turbulent processes of history (Chapters 4 and 5).[9] It is a reminder, too, that this contextual basis of the enquiry is also profoundly focused on religion. Not because this is a study of the contribution of religion to global change but because the predominantly secular literatures used in this research require its recognition. So, like the sociologist Bourdieu (reinforced by the theologian Tanner), we are now required to recognize religion as a discrete and relatively autonomous field of power and relationships alongside more secular fields (Chapter 4). For religion is not simply a recurring and important dimension of the multidimensional fields of empire, capitalism and globalization. This reality will be identified in each of these fields. It is also of profound importance in its own right in terms of the criteria for identifying a discrete field, and in terms of history and contemporary experience. So besides playing a key role in the major studies of civilizations, for example in Braudel and Huntington's work,[10] its relative autonomy is substantiated by a series of endogenous relationships. For example, there is considerable agreement that the centre of gravity in Christianity is likely to be moving from the North to the South, from Europe to Africa. More interestingly, this also represents the resurgence of the phenomenon known as furious religion,[11] which stretches across major faiths, including Islam. Yet although the concentration of religious energy has moved Southwards, there may well be an equally interesting reformulation of religion occurring in the West, particularly in Western Europe. This latter development is of some interest for this enquiry as a manifestation of faith-based endeavours. That significance is reinforced by the growing interest in social capital which I will recognize as a relatively autonomous field of influence (Chapter 5). Very clearly and substantially linked to this is the growing interest in religions and spiritual capital.[12] I will argue that this is a subset of religion more than it is of social capital, and I will develop it as *faithful capital*.

What I have therefore attempted is to recognize religion as a field of influence in it own right, with clear strong links to social capital but distinct from it. The development of faithful capital only reinforces that connection of overlapping fields. This is of twofold significance. First it links directly to the other fields, particularly globalization and capitalism, as an extension of the multidimensional nature of global capitalism in its various forms (for example, as human, natural, institutional and social, and now including faithful). Second, it constitutes a substantial and formative connection to the well-being literatures most of which I have located in Parts 2 and 3.

Running through all the conversations over these fields is the issue of social constructs and their role in the development of Christian social ethics in this enquiry. By this is meant the argument, for example, that modern economics and market economies are a natural construct.[13] Both secular and theological opinion reject this postulate. That is, there is a recurring concern in much of the literature to recognize these determinative realities as *social* constructs as both empirically accurate realities and as allowing for human interventions to change social structures for the better.[14] It becomes a clear rebuttal of the claim that there is no alternative to market economics and economies, to empires or globalization. However, as I reflect on these literatures and arguments I have become increasingly aware that social constructs cannot be accounted for by simply human endeavours however socially organized they are. Studies of institutional capital, for example, equally highlight the *systemic* character of social processes. This is of profound importance when reflecting on the evolution of capitalism, for example, over a 500-year history. That overall systemic persistence as structures, processes, habits and cultures (including religion) is not readily susceptible to regular radical change by the ideologies, organizations and rhetoric of counter movements, whether political, economic or religious. Again, the well-being literatures will illuminate the understanding of structures from other perspectives. They will, for example, confirm that we are increasingly aware that there is a tension between what is significantly given to us in terms of human nature and systemic institutional realities, but also as environmental realities which are more open to influence in relation to human norms and goals.[15] That re-acknowledgement of nature as well as nurture represents an important challenge to, and certainly major qualification of, any overriding commitments to plurality, difference and post-modernity. Such are the various consequences for the contextualizing of this enquiry.

I

Empires

The Necessity and Necessary Limits of Politics:
The Politics of Political Economy

Wherever I probed in this broad enquiry, I continually came across the concept of paradox way beyond its prominent place in the well-being literatures, epitomized by the paradox of prosperity (that is, increasing prosperity is not associated with an increasing sense of contentment).[16] In this part of the enquiry, it emerges as the paradox of politics in the contemporary era, as the growing discontent with politics in the West in juxtaposition with the growing and wider recognition of the importance of politics, governance and state for strong economies. The latter has a long history, of course, featuring prominently in Adam Smith's work in the late eighteenth century. He was very clear about the important role of government in providing resources which the market could not provide and yet without which it could not prosper.[17] These non-market goods included government's role in promoting peace and security, laws and justice systems, including the protection of property and contracts, efficient tax systems and therefore competent bureaucracies, and those public goods like education. Importantly these limits of the market, which politics and government supply, also require the contribution of values and norms, like trust, truth-telling and reciprocity, and the associations which nurture them, like family and community – which leads later to the role of social capital, and religious capital, in providing them.

What the enquiry also generated, and on which this chapter will concentrate, is a recognition of the importance of the ways in which politics and governance is organized. Here the nature and power of empires represented the most 'extreme' or 'hard' version, and attracted significant attention in the literatures, and across a wide spectrum of opinion from left to right. The crucial role played by economic strength or weakness in the rise and fall of empires was universally acknowledged, but always interacting with other factors, particularly the military-strategic, and the form of the state. The emerging typologies in these literatures also have strong connections with those in the following capitalist chapter of the enquiry, and are illustrated with reference to the British Empire, but particularly the current debates over the nature and role of the USA as empire. However, I also became aware that the political dominance of empires was a necessary but not sufficient explanation of the central role of politics in the contemporary context. Other alternative centres of explanation are also therefore acknowledged, including civilizations, the long-term historical survey of Diamond, liberal democracy, and oppositions or countermovements to empire. And, running through all these arguments is a constant reminder of the contribution of religion, for good and bad, and particularly in the account of civilizations.

Empires: A Long Story which Has Not Ended?

The interaction of politics and economics crystallizes in the production of empires. It is not an account focused on the contemporary American version, which in some important respects lacks certain elements of an effective empire. The Americans have rarely conquered territories and remained there, unlike the British. Empires have existed for most of recorded history, but this enquiry concentrates on their history since the fifteenth–sixteenth centuries, and on the emergence of European empires and their American successor. For the economic historian Landes, empires represent 'the dominion of one country over others' in terms of military, economic and political power.[18] For the neo-Marxist geographer David Harvey, the modern history of empires, reaching a climax in the American, represents the process of an endless capital accumulation of productive power fusing the logics of politics and economics as a 'capitalist imperialism'.[19]

Yet such definitions only become more meaningful when elaborated in terms of historical understandings. Recent longitudinal studies have illustrated this requirement not simply in necessary detail, but usefully interpreted in terms of the stages involved in the development of empires since 1500.

Importantly, such interpretations cross disciplines and ideological stances, from conservative to radical, and with fruitful convergences around themes and factors. For example, the role of the economy is central in explaining the rise and fall of empires. For Arrighi, capital and capitalism play such a dominant role that it will be considered in the next chapter on capitalism. Yet his stages of the development of empires resonate so strongly with the political work of Bobbitt, Kennedy and Fukuyama that their cumulative impact warrants serious attention.[20]

Although economic factors represent a field of influence in their own right, it is their correlative relationship with two other fields which is most striking, namely, the military-technological strategic (military) field and the political-state field. Harvey works with the two fields or logics of capital and politics,[21] but the military logic also occupies too prominent and relatively autonomous a place not to figure in this analysis. As important, it is that correlative relationship between the three fields which is supplemented by a strong interactive relationship between them. It is this contribution of military, economic and political which is regarded as so decisive for the development of modern empires. That interactive character is also reflected within each of the three fields. So the development of military technologies, for example the cannon in the North Italian states around 1500, or naval design and muniments in Britain in the late seventeenth and eighteenth centuries, were firmly linked to economic capacities, and were strongly connected to the evolving formations of the state. Similarly, the economic field was resourced by military and naval developments in terms of the promotion of international trade, and how this could evolve, particularly in Britain's case, as the construction of colonies and then as an empire. But such commercial and geographical expansion depends on more than indispensable military and political support. Without the support of a strong economy, and increasingly of financial means and systems, they would not have occurred. This foundation of empire is best illustrated by the formative influence of financial developments first in the Netherlands in the earlier seventeenth century, and then in Britain later in the same century. In Britain's case, largely replicating the Netherlands, and not least through the politics of William of Orange's accession to the British throne in 1688–9, this financial revolution was built on key components including: the institution of the Bank of England in 1694; the facility for the purchase and sale of stocks, and the rise of joint stock companies; and the partnership between Bank and Government for raising long-term loans at low interest, and guaranteed by the state and an efficient taxation system. It was such an institutional framework which played a decisive role in the British victory over the French in the eighteenth century in the struggle for empires.[22]

In terms of the political field itself, the commentators carefully trace the stages in the development of the modern state, and its links to empire, normally from the North Italian city states in the late fifteenth century, to the present. I will use Bobbitt's work to illustrate this later. What he also does is to link these developments with the evolution of the relationships *between states* (again as the necessary and inevitable relationships between fields of power). These run, for example, from the Treaty of Augsburg in

1555, as the concordat between princely states, with each prince determining his territory's religion (*cuius regio eius religio*), to the Peace of Paris in 1990 which drew to a conclusion the long epochal war of the twentieth century between parliamentary democracies, fascism and communism, with the former emerging triumphant. What is missing in these commentaries is elaborated in detail in Ruston's study of the emergence of international law, and the rights of people and peoples, out of the aggressive empire-building of Spain in Central and Latin America in the sixteenth century.[23] The work of Spanish Dominicans, using Aquinas' natural law extended into international law, played a formative role in the development of the role of law in the development of the modern state, international relations and the development of the market economy.

The elaboration of the development of this interaction between military, economy and state, particularly as the formation of empires in the modern period, is most usefully described by Bobbitt, recognizing that he should be regarded as representative of a series of corresponding initiatives, in say the works of Kennedy, Fukuyama and Arrighi. Bobbitt traces this development through six stages, usefully extending the field of the state to encompass relations between states.[24] Like most of the other commentators, he begins in the late fifteenth century with the emergence of princely states, exemplified by the city states of North Italy, and linked to the introduction of cannon. The second stage is focused on kingly states, in England, from Henry VIII until the deposing of the Stuarts in 1688. The third stage witnesses the emergence of territorial states, led by the Netherlands, and pursuing balances of power in the relationships between states. The fourth stage focused on the arrival of the state-nation, illustrated by Britain, with people essentially at the service of the state. It is this form of the state which particularly engages in imperialism as a 'projection of nationalism beyond the boundaries of Europe'.[25] The fifth stage, the nation state, emerges in the late nineteenth and early twentieth century, and is committed to the welfare of citizens, adult suffrage and the promotion, therefore, of self-government. There is an important argument, as we will see later, which suggests these developments represent the beginning of the end for empires. From 1989, Bobbitt begins to detect the likely emergence of a sixth stage, the market state, committed to maximizing the opportunities of its people, increasingly as liberal democracies, although not exclusively, and evolving in a variety of forms from the more interventionist corporate states of Europe and South East Asia, to the more entrepreneurial United States. As the link between capitalism and democracy, resourced by the military capacity of the United States as the one remaining superpower, the market state's propulsion on to an international level across continents gives it the potential for hegemony. For Hardt and Negri, this represents the emerging empire of global capitalism.

These longitudinal studies of empires as interlocking fields also reveal their intrinsic ability to both rise and fall. Essentially, this represents a historical manifestation of the relationships between fields of power, in terms of the relative positioning of states. The decline of states and empires is always relative to the rise of others; it does not represent the end of states. For the German mercantilist van Hornigk in 1700, 'whether a nation be today mighty and rich or not depends not on the abundance or security of its power and riches, but principally on whether its neighbours possess more or less of it.'[26] For example Europe in 1500 was relatively weak in relationship to the Chinese (Ming) and Indian (Mogul) empires. That positioning was reversed in the nineteenth and twentieth centuries, and is now undergoing another likely correction with the rise of emerging economies to a dominant world position.

In the interactive process, economic factors play a prominent part in both rise and decline. We have seen how they influenced greatly the growth of the Netherlands and then the British empires, particularly in terms of the development of modern financial processes, instruments and institutions in the seventeenth century. They play a similarly decisive role for most commentators in their decline. So empires have a tendency, in their later stages, of overstretch, in that an increasing proportion of their resources is diverted from productive use into military functions. The relative decline of their economy in relationship to emerging empires confirms that positioning. Kennedy interestingly judged the USA to be experiencing such overstretch in the late twentieth century, but revised his opinion because of a resurgence in the American economy accompanied by the decline of its defence expenditure, particularly after the end of the Cold War.[27] That focus on economic strength is confirmed by Arrighi's observation that the decline of empires is associated with movements within the economy, with the transfer of resources from productive to financial outlets. For the Marxist interpretation of Modelski and Wallerstein, this represents the fourth phase of global hegemony, as declining hegemony (the other three are ascending hegemony, hegemonic victory and hegemonic maturity).[28] These four phases are found in each of the four cycles from 1450, namely Habsburg, Dutch, British and then American. What is clear from all these sources and surveys is that the histories of empires and political arrangements is an ongoing process: 'for it simply has not been given to any one society to remain *permanently* ahead of all the others, because that would imply a freezing of the differentiated pattern of growth rates, technical advance and military developments which has existed since time immemorial'.[29]

From Imperialism to Post-Imperialism: British and American Empires

In terms of the journey of modern empires from 1500 to the present, the end stages of Britain and America's are particularly significant not simply because they epitomize so clearly that interaction of military, economics and politics, but because they represent a likely transition from traditional empires of modernity to the post-imperialism of either a multipolar world or a post-imperial empire. The latter is particularly significant and represents a variety of interpretations, which will be briefly noted through their connections with the development of the American empire beyond America. It represents a movement beyond the logic of territory, so intimately part of modern imperialism, to a logic of space and flows. And running through them is a reading and misreading of the role of religion.

The British Empire represents the epitome and peak of modern imperialism. For Ferguson, it was 'the biggest Empire ever, bar none'.[30] By 1900, it occupied 12 million square miles, included 25% of the world's population, and was built on an omnipresent navy, colonies and bases linking all the main sea lanes and continents, and resourced by London as the financial centre of the world. By 1940, it still occupied 25% of the globe, but now with only 10% of world manufacturing strength. Its decline was inevitable.[31] Yet it is a remarkable story from the late sixteenth century to the mid–late twentieth century, a journey from pirate to trader to ruler. 'What had begun as a business proposition had now become a matter of government.'[32] And it may have taken three centuries to build but it took only three decades to dismantle. Yet its legacy, though highly contested, is strongly linked to the global debate over 'the free movement of goods, capital and labour', and 'the norms of law, order and governance'.[33] Although Ferguson's justification of British imperialism is rightly questioned, including his arguments for a new liberal imperialism, his thesis should be debated in terms of a serious contribution to understanding the contemporary context: so 'the world we know today is in large measure the product of Britain's age of Empire. The question is not whether British imperialism was without blemish. It was not. The question is whether there could have been a less bloody path to modernity. Perhaps in theory there could have been. But in practice?'[34]

As insightfully accurate but equally contestable, are his interpretations of the role of religion in empire. The misuse of religion in the accounts of empire are legion and disturbing, from the first modern empires to the American. So in the early sixteenth century, Pizarro's remarkable conquest of the Incan empire with 168 Spanish soldiers was a classic illustration of

Diamond's thesis about the proximate causes of European dominance in the modern history of empires, namely guns, germs and steel. Weaving together eyewitness accounts by Pizarro's companions, their comments included:

> Your Majesty, [the Spanish-Habsburg Catholic Imperial Majesty] . . . It will be to the glory of God, because they have conquered and brought to our holy Catholic faith so vast a number of heathens, aided by His holy guidance. It will be to the honor of our Emperor . . . that . . . such riches (have been) brought home for the King and for themselves; and that such terror has been spread among the infidels, such admiration excited in all mankind.[35]

That inhumanity in the name of God runs through the story of empire, and certainly deep into the British empire, including in India. After the efforts of evangelicals, led by the Clapham Sect, had been rewarded by a new East India Act in 1813, which opened India to missionaries, the promotion of Christianity in India was often accompanied by an equal determination to condemn indigenous religion, including Hinduism. For Wilberforce, renowned anti-slavery campaigner, 'Theirs [Hinduism] is a cruel religion. . . . All practices of this religion have to be removed.'[36] After the Indian Mutiny in 1857, that dark side of the paradox of religion was powerfully illustrated by the great evangelical Baptist preacher and theologian, Spurgeon. He issued what, for Ferguson, 'amounted to a call for a holy war . . .' 'the religion of the Hindoos is no more than a mass of the rankest filth that imagination ever conceived . . . Their worship necessitates everything that is evil and morality must put it down. The sword must be taken out of its sheath, to cut off our fellow subjects by their thousands.'[37]

Yet even J. S. Mill, major influence in the formulation of classical economics, including 'economic man', recognized the significance of religion in combination with economic development as capitalism: like Livingstone, 'Mill saw the cultural transformation of the non-European world as inextricably linked to its economic transformation. These twin currents of the Evangelical desire to convert India to Christianity and the Liberal desire to convert it to capitalism flowed into one another and over the entire British Empire.'[38]

That relationship between religion and the economic development of capitalism recurs throughout accounts of the British and then American empires. It is certainly disturbing, yet it is far more than that. The contribution of Christianity to the emergence of democracy and human rights is equally powerful, as is the whole complex area of the development of the habitus of norms, values, virtues and habits that are so influential not simply in economic development but equally, and maybe more influentially, in the growing recognition of the seminal contribution of social capital to human well-being. This is *much broader* than, although inclusive of, what has been traditionally and too easily summarized as the Protestant Work ethic. And its significance is epitomized in the dramatic resurgence of Christianity in *post-imperial* Africa, and, as evangelical Christianity in Latin America today. These developments, although they will be considered soon under the title of global resurgent religion, are profoundly concerned with the development of character and virtue. That in no way negates the destructiveness of religion in empire's story, but it does *gravely* question the absence of such counterbalancing constructive religious experiences in virtually all the sources used in this first part of this enquiry (interestingly, the only sensitive interpretation of religion's significance for human well-being is in the neo-Marxist Hardt and Negri's final pages of *Empire*). They all essentially fail to account for and elaborate the paradox of religion's contribution to national and imperial histories. They mostly neglect the constructive significance of religion as a total field of influence, needing therefore to be juxtaposed with their convergence of military, economic and political fields in the journey of empires and nations.

The rise of the American empire accompanied the decline of the British, and as such, it represented the end of European empires, the end of the Vasco da Gama era. Equally, however, it reflected a move from the territorial logic of empire, allowing some, therefore, to regard it as the epitome of the endless accumulation of capital.[39] This view of Harvey is complemented by Hardt and Negri's view of a new global empire of capitalism which is resourced by America but essentially transcending it into a global network of capital accumulation and associated values. Although this represents the dominance of one of the fields of influence, namely, the economic, it continues to be resourced by military and political fields. Yet the history of American imperialism is more complex and nuanced, not least in terms of an increasing awareness of its limits and strengths. For example, it continues to be powerfully rooted in military-strategic resources. Before the invasion of Iraq, it still had 752 military installations in 130 countries, with US troops in 65.[40] It remains the dominant economic power in terms of its productive and consumption capacities, its culture of technological innovation and research, and its financial hegemony. Sometimes simplistically referred to as the Washington Consensus, the latter links Wall Street, and the US Treasury, with the Bretton Woods international economic superstructures of IMF, World Bank and (now) World Trade Organization, in all of which the USA has substantial influence.[41]

When this is connected to the political resource, as the power of demo-cratic governance and its influence in international institutions, not least in term of human rights and its cascading out into international development, finance and judicial processes, then the total US impact begins to project a hegemony which can be more powerful than empire.[42] Its particular asso-ciation with the wider processes of capital, particularly globalizing finance, also suggests a considerable argument for a reformulation of the language and logic of empire. This is particularly the case when a fourth field, culture, and its connections with religion, interacts with the other fields of influence. Again, the concept of paradox more accurately describes this influence. From 1945 (and President Truman) to 2007 (and President Bush), there has been a continuing commitment to the struggle of what is perceived to be good against evil, saving the world from totalitarianism in 1945 to the current 'fight for freedom and against terror "in every corner of the world"'.[43] When that is allied with the global power of American brands like McDonalds, again the result is a strong sense of hegemony. In 1999, McDonald's 'empire' comprised 30,000 outlets in 120 countries, and its head, like Donald Rumsfeld, 'needs his map of the world, and it presents a striking alternative geography of American empire'.[44] It's that overlaying of two maps of empire, of military bases and McDonald outlets, which presents such a striking coordinating of fields of power. Yet the paradox lies particularly in the field of soft power, of the deep worldwide influence of political and economic values, summarized as market econ-omy and liberal democracy, and of cultural innovations, which makes American influence no simple exercise in the hegemony of imperialism. For example, intimately interacting with American economy, politics and culture is the field of religion. As the export of evangelicalism, particularly in its Pentecostal form, it represents American influence but even more the indigenization and thereby transformation of that influence. The later chapter of this enquiry on resurgent religion will elaborate this impact.

These processes of transformation apply equally to the political and eco-nomic fields, for example, in the very different forms of capitalism, includ-ing in Bobbitt's three versions of a global market society, the meadow (entrepreneurial), the park (managerial) and garden (mercantile).[45]

The paradox of American imperialism is confirmed by its limits, from militarily (revealed in Korea, Vietnam and now Iraq), politically (with its recognition of self-government and inability to export people, unlike the British) and culturally (with the tendency for the indigenization of its values) to its transition into a debtor economy dependent on Asian and Middle East finance, itself representative of the emergence of new centres of power located in the emerging economies, and particularly China. The paradox theme even leads into the emergence of new imperialisms based on human rights and cosmopolitan values,[46] or Ferguson's promotion of a US-led liberal empire, again promoting human rights and good government as bases for economic development and well-being.[47] All have the propensity to be an extended version of American hegemony, but equally, all contain the possibilities of indigenization, transformation and the gradual emergence of a multipolar international order.

Alternatives to Empire: Countermovements, Civilizations, Really Longitudinal Histories and Liberal Democracy

The paradox of American Empire, including moving beyond the traditional territorial logic of empire, is confirmed and elaborated by the recognition of four alternative interpretations of the politics of political economy.

The rise of countermovements to empires

These are usefully surveyed in Hardt and Negri's *Multitude*, complementing the historical survey of states and empires from 1500. In the nineteenth and twentieth centuries, these movements regularly assumed the character of opposition to Europeanization (including British) and Americanization. Commenting on the challenges to a Eurocentric world, in Egypt, Turkey, India and China, Kennedy observes 'the more that colonialism penetrated underdeveloped societies, drew them into a global network of trade and finance, and brought them into contact with western ideas, the more this provoked an indigenous reaction.'[48] That revolt against the West has continued to the present, and is likely to persist at least until the indigenization processes of a multipolar world, or as the emergence of new empires, become firmly rooted in the global context. Contemporary studies, for example, Hardt and Negri, and Harvey, focus on the resistance or revolt against the new imperial global capitalism's seizure of 'the commons', or 'accumulation by dispossession',[49] including through privatization programmes (for Harvey, 'a process of barbaric dispossession on a scale that has no parallel in history').[50] These resistances cross all of the first three chapters of this first part of the enquiry, namely empires, capitalism and globalization, forming often 'a diverse and seemingly inchoate but widespread anti-globalisation movement'. It will be examined later, in the globalization chapter. But its significance is not to be underrated, not least because of the links with religion as protest. When Stalin asked, dismissively, how many divisions the Pope had, he did not realize that in the 1980s, the Pope and the religion he represented would play a central part in the overthrow of the Soviet Empire in Poland. For the Pope, and religion, represent 'a kind of power which, under the right circumstances, was superior to that of the Red Army'.[51] It is a most potent reminder of the relative autonomy of the religious field, and its significance in a global context of political economy.

Civilizations: at least a parallel interpretative tool to empires

It is easy to be distracted from the important role of civilization by those who claim too much for it, particularly in the contemporary context. For Huntington, 'In this new world . . . global politics is the politics of civilizations. The rivalry of the superpowers is replaced by the clash of civilizations.'[52] Yet the value of strong judgements which question traditional understanding is that they open up new perspectives; they offer new ways of interpreting contexts. In the section on furious religion, Jenkins plays a similar provocative role in terms of recognizing the growing influence of a resurgent Christianity in the South, and the present reality of, and potential for, conflict between Christianity and Islam.[53] Both Huntington and Jenkins use demographic trends to illustrate the changing shape of power within and between nations.

Yet however questioning and questionable such theses are, they cannot detract from the significance of civilization as a key interpretative tool for understanding our evolving context. The seminal work of Braudel only follows on the earlier studies of Weber, Durkheim and Toynbee, into civilizations, as the 'broadest identifications for peoples'[54] in terms of how 'to define their borders, their centers and peripheries, their provinces and the air one breathes there'.[55] Like empires, they can rise and fall, yet they frequently persist over many centuries. Indeed, unlike empires, they routinely survive political, social economic and ideological upheavals. Importantly, their definition includes 'a collection of cultural characteristics and phenomena',[56] a 'kind of moral milieu encompassing a certain number of nations, each national culture being only a particular form of the whole'.[57] And central to that is the role of religion as an integral and intimate part of cultural identity. Interestingly, Braudel's great work on civilization as a means for interpreting history was complemented by his study of the emergence of capitalism.[58] Modern commentators who overindulge in the heady waters of post-modernity and the empires of global capitalism would do well to take Braudel's multidimensional studies more seriously.

In terms of the longitudinal history of civilizations, most scholars work with eight: the Sinic-Confucian; the Japanese; the Hindu-Indian; the Islamic-Arab; the Orthodox-Russian-Byzantine; the Western-European-North American; the Latin American; the African, particularly non-Islamic sub-Saharan Africa. The contemporary post-1989 examples include: the USA, Europe, the West; Islam; Africa; Latin America; Hindu-India; and Buddhist-China.[59]

What is striking in these surveys is the recognition of the decline of the West relative to the resurgence of others: 'As the world moves out of its Western phase, the ideologies which typified late Western civilisation decline, and their place is taken by religious and other culturally based forms of identity and commitment.'[60] And in these transformations, religion, as Edward Mortimer suggests, is 'increasingly likely to intrude into international affairs'.[61] Like Jenkins, Huntington uses demography to illustrate this potential for conflicts linked to religious difference interacting with national and economic arenas.

For example, in terms of 'shares of world population under the political control of civilizations, from 1900–2025 (in percentages)': the Western declines from 44.3% in 1900 to 10.1% in 2025; the Islamic grows from 4.2% to 19.2%.[62] Not surprisingly, 'As Western power declines, the ability of the West to impose Western concepts of human rights, liberty, and democracy on other civilizations also declines and so does the attractiveness of those values to other civilizations.'[63] And that is a matter, not simply of civilization, but of hard economics, because in 2005 emerging economies overtook the advanced economies in terms of share of the world output.[64] Link that to the rise of furious religions in the South, and the decline of Christianity in the North, and you have a powerful mixture of powers quite unrecognized by most secular commentators on empires, capitalism and globalization.

The Islamic contribution to the religious field in general, and to this analysis of civilizations in the contemporary context is particularly informative. Its understanding of the *ummah* or Islamic community crosses national and economic boundaries. The first Islamic Summit in 1969 illustrated its distinctive implications for contemporary politics: 'Christian, Orthodox, Buddhist, Hindu governments do not have interstate organizations with memberships based on religion; Muslim governments do.'[65] It is almost a religious equivalent of Hardt and Negri's new empire of global capitalism as a transcending of the traditional limitations and logic of territoriality, particularly as the flows of financial capitalism. Yet for Islam, 'Consciousness without cohesion is a source of weakness . . . and a source of threat to other civilizations.'[66] However contested such interpretations are, and the later section on furious religion will only confirm their importance if not the way they are framed, it is becoming more and more apparent that 'The world is now as Arab, Asian, and African, as it is Western.'[67] The dominance of the West may well persist deep into the twenty-first century, but it will only be in the context of a multipolar world. The challenge of empires and of capitalism, as the dominant interpretative tools for the contemporary context is being profoundly modified.

The really longitudinal histories: putting even civilizations in context

The work of polymaths like Diamond, taking the growing significance of multidisciplinary working to new levels, locates contemporary contextual analysis in much wider longitudinal frameworks. Diamond's research question is why did history unfold differently on different continents in the last 13,000 years? Linking with the other historical surveys of empires and their beginning in 1500, for Diamond the die was cast by then. It was the different rates of development in different continents which led to the *proximate* causes of Western superiority when confronting Central and Latin America. These causes he summarizes as guns, germs and steel, with the addition of political structures and economic development. The more ultimate causes he traces back to at least two factors. First, the continental differences in domesticable wild plants and animals (six of the twelve major crops of the world were found in the fertile crescent, and four of the five animals). It was these resources which allowed the development of food production: 'the availability of domestic plants and animals ultimately explains why empires, literacy, and steel weapons developed earliest in Eurasia and later, or not at all, in other continents.'[68] Second, the diffusion of these key discoveries moved quickly and easily on an East–West axis, for example, Eurasia, as against the quite major obstacles presented by North–South axes, for example in Africa and the Americas. Interestingly, this reinforces and elaborates Wilkinson's emphasis on hunter-gatherer societies as models for his economy of regard (in the final part of this enquiry),[69] although both recognize their interaction with the development of agricultural societies, and their tendencies then to hierarchy, inequalities and models of dominance. Equally important, such societies also developed exchange models: 'In general, societies that engaged in intense exchanges of crops, livestock, and technologies related to food production were more likely to become involved in other exchanges as well.'[70] The deep roots of modern capitalist exchange are therefore located way before 1500. And the division of labour associated with the surplus generated by agricultural production also powerfully shaped the emergence of the religious field in terms of the development of that surplus to support the development of religious institutions, hierarchies and power. Taken altogether, it can be regarded as a useful additional dimension to contemporary contextual analysis as a series of interacting fields broader than traditional interpretations.

The growth of liberal democracy as challenge to empires?

For Dunn, the rise of democracy represents an enigma, from its complex origins in ancient Greece, through its continuing marginalization and opprobrium for most of recorded history until the twin revolutions in the United States and France in the late eighteenth century.[71] Its slow development in the nineteenth and immense struggle with totalitarian ideologies and systems for most of the twentieth century have reformulated its expression and interpretation at significant variance from it original meaning. What is clear is its remarkable resurgence as liberal democracy from 1945, in Southern Europe (Portugal, 1974, Greece, 1974, Spain, 1975, and Turkey, 1983), Latin America (Peru, 1980, Argentina, 1982, Uruguay, 1983, Brazil 1984, Chile and Paraguay by 1990, and Nicaragua in early 1990), East Asia (the Philippines, 1986, South Korea 1987, Taiwan, 1988) and South Africa (1990); the break-up of the Soviet Union after 1989 propelled the nations of Central and Eastern Europe and the Baltic states into democratic regimes.

Given such an outburst, it is not surprising that analysts like Bobbitt regard the emergence of market states as the great achievement consequent on the victory of parliamentary governance, in the long epochal war of the twentieth century, over the totalitarian systems of fascism and communism. It is easy to forget that achievement, not least what the alternatives would have been if democracy had not triumphed. More importantly, for Fukuyama it represented the end of imperialism through the success of democracy as self-government. Indeed, for Fukuyama it ensured the end of history in terms of Hegel's universal history. The provocative character of his claim should not detract from convergences across ideological divides, because Bobbitt's emerging market state is essentially democratic, and Hardt and Negri's *Multitude* is essentially a resurgence of a popular democracy of the people by the people, as a self-government of the multitude which therefore rejects global capitalist imperialism.[72] This, in turn, links with Dunn's argument for a movement beyond the political elitism of representative democracy to a deliberative democracy of self-government by the population. Importantly, this commitment to democracy, and particularly to its reformulation into more open, inclusive, participation, is a key feature of the happiness hypothesis, and of the wider well-being concept. In the latter, for Kenny, that includes the promotion of human dignity, including as human rights.[73] Within that same concept, the pursuit of moral norms and codes, and, in the happiness literature, also as the significance of religion, points to the important role played by Christianity in the historical development of democracy. For Fukuyama, using Hegel, and confirmed by Weber and Nietzsche, the evidence indicates 'the *objective* historical relationship that existed between Christian doctrine and the emergence of liberal democratic societies in Western Europe.'[74] Hegel's secularization of that religious impulse to participation developed into contemporary human rights concerns. However, the social capital literatures clearly recognize the continuing importance of Christianity in the nourishing of democracy, both in terms of nourishing values and norms supportive of reciprocity and participation, and providing the arenas for developing participatory skills and values, the classic schools of democracy argument.

Yet the promotion of liberal democracy as alternative to empires is severely complicated by its significant association with market (capitalist) economies. For some, like Fukuyama, it is essentially a positive and productive relationship, so 'the growth of liberal democracy, together with its companion, economic liberalism, has been the most remarkable macropolitical phenomenon of the last four hundred years'.[75] To the sociologist Talcott Parsons, the connection or interaction between these political and economic fields is not surprising since 'democracies are best equipped to deal with the rapidly proliferating number of interest groups created by the industrialization process'.[76] Indeed, the argument that the relationships between liberal democracies are essentially peaceful, removing or reducing the threat and likelihood of conflict between them, is a major contribution to flourishing market economies.[77] Adam Smith recognized the importance of governments producing peace, stability and security; Cobden argued that free trade would generate peaceful relationships between states, as 'the best human means for securing universal and permanent peace' (1842).[78]

Standing against this undue linking of liberal democracy and market (capitalist) economy, interpreted as a predominantly benign interaction, is a profusion of arguments highlighting the intrinsic tendency of market economics to erode the virtues and values on which it relies, but equally, which are also important for the development of inclusive democracies. So Dunn is deeply critical of what he describes as 'the order of egoism' represented by capitalism, and its tendency to generate grave inequalities.[79]

These themes are also powerfully part of the happiness and well-being literatures. Addressing these paradoxes of liberal democracy will form an important theme in the final part of this enquiry, including the central role of religion in it. Featuring also in that conclusion will be a recognition and reformulation of a renewed anthropology, of what it means to be human, and its links to human rights and dignity discourses. Havel, fighter for democracy and against communism, and then leader of the Czecho-slovakian movement into liberal democracy, summarizes these linkages very clearly: 'The essential aims of life are present naturally in every person. In everyone there is some longing for humanity's rightful dignity, for moral integrity, for free expression of being and a sense of transcendence over the world of existences.'[80]

2

Capitalism

Transforming Economic Systems:
The Economics of Political Economy

In the long frame of human history, the last 200 years, and particularly since 1945, have witnessed an outburst of economic achievements which has enabled human well-being to begin to make the historic transition from absolute want to astonishing levels of health, education and income.[81] Between 1945 and 2000, the world economy grew fivefold, income per capita by 2.6 times, and life expectancy from 35 to 58. For the great economist Keynes, 'From the earliest times of which we have record – back, say to 2000 years before Christ – down to the beginning of the eighteenth century, there was no very great change in the standard of life of the average man living in the civilised centres of the earth.'[82] The transformation of individual and social well-being since 1750 represents one of the decisive changes in human history. And economics is at the heart, as that 'natural progress of opulence' for Adam Smith, founder of modern economics.[83] For the changes affected human lives and social systems, but also economics itself: 'The Industrial Revolution in England changed the world and the relations of nations and states to one another. For reasons of power, if not of wealth, the *goals and tasks of political economy* were transformed.'[84] It is that combination of economics, industrialization and political relations which come together in the transforming power of capitalism. And it is 'free market capitalism, as an economic system, [which] has enjoyed unrivalled practical success at wealth creation'.[85] It is not economics in general, or market economics. Naming the central role of capitalism is absolutely essential for any adequate interpretation of the contemporary context. Without it, this enquiry ceases to function effectively. For the highly contested nature of capitalism, including its deep intrinsic contradictions, so harmful to that human well-being which it has also benefited, interacts most tangibly and significantly with the religious field of power. Unpicking this interaction and then reconstituting it for the more adequate promotion of human well-being is the primary objective of this enquiry.

Terminology and definition

Because it is such a contested concept and reality, accepting and understanding its complexity in itself and in its connections with other fields is of some importance.

Capitalism, certainly since the fifteenth century, has been intrinsically related to, and constituted by, interactions with markets and the accumulation and development of wealth, and therefore of power, including in its political form. From the eighteenth century, it powerfully interacted with the emergence of the industrial revolution, and the technologies associated with it. And it became closely linked to the development of modern economics and economic systems as the free market economy. It is their powerful *interlocking*, with significant focusing on the evolving processes of capital accumulation, which in turn informed a series of social relationships and hierarchical arrangements.

Apologists from both left and right have regularly collapsed these areas of influence into one reality, whether capitalism or free market economies. Yet to understand the complexity of the contemporary context it is, I believe, important to understand these different tributaries which now constitute the capitalist market economy. First, and not in order of importance, is the market itself, and particularly as market mechanism, essentially as a coordinating system of economic activity. 'It regulates what things are produced and by what means. It determines who receives them in return for which contribution',[86] and particularly through the price mechanism. Because it involves millions of consumers and producers, that coordinating function is absolutely essential for economic well-being. In the most sharp and decisive contrast to the state command economy, it is rightly seen 'as uniquely capable of overcoming the informational constraint'.[87] Incentives and profits are intimate parts of these mechanisms. The market mechanism can clearly be located and utilized in a variety of political systems, from the USA to China.

Second, modern economics emerged alongside and deeply interacted with the development of what became the industrial revolution. It has undergone a series of mainstream developments from classical to the current neoclassical arrangement, becoming, in the process, more focused on the technical or positive side of economics, what Sen has usefully called engineering economics. As such it has regularly been defined as 'The science which studies human behaviour as a relationship between ends and scarce means which have alternative uses'.[88] Within certain firmly defined limits, (and these will be explored throughout the enquiry), it therefore has an indispensable contribution to make to modern well-being, particularly, as we will see, in critical interaction with other disciplines. These conversations will centrally include frequent reference to the more neglected and yet increasingly essential part of economics described as normative or ethical. These link directly into the essential contribution to well-being made by other capitals, namely social and religious.

Third has been the growing significance of capitalism itself, as the pursuit of profit and therefore the accumulation of capital, particularly now in its financial form. As such it generates distinctive social arrangements, including class or social stratification structures, firmly linked to inequalities, such an important part of the well-being literatures. In this deeply interlocking form, it represents one of the strongest, if not strongest, field of power, affecting relationships within political economy and way beyond it. Increasingly, its systems of accumulation operate across space and time, resourced by new communication technologies and globalization processes. Its focusing and projection of power can easily be overlooked, leading to fundamentally inaccurate analyses not least by the discipline of economics itself. For Galbraith,

> Power – the ability of some in the economic system to command or otherwise win the obedience of others and the pleasure, prestige and profit that go therewith. It is a reticence (to speak out about power on the part of the classical tradition) that persists to this day. The pursuit of power and its pecuniary and psychic rewards remains . . . the great black hole of mainstream economics.[89]

When that power is coincided with political power, and particularly in its more imperialist form, it can effortlessly assume hegemonic proportions. That is why capitalism has to be considered, not simply in relation to market mechanisms and economies, but also in connection with the state.

The state, including as capitalism

There is considerable agreement across a wide spectrum of opinion that the state, in its various forms, made an increasingly central contribution to the development of commercial and then industrial capitalism, the transition of weight moving from the former to the latter in the early nineteenth century. For Polanyi, 'The road to the free market was opened and kept open by an enormous increase in continuous, centrally organised and controlled interventionism.'[90] That significance of the state persisted into the current global financial capitalism. For Braudel, whose historical surveys of medieval and early modern capitalism have been so richly rewarding, 'Capitalism only triumphs when it becomes identified with the state, *when it is the state*'.[91] For Bobbitt, the latest stage of that journey, at the end of the long war of essentially the whole twentieth century, is the *fusion* of capitalism and state in the market state, including as its concert of nations. Yet Ferguson insists on continuing to recognize the 'nexus between economics and politics' as the key to understanding the modern world, and as an interaction between two distinct fields, not least because 'political events and institutions have often dominated economic development'.[92]

Capitalism as contested ground

Religious, like secular opinion, is deeply divided over capitalism as ideology and as system. The American Roman Catholic scholar, Michael Novak, argues fluently, in his *The Spirit of Democratic Capitalism*, that capitalism 'is the superior political-economic option for contemporary societies'.[93] The Lutheran feminist scholar Cynthia Moe-Lobeda, in her *Healing a Broken World: Globalization and God*, vehemently attacks 'the prevailing paradigm of (capitalist) economic globalization' as intrinsically hostile to the marginalized and the environment.[94] That deep unease with the unsustainability, ethically and practically, of capitalist economics was shared even in the 1840s by Carlyle, Wagner, Marx and Dickens, and continued into the historian Hobsbawm's survey of the twentieth century in the *Age of Extremes*.[95] All reflected the view, so pungently expressed by Carlyle, the prophet of Ecclefechan, that 'Cash-payment is not the sole relation of human beings'.[96] Yet even Marx recognized 'something progressive about capitalist development' even in British India.[97] That is a judgement repeated in the next section on globalization, again highly contested, often revealing the complex and paradoxical nature of contemporary economic processes. So the charge of the exploitation of labour in developing economies, powerfully central to Moe-Lobeda's case, can also contribute to the quite essential enhancement of women's roles in domestic and public arenas. A more detailed examination of the very varied understandings in Christian social ethics of both capitalism and market mechanism, which parallel secular discourse, is undertaken in my *Through the Eye of a Needle: Theological Conversations over Political Economy*, itself intentionally undertaken as a research resource for this enquiry.

Like empires, capitalism's winners and losers

The recognition of capitalism as a relatively autonomous field of influence and power carries with it the importance of structured relationships within it, and with other fields. Like empires, therefore, its different formulations rise and decline in relation particularly to other capitalist forms. For example, in 1960, the per capita GNP of South Korea and Ghana was the same, at $230. South Korea's is now 10 to 12 times greater.[98] Of more significance is the historic change in the relationship between developed and emerging economies, with the former being dominant from the later nineteenth century to virtually the present. In 2005 that position changed, with the foremost 27 emerging economies recording slightly more than half world output (measured at purchasing power parity). It is a profoundly historic rebalancing, '*returning* the world to the sort of state that endured throughout most of its history. People forget that, until the late nineteenth century, China and India were the world's two biggest economies.'[99]

Modelling Capitalism's Transformation

Reflecting on the different sources for this section of the enquiry, the resonances between empires and capitalism become very pronounced. It is not simply that they represent two sides of the same coin, as politics and economy. Both have also developed very similar modellings to describe and account for the development of empires and capitalism from the fifteenth century to the present. Using for this exploration Arrighi's typological history of capitalism as a basic framework with its focus on four cycles of capital accumulation, each with three stages, I will supplement it from three other sources. First, I will use brief reflections on contemporary financial capitalism, because Arrighi, like Braudel, identifies the final stage in each cycle as the movement into financial from industrial or commercial capitalism. This is regarded as both symptom of decline and seed of the transformation of capitalism into the next stage. To illustrate this role of finance with reference to contemporary experience and analysis, I will use Cowley's *The Value of Money: Ethics and the World of Finance*, not least because further use will be made of it in the third stage of my enquiry, because of its contribution to ethical economics, virtues and common good out of a reformulated natural law tradition. The second and third additional sources take Arrighi's fourth and final contemporary stage into new and alternative scenarios: Bobbitt's market society, and Hardt and Negri's

Empire of global capitalism. The three additions, with Arrighi, illustrate the necessary and valued multidisciplinary and multiperspectival approach to the global capitalist economy.

The longitudinal survey: a preamble

As with the study of empires, through say the work of Diamond, reflections on capitalism can usefully refer to much longer time frames, in this case Jay's. His view is that, since there has been no development in our genetic evolution for 40,000 years, economic development becomes of central importance for human well-being. The study of why our wealth advances and retracts, particularly since the end of the last ice age (11,000 BC), lies for him, in 'a rounded view of man's total social context, political, psychological and ethical as well as economic'.[100] It is a multidisciplinary approach remarkably similar in its constituent parts to contemporary well-being research. Like Diamond, he recognizes the decisive breakthrough from hunter-gatherers into agricultural production, with the associated rise of politics and then empires, and of organized religion. But he then focuses on the emergence of money and trade. By the time of the Roman Empire, key parts of capitalist economics in Arrighi's survey of much later periods had emerged, including finance, money, loans (banks), ways to finance risky trade voyages, maritime commercial loans and insurance secured on ship and cargo, commercial law, private property, contracts and the associated recognition of legal persons. It is a reminder of the long history of the emergence of production, consumption, exchanges and market, as preliminary to the relatively recent evolving of capitalism.[101]

Arrighi's four systemic cycles of accumulation as historical capitalism

There is considerable convergence over the importance of the 1970s in terms of the take-off of financial capitalism globally. The decoupling of the US dollar from the gold standard in 1971, and the consequent floating of exchange rates, when combined with the liberalization and deregulation of financial markets, generated a most powerful development of financial markets. It was supported politically by what became known as the Washington Consensus of the US Treasury, Wall Street and the Bretton Woods institutions (IMF, World Bank) with GATT (later to be the WTO). Certainly, at times, this strongly linked to what critics have described as an

American-led 'neo-liberal hegemony' (1970–2000), and which for Harvey became the epitome of capitalist imperialism. What interests Arrighi is the prominence of this emergence of financial capitalism out of American manufacturing and trading global dominance. Its character, resourced by new communications, especially information technologies, represented, for Harvey, 'a dematerialized monetary system' with capital flowing freely in the world, liberated from state controls.[102]

Inspired by Braudel's magisterial historical survey of capitalism in its early modern phases, Arrighi began to carefully construct his own longitudinal study of modern capitalism. He quickly observed how the development of American financial capitalism from 1970 was in fact a recurring phenomenon across that history. At the end of each cycle the movement to concentrate on financial processes for capital accumulation was seen to signal both the end of a cycle and its transition into a new one: they represented 'integral aspects of the recurrent destruction of "old" regimes and the simultaneous creation of "new" ones'.[103] They indicated the movement from capital accumulation through manufacturing and trade through profit accumulation to through financial transactions.

Like Braudel, what emerged from his study was a long historical survey unnecessarily described as 'a source of inspiration rather than a model of analysis'.[104] For although it certainly inspires my enquiry, it resonates empirically too much with other surveys, not to be taken very seriously.

The consequent story of capitalism's long journey reveals its flexibility and adaptability, almost suggesting an intrinsic propensity to re-create. It certainly acts as major challenge to theological and secular opinion which regularly predicts its demise. It certainly requires major adjustments to the British tradition of Christian social ethics, and its examination of the relationship between religion and capitalism. Its three protagonists, Tawney, Demant and Preston, were not able to enter into conversations with such historical contextualizing because they pre-dated them.[105]

For Arrighi, that history is divided into four cycles, Italian, Dutch, British and American, covering the period from the fifteenth century to the present. Each cycle has three stages modelled on Marx's analysis of capitalist development, moving from emphasis on capital accumulation through production and trade, into a mixture with financial capitalism added, and finally, into financial transactions as a dominant means of profit and capital accumulation. It is that last stage which heralds both the end of a cycle and the transition to the next. So the Italian city states, and particularly Genoa, represented the concentration of wealth and power in oligarchies. They journeyed, from the fifteenth to the sixteenth and early seventeenth centuries, from capital accumulation through long-distance trade to capital accumulation through high finances, war and diplomacy. The making of money, as profit, for accumulation and reinvestment, moved from profiting out of making and selling things, to profiting from money transactions, to making money out of money.

The second cycle, the Dutch, represented the emergence of state-supported capitalism, transforming the European system to capital circulation on a world scale, using trade, colonies and war as key instruments, resourced by modern financial systems and resources. The third cycle, the British, linked capital and territorialism even more strongly, as did the fourth, the American. In each cycle the movement was from capital accumulation through production and trade, to finance.[106]

Contemporary financial capitalism: the globalization and de-materializing of money

Arrighi and Braudel both agree that the movement of capitalist accumulation into the dominance of financial transactions represents a decisive stage as transition from one cycle to the next. Developments in financial affairs since 1970 both confirm and take them to new heights, in terms of transforming their nature and extending their significance. Although I will use Cowley's work, it is substantiated across a wide field of studies. They talk of finance moving effortlessly across national boundaries, creating a 'borderless world'.[107] For Ferguson, this 'financial globalization' exhibits remarkable features:[108]

- Cross-border transactions in bonds and equities were equivalent to 9% of American GDP in 1980, in 1998, it was 230%.
- International bank lending has also expanded exponentially. Between 1993 and 1997 'gross international bank claims rose from $315 billion to $1.2 trillion.'
- 'The daily Turnover on the world's foreign exchange markets rose from $1.6 trillion in 1995 to $2 trillion in 1998, implying annual flows of more than $400 trillion.'
- 'The total amount of futures and options instruments rose from $7.8 trillion' in 1993 to $13.5 trillion in 1998.

For Cowley, such figures are now beyond our comprehension. As economics drives globalization, so finance drives the economics, and especially as money. Yet it is an essentially different reality from Aristotle and Aquinas's understanding of money. It is now almost unimaginably more dynamic, and nebulous, often 'merely electronic traces in computer memories', with no physical existence, and in 'a constant state of flux'.[109] For her, she notes the sheer size and complexity of global finance, its potential destructiveness and particularly for the poor, its challenge to imagination with talk of trillions of dollars a day, and the lightning speed of processes. It represents a profound challenge to the promotion of human well-being in general, and to Christian social ethics in particular. The latter, as she rightly observes, is singularly ill-equipped to contribute to such well-being, although her own work provides an important basis from which to develop that necessary religious and ethical contribution.

Empire or market society: another cycle for capitalism?

The historical surveys of empires and capitalism generate various points of convergence between them, from shared origins in the fifteenth century, the cycles of their evolution, and the regular interactions of politics and economics. Both also suggest we now inhabit a period of transition from an American-dominated era. It is in speculating what the new era will be that two sources, from Bobbitt and Hardt and Negri, from different standpoints and disciplines will be deployed to suggest complementary possibilities, not least for my task of formulating a religious contribution to the transformation of capitalism.

Bobbitt's *The Shield of Achilles: War, Peace and the Course of History* emerges out of a tradition of history, constitutional law and policy advice to recent US administrations. His survey of the history of the relationship between political regimes, war and technology, and economic development reflects a firm commitment to political economy: 'The political and economic, far from being decisive causal factors on their own, are really two faces of the same phenomenon.'[110] For him, the end of the long epochal war of the twentieth century, between parliamentary democracy, fascism and communism, ended in 1989–90 with the defeat of communism and the emergence of democracy as the legitimate and preferred option for human governance. That political system was also clearly linked to economic governance informed by the market mechanism. The year 1990 represented not simply the emergence of one political system as the dominant feasible way forward, but also of a preferred economic system, given the collapse of command economies as unfit for purpose: it had therefore become clear that 'the complexity of modern economics proved to be simply beyond the capabilities of centralized bureaucracy to manage'.[111] This commitment to market mechanisms and open economies, including participation in the global economy, for example through membership of the WTO, includes regimes like China. For Den Xiaoping (1982): 'Not a single country in the world, no matter what its political system, has ever modernized with a closed-door policy.'[112] Despite that juxtaposing of political authoritarianism and market mechanism, Bobbitt clearly argues for the combination of market economy and liberal democracy, therefore resonating with Fukuyama's thesis that this provides the preferred, feasible and tested way to deliver human well-being in the contemporary context. Bobbitt describes this emerging option for the early twenty-first century as the market state. By this he means a form of political economy and constitution to provide, promote and 'maximise the opportunities enjoyed by all members of society'.[113] This contrasts with the objective of the welfare of people of the previous nation state, and connects with Baker's criterion of adequacy, adapted as, 'by the fruits of opportunity for all ye shall know them'.[114] Bobbitt acknowledges that this commitment to market economies and liberal democracy as a market state of individual opportunities, has clear limitations, including the generation of inequalities, job insecurity, the problem of social cohesion fed by undue personal consumption, and encouraging more women into the labour market with detrimental consequences for wages.[115] These limitations connect strongly to the indications of social disease in the well-being literatures, and their designation of market economics as selfish capitalism or the order of egoism.[116]

The varying ability of the market state to address such deformities is linked to his three types of market society: the entrepreneurial (USA and UK partly), the mercantile (Japan) and the managerial (EU).[117] Recent performance and projections suggest the last two, and particularly the managerial, are likely to engage more effectively the diseases of what James calls 'affluenza'. This is confirmed by Bobbitt's recognition of the emerging erosion of market states on national lines by international production and distribution processes, epitomized by transnational corporations, and by the processes of global financial capitalism.[118] His international concert and networks of market states could offer ways of addressing such global problems including inequalities, disease transmission and financial instabilities. The virtue of more mixed market states is confirmed by his recognition of the great dangers of the market's systemic 'indifference to community and to culture'.[119] Reducing all to the market 'will invite revolt'.[120] This can best be counterbalanced in the mixed type by underwriting the importance of public goods, including the values and norms located in relationships and more locally based associations. Again, this links directly into the well-being literatures in general, and social and religious capitals in particular.

45

Hardt and Negri's *Empire* marks an impressive collaboration between an Italian political scientist, imprisoned for his radical beliefs, and an American academic in the field of literature. The result is an alternative to modern capitalism as empire, which bears the marks of a version of neo-Marxism. For them, what has emerged out of the late twentieth century is a radically new form of capitalism, reshaped by globalizing processes, including communication technologies, and which is formed by and committed to new hegemonic forms of world dominance. As an empire of global capitalism it links my three sectors of empire, capitalism and globalization into an interlocking reality, conceptualized as empire: it becomes a 'global order, a new logic and structure of rule – in short, a new form of sovereignty. Empire is the political subject that effectively regulates these global exchanges, the sovereign power that governs the world.'[121] As a combining of fields of power into a new cycle of imperial capitalism, it becomes a new cycle for Arrighi's typology, not least because the USA's privileged position in his fourth stage becomes a basis, but only that, for this new post-capitalist world market society (like Bobbitt) or state. I say state, because what is being argued for here is a profoundly political economy, a new fusing of state and economy in a new system of global domination, resourced particularly by the power of new forms of capitalist accumulation. As a 'moral, normative and institutional order of Empire',[122] Hardt and Negri claim 'Empire is better in the same way that Marx insists that capitalism is better than the form of society and modes of production that came before it'.[123] It is this recognition which allows them to argue for the essential transformation of empire because of its fundamental contradictions and oppressions. What interests me is their commitment to such change primarily from within the existing system – that 'the real alternatives and potentials for liberation that exist *within* Empire. We should be done once and for all with the search for an outside, a standpoint that imagines a purity for our politics.'[124] The sheer weight of the historical processes elaborated in these sections on empire and capitalism combine to confirm that judgement, and question the analytical adequacy of many radical theologies. For Hardt and Negri are arguing in their last pages, remarkably using St Francis, for 'the ontological power of a new society'[125] by harnessing the resources of the *Multitude*. That process of transformation has remarkable connections with important features of Part 3 of this enquiry, and its model of transfiguring capitalism. The difference is that their resort to Christian spirituality can appear as a last resort. Engaging empire is more complex than that, and particularly because it needs to engage with religion in a far more substantial way.

Restraining Capitalism: Limitations of Resources and Behaviours

Across a wide spectrum of opinion, there is much agreement that the great contributions of capitalism and market economy to human well-being do not diminish its profound limitations. It is these which formed the basis, as motivation and agenda, for the emergence of widespread protest and countermovements in the late 1990s. Particularly focusing on Seattle and the WTO in 1999, they continued and proliferated as coalitions of very different interests and concerns, and all relating at some point to the anti-globalization, capitalism and empire themes. Hardt and Negri's promotion of *Multitude* is a composite of such varied forces.

Given this complexity, I have decided to focus on two constraints on or limitations of capitalism which illuminate particular problems and possibilities of capitalist political economy. The first is a brief reflection on demographics and environment, their relationship, and their roots in early Christian political economy. The latter relates to the work of Malthus, and includes Darwin's deployment of his arguments in his construction of the *Origin of the Species* (1859) as profound apologetic for ecological diversity. The second, dealt with again briefly, examines the role of religion in capitalist development, initially through the obvious debates over the Protestant work ethic, but then cascading out to embrace the inadequacies of capitalist and economic behaviour in terms of broadly accepted understandings of human behaviour.

Finitude and limits: lessons from demography and environment

Thomas Malthus, one of the early founders of political economy with Smith and Ricardo, was a committed Christian and a seminal influence on the formation of the early religious tradition of Christian political economy.[126] He began his studies with the research problem created by what he perceived to be the potential clash between rising populations and limited resources (required to feed, clothe and house people). What he failed to account for in his analysis, understandably given his death in 1834, was the seismic shift in the production and distribution of wealth provided by new technologies. So the population of Britain increased astonishingly fourfold in the nineteenth century, yet GNP accelerated fourteenfold. That problem of population pressures and resources remains a continuing problem exacerbated by two emerging modern forces, on the one hand, the dramatic demographic explosion from the mid eighteenth century and accelerating through the twentieth and into the twenty-first century; and on the other hand, the irruption of new constraints as the limits of the planet to support such population size. The connection of population and environment links Malthus and Darwin, as already noted.

The demographic constraint

For most of recorded history – again, a longitudinal understanding is required, as beyond the routine histories of empire and capitalism – there existed an emerging constraint on human well-being because energy was restricted to finite human efforts and existing plants and animals. That limit of land and human was exploded by the industrial revolution, through the discovery of inanimate energy. The result was that, in the long run, 'demographic growth, moves in tandem with the growth of available resources, the latter imposing an impassable limit on the former' (but regularly overcome by new knowledge).[127]

It is this development from the restraints of a finitude restricted by land and human energy to abundant inanimate energy and other resources, and its sustaining of large population growth, which is known as the *demographic* transition. This, I believe, has a decisive connection with at least two other comparable transitions in human history; the epidemiological (as the breakthrough in health), and the prosperity paradox one (the regularly attained income level above which well-being does not occur). All three transitions are intimately connected to economic and income growth. The latter two will be discussed at the beginning of Part 2. The first, the demographic transition, illustrates the move from large families with the early death of children to smaller families living longer, essentially from disorder to order, from waste to economy. This transition has been achieved in Europe and the West (it took France 185 years, Sweden 150 years), and in the Far East (China and Taiwan took 70 years), but it is still in progress in Africa.[128] The transition has quite major consequences for demographic growth and human well-being. For example, it is accompanied by the decline in mortality which generally precedes fertility decline. When the latter does occur, as it invariably does, decline slows. The result in such economically developing societies is natural population increases at a low level. The accompanying increase in life expectancy is regarded as a prerequisite for human development, and forms one of the three criteria used in the UN's Human Development Index, the key test of national well-being. In other words, there is a 'long-term relationship between life expectancy and material well-being',[129] in terms of the link between rising GDP and fertility decline. The demographic transition is therefore an integral part of the transformation of Europe and then increasingly of world societies. This has stark implications for poverty reduction, so intimately part of the promotion of greater well-being: for 'no population has maintained high levels of fertility for long in the face of increasing well-being and declining mortality.'[130]

The sustainability of extended survival?

This issue again develops the relationship between economics and demography, including as limits of capitalism. For increasing life expectancy proceeds apace: for developed economies, it is projected to rise from 75 years (2000) to 81 (2050), and for the least developed economies from 63 to 76. This sustainability is threatened by three factors:

- biological sustainability – with the irruption and now rapid global transmission of new or reformulated diseases: by 1999, 34 million were infected with HIV/AIDS; 66% in sub-Saharan Africa;
- political sustainability – major political upheavals or collapses, as in Russia in 1990, continue to reduce life expectancy;
- economic sustainability – in terms of the growing ageing of the population and the resulting pressures on health care and pensions (by 2050, 28% of developed economies will be over 65).[131]

Sustainability as the carrying capacity of the world as finite system: the emergence of environment as challenge to world and capitalism

Estimates of the ability of the earth to carry a specific population (Malthus's original hypothesis) were made by King in 1695, with his proposal of 4 billion rising to 13.9 billion. Modern estimates suggest around 10 billion by 2100. The sustainability of the interaction between population and environment normally uses a number of variables including impact on the environment, population size, goods consumed per person (as affluence – linked therefore to philosophy of life, as organization of society and lifestyles) and levels of technology.[132]

Given current understandings of this relationship, it is normally predicted that, in the next *two* generations only, the following challenges are likely to occur:

- The inevitable growth in the consumption of non-renewable resources, and particularly of the deep inequalities between LDCs and developed economies. Since addressing this gap initially requires more resources with high energy inputs, and 99% of current big population growth is in poorer economies, 'it is easy to understand that this indispensable growth will hardly be sustainable for a very long time'.[133]

- The impact of population growth on the demand for food will severely impact land, sea-fish, water and timber, including accelerating waste and pollution.
- The changing allocation of space will conflict with environmental integrities, in terms of the intensification of agriculture and fisheries and increasing urbanization, particularly in coastal areas already threatened by global warming.
- The contribution of population growth, and increased human activity to sustain it, will increase the concentration of greenhouse gases in the atmosphere, contributing to global warming with its likely profound impacts on environment and human activities.

This threat posed by the issues of sustainability in relation to the carrying capacity of a finite world probably presents the greatest challenge to, and maybe limitation of, capitalism today. Much of the material on empires and capitalism relates to long-term developments. The dramatic changes represented by the impact of population activity on environment is now measured in 'periods of time measured in decades rather than centuries'.[134] It represents a remarkable reformulation of Malthus's original research question in dramatically new contexts with possible consequences beyond his comprehension.

The limits of behaviour: capitalism and additionality factors, and the role of religion

The connection between religion and capitalism is not just a major theme in the parochialness of British Christian social ethics. For its academic origin in Max Weber's *The Protestant Ethic and the Spirit of Capitalism* is of profound wider-reaching significance. So it provided not simply the stimulus for an evolving debate over religion's relationship to the rise, decline and persistence of capitalism. It also inspired a much wider argument over the significance of religion's role in capitalism's development as outlined in the chapters on empire and capitalism in this enquiry. In my earlier *Public Theology for Changing Times*,[135] that relationship is illustrated in some detail, as the correlation and interaction between the fields of religion and politics from the mid eighteenth century to the present.

Although Weber's hypothesis on the relationship between capitalism and religion continues to be highly contested, it is interestingly gaining new force from what I will soon examine as the recent rise of a globally furious religion in general, and from its manifestation as Pentecostalism in Latin America in particular. Commentators on the latter note how commitment to such a faith community is associated with character change and the nurturing of virtues that certainly are conducive to economic behaviour supportive of capitalism, but also of family and community life. It is that latter which broadens this debate beyond the confines of religion and capitalism, and into the social and religious capital arena. This also then cascades out into the challenge to the anthropology of mainstream neo-classical economics.

The Weber thesis itself examines the relationship of Protestantism (particularly in its Calvinist and Puritan forms) and capitalist economies in Northern Europe from the sixteenth century (resonant of my surveys of empire and capitalism). Essentially, he treats it as an elective affinity, as sympathetic not causal. Like de Tocqueville's observations on mid nineteenth-century America, it was as though 'there was an inner relation between the religious spirit and the strength of the capitalist impulse in America, and that the single-minded pursuit of wealth and personal prosperity was linked with the single-minded quest of God.'[136] Yet that link was not concerned with a direct religious requirement to create wealth. It was rather that belief in God was sympathetic to 'defining and sanctioning an ethic of everyday behaviour that was conducive to business success'.[137]

That sympathetic relationship between one's understanding of what God requires of human living and economic impulses, such as hard work, thrift and not profligacy, trust and truth-telling, and responsibility, is not confined to Protestant Northern Europe as Weber's initial study suggested. The contributions of Roman Catholic Northern Italy to the development of early capitalism and the presence of such religiously inspired ethics in other faiths and continents is rich testimony to the contribution of religion to economic life. Commentators have particularly noted the religious sources of a work ethic in Japan.[138] So the Zen monk Suzuki Shosan (d.1655) saw 'greed as a spiritual poison; but work as something else: "All occupations are Buddhist practice; through work we are able to attain Buddahood."' As Landes rightly comments 'One does not have to be a Weberian Protestant to behave like one.'[139]

It is important to recognize too, that the relationship of religious ethics and economic endeavour continues to play a significant part in emerging economies, not least in Latin America, as already noted. As important, however, is the extension of this relationship to also include arguments for the connection between religion and the rise of democracy. Indeed Fukuyama links religion to both: 'Just as in the case of political democracy, the success of capitalism depends in some measures on the survival of pre-modern cultural traditions into the modern age. Like political liberty, economic liberty is not totally self-sustaining but depends on a degree of irrational thymos.'[140] In passing, this is a reminder that these virtues are not simply accounted for in Weberian rationalist terms. For Weber also understood that in Calvinism 'Work was undertaken for a totally non-material and "irrational" goal, that is, to demonstrate that one had been "elected".'[141] The relationship between Christianity and democracy, including the support of reformed traditions for it in the English Civil War, also played a role in the Scottish Presbyterian tradition, and its evolution into the Scottish Enlightenment, say in the work of Adam Smith. He argued for 'The natural effort of every individual to better his own condition, when suffered to exert itself with freedom and security.'[142] De Tocqueville's later careful examination of American democracy also included the decisive contribution of Puritan traditions and ethics to those virtues and civic associations which had such a formative influence on the democratic way of life.[143] It is a linkage which Putnam's recent work on social capital builds on, including in terms of the contemporary significant role of churches in the formation of social *and* political capital.[144] A Freedom House Survey takes this even further, by deducing from a survey of 88 countries, qualified as 'free' in their 1998 edition, that 'no fewer than 79 are "majority Christian"'.[145] Only one country with a Muslim majority was free. Of course, this proposed correlation is highly contested and does not involve a causal relation necessarily. It also overlooks the Eurocentric contribution to two World Wars, as Christian nations. In addition, for Ferguson, the answer to the question 'Does economic globalization imply the globalization of democracy' was also sceptical since 'both economic growth and political democratization seem to be dependent more on the existence of education, the rule of law and financial stability than on one another'.[146] That same judgement could also apply to the question does Christianity imply a commitment to democracy and capitalism? *Yet* what does emerge from the literatures is a recognition that capitalism erodes those values, virtues and associations on which it is dependent for its flourishing. What is equally convincing is the evidence from the social capital literatures that Christianity in America and Britain has a strong relationship with the development of those values and associations that play an important role in both market economics and liberal democracy. This issue of behaviour will figure large in the following discussions of social capital, well-being and religion, including their recognition of the limitations of the view of the human in neoclassical economies, and in contemporary affluent societies shaped by what one commentator has described as selfish capitalism.[147]

These limitations of capitalism, across demography, environment and behaviour are therefore beginning to reveal a series of connections which will require serious examination as this enquiry now begins to unfold.

3

Globalization

The Operating Context of Empire and Capitalism

Globalization provokes a contest of opinion of greater passion and reason than empires or capitalism, not least because it so frequently acts as their proxy. As a contemporary Roman gladiatorial amphitheatre, the sources of such positional play can be revealed as much in subtitles as main statements: for Wolf, *Why Globalization Works* becomes *The Case for the Global Market Economy*; for Gallagher *The True Cost of Low Prices* becomes *The Violence of Globalization*.[148] Yet explorations of its definitions and histories, and of its detailed apologetics, reveal a complex multi-dimensional reality which adds considerably more added value than a summary of capitalism and empires. It provides an operating context which is both informed by them but in turn increasingly shapes them. It is a field of power and influence in its own right.

Of course the use of globalization as surrogate for capitalism and empire rightly carries some weight. A study of empire confirms the importance of global reach, and capitalism embodies the importance of the global reach of economies for well-being. Indeed well-being literatures, and particularly on social capital, powerfully reinforce the significance of mutuality and reciprocity as interdependence. Globalization encapsulates such features, yet by gathering them in an interacting whole it then provides additional dimensions which extend our understandings of empires and capitalism.

This interpretation of globalization as an operating context is revealed in the structure and content of this section. For example, the historical development of globalization again from the fifteenth–sixteenth century emphasizes particular features of the histories of capitalism and empires but from a different vantage point. That understanding of globalization as similar to yet different from previous fields also pervades the definitional work. The argument moves on to consider the contested opinions on globalization, beginning with the opposition, and then examining some of its key criticisms by giving economic experience a voice. Engaging mainstream political economy in this way is a reminder of the enquiry's emphasis on it.

It also counterbalances the undue emphasis on sociology and literature by the protagonists of anti-globalization thought. The sharp questions posed by the discipline of economics need to be at least heard even if not answered adequately. This voice will also be heard in the discussion in Part 2 of religious views on the contested area of usury. Again, religion also impinges at various points of this exploration. There is a profound conversation which emerges out of Christian understandings of stewardship in New Testament Greek, as *oikonomia*, as engaging the household, the root meaning of *economics*, and also as *ecumene*, to the whole inhabited world, including ecumenical. That commitment to catholicity, to a world-view, and to interdependence and interrelationships, leads theologians like Tanner to engage constructively with globalization, particularly its decisive economic dimension. Others, like Gillett and Peters use such basic theological understandings to essentially reject these processes.[149] This also links to the role of religion in identity construction (seen particularly in the role of Islam since the 1960s) which provides a basis for a critical engagement with the homogenizing forces of globalization. And this, in turn connects with the later discussion of Pentecostalism, regarded as a truly global, both as globalized and globalizing, religion.

History and Definitions

History

A brief note on the history of globalization both connects it to the histories of empires and capitalism, and identifies features central to the distinctiveness of global processes.

Commentators routinely begin with the innovatory global sea journeys of the late fifteenth and sixteenth centuries. For Frank, it is a transformative development against the relatively isolated regions of the world before 1500. After that, he notes the emergence of 'a single global world economy with a world-wide division of labor and multilateral trade from 1500 onwards'.[150] In that development, the role of shipping and technologies played a decisive part, including in the emergence of the Dutch and then British empires. The linking of military-strategic, commerce, capital accumulation and colonization became roots of 'a modern world system' reinforced by the industrial revolution.[151] The latter, as a rapidly evolving global force in the nineteenth century, was particularly resourced by technological achievements which reinforced and provoked further globalization. These included communication systems clustered around telegraph, telephone, wireless, railways, steam shipping and aeroplanes. Together, they constituted what Landes has elsewhere described as 'genesis'[152] factors, and contributed to that annihilation of distance which has become such a feature of recent globalization processes.

It was the British empire which is widely seen as providing a decisive leap forward in this history of globalization, particularly in the period 1880–1910. Its commanding industrial, commercial and imperial presence allowed it to develop its powerful financial systems, particularly through its integration of capital markets, and the power, and wide spread, of its foreign direct investment (FDI). Although some have argued that the globalization of the late twentieth century is essentially making up for the lost ground of the depression and protectionism of the 1930s, there are convincing arguments that suggest this later recent stage is much more significant, broader cast, more plural, much more sustainable. Its achievements in world trade, production and finance far outweigh the earlier phase, not least because of the deployment of new communication technologies and the resulting conquest of time and space. That dominance, particularly American led, was only reinforced by the collapse of command economies in 1989. What is arguably a retrograde development, is the unwillingness to promote migration today, generally recognized for its contribution to eroding world income inequalities in the early twentieth century. That absence is compounded by an undue emphasis on capital flows, meaning that 'the gap between rich and poor countries tends to widen'.[153] This growing focus on financial globalization is confirmed, as noted above, by Arrighi and Braudel's analysis, as a phenomenon of the last stage of a particular cycle of capital accumulation.

Definitional interpretations

'The exploration of the world market has given a cosmopolitan character to production and consumption in every country . . . In place of the old local and national seclusion and self-sufficiency, we have intercourse in every direction, universal interdependence of nations. And as in material, so in intellectual production . . . National one-sidedness and narrow-mindedness become more and more impossible.'[154] Not a contemporary comment on globalization, but Marx and Engels in the *Communist Manifesto* in 1848. For in the history of globalization, they detected economic processes as continually evolving structures with clear benefits for human well-being and even greater costs. Yet the concept of globalization itself only emerges in the 1960s, somewhat fittingly given the significant defining of globalization by the post-1945 economic and political trans-formation.[155] Held argues, with some accuracy, that these two fields of power and influence provide the core of globalization processes.[156]

In *economic globalization*, he recognizes:

- the role of increasing trade and exports with the erosion of barriers to trade. The Chinese rightly recognize that openness to and integration into the global economy is essential for economic growth and poverty reduction.
- the astonishing acceleration in production and investment, the latter as FDI, across economies, and includes the growing significance of trans-national corporations (TNCs), contributing 25% of world production and 70% of trade (25% being internal to the firms). Their importance for production and trade in a global market economy, characterized by commitments to free markets and trade, although much contested should not detract from the significance of the company itself for wealth creation and human well-being. For economist and Nobel laureate, Kenneth Arrow, it represents one of man's 'greatest and . . . earliest' innovations.[157] Yet there is increasing unease that the leaders of global companies are increasingly disconnected from the commitments to place and people and inhabit a created borderless world, as global 'cosmo-crats'.[158] For Castells, 'Elites are cosmopolitan, people are local'.[159] It was a trend Adam Smith observed disapprovingly in its very early stages: unlike the proprietor of the land – 'necessarily a citizen of the particular country in which his estate lies . . . the proprietor of stock is properly a citizen of the world, and not necessarily attached to any particular country'.[160]
- global finance, as increasingly significant in the global economy as both global process and product, and as strongly connected to new com-munication technologies. It is recognized as a source both of global eco-nomic turbulence and turmoil, witness the 1997 Asian financial crisis, and of economic feasibilities (in terms of mobilizing savings, allocating capital investment productively, monitoring managers and transforming risk[161] – the latter through an increasingly complex development of financial instruments, including derivatives and hedging).

Political globalization, for Held, is primarily a recognition of the nation state (for Bobbitt as transmuting into market states) now intersecting internationally to manage trade and finance, and including through the development of multilateral agencies.[162]

It is these processes of integration which are, it is argued, evolving into a more globally interconnected political economy. At times this implies a move to a 'single market'.[163] Yet a more accurate, not least because more cautionary and careful, description of globalization is 'the significant expansion of international trade, investment, transportation and communication', and characterized by the increasing use of the language of *flows* to describe movements of capital, labour and knowledge across national boundaries.[164]

Although globalization is a contested concept and reality, there is an increasing weight of opinion which recognizes the contemporary experience of 'an ever-denser web of exchange spreading over an ever-widening geographical area'.[165] It can also be argued that these processes are 'almost certainly irreversible'[166] because they represent a long-run history of economic and political processes beginning in the fifteenth century. Yet the important and well-substantiated argument for the likely irreversibility of an ever increasing web and geographical spread of economic and political exchanges should not be restricted to the increasing dominance of politics as liberal democracy and economics as market economy. There is rather much argument suggesting the growing importance of varieties of constructive engagements with globalization processes. These occur even within the relationship between liberal democracy and the market economy, as suggested, for example, by Bobbitt's three varieties of market states. Widening this argument further, Braudel clearly distinguishes between modernization and westernization: he regards it as 'childish' to think that modernization – or the 'triumph' of a civilization – would lead to the end of a plurality of cultures and civilizations.[167] That judgement is confirmed by the view that 'Neither the WTO nor the IMF can force countries to do what they would prefer not to do.'[168] The degree of protectionism in both advanced *and* emerging economies confirms that cautionary judgement. This recognition of both the universalizing tendencies of globalization and the equal pressures of plurality and difference recurs throughout this enquiry. I describe this as the Hollenbach question because he frames the problem so clearly: 'This poses the most challenging question raised by the phenomenon of globalization – how to achieve effective and universal respect for the common humanity of all people even in the midst of their differences. Neither a commitment to universality alone nor to cultural differences alone will provide an adequate moral stance toward a globalizing world.'[169] It is that relationship between universality and difference, embedded in globalization processes, which is also prominent in the well-being literatures, as we will see. And it also features in Part 3 of this enquiry as the relationship between a global ethic and global ethics.

Although politics and economics form the central core of globalization processes, other features or factors reinforce that ever denser and wider web, including culture. However, I will simply select three, which certainly have links with empire and capitalism, but which also provide additional perspectives.

First, the demographics of globalization generate understandings which do overlap with capitalism's. For example, predicted population growth will be predominantly in the South, and not in the North, confirming the judgement that globalization will increasingly not be Western. Emerging economies overtaking advanced economies in world output supports this judgement. The potential for global pandemics is also accentuated by the growing ease of movement, including as migrations. The rapid spread of HIV/AIDS epitomizes this threat. Interestingly the source of such diseases still relates to the original small group of animals used in agricultural production, and identified by Diamond as part of the transition from hunter-gatherer 10,000 years ago. What is equally thought-provoking is the challenge of population migrations. The contrast already made between their encouragement in the nineteenth century, and their discouragement today is seen to be a contributory factor, along with the growing dominance of financial capital, to the inability to moderate global income inequalities.[170] Some counterbalancing to this restriction of migration is provided by the growth of global remittances provided by migrants back into their countries of origin: the estimate is between $63 billion and $80 billion in 2000.[171]

Second, technology continues as central to the continuing development of global processes, particularly as transport and communication, and now including 'the annihilation of distance', with its profound impact as financial globalization.[172] For Schumpeter, entrepreneurial technological innovation became the destructive driving force of capitalism,[173] which later economists still estimate to be of greater importance in job losses in advanced economies rather than the politically popular view that globalization processes are the principal cause.[174]

Third, the continuing importance of the state in promoting globalization processes connects to the wider contributions of governance to economic processes. The significance of 'right, legal, financial and political institutions'[175] are supplemented, as we have discussed under capitalism, with the support of values and associations generated outside the economic mechanisms. The contested link between free markets and liberal democracy has also been explored, not least in terms of the correlation between accelerating globalization and the spread of democracy in the late twentieth century.[176] The contribution of values and associations to both these political and economic forms raises the wider concerns of governance, not least the growing significance of civil society. As an important source of social capital, including through religion, civil society is also a major source of the critique and promotion of alternatives to globalization. As a constructive apologist for globalization, Bhagwati's recognition of the important role of Non-Governmental Organizations (NGOs)[177] as critic and monitor of globalization has important links with Hardt and Negri's commitment to the deep and radical reconstruction of globalization, not least through the operations of the *Multitude*. For Keane, the development of NGOs into global institutions adds to the relevance of arguments for their contributions to constructive countervailing global processes.[178] This leads naturally into the following reflections on contesting globalization.

The Empire Fights Back: Economic Reflections on Anti-globalization.

An account of anti-globalization needs to recognize three interacting institutional agendas in the late twentieth century: first, the acceleration of globalization and its associated agencies such as the IMF, and second, the growth of protest movements combining anti-capitalism, anti-empire (American) and anti-globalization. The 1999 Seattle protests against the WTO with accompanying violence acted as catalyst for them, and reflected the third agenda as the growth of NGOs nationally and internationally (in France, '54,000 private associations' were formed in 1987 alone, whereas 11,000 had been formed during the 1960s).[179] The acceleration of this organizational coagulation in the 1990s is linked to a series of developments, including the collapse of command economies as the only feasible alternative to global capitalism and leading to what Bhagwati has called 'the tyranny of the missing alternative'. It also relates to the important developments in culture, particularly intellectually, in 'fields other than economics, English, comparative literature, and sociology', to which I would add anthropology and geography.[180] For example, the deconstructionism of post-modernism advocates 'an endless horizon of meanings'. For Eagleton, commenting on modern literacy theory, 'Derrida is clearly out to do more than develop new techniques of reading: deconstruction is for him an ultimately political practice, an attempt to dismantle the logic by which a particular system of thought, and behind that a whole system of political structures and social institutions, maintains its force.'[181] And its objective almost invariably focuses on capitalism, often connecting to other disciplines' creative use of neo-Marxist thinking, say in Hardt and Negri's *Empire*, and to post-colonial traditions with their profound suspicion of much Western scholarship, sometimes with good reason. The cumulative effect of such discourses was to give strong support, in the 1990s, to anti-globalization movements as proxies for the 'missing alternative'.

The focus of anti-globalization represents a convergence of a variety of groups, which Wolf usefully divides into more traditional economic interests – the trade unions (lobbying on jobs and labour standards), the farming lobby (US and EU), and critics of trade liberalization and the WTO; and more recent single-issue groups, often NGO-led, and including religious groups, and others covering environment, gender, peace, human rights, indigenous issues and debt.[182]

This context for protest and countermovements provokes Bhagwati to describe them in terms of a spectrum of opinion, from an essentially rejectionist position, reflecting 'deep-seated antipathy to globalisation', to critics of globalization who do not comprehensively reject it, acknowledging that globalization may be economically benign yet socially malign.[183] It is important to note that the former, the more hard core militants, include right-wingers like Buchanan in the USA, and the more xenophobic religious – cultural – nationalists like the Indian Bharatiya Janata Party. Both have aspirations for self-reliance, for autarky. Some Christian opinion is in a similar area on the spectrum, for example, Rebecca Peters.

Peters's work reminds us that theological opinion operates across a similar spectrum, from rejectionist to critical engagement. In my *Through the Eye of a Needle* this spectrum is developed in detail and can move from the more radical stance of Gorringe, Duchrow, Gillett, Moe-Lobeda, Peters, Long and Goodchild to the balanced criticism of global capitalism by more mainstream liberal theologians like Preston, Hay, Wogaman and Niebuhr.[184]

What is also interesting is how mainstream churches, particularly in the USA and denominational world bodies, have sometimes moved to a rejectionist stance, publishing statements often reflecting the passion and emotion of deep convictions disconnected from engagement with hard reason, economically based. So the Lutheran World Federation, at its Tenth Assembly in Geneva in 2003, addressed the new global market-oriented philosophy:

> This false ideology (neo-liberalism) is grounded in the assumption that the market, built on private property, unrestrained competition, and the centrality of contracts, is the absolute law governing human life, society, and the natural environment. This is idolatry, and leads to the systematic exclusion of those who own no property, the destruction of cultural diversity, the dismantling of fragile democracies and the destruction of the earth.[185]

For the Evangelical Lutheran Church of America in 2001–2, 'economic globalisation has seemingly taken control of our communities from our hands'.[186]

Yet such unequivocal language can move churches beyond dialogue with strong critics of globalization within the discipline of economics. Scholars like Bhagwati recognize the valuable contribution of NGOs as critics and monitors of globalization. They seek engagement with 'serious NGOs with real knowledge and serious policy critiques'.[187] To illustrate the possibility of such dialogue, I will therefore briefly use key criticisms of globalization, in conversation with mainstream economists. This will have the additional value of illustrating some constructive alternatives to contemporary globalization. It also addresses Hardt and Negri's view, as radical critics of globalization, that such historically embedded processes cannot be bypassed but have to be transformed for the sake of human well-being. This will connect with Part 3 of this enquiry, and its consideration of social philosophy and policies supportive of the transfiguration of capitalism. I have drawn four criticisms of globalization from the work of the economists Bhagwati and Wolf, with their responses, in abbreviated form simply as illustration of the potential for such a critical conversation.

Does globalization enhance or diminish poverty and inequality?

The United Nations historic Millennium Goals centrally included the commitment to reduce absolute poverty (as measured by the billion living on $1 a day) by 50% by 2015.

That is a commitment which powerfully resonates with much in economic tradition. For Malthus, 'the causes of the wealth and poverty of nations (was) – the grand object of all enquiries in Political Economy'.[188] The commitment to poverty reduction was an integral part of, and motivation for, the search for economic prosperity for all. For Adam Smith, it is when society is 'advancing to further acquisition . . . the condition of the laboring poor, of the great body of the people, seems to be happiest'.[189]

Yet for the critics of globalization, the results of such economic processes have been the increase of poverty, ill-being in its key form, and growing inequality between and within nations.

The economists address these charges systematically. Their task, based on much research, recognizes that 'appropriate policies will always enable us to profit from growth and to moderate, even prevent, unpleasant outcomes for the poor'.[190]

Much weight is placed by them on the experiences of India, Egypt, Chile,

Brazil and Mexico in adopting autarkic economic policies in the 1960s and 1970s – as essentially inward looking, and not welfare embracing. Major growth and poverty reduction occurred when outward oriented policies were adopted in terms of trade with the world economy and the promotion of FDI. This profound change of economic direction was linked to annual income growth between 1980 and 2000 in China of 10%, and 6% in India, with associated reductions in poverty from 28% in 1978 to 9% in 1998 for China, and India's following from 51% to 26%.[191] Dollar and Kraay's survey of 1977 to 1997 observes 'that while growth rates in the non-globalizing developing countries have generally slowed down in the past two decades, globalizers have shown exactly the opposite pattern, with their growth rates accelerating from the level of the 1960s and 1970s'.[192]

The contrast between Asia and Africa was particularly stark: 'Poverty reduced remarkably in Asia because Asian countries grew. Poverty increased dramatically in Africa because African countries did not grow' (Sala-i-Martin).[193]

Inequality, so associated with the poverty charges of globalization critics, is a much more complex matter. The key questions become: 'Is human welfare, broadly defined, rising? Is the proportion of people living in desperate misery declining? If inequality is rising, are the rich profiting at the expense of the poor?'[194] Wolf's analysis is substantial and complex, and his summary of the evidence builds a multidimensional reality which globalizing critics would do well to dissect. His conclusions are:[195]

- 'the ratio of average incomes in the richest countries to those in the very poorest has continued to rise in the age of globalization'.
- 'the absolute gap in living standards between today's high-income countries and the vast proportion of developing countries has continued to rise'. This is inevitable, given the starting point two decades ago.
- Global inequality among individuals has not risen. In all probability it 'has fallen since the 1970s'.
- The number of people in extreme income poverty has not risen. It may well have fallen since 1980, 'for the first time in almost two centuries, because of the rapid growth of the Asian giants'.
- The proportion of people in extreme poverty in the world's population has *not* also risen, but almost 'certainly fallen'.
- The poor of the world are *not* worse off in terms of a wide range of indicators of human welfare and capability. 'The welfare of humanity, judged by life expectancies, infant mortality, literacy, hunger, fertility and the incidence of child labour has improved enormously' (but it has improved least in sub-Saharan Africa).

- Income inequality has *not* risen in every country because of exposure to global economic integration: it has risen in China. Inequality has risen in high-income countries, but 'the role of globalisation in this change is unclear and, in all probability, not decisive'.

Does economic globalization damage the most vulnerable in terms of child labour?

Child labour figures remain unacceptably high according to the ILO, at 100 to 200 million, with 95% in poor countries. It is a phenomenon rooted in poverty, and pre-dates recent globalization.

Again, evidence is clear: that when incomes improve, through economic growth policies, then 'parents can generally be expected to respond by putting children back in school' – essentially 'the income effect', that 'education of one's children is a superior good, the consumption of which rises as incomes rise'.[196]

Does globalization threaten wages and labour standards?

Marx predicted the progressive immerseration of the working classes. Yet in the nineteenth century because of industrialization and economic growth, their real wages and conditions improved.

The contemporary version of Marx's theory is that globalization provokes 'a race to the bottom', with particularly damaging consequences for workers in advanced economies. Yet the majority of economists are agreed 'that the role of trade with poor countries in depressing wages is small, perhaps even negligible.'[197]

Transnational corporations are essentially predatory

As the 'B52 bombers' of globalization, transnational corporations (TNCs) invariably attract the 'flack' of secular and religious critics. They are seen as provoking a 'race to the bottom' by exploiting cheap Third World labour. However, evidence suggests that the wages paid by them in developing economies are higher than in alternative jobs, exceeding the going rate: Lim's research from Bangladesh, Mexico, Shanghai, Indonesia and Vietnam overwhelmingly confirms 'the existence of such a premium'.[198] Another argument accuses TNCs of violating labour rights. Again, the evidence is that TNCs 'pay more – and treat their workers better – than

local companies do'. ILO surveys also indicate that workers in export processing zones (EPZs), with their sweat shops, received pay which 'while
extremely low by the standards of developed countries, is higher than
what would be available in the villages from which the workers come . . .
Other surveys have found that, on average, jobs in foreign-owned, export-
oriented factories offer higher pay and better working conditions than
comparable jobs in domestic companies.'[199]

Examination of other criticisms relating to financial globalization and
environment are similarly addressed. What is particularly interesting is
how an economist like Bhagwati then begins to explore ways forward out
of these dialogues. Here, he usefully picks up the concept of *ethical* globalization from Mary Robinson, former UN commissioner for human
rights.[200] This powerfully resonates with the reflections in Part 3 of this
enquiry on ethical economics in general, and on moral or ethical growth
in particular, significantly and necessarily locating these processes in a
globalizing context. Since trade is such an integral part of globalization, I
will explore Bhagwati's proposals for it. Again, this will also connect with
Part 2 of the enquiry, and its references to pro poor economic growth
philosophies and policies.

What he works with is what I will later describe as promoting virtuous
circles for well-being and attacking vicious circle obstacles: so he talks of
devising 'benefits-enhancing policies', in conjunction with developing
'institutional mechanisms to cope with the occasional downsides'.[201] This
can be usefully elaborated using his rightful concern to develop more
appropriate measurement systems in relation to such ethical globalization,
again an important conclusion elaborated in my Part 3.

The constructive virtuous circle leans on a strong promotion of global
economic growth, including free trade, as central to enhancing human
welfare, not least indeed significantly through poverty reduction. The
managing of the free trade component he regards as more achievable than
trying to control financial globalization. The proven benefits of such economic policies have been described with reference to the contrast between
Asia and Africa. Yet he does recognize that there is an equal task of damage limitation, particularly to protect the most vulnerable in the face of
such processes. As I will elaborate later as pro poor economic growth, he
has four proposals:[202]

- Adjustment assistance for workers and industries affected by import
  competition. Free trade is welfare enhancing only if losers are compen-
  sated by the beneficiaries, but leaving the winners also better off.

- Improving the WTO's dispute settlement mechanism – for example to compensate Caribbean nations for losses when trade in bananas was opened to free trade.
- Addressing price volatility in agriculture – particularly for nations (normally the poorest) dependent on two or three primary commodities, like coffee – and using the IMF Extended Fund facility for special loans to poor economies for transition support when prices drop significantly. This links to the fair trade reflections on coffee in Part Two.
- Economic insecurity – to be engaged by domestic institutional support particularly for farmers losing markets to foreign competition.

His conclusions on global finance are also very relevant to this enquiry. The Asian financial crisis of 1997, with a rapid one-size-fits-all imposition of deregulated financial markets, he regards as an exercise in the bad economics of the Washington Consensus elites. He clearly recognizes that past great economists were uniformly 'against shock therapy'. For example, Adam Smith, faced with the need to promote free trade, and the dislocation this would initially cause, advocated gradual transitions to the preferred economic policy: 'Humanity may in this case require that freedom of trade should be restored only by slow graduations, and with a good deal of reserve and circumspection.' For Keynes, 'The economic transition of a society is a thing to be accomplished slowly . . . For *it is of the nature of economic processes to be* rooted in time. A rapid transition will involve so much pure destruction of wealth that the new state of affairs will be, at first, worse than the old, and the grand experiment will be discredited.'[203] The lessons were clear; gradual transitions to trade and financial liberalization, with protection for the vulnerable but not protectionism, and a recognition that one size does not fit all, that the general processes can and should relate to a variety of approaches linked to context.

All in all, these economists present us with the overall possibility of an *ethical* globalization, but achieved in relation to examinations of longitudinal and contemporary evidence. It is an important lesson, that 'Public action . . . will not succeed unless it reflects not only passions but also reason.'[204] It is a long journey through empires, capitalism and globalization, but that is not an unfitting expression of what is beginning to emerge as an adequate response to global change.

4

The Resurgent and Reformulating Religious Field as Study of Overlapping Concentricity

As the twentieth century was a profoundly secular era, so the twenty-first century is 'dawning as a century of religion . . . in full swing' – the powerful judgement of Gilles Kepel in *La revanche de Dieu*.[205] Any contesting of the rhetoric of such claims should not detract from a more substantial and empirically verifiable judgement. That is, it is now as implausible and inaccurate to develop secular interpretations of the emerging contemporary context divorced from religion, as it is to generate religious interpretations which do not take the contemporary context and its disciplines seriously. Both defective analyses still occur with unhappy and unfortunate regularity. Both are profoundly imprecise and unhelpful. They are actually just plain wrong. This enquiry began with that hypothesis, tested against evidence drawn from more secular sources, including the well-being literatures, but also much wider, as this study has already begun to reveal. Parts 2 and 3 will substantiate this acknowledgement of the place of religion in contemporary discourse. This first part will therefore conclude by continuing to elaborate that claim. For religion is both recognized by say Bourdieu and Tanner as a relatively autonomous field of power and influence, sharing the characteristics of other fields, but likewise with its own distinctive elaborations. And, like other decisive fields, like the economic as capitalist markets, so the religious also develops in interactive relationships with other fields. The explorations of three similar secular fields, the political as empires, capitalism as economics, and globalization as process and product, all contain important points of such interactions. For example, the complex of interpretations and arguments around the Protestant work ethic engages with capitalist economics through the dimension of human behaviour and its social impacts. This will engage powerfully with the well-being examination in Part 2, and with the reformulation of political economy, including as a revised anthropology, in Part 3. In the ways of interpreting political economy other than empire, civilizations were significantly defined by religions. Similarly, the exploration of globalization revealed the contribution of religion to counter-movements, illustrating the importance, among other things, of collaboration, often as partnerships, between faith groups and civil society. We will soon see how partnerships play a wider formative role in development economics and environmental sustainability in Part 2. All exhibit not just the importance of interacting fields, but its embodiment in institutional and programmatic forms.

Such processes should not, however, divert attention from the significance of the integrity of religion as a relatively autonomous field, alongside those more centrally located in the arena of political economy. And although this enquiry has focused on the Christian perspective and dimension of the religious field, it will gradually exhibit the rich variety of faiths which actually constitute that integrity. The later material on environment and development economics draws from 11 world faiths, and the reflection on the emerging significance of interfaith religious ethics in the final part, both confirms that rich source and begins to tentatively uncover possible shared understandings. These include the nature and significance of the human as multidimensional reality in itself and as located in a context of world, universe, spiritual and divine. The potential for common views on complex contemporary problems, for example, poverty reduction, economic development and environment, is significant but without in any way detracting from the relative autonomy of the faiths themselves. It is a replay of Hollenbach's seminal question on commonality and singularity. It is a reminder of the later discussion of global ethic or global ethics, of the role of contextual in relation to universal, a concern also engaged deep within the well-being discourse. There are also different emphases in the histories of empires, capitalism and globalization, yet their shared understandings do not detract from these differences. So there are diverse religious histories which also contain actual and possible interconnections. Such multiple operating of the religious field in itself, and in its *inevitable* relations with others (inevitable because, like globalization, probably irreversible), confirms and elaborates its rightful field positioning in this wider contextual exploration of Part 1.

An understanding of the religious field as a concentricity of a series of overlapping experiences in its wider context has begun to shape this introductory note. The resulting analysis elaborates that understanding further. It therefore begins with the emerging significance of globally furious religion, of the remarkable resurgence of religion, particularly in the South, and increasingly intruding into the West, not least through migrations. It is this centring of religious revival in a different location, in the South, away from the historic North, which could constitute a new stage in religious history. It is the religious field equivalent of the transition between cycles in the histories of capitalism, empires and globalization at the end of the twentieth century. The contrasting remarkable decline of mainstream churches in the West only reinforces that repositioning (and forms the second stage of this account of the religious field). Yet it is unlikely that this new cycle will be restricted to the phenomenon of furious religion, though it is likely to play a central part. It constitutes a reminder that the character of Western religion, especially as institutional decline arguably in the face of the modernizing and secularizing forces of global capitalism, should not be regarded as the emergence of another universal model, an intimate part of a new global empire. It may well rather be an *exception* both to current and historical experience. Yet it may also contain understandings which will form, with resurgent religion, an important part of this new cycle in the history of the religious field.

The analysis therefore then focuses on the interpretation of Western Christianity which presents a much more complex and plural understanding than simply institutional decline. The third and final stage of this religious account takes one aspect of that possible reformulation of religion in the West, the concept of social capital (recognizing that the discovery is in the West but the phenomenon is global, and increasingly supported by research like the World Values Survey). Although it can easily become the classically morally obvious bandwagon beloved by religious apologists (and therefore almost invariably morally wrong), its selection in this enquiry rather emerges out of the detailed analysis of secular change in this contextual analysis. For example it links to explorations of the limits of global capitalism, but as a form of capital essential to its efficient long-term functioning. In that very complex of processes it therefore has the potential for being a transformative element from within the political-economic system itself. Indeed, I suggest it may well constitute a field in its own right. As important is its actual and potential religious dimension which, as it will be argued, may be metamorphosing as at least a distinctive religious or faithful capital. As a key component of the religious field, including its interaction with the secular fields of capitalism and globalization, it has the seminal added value of connecting us with the complex research area of well-being and happiness (again, valued intrinsically and as interaction). An extended reflection on this area introduces the second part of this enquiry which then moves into an examination of the contributions of the religious field to human well-being.

Furious Religion: The Resurgence of Faith in the Late Twentieth Century

I first came across the vivid concept of furious religion in Duncan Forrester's work.[206] Although he rightly uses it to describe a global phenomenon, I was asked not to use it in publicity for a lecture at Edinburgh University because of the delicacy of faith relationships particularly with Islam. Rather predictable, rather sad because the concept refers as much to Christianity and other faiths, as Islam, as we will see. That wider understanding is revealed in Berger's work, *The Desecularization of the World: Resurgent Religion and World Politics*. In it, he talks of his change of mind: 'the assumption that we live in a secularized world is false. The world today, with some exceptions . . . is as *furiously* religious as it ever was',[207] a state particularly reinforced by the remarkable decline of irreligion, what McGrath calls 'the twilight of atheism'.[208] In fact, the concept of 'resurgent religion' is more accurate because it allows us to locate furious religion on a wider spectrum describing the astonishing outburst of religious growth in that astonishing post-1945 generation. It accounts for the further globalizing of religions as an evolution of their historically embedded universalizing tendencies. Islam and Christianity particularly are 'religions made to travel'.[209] It reflects their entry into a new and seismic cycle of change and growth. When you survey this remarkable evidence, then religion is more globalizing than the global economy.

This brief account of globally resurgent religion is based on accumulating evidence from across disciplines and perspectives, including sociology, history, political science, philosophy and theology. I will use a critical conversation with Jenkins's[210] work as entry point into these wider literatures. Although this survey is embedded in these different discourses, some important secular material used in this Part 1 ignores this religious resurgence in its wider sense. So Hardt and Negri, Arrighi, Wolf and Bhagwati all address globalizing processes essentially without reference to one of the most significant. To some extent, this reflects the malign influence of the secularization thesis, addressed later in this section. As the twenty-first century unravels, that will change. The neglect of religion in contemporary contextual analysis will become increasingly unsustainable. Indeed, Jenkins argues the opposite: 'it is precisely religious changes that are the most significant, and even the most revolutionary in the contemporary world'.[211] Given what has emerged so far in this contextual analysis, that claim, when its unequivocal language is significantly moderated, does correlate with, and indeed is corroborated by other emerging findings in the research. Here I think of the changing balance of economic power from developed economies to emerging economies. That transition is powerfully supported by imbalanced demographic change, suggesting in total, the move away from the Western domination of empire, capitalism and globalization. Interestingly, the demographic evidence for both such secular and religious change is central to this emerging analysis. In 1950, only four nations had a population more than one hundred million (USA, USSR, China, India). By 2050, it is projected there will be seventeen, with only three being in the West (USA, Russia, with Japan), the rest including Iran, Egypt, Indonesia, Nigeria, Pakistan, Ethiopia, the Democratic Republic of Congo, etc.[212] And it is in that increasingly populous and dominant South that religion will also be dominant.

Not surprisingly that changing equilibrium is revising the traditional (that is, from 1800–2000) influence flow, as the South increasingly intrudes into the North not least through migration flows. It is represented religiously, as 'reverse' missionary endeavours, epitomized by GATE, the 'Gospel from Africa to Europe'.[213] Indeed, such is this reversion of power, that the era of Westernization, 1800–2000, may become seen as an *exception*, as an aberration in the longer frame of history. That concept of exception is particularly seminal and fruitful, describing, as it does, a series of overlapping consensuses. For example, it refers to the argument that the secularization processes of the West are an aberration in historical *and* contemporary terms – that for most of recorded history, religion and life, both individual and public, including as state, were inextricably bound together.[214] Their division in the West was the exception. Attempts to therefore assume that Western secularization processes are a prototype for the rest of the world through globalization are severely questioned, for example in Davie's fittingly titled *Europe: the Exceptional Case*. It is this reversion back away from Western domination that is being confirmed by the demographics of population and religion, and the economics of emerging economies.

What may modify 'the exceptional' claim is the growing significance of social and religious capital, and its empirical basis in well-being, and including as limits of globalization processes.

Although most of the material in the following account is drawn from Christian sources, the resurgence of religion, as it impacts on other faiths, has to be acknowledged, and will be illustrated with reference to Islam.

As with histories of empires, capitalism and globalization, the furious religion proponents in general, and their 'new Christendom' variants in particular, argue for the later twentieth and early twenty-first century as 'one of the transforming moments in the history of religions worldwide'.[215] At this point, note that it is the inclusion of this religious interpretation in wider secular discourses which gives added value to the enquiry in general and the religious section in particular, and that relevance and significance is confirmed by its interaction with the other fields.

The central part of this 'transforming moment' is provided by the resurgence of Christianity in the South, the emergence of what Buhlmann has called 'the Third Church', on the 'analogy of the Third World', as centre of tradition comparable to the movement of that centre from East to West in the first millennium.[216] It is what Jenkins describes as an emerging 'new Christendom', thus linking his ecclesiological 'emerging' with emerging economies as a cumulative weight of interpretation.[217] For Kenyan scholar John Mbiti, 'the centers of the church's universality (are) no longer in Geneva, Rome, Athens, Paris, London, New York, but Kinshasa, Buenos Aires, Addis Ababa and Manila'.[218] And as Christianity moves southward, it will be changed by 'immersion in the prevailing cultures of those host societies'.[219] Again, the comparison with the development of a variety of models in the equivalent new cycle in the empires–capitalism surveys is revealing.

Resurgent religion, causes and definitions

Resurgent religion refers to the massive growth of Christianity in this global context, and particularly to its increasing concentration in the South, a transition made all the sharper by the contrasting decline of mainstream churches in the North (except the USA).

Counting the sheep

Of the 2 billion Christians today, Europe has the most (560 million), with Latin America close behind (480 million); Africa has 360 million, Asia 313 million. Extrapolating from these figures gives us, in 2025, 2.6 billion Christians, but now, with 633 million in Africa, 640 million in Latin America, 460 million in Asia, and Europe with 555 million. 'By 2050, only about one-fifth of the world's 3 billion Christians will be non-Hispanic Whites'. That redistribution will continue apace for the rest of the century.[220]

Why the resurgence?

Three reasons particularly recur in the literatures. First, the demography of religious redistribution. Given the continuing world population growth, of historic proportions, then the fact that 99% will be in the South provides a material basis for religious revival. Second, Islam and Christianity are particularly experiencing a religious renewal, a new vibrancy, commitment and confidence, which confirms and accentuates their innate mission–expansionist character. Third, this becomes a decisive factor when inter-secting a turbulent environment caused by globalization processes and the rapid urbanization of traditional rural populations.[221] Religions that are able both to adapt to such change and to challenge it by offering alterna-tives can flourish. By providing 'warm' communities offering the hospital-ity of bonding social capital, as friendships and as health care, education and welfare, they develop identities which counter the identity-dissolving processes of globalization. The resource of a philosophy of life for personal and communal identity has historically proved to be an essential support for people encountering major social change. As al-Turabi observed, all religions provide 'people with a sense of identity and a direction in life' – 'In this process, people rediscover or create new historical identities'.[222] It is that 'direction in life' which is also now regarded as an essential factor in contemporary happiness and well-being literatures.

Profiling resurgent Christianity

Because more traditional religions are 'unable to adapt to the requirements of modernization' then 'the potential exists for the spread of Western Christianity and Islam'.[223] Realizing that potential has been the task of a resurgent Christianity which is markedly different from traditional Western mainstream Christianity and Church: it would need to be, given the major decline of the latter. It is almost as though the resurgent Christianity of the South is defined by what it is not. Unlike the 'cooler' North, it is not essentially a 'propositional Protestantism', but experien-tially based on a daily encounter with the living Christ.[224] In the West, that understanding of faith is identified with an evangelical, charismatic and Pentecostal mode, and as deviant from the mainstream. In the South, it is mainstream. A modern follower of the Shona prophet Johane Masowe vividly describes the two contrasting experiences:

> When we were in these synagogues (European Churches) we used to read about the works of Jesus Christ . . . cripples were made to walk and the dead were brought to life . . . evil spirits driven out . . . That was what was being done in Jerusalem. We Africans, however, who were being instructed by white people, never did anything like that . . . We were taught to read the Bible, but we ourselves never did what the people of the Bible used to do.[225]

The difference is that now they do. And that is resurgent religion. For the theologian Borg, on encountering this, 'it is as if we are seeing Christianity again for the first time' – 'not just for what it is, but what it was in its origins and what it is going to be in the future'.[226] There is a profound sense of replaying a vivid reappropriating of the apostolic church, a striking return to the Book of Revelation as a reliving experience of a local and global context 'ruled by monstrous demonic powers'. For Latin American liberation theologian Miguez, 'The repulsive spirits of violence, racial hatred, mutilation and exploitation roam the streets of our Babylons in Latin America (and the globe) . . .'[227] That utter dependence on the living Christ in and through the living Word of God (as both Old and New Testaments) provides the detailed guidance for personal and social living. It leads to the transformed lives of individuals, families and communities, often exhibiting a profoundly conservative character – a lifestyle linked intimately to a conservative understanding of Bible, doctrine and Church. It is a Christianity of the daily lived experience of an encounter with the Transcendent, a God who intervenes directly in all areas of life, a religion 'much more centrally concerned with the immediate workings of the supernatural, through prophecy, visions, ecstatic utterances, and healing'.[228] And it is a religion of the poor and for the poor. 'Contrary to myth [particularly in academia] the typical Christian is not a White fat cat in the United States or western Europe but rather a poor person, often unimaginably poor by Western standards.'[229]

Resurgent religion as spectrum

The concept itself covers a variety of experiences and traditions, again confirming the relevance of the Hollenbach question for this analysis, and its connection to the earlier findings on capitalism and empires. In the procedural context of their histories and of globalization, what is emerging is a new cycle but encompassing a variety of forms. The features themselves of resurgent religion allow for a broad series of interpretations and embodiments. These move from a more fundamentalist mode to a conservative form, from Pentecostalism, through African Independent Churches, to Roman Catholicism, from the Philippines to the USA. What cannot be allowed is the appropriation of the concept as furious religion, particularly as fundamentalism. Since these other forms will be developed briefly as Roman Catholicism and Pentecostalism, with reference also to the Islamic tradition, I will quickly sketch the fundamentalist and US models.

Fundamentalism

The concept itself emerged in the USA, in the first decade of the twentieth century, and portrayed a variant of conservative Protestantism. (A major study of it was conducted in Chicago in the early 1990s, producing Marty and Appleby's *Fundamentalisms Comprehended*.) Some 60 or 70 years later, it was now used to describe 'a series of trends visible in a variety of world faiths'.[230] Essentially reactive to, and sometimes resisting, modernizing projects, it developed into a range of conservative religious movements – incorporating the 're-Islamization', Hinduization and Confucianizing of society, along with Christian, ultra-Orthodox Judaism and some variants of Buddhism.[231] Interestingly most of the Chicago case studies were located outside the West and Europe. There can therefore be a strong focus on anti-Western values, particularly of a more liberal kind. There is a firm tendency to return to sacred texts and traditions, reinforcing the role of criticism of, and developing alternatives to, globalization, capitalism and (Western) empires. Yet as one commentator has observed, they are also 'quintessentially modern in the manner in which they set their goals and in the means that they adopt to achieve them: their outlooks, for example, are truly global, and their technologies highly developed'.[232] They thereby represent a reappropriation and reformulation of the modern. Their anti-modernism becomes essentially a post-modern project, a refusal of modernity.[233]

Conservative Christianity in the USA: the new Christian Right

In what is an exception to the exceptionalism of Western-Europeanized Christianity, the USA is a remarkably religious society at the heart of the processes of empire, capitalism and globalization. It is a strong caveat to the assumption that resurgent Christianity is simply an account of the South. The significance of religion in US life was evidenced by an International Social Survey Programme in 1991, covering 17 countries. This placed the USA ahead of even Ireland and Poland. The more useful World Values Survey (1990–3) covered 41 countries, with the most religious being, in order, Nigeria, Poland, India, Turkey and then the USA.[234] Surveys regularly reveal around 40% of Americans say they attend church or synagogue weekly, and 90% say they believe in God.[235] It is within that broad context of believing *and* belonging, that the resurgence of belief as conservative Christianity is so pronounced. Again this is reflected in numbers: between 1990 and 2000, the fastest growing denominations were the Mormons (+19.3%), conservative evangelical churches (18.6%), the Assemblies of God (18.5%) and the Catholic Church (16.2%). Mainline Protestant churches declined.[236] It is the manifestation of such resurgent religion in political form, as the New Christian Right, that is particularly interesting. Essentially, it is a 'social movement of conservative Christians' that has influenced the political-electoral map of the USA.[237] In the 2004 presidential election, 78% of evangelicals voted for Bush (23% of the electorate). For *The Economist* it was 'The triumph of the religious right'.[238]

Focused on a literal interpretation of the Bible to provide direction and inspiration for life in personal relationships, but now also in the political arena, it became a movement of born again Christians promoting traditional Christian values. Conversely, it was vehemently anti-secular and anti-liberal. Yet as with fundamentalism, it readily utilized modern technologies, particularly as televangelists. Beginning in the 1970s with a focus on family values, with Falwell's Moral Majority, it moved through the campaigns for a Christian presence in the public realm in the 1990s, with Pat Robertson's Christian Coalition, to a broader involvement today, also engaging with campaigns on poverty, HIV/AIDS and the environment. It has been deeply involved in developing government recognition of the contribution of faith-based organizations on public welfare issues. So Clinton's Welfare Reform Act (1996) contained a 'charitable choice provision' enabling States to contract with churches for the delivery of welfare programmes. Bush went even further, with his White House Office of Faith-Based and Community Initiatives, prohibiting federal agencies from excluding religious organizations from funding for community programmes and social services. For the *New York Times*, Bush reflected the development of a personal and public conviction 'that religion can and should occupy a central place in public and private life'.[239]

The new resurgence of Christianity in the USA has been a remarkable journey, coinciding with the intensifying of globalization, and with the transition to new cycles of capitalism and empire. In 1984, Richard Neuhaus wrote *The Naked Public Square: Religion and Democracy in America*, bewailing the absence of religion in public life. The square is no longer empty.[240]

Roman Catholicism and Pentecostalism: the (not terrible) twins of resurgent Christianity

Roman Catholicism

Although this section will focus on Pentecostalism, Roman Catholicism cannot, and must not, be ignored, as is often the case in academia. For a start, it is the biggest Christian church by far, with one billion members in 2000, a sixth of the world population.[241] And, like other forms of resurgent religion it has experienced dramatic growth since 1945, concentrated in the South, and particularly in Latin America and Africa. For example, in Africa, in 1955, it had only 16 million members.[242] Today, there are 120 million, which could rise to 230 million by 2025 (a sixth of all Catholics). Astonishingly, 37% of all baptisms are adults, clearly converting from other faiths.[243] As an illustration of this outburst of Catholicism, Tanzania's Catholics have grown by 419% since 1961, to four provinces with 29 dioceses, all now headed by bishops from the local population. Latin America is the core of the church, with 424 million members (more than Europe and North America together). By 2025, Africans and Latin Americans could constitute 60% of Catholics, with Europe, the traditional home and centre of the faith, forming a very minor part. Even today, baptisms in Nigeria and the Democratic Republic of Congo are each higher than the total from Italy, France, Spain and Poland. 'The twentieth century was clearly the last in which Whites dominated the Catholic Church: Europe simply is *not* The Church, Latin America may be.'[244]

For a church with 40% of cardinals now from the 'Third World', and the largest Jesuit province now being India (no longer America), the character of the church is also changing, essentially to a reconfirmed conservatism. It is not the recent papacy which drives that trend, but more a resurgent South-based religion: 'African Catholicism is far more comfortable with notions of authority *and* charisma than with newer ideas of consultation and democracy.'[245] That mention of charisma also reminds us that resurgent Catholicism incorporates a wide spectrum of understandings and forms. In the Philippines that moves from charismatic revivals to an 'amalgam of Christian and folk elements' in the Morian festival on the island of Marinduque during Holy Week.[246]

Pentecostalism

This constitutes the other major focus of Christian resurgence, again particularly in the South, and emerging as both a formative symbol of globalization and a deep change from traditional mainstream Western Christianity. It is now claimed to have half a billion members, and in 2000, was expanding at a yearly rate of 19 million. It is particularly strong in Latin America, Africa and increasingly in Asia – all major centres of population growth *and* of resurgent Christianity, the double pressures for religious growth.[247]

Like fundamentalism, with which, like resurgent Christianity, it shares some features, it emerged in the first decade of the twentieth century in California. 'These awakenings were themselves *harbingers of global society* and their spread corresponded to the movement of lay people around the globe, to South Africa, Norway, Sicily, Korea or the Southern Cone of Latin America. No sooner converted than en route.'[248]

As I reflected on this kind of material, in this case from a major academic source, I was struck repeatedly by the references to the global of globalization, the international of empires, and the marketplace of capitalism, as key features of Pentecostalism. Martin's analysis illustrates this par excellence, and he continues in the same mode, reflecting on its spread through 'earlier' messengers of 'a global faith' empowered by the Holy Spirit and not by an institutional church or theological education. For 'Frontiers meant little', and 'they exploited the intimations of (a) global society' spread by the English language and culture in the British and American empires, and then Spanish. So 'what began with minor hints of global religion' in Nicaragua, Mexico or Sierra Leone, expanded 'until the world capital of Pentecostalism was not the City of Angels (it began in Los Angeles) but Sao Paulo or Seoul', and all 'competing on an open market'. In major academic treatises on globalization, you never encounter this. They are profoundly inadequate as a result. Pentecostalism, as epitome of resurgent religion, is equally the harbinger of globalization.[249]

In many ways it shares the marks of a resurgent Christianity in that it engages particularly with the poor, and especially in rapidly expanding urban centres, attracting ever-increasing numbers from rural areas. In Rio de Janeiro, 700 new Pentecostal churches opened between 1990 and 1993. The mega Church of the Kingdom of God in Brazil now controls the largest TV station, a political party and a football team, and it is present in 40 other countries.[250] It's that intersection of meeting and exploiting human need using modern techniques and systems which has so contributed to its success in Latin America. In Africa it again meets the needs of a rapidly expanding demographic and urbanizing context. Spearheaded by the Assemblies of God, as in Latin America, it has achieved astonishing growth of multiple congregations and denominations. Across nations and continents it exhibits a 'free-wheeling, Spirit-filled worship style' embodying 'all the features of Pentecostal spirituality' from Boston to Rio de Janeiro to Seoul (the latter has the biggest congregation in the world, the Full Gospel Central Church, with half a million members).[251]

The classic marks of resurgent religion, as free and open style worship, as the interaction of indigenous and international, as committed to the Holy Scriptures as basis for a way of living deeply affecting personal and communal lifestyles, are all encompassed, transcended or transfigured by its central commitment to the Holy Spirit, as Spirit-transforming worship and being, as lived immediacy and enduring life-long commitment.

It is the impact on personal and so on communal living which is particularly striking, interacting in a positive *and* yet also critical way with global capitalism. Living spirit-filled lives is about conversion and transformation, in constant contact with communities disfigured by crime, drugs, poverty and unemployment.

Not surprisingly, it offers, and can become, and particularly for young people say in Nigeria, a gospel of success. Offering personal communal support, it generates independence, self-worth and self-help. It allows 'hope for material betterment in a capitalist economy to burgeon without selling out to worldly seductions'.[252] Of course, that boundary between resurgent religion as countermovement to or accommodation with global capitalism is regularly crossed intentionally, and in the longer term unintentionally, as the Protestant work ethic becomes more secularized. For Martin, Pentecostalism, despite these possibilities (or almost because of them), remains a 'major meta-narrative of global modernity', as alternative route to modernity, not as the rationality and bureaucratic Weberian Protestantism, but as 'rather . . . story and song, gesture and empowerment, image and embodiment, enthusiastic release and personal discipline.'[253] For Bernice Martin, in her 'New Mutations of the Protestant Ethic', where Pentecostalism differs most from classical Western Protestantism is its embrace of a religious version of the 'Expressive Revolutions' – 'they "let go" in their services, just as they also exercise control in earning their living. They also anticipated later developments . . . in their holistic approach to healing' (of body and mind together, supported in the community).[254]

It is this 'potent combination of empowerment with release' which, for Martin, is 'just as viable in terms of advancing modernity as rationalization'.[255] This is a remarkable judgement in terms of this enquiry. For it endorses features of the global scene, namely, economics, politics and the international, *but* from an alternative basis. It is not counter-rational, but recognizes other equally important centres of being human. One of the fundamental discoveries of the well-being and happiness studies endorses this finding of Pentecostalism. The rationality of income delivery in market economies and economics will not alone deliver well-being as profoundly holistic reality.

Islam: resurgent religion as transfaith phenomenon

Christian social ethics does not normally equip you with serious knowledge concerning religion in general, or its sacred texts, history, doctrines and ecclesiology. Learning a little about resurgent religion has been an 'eyeopener', not least because of its remarkable resonances with so many of the themes and disciplines central to this enquiry. That religious knowledge becomes even less adequate when considering faiths other than Christian. Yet this enquiry has provoked such an engagement as the beginning of a personal journey. Its initial results will become apparent in Parts 2 and 3, but equally here. For Islam, and Christianity, are the two most successful globally resurgent religions. A brief reflection on Islam is therefore quite indispensable both to embody the transfaith nature of globally resurgent religion, and also as a preliminary introduction to an important case study, in Part 2, on Muslim economics and finance, which I conducted in Manchester.[256]

Islam is widely regarded as the epitome of furious religion. Yet although Islam attracts national and world attention as a globally resurgent religion, this study clearly confirms Christianity as *equally* resurgent. Both are intentionally, historically and in the contemporary context, profoundly mission-oriented faiths, able to adapt across a wide variety of cultures and continents, particularly in Africa and Asia. For both, this current resurgence is essentially post-1945 – again in that historic generation of global change. Both expansions were fed by the same demographic factors in the South. For Islam, that has particularly occurred in the Middle East, Asia (both Central and East) and Africa.

Like much in resurgent Christianity, Islam's resurgence is both a return to sacred texts and traditions and a new creation, not least through its interaction with such a changing contemporary context. Yet it is a resurgence which is more profoundly mainstream than the Christian, not extremist or isolated, but pervasive. It is therefore 'a broad intellectual, cultural, social and political movement, prevalent throughout the Islamic world'.[257] In many ways, it is the latest phase in the adjustment of Islam to the wider world. It is also profoundly multidimensional, affecting personal, family, community, national and international life. It is driven by and represents a reawakening in personal life, with greater religious observance, reflected, for example, in a great emphasis on dress, codes and values. It can lead to the creation of countermovements and systems. For example, the Muslim Brotherhood has developed parallel (to the state) provisions of education, health care and welfare, centred on the mosque but cascading out from it – as a thick form of Islamization. It therefore speaks powerfully to the marginalized, particularly in new urban situations, for example in Gaza, and to young people and intellectuals. Again, demographic factors reinforce these trends, with the rapid expansion of Muslim populations, with the under-eighteen constituting 30–50% of the population, creating a truly explosive mix of demography and deprivation.

A further feature of this mainstream Islamic resurgence, and currently of increasing importance is its reawakening to and reassertion of *ummah*, as the community and solidarity of Islam, increasingly stretching across nations, so a threat to any (whether Palestinian, Iraqi, Chechnya or Bosnian) is a threat to all. It is therefore both global religion and total system (the two aren't coterminous but do feed each other) because it 'makes a point of being a complete system coextensive with society (including as a society of societies) and with ambitions to become the global faith'.[258] It is this completeness which is so alien to Western experience with their tradition of separating religion from politics and economics. In contrast, 'For Muslims . . . religion was not only a system of belief, worship and communal organization. It was the ultimate basis of identity, the primary focus of loyalty, the sole legitimate source of authority' over nation and economy.[259] It informs both personal, family and community life but also politics and economics, in and through the role of religious based law.

Against that backcloth of mainstream resurgent Islam, there are a variety of modes of understanding and operating, from strong tolerance to strong fundamentalism. The latter is not coterminous with Islamic resurgence, but is a significant form of it. Again it has a long history, undergoing a series of revivals in the eighteenth–nineteenth centuries, and again, post-1945. Resolutely opposed to the West and to much in modernity, it is particularly provoked by 'the progressively changing secular forms of modernity'.[260] Its most virulent form is epitomized by Al Qaeda, and its declaration of a global 'jihad against the Jews and the Crusaders' with the killing of 'Americans and their allies, civilian and military . . . as an individual duty for every Muslim who can do it in any country in which it is possible to do it'.[261]

It is the contribution of resurgent religion, including in its more fundamentalist forms, which has drawn scholars like Huntington to use the rhetoric of a clash of civilizations. Yet Jenkins's cool demographic analysis also indicates the potential for conflict, religiously based, in the emerging global context. For him, of the world's biggest nations by 2050, 20 are predominantly or mainly Christian or Muslim: 9 are Muslim (Pakistan, Bangladesh, Saudi Arabia, Turkey, Iran, Yemen, Indonesia, Egypt and Sudan), 8 are Christian (USA, Brazil, Mexico, Russia, Philippines, Zaire/Democratic Republic of Congo, Germany and Uganda) and 3 are deeply divided (Nigeria, Ethiopia and Tanzania).[262] His conclusion is disturbing: 'Demographic projections suggest that religious feuds will not only continue but will also become worse.'[263] Yet this fails to recognize the subtleties of Islam and its interaction with wider and varied contexts. In other words

> Islam may . . . be the prime form of political and social identity, but it is never the sole form and often not the primary one. Within Muslim societies, divisions of ethnicity matter much, often more than a shared religious identity . . . No one can understand the politics of, say, Turkey, Pakistan or Indonesia on the basis of Islam alone. Despite rhetoric, Islam explains little of what happens in these societies.[264]

The judgement that Islam explains little can be strongly contested. What it does remind us of is the complexity of a resurgent religion in its varied forms *and* in its interaction with environments. But that is the story of globally furious religion as a whole, from Christian Roman Catholicism and Pentecostalism to Islam, all as a profoundly post-modern embodiment, as a fusion of pre- and post-modernity, as a unique form of globalization.

What's Happening in Europe? Decline or Reformulation: A Contribution to the Global Field of Religion

For some years I have been interested in how traditions, particularly religious (although also socialist), reformulate in the light of a changing context.[265] What is becoming clearer, in the light of this enquiry, is how wide-ranging that reformulation now has to be. For example, the interactions between the fields of politics, economics, globalization and resurgent religion both confirm the importance of that task and what needs to be included in it. What is also becoming clear to me is the importance of the European experience as a contribution to the religious field. The growing power of the religious South, accentuated by institutional decline in the North (as Europe and Canada), can too easily suggest that the future lies only with the former. Yet evidence emerging from Europe both complements material from the South and formulates a unique experience into a new religious model of central importance, I will later argue, for the religious engagement with global capitalism. The development of that model into a critical conversation with capital, in the form of social and then religious capital, will begin to develop that connection. It will also lead firmly into Part 2 of this enquiry and its introductory exploration of human well-being and happiness, and the religious contribution to such an agenda.

The European experience

A brief profile of religious change in Europe is a necessary addition to any consideration of the global religious field of influence and power. For Europe has provided a historic centre of Christianity and an important avenue, through empires, for its worldwide transmission. It will continue to be a centre of geopolitical and economic power in a global context. And the nature and *intrinsic* significance of its changing religious experience confirms and extends that significance.

Any brief description of European Christianity enters into the highly contested arena of interpreting religious trends. The main features themselves are widely accepted, particularly the decline of the mainstream churches, and especially since the 1960s. For example, Anglican membership in England dropped from 2,297,571 in 1975 to 1,808,174 in 1992.[266] Hastings casts his net wider, with Anglicanism effectively halving in 30 years. I calculated a 70% drop in the Diocese of Manchester, 1960–94.[267] Yet the low levels of religious practice and credal assent, confirmed by the European Values Study surveys[268] from 1981 to 1999, need to be read alongside persisting high levels of residual belief. In the 2001 British Census, 72% of the population (42 million people) defined themselves as Christian, 'a remarkably resilient and enduring part of the social and intellectual order'.[269] This more subjective religious disposition when considered alongside declining church attendance leads Davie to correlate with her premise of 'believing without belonging' to describe the British approach to religion.[270] It is an experience widely present across Western Europe. In a marketplace of religious choice, reinforced, if not promoted, by an increasingly post-industrial capitalist society of consumerists' choice, the individual becomes more prominent, as does a more consumer approach to religion, as pick and mix. What interpreters like Davie realize is that this transition to believing rather than belonging (my modification, because over 10% still go to church) can be and is re-energized by major public events like the death of Princess Diana and the sinking of the Baltic ferry *Estonia*.[271] In other words, the development of vicarious religion, of regarding the Church as a public utility, always there, including when needed, is not the end of religion but a possible metamorphosis.[272] And, as such, it represents a profound challenge to the secularization thesis of the sociology of religion, as developed in the 1960s and 1970s by Bryan Wilson and later by Steve Bruce. That thesis argued 'that there is a necessary connection between the onset of economic and social modernization and the decline of religion as a significant feature in public (if not always in private) life'.[273] The argument therefore assumes that the rise of secularization and the decline of religion will accompany globalization processes and become a world phenomenon. It is thus a thesis significantly contradicted by the evidence of a globally resurgent religion, particularly in the demographically dominant South, *but* also by the widespread persistence of belief and the continuing but reduced importance of the institutional church in the North.

Matters arising from changing religion in Britain

The mutation of religion, as Christianity, in Britain is both complex and inclusive of indicators of potential importance for this enquiry as it is beginning to evolve. Four examples illustrate the insightful capacity of this potential.

First, there is the likely growing public awareness of not simply the significance of residual belief, but also that its erosion as belief and its institutional (church) support is a threat to this 'keystone' of the arch of European values.[274] In other words, vicarious religion depends upon the maintenance of an effective Church, and that, as we will see later, is dependent on faith communities and traditions. This unease should be linked to the Great Disruption thesis of the social capital literatures – essentially, that the 1960s to 2000 witnessed a severe decline in social capital as volunteering and trust and, conversely, an increase in social and personal 'disease' as family breakdown and crime. Since the churches are a major contributor to social capital, then their decline is part of that wider problem. Since the turn of the century therefore that unease translates into attempts to reinvigorate social capital, including through the role of faith-based organizations now promoted actively in and by public policy. In 2001, Prime Minister Blair argued that faith groups are 'playing a fundamental role in supporting and propagating values which bind us together as a nation . . . In carrying out this mission [they] . . . have developed some of the most effective voluntary and community organizations in the country.'[275]

Second, there is an emerging recognition of the importance of faith traditions and communities, as religions, in personal and public ethics. It is confirmation of the importance of rationality but also of the additionality provided by a wider framework for understanding the complexity of behaviour. It therefore recognizes the role of sacred story and place, that 'religion acts as a repository of human values and transcendental reference which can be activated in the realm of civil society' and beyond.[276] For Martin, Christianity is not simply about neighbour care but the importance also, as resource and motivation for such care, of faith embodied in 'story and image'.[277] Here there is already a strong connection with resurgent religion as Pentecostalism, but also with the following reflections on religious capital, and then well-being and happiness.

Third, there is increasing recognition, in Europe and Australia, of the growing importance of spirituality. Tacey's *The Spirituality Revolution* charts this phenomenon among young Australians, describing it as 'a deeper and more profound experience of our ordinary lives', a search for meaning, particularly by younger people, outside traditional authority structures of Church and religious doctrine.[278] It is a search, in Europe, which is 'highly personal', leading to 'therapeutic engagements and small intimate cells',[279] confirmed by Woodhead's pioneering research in Kendal indicating spirituality networks almost as influential as the Church.[280] This leads to the acknowledgment of prayer's importance in health, essentially as a clear *added value* of religion, and confirming the distinctive character and contribution of the religious field. It is this concern for spirituality which will feature later in the well-being analyses.[281]

Fourth, although the trend to the individual through choice is deep rooted in the post-industrial and post-modern societies of Europe, there is an increasing unease over its links to materialism, what James calls 'affluenza'. For him, the answer is to promote being not having. Again, there are strong links with this material, with the individual as moving beyond choice as materialism, to the countermovements noted earlier, including religious involvements in environmental and other movements. It is the recognition, central to the happiness literatures, that the increasing incomes and choices of post-industrial societies are not commensurate with increasing happiness. For Davie's reflections on European religion, it is the transition of post-industrial populations 'to place far more stress on *post*-materialist values, not least an increasing emphasis on well-being and the quality of life'.[282]

Europe: *the religious field as a variety of models*

Davie makes a convincing case, supported by this emerging contextual analysis, for regarding European religion not as 'a model for export' but something 'distinct and peculiar', essentially to be regarded as 'parallel trajectories' (quoting Baker)[283] running alongside and interacting with other models, like resurgent religion, in the religious field. It is a strong commitment to a 'multiplicity' of perspectives, of 'multiple modernities' (using Eisenstadt).[284] The mutations of European religion therefore make a major contribution to the profiling of the religious field, confirming conclusions from the empire, capitalist and globalization fields of recurring commonalities and pluralities, and particularly with regard to the early twenty-first century. It is strong confirmation of the significance of a distinct and credible religious field as an integral part of any adequate global contextualizing.

5

Social Capital
Operational Interconnectivity

Social capital is a recognition of the importance for human existence of constructive relationships resourced by associations, networks, norms and sanctions. Its attraction for academic discourse and practical politics struggling with seemingly intractable forces is that it restores human behaviour and its social embodiments in families, communities and nations to the centre of our agendas. It is profoundly at the heart of human living, of human experiences in relationships enfolding the intimacies of family life and friendships, and cascading out to neighbourhoods, institutions like companies and the NHS, and into national strategies and ethos. One can't be more practical than that. But then, of course, there is nothing more difficult than building good lasting relationships and networks. There is a profound disquiet rooted in empirical evidence of a most widespread and in-depth kind, over the significant decline in and erosion of social capital again in that epochal generation from the 1960s to the present. Very significant endeavours are underway to reverse that trend for everybody's well-being.

Reflection on social capital could quite naturally have been located in the section on capitalism. After all, it is an acknowledged, if contested, subspecies of capitalism. Yet a note of four functions which it performs justifies its location at the end of the first part of this enquiry. For social capital as human networks is a field of influence in its own right but equally that very relationality is embedded in all the other fields. It is that intrinsic relational existence which characterizes it as operational interconnectivity. That is what it is and does. The four such functions which social capital performs are: first, it enables the more effective operating of economies in general, and particularly in such emerging forms as information technology and small/medium sized enterprises (SME), so heavily reliant on networking. It is similarly central to more adequate modes of political participation and global processes. Second, it is central to questions of human behaviour, including the enlarging if not reformulating of economic understandings of the human, thereby also informing the sections

87

on globalization, capitalism and empires, not least because of the profound emphasis it places on historical contextualizing as an indispensable part of contemporary social analysis. Third, social capital is fundamentally practical, and yet centrally concerned with values, normative communities and sanctions. That in itself, as the inextricability of *ethics* in human tasks and constructions, is an emerging lesson for all sections of this contextual analysis. It is particularly focused on, and reinforced by, the contribution of social capital. Fourth, that firmly integrated normative dimension of the social task is informed and resourced by the equal recognition of the central and indispensable part played by religion in contemporary as well as historical experience. That religious field, interacting with social capital, suggests the development of a function of that religious field as *faithful capital*.

An examination of social capital therefore connects with and through every section of this contextual analysis. It is both entity, or field of power and influence in its own right, and through its strong relationship with other fields in this Part 1. It also leads naturally and logically into Part 2, with its focus on the detailed nature of that religious contribution to global change with its introductory exploration of well-being and happiness. This encapsulates a number of themes, recurring throughout the enquiry, including: measurement systems for wider understandings of political economy and more subjective states like happiness; an increasing recognition of multidisciplinary perspectives; developments of reformulated anthropologies; a revived emphasis on nature as well as nurture; the role of norms and virtues in behaviour and economics; and the central contribution of religion in interdisciplinary formations.

Historical Contextualizing: Old Continuities and New Disruptions

Most commentators trace the origins of the constituting of social capital to the late eighteenth and early nineteenth centuries – to Adam Smith's recognition that markets needed to be sustained by natural sympathies like benevolence,[285] and to de Tocqueville's related identification of the importance of the associational form of such sympathies, with 'Americans . . . for ever forming associations' and of 'the reciprocal action of men upon one another'.[286] That acknowledgement of reciprocity and association should also be traced to Edmund Burke's advocacy of 'the subdivision . . . the little platoon we belong to in society, is the first principle, the germ as it were, of public affections. It is the first link in the series by which we proceed towards a love to our country and to mankind'.[287] One hundred and fifty years later, William Temple similarly emphasized such intermediate groupings or associations using the same arguments.[288] From the 1960s onwards the concept of social capital was further refined by the work of Bourdieu, so important for this enquiry, and by Coleman and then Putnam.[289] Yet once again, as with the above study of empires and capitalism, a much longer time frame is used particularly in terms of identifying the nature and origins of the human propensity to co-operation and the development of social norms and rules, for example, in the pre-agricultural era.[290] This links with contemporary research into the role of genetics and neurophysiology, and their cumulative generation of capabilities for co-operation and social capital. These therefore become both intrinsic to human behaviour and also constructed through experience and interaction with the social environment. Such combinations will figure large in the later discussion of well-being and happiness. It suggests an important corrective to an overemphasis on environment and a consequent neglect of natural instincts as shared human capabilities and propensities.[291] It constitutes a strong challenge to post-modernism's stress on difference and its complementary rejection of universals.

For current historical accounts and interpretations of social capital, a particularly prominent part is played by what Fukuyama has vividly but accurately named the Great Disruption. It is centred, once again, on that historic era of change from the 1960s to 2000. Using data from developed economies, and principally from the 1950s, commentators began to observe both the severe decline in the classic indices of strong social capital, principally relating to voluntarism and trust, and an accompanying very marked increase in the erosion of social capital through the growth of crime and family breakdown. Fukuyama also recognizes that the Asian societies in the survey (Japan and South Korea) do not necessarily follow the American and European trajectories, suggesting the particular selective influences of cultural differences. Yet he concludes that 'all Western societies were affected sooner or later by the Great Disruption'.[292] It is also generally agreed that the surge in damaging social capital factors began to moderate, if not decline, in the 1990s, but from a very high base.

Interestingly, Putnam's magisterial and field-leading survey of social capital compared this social capital decline with the late nineteenth century in America, what he calls the Gilded Age.[293] The latter experienced similar major socio-economic disruption, but nationally rather than globally provoked. So Himmelfarb's insightful analysis of later Victorian England paints a very different picture to the American, one of emerging strong social capital based principally on the development of working as well as middle class personal, family, community and civic virtues and sanctions.[294] For Carlyle, writing in the middle of the century and on what he called 'the Condition of England' question, the key test of a nation's success was not measured by 'figures of arithmetic' about the economy, but the 'condition' and 'disposition' of the people: 'their beliefs and feeling, their sense of right and wrong, the attitudes and habits that would dispose them either to a "wholesome composure, frugality", or to an "acrid unrest, recklessness, gin-drinking, and gradual ruin"'.[295] By 1900, much of the British population had chosen the former course of high social capital. It was such positive indices which provoked Himmelfarb to *contrast* the latter stages of the nineteenth century in England with the equivalent era in the twentieth century in England and the USA, in sharp variance to Putnam's *comparison* of the American Gilded Age and the Great Disruption. Where Himmelfarb and Putnam do agree is on the latter, as a shared disturbing experience between Britain and America, what she calls in Britain, 'the de-moralisation of society'. Like Putnam she also uses the crime indices of social disruption, but more longitudinally, from 1857 to 1991.

So from 1857 to 1900, indictable offences in Britain decreased from 480 per 100,000 people to 250 (a 50% decline in 40 years, reflecting the effects of religion, education and environmental reforms). By 1931 the figures had climbed to 400 per 100,000, to 900 in 1941, and to 1,756 in 1961. But then they really do rocket up to 10,000 by 1991, a 40 times increase from 1901.[296]

Because of the significance of multidisciplinary work in such studies, it is justified, I concluded, to deploy a major historian into a field dominated by sociologists. That judgement, given the above comparative insights, begins to pay dividends. For her indices for social capital decline are similar to the sociologists, but as a historian she focuses more clearly and firmly on the central role of character and virtue formation, through norms and sanctions, including the formation of religion. Although more vividly expressed, her statistics and interpretations bear strong comparison with such important contemporary sociologists as Putnam and Halpern. An emerging consensus is being constructed, that 'we are discovering that the economic and social aspects of that problem (social capital decline) are inseparable from the moral and personal ones'.[297]

Confirming that judgement is the fact that alongside the figures for the severe increase in crime, the Great Disruption is also marked by the equally severe decline in *trust*, a core feature of social capital and of its measurement. This uses the survey question 'Generally speaking, would you say that most people can be trusted or that you can't be too careful in dealing with people?' (replicated, as we will see later, in the happiness survey).

Fukuyama therefore observes that while 10% more Americans evinced trust than distrust in the early 1960s, by the 1990 the distrusters had a 20% margin over the trusters.[298] All commentators express profound unease over this strong decline in such a foundation of social living. For, although 'trust . . . is not in itself a moral virtue, but rather the by-product of virtue . . . it arises when people share norms of honesty and reciprocity and hence are able to cooperate with one another'. Again, most commentators begin to trace that decline to the rise of an 'excessive selfishness or opportunism', of a possessive individualism which we have already linked to socio-economic changes.[299] It will also feature prominently in the later well-being and happiness analysis.

The Great Disruption, the analysis of which is far more substantial and widespread than figures on crime and trust indicate, is therefore far more penetrating than an analysis of the health of social capital. It also informs the examination of capitalism, globalization and empires, even if contained and restricted. Himmelfarb has vigorously reminded us that the covert, when so significant as norms and sanctions, cannot be so contained. Resurgent religion, among other factors, is another strong reminder of that truth.

What is Social Capital? Definitions and Elaborations

For Putnam, the most acclaimed and accomplished social scientist currently in this field, social capital refers to the 'Features of Social Life – networks, norms and trust – that enable participants to act together more effectively to pursue shared objectives . . . Social capital, in short, refers to social connections and the attendant norms and trust.'[300] It is a series of factors which featured prominently in the analysis of the Great Disruption in terms of social capital's erosion, and in their central role in its rehabilitation. And, for Halpern, not surprisingly, it is a concept which therefore 'captures the political Zeitgeist of our time: it has a hard-nosed economic feel while restating the importance of the social'.[301] That recognition of the combination of economic and social forms the basis of social capital's interconnectivity. And, because Halpern also recognizes the need for a more nuanced approach to both disciplines, economics and sociology, and incorporates them into his study of social capital, this section will rely on his work in conversation with Putnam and Bourdieu. The latter particularly reinforces that interdisciplinary approach. Halpern, in addition, usefully epitomizes important differences of emphasis in the European as against the American perspectives, particularly and importantly giving greater prominence to the role of government and inequality in analysis and policy formation. This difference features strongly in the later well-being study.

Having acknowledged the relevance of the concept to the prominence of political economy in contemporary context and discourse, Halpern rightly then locates it in a dissection of capital itself. In general usage, *capital* for him is any 'form of material wealth used, or available for use, in the production of more', but then it is expressed in different forms, as *financial* (to purchase factors of production), *physical* (stocks which contribute to the purchase of others), *human* (the stock of expertise accumulated by the worker), *institutional* (organizational, including as company) and *social* (networks and norms).[302] To this clarificatory list should now be added *natural* capital as environment and ecological resources, *cultural* (not to be confused with human) and, as I will later argue, *faithful* capital (the distinctive resources of faith communities and traditions).

For Halpern, social capital itself has three *components*: first, networks (as communities, neighbourliness); second, social norms and values as behaviour – including helping others, courtesy, habits of reciprocity – such as keeping an eye on children and homes; third, sanctions – to maintain social norms, and often informal.[303]

He then divides social capital into three *types*: first, *bonding*, as the property of more inward looking groups, reinforcing their identity, as like with like, and so can be hostile to strangers, as bad social capital (for Putnam, bonding social capital represents the *superglue* of capital); second, *bridging* social capital, connecting groups and networks – as a sociological WD-40, and essential, because it goes beyond bonding, for healthy social capital; third, *linking* social capital, connecting to those with more power, often institutionally as economic and political power.[304]

He then usefully works with three *levels* at which social capital operates – individual and close relationships (micro), associations and firms (meso), and national (macro).[305]

Having defined it, including through locating it in relation to other forms of capital, he acknowledges the problem posed by connecting the warmth and intimacy of social relationships with the hard realities of economics. In other words, is social capital really capital? For prominent economists like Arrow and Solow, the answer is no, even though strong social capital does reduce transaction costs (making it easier to work together economically because of trust and truth-telling).[306] In addition, you can choose to invest in social capital: a manager can invest in new machines (physical capital), train people (human capital) *or* send a group on a weekend course (social capital – as network and trust building). Yet you cannot sell it. Yet, for Halpern and many others, including global institutions like the OECD, 'An Economic model that ignores social capital, human capital and investment in public goods would be a pretty poor model.' Given such reports as the OECD's 'The Well-being of Nations: The Role of Human and Social Capital' (2001), then 'by 2010 the term (social capital) will be at least no more controversial than "human capital" is today', across developed and developing economies.[307] That said, there will always be some unease over the economicization of social relations. Yet that interaction of economic and social – and I would add, of religion – is becoming an increasingly vital area to seek that common ground between disciplines and experiences in relation to an inclusive global well-being.

As an illustration of the central importance of social capital, as normative paradigm, to this total process, and including its strong links with religion, *trust* embodies the indispensable character of social capital for well-being. In all the literatures it occupies a most prominent place as a key constituent of social capital and wider socio-economic processes, and of the measurement of its health or ill-being.

For Fukuyama it is a 'key by-product of the cooperative social norms that constitute social capital. If people can be counted on to keep commitments, honor norms of reciprocity, and avoid opportunistic behaviour, then groups will form more readily, and those that do will be able to evolve common purposes more efficiently.'[308] As a by-product of virtue it therefore arises when shared norms of honesty and reciprocity resource the ability to co-operate with each other. And, most disturbingly, there is again much evidence that this controlling norm for well-being is eroded by excessive selfishness and opportunism.[309]

This operational interconnectivity of social capital is also embodied in key areas of human living, for example, in health, education and democratic government. Again, all three feature in the later well-being examination.

Health is a crucial indicator of well-being and happiness, and is intimately and powerfully correlated with the presence of strong social capital. The early research, led by Durkheim, had already noted the link between suicide and the paucity of the close social relationships and networks of social capital: so 'suicide varies inversely with the degree of integration of the social groups of which the individual forms a part'.[310] Throughout these literatures, the role of the individual in social networks provides a vital buffer from life's turbulences in all three of Halpern's levels. For example, good personal relationships, especially as marriage and close friendships, play central empirically verifiable roles in both promoting good health and overcoming ill-health from common cold to breast cancer. (Indeed, for the economist Oswald, marriage is equivalent to an additional $100,000 per annum for well-being.)[311] Again, health and ill-health are strongly correlated with inequality, in this case with where you live. The death rate from heart disease for the under-65s is three times greater in Manchester than Kingston and Richmond (2000), strong evidence of the detrimental impact of inequality on social capital (and later, on well-being).[312]

Education registers the same positive correlation between performance and social capital. Where families and schools cooperate, greater educational achievements occur, reflecting the importance of networks linking parents, children and school as the development of shared values and sanctions.[313] Again, involvement in higher education generates similar results, with students learning social capital skills, such as reciprocity and co-operation, as in one's best interest, and thereby as contributions to common norms and social cohesion. In the happiness literature, particularly in the work of the economic historian Offer, such education is an integral part of the crucial development of self-control, of particular importance in a post-industrial consumer-driven society.[314]

Finally, social capital firmly correlates with increasing participation, reduced corruption, and greater government efficiency. In the USA, 'states with higher social capital as measured by social trust, volunteering and census response . . . had significantly better governmental performance'.[315] The World Values Survey corroborates these findings – that higher social trust (between strangers) is associated with low corruption, high bureaucratic quality, higher tax compliance, infrastructure quality, and the efficiency and integrity of the legal system.

Similarly, the Surveys indicate that social trust fosters democratic governance as well as economic growth – that higher social capital is associated, for Halpern, with '*virtuous citizenry*'[316] (or moral citizenry as a clearer link to the moral growth, economics and globalization to be discussed later) – as reflecting, for Putnam, our 'better more expansive selves'.[317] Further reflection even suggests, for Halpern's concluding thoughts on participatory governance and social capital – that 'it would seem communities with high and egalitarian social capital foster more civic citizens who are easier to govern, a ready supply of co-operative political leaders, and a fertile soil in which government institutions can grow.'[318] These institutions then reinforce values and behaviour further, as a continuing interactive development. Indeed, for Halpern, some may view such democratic and participatory governances as a form of social capital, especially as the common normative framework they embody gradually spreads into a shared global understanding of how people should trust and respect each other. It is a powerful illustration of the nature and potential of social capital in itself and through interaction with economics and politics in global frameworks. This resulting implication for a global ethic or ethics will be addressed in Part 3.

Further Reflections on Social Capital as Being Human and Practical: 'Economic Anthropology' and Government Policies

A number of matters for further consideration have begun to emerge from the overall contextual analysis, some of which have been confirmed and elaborated by this social capital material. I have chosen two, first, the implications of social capital for what Bourdieu calls an 'economic anthropology',[319] essentially addressing the limits of the mainstream economic tradition's understanding of human behaviour, and the critical role which, it can be argued, social capital performs in that readjustment. The second briefly reflects on the contribution of government to rebuilding social capital. Both also act as preambles to the matters addressed in Part 3, but also to the well-being section in Part 2.

Rethinking anthropology

An agenda of some importance has begun to emerge centred on human behaviour, and particularly its deployment in economics. Social capital contains resources for critically engaging its formulation in capitalism and mainstream economics by bringing the decisive social nexus of human relationships into the forefront of any reformulation of anthropology.

Bourdieu's work is particularly useful for exploring these relationships because of his critical but constructive conversation with mainstream neo-classical economics. Out of this, ways can also be developed into wider relationships with today's empire as epitome of neo-liberal economics and politics, but also, more importantly, with orthodox economics. Confirmed by this enquiry is also his emphasis on historical contextualizing as an essential part of such analysis and interpretation. Bourdieu clearly argues that 'the social world is present in its entirety in every "economic" action' and theory, including the mainstream neoclassical.[320] Most importantly, *this does not unduly erode* the significance and achievements of economics, but carefully acknowledges its limitations. For what economics does is to universalize a particular case, namely modern economics and the context out of which it arose. It is when that is elevated into a 'de-historicized and de-historicizing science' imposed on the world that it becomes unaccept-able.[321] Much theological opinion would support that judgement.

Out of this critical conversation with mainstream economics, Bourdieu develops what he describes as 'Principles of an Economic Anthropology'. This addresses a foundation of modern economics in terms of its view of human behaviour in economic life (as 'economic man', the rational, self-interested individual maximizing its utility in an open competitive free market). His task is 'to break with the dominant paradigm' through an 'expanded rationalist vision', of 'the historicity constitutive of agents and of their space of action' – an attempt to construct 'a realist definition of economic reason as an encounter between dispositions which are socially constituted'.[322]

His aim, like Tanner's theologically (as we will see in Part 3), and mine in Christian social ethics, is to develop an understanding of human behaviour in the field of economics which is both a more accurate representation of social behaviour because it takes account of its embeddedness in networks of social relations, and yet engages in a constructive conversation with economists who understand the possibilities in economics for such an enlarged discourse on economic anthropology.[323] Essentially it represents the consideration of a profound realism in economics, at least in its reformulation of economic man. For the traditional view of economics is increasingly disconnected from major discourses in modern social sciences. As Durkheim, very early in this dialogic process observed:

> Political economy . . . remained an abstract, deductive science, concerned not with the observation of reality, but with the construction of a more or less desirable ideal. For this abstract man, this systematic egoist whom it describes, is solely a creature of reason. Real man – the man whom we all know and whom we all are – is much more complex: he is of a time, of a country; he has a family, a city, a fatherland, a religious belief and political idea'.[324]

What Bourdieu does is to bridge that gulf between economics and sociology by observing and then developing empirically based *correspondences* between the regularities observed in economic behaviour by economists and the behavioural dispositions generated by social networks.[325] What emerges out of this interactive process are *reasonable* (not rational) expectations of human behaviour.[326] It suggests an economic anthropology that fits more carefully with both an evolving economics and the mainstream understandings of social capital. It is a combination which resonates with Sweden's *'solidaristic individualism'*,[327] as a combination of neoclassical economics' individual and Bourdieu's social. It is a view of human behaviour that recognizes that the narrow definition of economic behaviour – of Becker, for example – contradicts the 'best-established findings of the historical sciences'. It also recognizes that many of the 'established findings of economic science are perfectly compatible with the philosophy of agents, action, time and the social world' and that this is quite different from 'the one normally accepted by the majority of economists'.[328] That recognition of *agency*, so central to Christian social ethics as noted in the introduction, is equally central to social capital as constructing adequately normative relationships, but equally to economic behaviour. When that agency is also located in fields of power, as it must be, it accepts that it is then informed by wider structures and relationships of power. This is also an important corrective to social capital understandings when they are described in apolitical terms, and not rooted in the historical details of a sociopolitical context informed by capitalism, empires and globalization. Such an evolving reformulated anthropology is therefore a challenge to both mainstream economics and to the mainstream sociology of social capital. And it also projects an informative bridge into Part 3 of this enquiry and its concern with developing a Christian anthropology.

Government and social capital

The intrinsic interconnectivity of social capital lends itself to an important formulation of the processes of policy-making, which Halpern calls the 'Catherine wheel model', and which he rightly describes in the language of virtuous and vicious circles: for example, the latter reflects how a society of low trust will normally fail 'to build trusted institutional structures'[329] as we have seen societies like Sweden settle into – as structural frameworks promoting public goods like education and welfare state, which erode inequalities and promote environments of such trust, community and associational life. The practice of promoting virtuous circles supported by strong measures against vicious circles will also feature strongly in Part 3, including through the work of Tanner. It is a reminder, too, that public policy committed to promoting social capital will address, as a matter of fundamental importance, the presence of grave inequalities. The literatures are very strong in their deep unease over the clear consequences of economic and social inequalities for social capital – and therefore for how this impacts on health, education and democracy. Although Halpern emphasizes the attack on inequality, and the role of the state in it, more than the American commentators, he does note how Putnam very firmly judges that 'Inequality and social solidarity are deeply incompatible',[330] that, as Bourdieu recognizes, unless such inequalities of structured power relationships are addressed, then relationships and networks will continue to be severely restricted in terms of attaining a societally inclusive well-being.[331] Putnam's and Halpern's resulting agenda for 'moral entrepreneurs' or social capitalists (so reminiscent of James's 'unselfish capitalism' in the well-being literature) in fact focuses on policy areas which lend themselves to addressing inequalities – namely, child welfare and education, health and productive neighbourhoods, wealth, and democratic citizenship.[332] Indeed, Halpern picks up six strategies from Putnam's later *Better Together* (that is, how to reverse the Great Disruption of social capital) which Halpern then develops through his three levels of society, of micro, meso and macro, in ways which clearly include engaging inequalities and their negative implications for social capital. For example, at personal micro level he focuses on more support for families through better child-care facilities and more effective entrances into and support for employment. What Halpern could have developed further was to translate his recognition of the role of norms, values and sanctions in the better functionings of both social capital and market economies into a supportive political economy itself, for example, by using his work with Putnam's *Better Together* and its concept of enforcing *a moral economy* and its sustainability including as embodied in working relationships (taken from United Parcel Service team working).[333] Again, it is a forceful reminder of the emerging ways in which reformulating economic behaviour as a more social and *moral* anthropology connects with developing more social capital informed political and economic strategies. A further development which Halpern could have encouraged, which is also part of Putnam's six *Better Together* strategies, is the recognition of the formative role of religion in that preferred resurgence of social capital: British academia, like the American, is regularly overinfluenced by the intrinsically defective secularization thesis, and therefore regularly underrates or ignores the religious contribution. Empirical credibility will increasingly challenge that persistence.

Religion and Social Capital: The Unlikely but Logical Bridge into Faithful Capital as Subspecies of the Religious Field

There is considerable agreement in the social capital literatures over the significant contribution that religion, as Christian churches and members, has made to the flourishing of social capital, and should make in its hoped for recovery from the Great Disruption. It is an argument which recognizes both the weight of that contribution, but also its nature or character, particularly with reference to its actual and potential *added value*, that is the distinctively different character, which is intrinsically part of Christianity, and which adds a unique dimension to its contribution to well-being. It is this total religious contribution – as what it shares with others in promoting social capital, and what it additionally brings to the table – which, I will argue, leads into a recognition of it as *faithful capital*. And that is an intimate part of the religious field, and not of social capital, although it clearly overlaps with social capital. The sheer weight and significance of the religious field, including its historical and contemporary plurality and complexity, for example today as resurgent and Western Christianity, both confirms that locating of faithful capital and its significance.

The evidence is clear and unequivocal that 'Faith communities in which people worship together are arguably the single most important repository of social capital',[334] certainly in America, as Putnam is here arguing, but also in Britain – for example, as described in detail in the report *Faith in England's Northwest: The contribution made by faith communities to civil society in the region* (2003) and its subsequent report, *Faith in England's Northwest: Economic Impact Assessment* (2005), the latter of which measured the economic value of the two assets of faith communities in the region, their buildings and volunteers, suggesting the overall figure of between £90.7 million and £94.9 million per annum.[335] In the USA, similarly, half of associations are church-related, half of personal philanthropy, and half of volunteering.[336] The list of organizations promoted by the Crystal Cathedral, an evangelical church in California, included in 1991, sessions devoted to Women in the Marketplace, Stretch and Walk Time for Women, Compulsive Behaviours, Career Builders' Workshop, Cancer Conquerors, Positive Christian Singles, Gamblers Anonymous, Women Who Love Too Much, Overeaters Anonymous, and Friday Night Live (for junior high schoolers). The complex also includes restaurants and a Family Life Centre with a swimming pool, saunas and steam rooms.[337] Such an audit reminds me of a similar array of associations hosted in churches in Halifax in England in 1890: the Northgate End Unitarian Church had a large choir, a strangers committee, a poor fund, a Sunday School, a Band of Hope, a Penny Bank, Elocution Society, Guild of St Christopher, a Rambling Society an Orchestral Society, and a Mutual Improvement Society.[338]

From that base as and in church, essentially as schools of social capital formation as well as of democracy, churchgoers were 'substantially more likely to be involved in secular organizations, to vote and participate politically in other ways and to have deeper informal social connections'.[339]

And it is an influence which bears some correlation with the type of church – so more conservative evangelical churches are stronger on bonding social capital, on fostering the relationships of like with like, than they are with the bridging social capital serving the community. 'Historically, (and contemporarily) mainline Protestant church people provided a disproportionate share of leadership to the wider civic community, whereas both evangelical and Catholic churches put more emphasis on church-centred activities'[340] (the differences between the Californian and the Halifax churches reflects more than a historical and contextual contrast; the latter included more community-oriented organizations). Interestingly, the social capital literatures also detect a relationship between more hierarchical and authoritarian faiths like Catholicism and Islam and lower social capital.[341]

It is when attention is drawn to the religious motivation for such civic behaviour that the *distinctive* character of the religious contribution particularly begins to emerge and becomes clearer. Putnam therefore recognizes 'the tie between religion and altruism' as embodying 'the power of religious values'. For Wald, 'Religious ideals are potentially powerful sources of commitment and motivation' so that 'human beings will make enormous sacrifices if they believe themselves to be driven by a divine force'.[342] This *difference factor*, I will call it, ensures that whereas 75–80% of church members gave to charity in the USA, only 55–60% of non-members do, and 50–60% of church members volunteer, while only 30–35% of non-members do.[343] That difference factor is further enlarged by research which is beginning to suggest that religious activities, like prayer, have 'beneficial psychological and social effects' among young people, including developing 'pro social attitudes' and an enhanced 'sense of purpose in life'.[344] This also correlates with greater happiness findings.[345]

Faithful Capital: Why the Additionality Factor?

Explaining the enhanced contributions of faith communities to social capital in general, and to the additionality factor in particular, is exercising a growing number of researchers. For example, Gill's analysis, based on the European Value Systems Study Group and other research studies, suggests that 'beliefs of churchgoers are more distinctive than has often been realised by theologians, by sociologists or even by the public at large'.[346] It is that distinctive character which arguably forms a principal foundation of the religious contribution to society. This feature accounts significantly for the distinctive and discrete integrity of the religious field in general, and therefore of its contribution to social capital, among other things. And it was the major Church report, *Faithful Cities*, which described it as faithful capital.[347]

In terms of the serious development and elaboration of that concept, I have found the work of the William Temple Foundation to be most useful. Its three-year research project, culminating in the report *Faith in Action: The dynamic connection between spiritual and religious capital* (2006), distinguishes between two dimensions of faithful capital: first, *religious* capital is *what* religion contributes as concrete actions and resources. This is well documented, including with regard to social capital, as noted above. Further elaboration will occur in Part 2 of this enquiry, both as partnerships with others, and as more distinctively faith based (as Fair Trade, Jubilee 2000, and Muslim interest-free finance).

The second dimension is *spiritual* capital as the *why* of the religious contribution, 'the motivating basis of faith, belief and values (sometimes expressed in tangible forms as worship, credal statements and articles of faith, or more intangibly as one's own 'spirituality') that shapes the actions of faith communities'.[348] Gill's study adds to this with reference to regular hymn singing together as congregation, as an important element in the formation of the spiritual character of Christians.[349] For the William Temple Foundation (WTF), embarking on a major three-year Leverhulme Trust funded research project on religious and spiritual capital, spiritual capital warrants further elaboration, given the centrality of the additionality factor to this enquiry. For the WTF, it refers to 'the values, ethics, beliefs and vision which faith communities bring to civil society at the global and local level. It also refers to the holistic vision for change held within an individual person's set of beliefs.'[350] It is that tracing from commitment to God and therefore to caring for others, which is a transformatory experience derived from the transformatory encounter with and worship of God. The detailed research into churches in Manchester and their involvement in the urban regeneration of some of the most deprived communities in England, confirmed and formulated this understanding of the motivational power of religion. Seven strands were particularly identified as integral to that spiritual formation (and therefore to religious social outputs), namely: (1) transforming people personally and spiritually, with an 'over-arching hope that the transformation will occur', (2) valuing personal stories about how individual regeneration occurs (and so beyond rationality); (3) belief that God is at work within urban regeneration; (4) acknowledging the importance of feelings – of anger, frustration, weariness, cynicism and fragility; (5) introducing into the discourse values of self-emptying, for-giveness, transfiguration, risk-taking and openness to learning; (6) accept-ing those rejected elsewhere; (7) valuing people's inner resources, and 'seeing people as capable of creating their own solutions to problems'.[351]

The WTF's conclusions are particularly interesting, emphasizing that religious capital is not simply a 'bankable commodity', to be 'stored, counted or controlled'. It is rather 'continuously created within a society increasingly interested in and shaped by the values of faith and spiritu-ality'.[352] This confirms my earlier conclusion that it is likely that Western European religion and society is undergoing a reformulation likely to lead to a renewed contribution to and understanding of religious contributions.

Like social capital's question, is it really capital, is faithful capital really religion? Some, like Davey, are at least unsure, if not rejecting – because religion's core values are likely to be unacceptably distorted by the eco-nomic rationalities of capital.[353] A recognition of the variety of capitals, which vary in the nature and extent of their materiality, questions this negative judgement, as does the profound materiality of Christianity, centred on its incarnational beliefs and practices. My judgement is clear. As an important component of the religious field, interacting with other fields identified say in the first part of this enquiry, both understandings substantiate its claim and indeed require it. Indeed, like F. D. Maurice, I regard what some see as faithful capital's provocative nature as a plus not a minus. For Maurice courageously brought together, in 1848, two totally contradictory realities, so the contemporary context and opinion per-ceived, namely Christianity and socialism, essentially the oil of religion and the water of atheism. Yet Maurice used the concept of Christian socialism as a profound two-headed challenge, on the one hand to 'unchristian socialists' (or the secular), and on the other hand to 'unsocial Christians' (or the churches).[354] In other words, faithful capital is a challenge to capi-talist political economy and economics to recognize the importance of the moral, a recognition reinforced by these reflections on social capital, including as religion, and a challenge to religion to engage with political economy. And that of course, is the task of this enquiry in general, and of this particular part, of the contextualizing of interactive fields.

Part 2

The Religious Contribution: A Complex in Complexities

Introduction

Over the years of this research project new openings and possibilities frequently presented themselves. For example, awareness of the value of economics and economies for human living was both historically rooted and contemporarily expressed. Yet studying that significance also revealed its limits. Its juxtaposition with other fields of influence and power, whether the politics of empire or the processes of globalization forcefully embodied such locational constraints. Interacting with social capital focused attention on another kind of widespread limit, that of a social relationality which is both an essential addition to economic understandings and a challenge to them. The religious field and its faithful capital subdivision reinforced that constraint and added further enlarging perspectives.

As this research unfolded the trail regularly led into what I have referred to as the well-being happiness literatures. Their creative function was to both crystallize these arguments about the strengths and limitations of political economy in the emerging contemporary global context, and to take them forward. They enriched existing understandings and suggested new directions. Then suddenly, in an insightful study of emotional ill-being in global elites, I came across three jokes. In these literatures, there are very occasionally pictures, more frequently graphs, and invariably heavy densely printed texts. But never jokes. What delighted me, and the congregation in my local church in Blackrod, a large village 20 miles north of Manchester, will make you smile. For the conclusion is totally unexpected, and quite delightfully mad. Most importantly, it should inject a slight touch of happiness into your life. And that will lead into my examination of the happiness and well-being literatures.

It is a joke told by a New Zealander against the Australians.[1]

The great Aussie game-hunter was stalking the jungles of Africa when he stumbled across a beautiful woman lying provocatively on her back in a clearing.

'Wow!' he said. 'Are you game?' With a seductive smile she replied, 'Why, yes, I am'.

So he shot her.

Part 1 has established the religious field as a field of influence and power in its own right and through its inevitable interaction with other fields. It behaves, in other words, like any other relatively autonomous field.

As the religious field, it is in itself a complex: I have simply noted the importance of resurgent religion, the reformulation of Western religion, and the conversation between social capital and faithful capital. All have historical and contemporary dimensions.

Its relationships with other fields, including empires, capitalism and globalization, and including its role in the recognition of the strengths and limitations of political economy, add significantly to its weight. The cumulative effect highlights the integrity and relative autonomy of the religious field and therefore its indispensable place in the total global context. It is a complex in itself located in the midst of complexities.

What Part 2 of this enquiry seeks to do is to fill that religious field out further with reference to the contemporary context (Chapter 7). It will therefore examine some of the features of its contributions to global change from two perspectives. First, as basic account, empirically based, and covering such activities as religious involvement in partnerships in such areas as poverty reduction through economic development and environmental involvements. Second, it will also consider the nature of that contribution, including how it represents a spectrum of faith contributions from overlapping between faith and secular in partnership to the ability to discern the difference or additionality factor in these and other involvements. That factor was identified towards the end of Part 1. Here, it will be particularly illustrated through three examples, fair trade, international debt relief and interest-free finance. The latter is important because it represents Manchester-based research through Christian–Muslim conversations on finance.[2] This also generated an economic critique of such faith-based economics which also relates to fair trade and debt relief. The Manchester example additionally illustrates a dimension which runs through these explorations of the religious contribution, namely the importance of drawing material from a number of world faiths. They also illustrate the relevance of the Hollenbach question in the religious field. Each faith is clearly autonomous yet when engaging in poverty reduction or environmental rehabilitation, they also reveal significant correspondences between them. This material then feeds into the reflections on the problems and possibilities of interfaith social ethics in Part 3.

However, before this chapter on religious contributions, there is a substantial reflection on the happiness–well-being material (Chapter 6). It will constitute both an entry point into the religious contributions, but also a strong link between Parts 1 and 3 of this enquiry. Its function both reflects the emerging character of the enquiry and the opportunities for transforming the global context. It therefore embodies a complex of disciplines and perspectives, within which the ethical and religious occupy a significant place. Most importantly, it therefore provides a bridge between the account of what is, in Part 1, to what needs to be, in Part 3. It illustrates the capacities of the global market economy for promoting human well-being but also its equally formidable limitations. To overcome both, because the limitations interact with the strengths, is the task of the final part of the enquiry. The well-being literatures contain resources for such an objective.

6

The Happiness Hypothesis as Paradigm for Global Change and Religion's Contribution
The Development of Faithful Economics

The evidence for the strengths and limitations of economic processes is increasingly evident in the current global context. They are a profoundly costly benefit. The happiness hypothesis focuses on that paradoxical character of contemporary prosperity. So, the astonishing increase in global wealth since 1945 is centrally linked to increasing well-being through better health, education and income as measured by the Human Development Index of the United Nation's Development Programme (HDI of the UNDP).[3] Yet most importantly it has not resulted in any increased happiness particularly in advanced economies like our own. The evidence for economic growth as both opportunity for and obstacle to human well-being is informed and elaborated by an accumulation of disciplines and experiences, which includes economics but spreads wider and wider encompassing traditions such as psychology and epidemiology. An Oxford philosopher and a World Bank economist have recently convincingly demonstrated that 'Beyond some minimal level, increasing income appears at best weakly correlated with improvements of welfare, dignity or contentment (happiness) within or across countries over time.'[4] Indeed, they go much further in their reflections questioning, in effect, whether a free market economy on its own, as the predominant social arrangement in the world today, can deliver adequate and sustained well-being: for 'there is evidence that income equality, gender equality, and measures of civil rights may all be *causally related* to welfare outcomes including infant mortality and life expectancy'.[5]

The happiness hypothesis crystallizes this complex and contested debate particularly as entry point into a series of arguments which range far wider, embracing economics, economic history, psychology, sociology, epidemiology, philosophy and religion. Some of these, although evidencing striking correspondence of analysis and policy implications with much in the hypothesis, can be very critical of it.[6] All acknowledge the strong role of ethics in diagnosis and solution. Some go further and also accept the complementary contribution of religion. An exploration of the happiness hypothesis therefore summarizes many of the findings of the first part of this enquiry and clearly leads into the second. For the contribution of religion to global change is both part of wider collaborations and in itself also something quite different.

There are other reasons why I have chosen to begin this part of the enquiry with the happiness hypothesis. Managing such complex materials was becoming more and more difficult. The trail begun by the hypothesis, leading as it did into such very varied yet related materials, thereby presented me with a kind of archaeological trench dug into such a profusion of fields of power, experiences and academic disciplines. Because it also offered strong evidence for the importance of the contribution of religion to well-being, it provided not simply an entry point into this survey of religion's contribution to society. It also contained the possibilities for shaping religion's role in the transformation of capitalism. That is no wild claim. For the empirical evidence for the valued part religion plays in happiness–well-being has been confirmed and enhanced by the weight of evidence from Part 1 of the integrity and substance of the religious field as equal force with the other fields. Religion can no longer be discounted in contemporary debates. The task now is to explore in detail what it can offer to human well-being.

A definitional cautionary explanation. This examination begins with the happiness hypothesis as elaborated by the economist Layard, with the concept itself drawn from the work of the psychologist Haidt.[7] The development of the argument *in* and *through* the circles of academic disciplines, which significantly overlap with the original hypothesis but clearly add new material, widens both the evidence base and its conceptual definition. A major problem with the hypothesis is what is regarded as its subjective nature. When it is linked with the 'harder' resources of welfare and dignity (or rights), their combination as well-being reinforces its strengths and balances its limitations. That is the Kennys' argument, and it carries much conviction. Its links with another related (in terms of findings) discipline, namely epidemiology, and Wilkinson's study of health and inequalities, continue that process of refinement and elaboration.[8] This includes confirming Bourdieu's essential criticism of much social capital literature, that the conduct of individuals in their relationships cannot be divorced from their location in fields of power. The happiness hypothesis contains insights which consider this role of inequalities in the actual deformation of well-being and in its possible rehabilitation. No comprehensive consideration of market economies and economics should ignore these findings from such a wide complex of disciplines and experiences and their remarkable consistencies. So, we begin with the happiness hypothesis, and then connect with the wider well-being concept and literatures.

The argument of this section will progress from, first, further reflections on definitions, representing paradoxes and transitions drawn from different disciplines, second, a brief historical contextualizing of the subject from hunter-gatherers to contemporary American economists, third, descriptions and elaborations, bringing together corresponding profiles of what constitutes happiness and well-being, and their embodiment in health, marriage and teenage pregnancies, and inequality; and finally, selected matters arising from the happiness material which are of critical importance for the religious field's contribution to global change, including through the development of faithful economics.

Definitional Explorations: Transitions, Paradoxes and Histories

The happiness hypothesis, and its evolving interaction with related areas of interest, is a recognition of the essential contribution to well-being of economics in general and economic growth in particular – as both historical phenomenon and contemporary and continuing necessity and reality. Like the modern demographic explosion the economic advance occurs in a roughly similar time frame, in the nineteenth and twentieth centuries. The results have been widespread and far-ranging, not least in terms of environmental consequences, and centrally including the liberation of the human from the scarcity of absolute poverty. Yet the price of that liberation, so epochal for well-being, has been the progressive inability of increasing income to deliver corresponding increases in happiness. Indeed, some argue that these economic processes, in the form of the market economy, themselves generate obstacles to happiness. To describe this predicament, the literatures use the two languages of transition and paradox.

Transitions

The concept of transition has already featured in this enquiry in relation to demographic change. Alongside the development of the industrial revolution, the demographic transition referred to the evolving global population explosion from one to six billion (1800–2000), but which in its source, Europe, has now gone into reverse, with the average number of children per woman dropping from five to two. That transition is now occurring in developing economies at varying rates, now achieved in China and only beginning in sub-Saharan Africa. What took 150 years in Germany, took 70 in China.[9] The relationship between economic growth and the demographic transition is complex and interactive. The language of demographers reveals that. So for Livi-Bacci it is a journey from 'waste to economy', from 'disorder to order', from high birth and death rates to a sustainable low rate of natural increase.[10] And it is a transition with profound consequences across many fields, substantially shaping, for example, the changing power relationships within the religious field with the centre of influence moving from the North to the resurgent religion of the South.

The following three transitions are drawn from the literatures. They suggest a gradient from basic needs, through disease to behaviour. Like the demographic transition, all are connected to economic change and relate to the consequences of overcoming absolute poverty, one of the great achievements in human history. The transition to agricultural production was of a similar order of importance, and like the demographic transition was closely linked to population growth and the ability to now resource it, but at very low levels either in or on the edges of absolute poverty for most.[11] To break that constraint was the achievement of the industrial revolution. Its increasing effectiveness in delivering resources for living generated, however, new problems for a post-scarcity age in terms of promoting happiness (the basic human needs transition), health (the epidemiological transition) and co-operative arrangements (the behavioural transition). Together, they present another major challenge for human development, intimately linked to economic change, and offering important possibilities for the contribution of faithful economics.

First, the basic human needs transition occurs, as Offer observes, when 'basic deprivations are remedied and basic needs are satisfied'.[12] Beyond this point, other challenges arise, including the happiness hypothesis, because 'once subsistence income is guaranteed, making people happier is not easy'.[13] The point at which this transition occurs may vary according to the stages of economic growth in developed and developing economies. Most of the happiness hypothesis literature has focused on the former. For example, Layard concludes that once a nation's per capita income is over $15,000–18,000, the level of happiness is independent of rising income. Interestingly, this links to measurements of poverty as relative deprivation: the US Federal Poverty level for a family of four is $18,400, and $17,500 in Britain.[14] That connection is important because the happiness hypothesis works with a spectrum from happiness to unhappiness, with the complex of features associated with relative deprivation clustered at the negative end. Poverty reduction is therefore an important contribution to well-being in advanced as well as emerging economies. With regard to developing economies, the transition point to well-being could be much lower. I have encountered several sets of figures which provide interesting perspectives on the issue. On the one hand, in relation to health, Kenny uses Diener and Diener's (1995) research which suggests an index of basic needs 'which includes factors such as access to clear water and infant mortality' as 'significantly related to income only up to a GNP per cap of about $4,000'.[15] That corresponds, interestingly, to Bhagwati's observation on environmental concerns, using the economists Grossman and Krueger's work, that 'sulfur dioxide levels' peaked 'at per capita incomes of $5–6,000' and that as people become richer, they became more likely to become environmentally concerned, although the economic processes themselves are key contributors to that environmental crisis.[16] The basic human needs transition is both necessary achievement and accompanying problem.

The second epidemiological transition is much more substantially elaborate, with hard detailed evidence, particularly provided by the work of Wilkinson. Essentially, it refers to 'the changes in health brought about by economic development as it lifted populations out of absolute material want',[17] one of the greatest achievements of the twentieth century for an increasing proportion of the world's population. Most interestingly, he then observes 'Health in societies that have gone through the epidemiological transition ceases to be as responsive to further rises in material living standards as it had been earlier. Once you have enough of everything, it doesn't help to have much more.'[18] Similarly for the psychologist James, 'once we have achieved a basic level of affluence, this will do little to make us emotionally better'.[19] This is reinforced by World Bank economist Kenny, reflecting on the achievements of the Least Developed Countries (LDCs) in health and education: despite inefficiency and corruption – 'their performance is historically incredibly impressive . . . We did not have to see huge increases in income to see very impressive gains in infant survival, life expectancy and education.'[20] Indeed, for Kenny, 'It is the failure of income to significantly raise contentment (happiness), dignity or welfare, which makes it an irrelevance to perhaps the majority of the World's countries.'[21]

The third behavioural transition is more speculative, but again begins with economic growth weakening the grip of absolute poverty, and particularly its social disciplining power. As a result, for Wilkinson, 'the most fundamental rationale for inequality is always scarcity'.[22] Based on both are a modern economics, driven by self-interest and resulting in inequalities; the movement beyond such scarcity by affluence may well erode both. At the moment, therefore that drive to more co-operative behaviour and accompanying social arrangements, what Wilkinson calls the 'new postscarcity humanity', is encountering its biggest obstacle, income inequalities.[23] In this connection, it is worth recalling that the Revd Thomas Malthus, early demographer and apostle of scarcity in the formation of modern economics, provided an important resource for Darwin's later work on evolution as the survival of the fittest.[24] It is a tantalizing thought that both may now be being transcended in some important ways.

Paradoxes

The regular use of the concept of paradox to describe the benefits and yet costs of modern affluence is strikingly reminiscent of the transition language. It reformulates its focus on the achievements of the progress beyond the scarcity of absolute poverty and also the new problems that creates. For the philosopher Kenny, the 'increase in education and sensitivity brings with it increase in the number of desires, *and* a corresponding lesser likelihood of their satisfaction'. In other words, 'To increase a person's chances of happiness, in the sense of fullness of life, is to decrease his chances of happiness, in the sense of satisfaction of desire.' Remarkably, he then concludes that 'in the pursuit of happiness, no less than in the creation of a world, there lurks a problem of evil'.[25] It is a replay of Malthus's acceptance of the inevitability of scarcity and its profoundly negative consequences for human aspirations and utopias.

As an economist, Layard particularly focuses on the happiness hypothesis as intrinsically paradoxical – literally in his opening words: 'There is a paradox at the heart of our lives. Most people want more income and strive for it. Yet as Western societies have got richer, their people have become no happier.'[26]

And echoing Kenny's diagnosis but formulated in economic logic, Offer concentrates on the modern economic process itself as generator and satisfier of increasing choice but which in itself corrodes human ability to cope with it. So 'The paradox of affluence and its challenge is that the flow of new rewards can undermine the capacity to enjoy them.'[27] That propensity to corrode the human capacity to cope with such economic change is confirmed and exacerbated by the association of free market economies with those grave inequalities which have such damaging consequences for human well-being. As another paradox of affluence, it argues that 'as affluence has increased overall, health has improved', yet 'inequality has risen as well', and 'the differences in health between the best off and the worst off have opened up as well'.[28] It is the necessity of market mechanisms for contemporary economic life and their erosion of individual social well-being which constitute the paradoxical core of the paradox of happiness.

A church document, using research commissioned from the Henley Centre, brings these different perspectives on paradox together in one report. The Salvation Army's *The Paradox of Prosperity* argues that on the one hand, economic growth has increased dramatically along with the standard of living, yet 'the economic fortunes of many people' have 'become decoupled from consumer confidence and quality of life' including 'a general loss of meaning in our lives'. On the other hand, these economic processes are associated with grave income inequalities, with their damaging consequences for health and wider life prospects.[29] The paradox of prosperity represents a close paralleling of the paradox of happiness, usefully locating it in a wider context of the ambiguities of affluence in capitalist societies.

Accounting for transitions and paradoxes: measuring happiness and well-being

The insights from the transition and paradox literatures present a formidable challenge to measurement systems of modern economic processes.

The problem is crystallized in the dominance of Gross Domestic Product (GDP) as the central measurement system of the economic life of nations, and as GDP per capita, of the standard of living of their people. It is a modern system, emerging particularly in the post-1945 period. Yet its limitations are increasingly apparent, not least its failure to incorporate productive endeavours that are not tradable, like household caring for children and the elderly, and the negative impacts of environmental damage. The rapidly growing research into social capital, and now happiness, and their increasingly recognized contributions to economic and social well-being is also not engaged by GDP accounting.

To develop more adequate ways of measuring well-being, clearly inclusive of its foundational economic character, three main approaches have emerged since the 1980s. Economists have played a dominant part in all of them.

The first is what Offer describes as '"*extending*" the national accounts to incorporate non-market goods and services and to eliminate detrimental components'.[30] Cobb and Daly have developed such a system, the Index of

Sustainable Economic Welfare (ISEW). This accepts the need to run environmental alongside social and economic indicators. When used to measure 'the true health of our economy over the past 36 years'[31] it reveals a growth rate considerably below the GDP rate; between 1975 and 1990, while GDP grew considerably, the American ISEW declined by 25%, and the British by almost 50%.[32]

The second system identified 'social norms, and evaluated their satisfaction by means of social indicators' – what Offer describes, creatively for this enquiry, as a more 'normative' system.[33] The work of the UNDP and the economist Amartya Sen, developed the Human Development Index incorporating the measurement of health (life expectancy at birth), education (proportion of population in education) and income (GDP per capita). This clearly identifies more closely with human well-being, corresponding with some of Layard's Big Seven features of happiness (to be identified later). Indeed, its normative character also aligns it more effectively with the contribution of social relationships to economic and social life, including their moral dimensions (as in social capital).

For Offer, this system, and Sen's capability approach, are 'congruent to some extent with non-utilitarian ethical frameworks – Buddhist, Hindu, Jewish, Greek, Christian, "Enlightenment", Romantic – which teach that acquisitiveness may be self-defeating, and which highlight other welfare criteria: virtue, stoicism, altruism, approbation, self-realization'.[34]

The third system is what Offer calls 'psychological indicators'[35] – or the measurement of 'subjective well-being'[36] – a recognition that well-being is derived to a great extent '*outside* the market, from human relations in the workplace, the family, and from other forms of attachment'.[37] Although some contest the adequacy of such measurements, witness their description as subjective in contrast to the 'hard' evidence of economics and sociology (crime and divorce statistics, for example), there is growing acceptance of their research basis accuracy across a number of disciplines, including economics, sociology and psychology. The happiness measurement is based, for example, on surveys of individuals in random samples of households, asking the question 'Taking all things together, would you say you are very happy, quite happy, or not very happy?' The answers have remained remarkably constant since the 1960s, despite the doubling of incomes. American and British, male and female, are very similar: in Britain, 36% were very happy, 57% quite happy, and 7% not very happy.[38] Despite their perceived subjective character, the answers are checked, independently verified, taken over significant time periods, and are increasingly regarded as reliable indicators of happiness, particularly when corroborated by brain studies.

If a conversation is developed across these three alternative accounting systems, they provide a useful accurate measurement of well-being which engages with the strengths and limitations of economic processes identified by the transition and paradox literatures.

Histories of happiness: a multidimensional narrative

The story of happiness matches narratives of capitalism and empires in longevity, complexity and philosophical depth. All converge on the late twentieth century. The negotiation between them may well determine the social and personal quality of the twenty-first century. Without the formative influence in that process of the happiness–well-being discoveries, it is unlikely that will be achieved.

It is impossible to disaggregate modern political economy without a major conversation with the history of moral philosophy in general, and of happiness's particular place in it. The roots of modern economics in utilitarian philosophy shape its particular understanding of the individual and therefore of the social arrangements associated with it. Located in the wider history of moral philosophy that choice of utilitarianism is illuminated and its profound limitations are revealed. It is a wider journey which Adam Smith, founder of modern economics, would have fully understood. He was a moral philosopher engaging with, among other things, political economy. His *Theory of Moral Sentiments* (1759) pre-dates and stands alongside his *Wealth of Nations* (1776). Without the two, his understanding of human behaviour and its virtues in its social context is *totally* inadequate. The happiness research confirms that judgement.

The philosophical origins of the happiness subject are Greek and are particularly informed by the work of Aristotle. His primary commitment was to the good life as a pursuit of happiness, or *eudaimonia*.[39] This constituted the ultimate worthwhile goal of life, or the *telos* which one pursued as 'an activity of soul in conformity with excellence or virtue'.[40] It was therefore a life lived in accordance with virtues, a life of study, political or public life, and pleasure. Augustine, and then Aquinas, located that commitment to happiness within a Christian philosophy of life, so that it becomes the gift of God, the supreme good only possible in the afterlife. The Greek or cardinal virtues of prudence, justice, temperance and fortitude were now located in relation to the primary theological virtues of faith, hope and love, informed, as they were, by the outflowing of God's grace.

The view of the journey of the individual soul to its authentic *telos* was radically reformulated by Scotus as subordinate to 'a natural law laid down by a creator God', a position which it continues to occupy in the work of Christian moralists.[41] Happiness was therefore interacted with justice, as the common good – the fundamental moral significance of balancing individual and social within a wider moral context. The work of Kant (as deontological ethics) and Bentham (as utilitarian ethics) greatly influenced the nineteenth century, with the former being dominant. Classical economics used the latter to provide its philosophical framework in terms of the rational individual maximizing its utilities in the context of a free market. That emphasis was confirmed and accentuated by behaviourist philosophy, a highly contested and deeply flawed understanding of human behaviour. The contemporary interest in happiness interacts the work of economists like Easterlin (1974), Oswald and Layard, with psychologists like Seligman and Haidt.[42]

Two additional currents contribute to the history of happiness. They exhibit strong similarities to the historical formats of capitalism and empires. First, the longitudinal framework is deeply informed by early prehistory, including new research in psychology and neurophysiology into heredity and genetic balances in relation to environment (to be considered later). Kenny also usefully locates his work in the last two millennia, thereby highlighting the significance of recent developments in economic processes with reference to changes in income and life expectancy (two important indices in the happiness hypothesis). These figures illustrate how 'more people have more of the constituents of welfare than ever before in history'.[43] For example, with reference to GDP per capita incomes, estimates suggest, in Western Europe, an income of approximately $450 in the first century AD, remaining the same in AD 1000, rising to $1,232 in 1820, to $18,742 today. Alongside these figures, life expectancy in the UK moved from 35.9 in 1800 to 48.30 in 1900, to 69 in 1950, and 77 in 1999. They are remarkable complementary indications of the impact, among other things, of economic growth on human well-being.[44]

But secondly, within that wider framework, the literatures again focus on the role of social capital's Great Disruption in the post-1945 era, reinforcing the strong relationship between the happiness and social capital research. It again reinforces the importance of the contribution and limitations of economic processes. Layard summarizes this paradox as increasing incomes but not increasing happiness, not least because of the grave impact of factors promoting unhappiness.[45] The literatures almost universally point to the major growth in this period of such factors which flow against well-being. These include the increase of mental or emotional disorder (by the age of 35, 15% of Americans 'have experienced major depression'), alcoholism, drug abuse, crime (in most developed economies 'recorded crime increased by at least 300%', 1950–80), and broken families (in terms of the major increase in divorce, out of wedlock birth and single parents).[46] For Layard, 'Since more and more people are separated, divorced, or never married, this exerts a steady downward pressure on the average level of happiness.'[47] Again, many of the commentators detect in these negative features a more significant underlying trend in the nature of the social experience and structures, as a shift from 'the common welfare and public service as sources of well-being and towards private benefits'.[48] Layard (and Putnam before him) also identify the rise of a more possessive individualism as a fundamental cause of this transition.[49] I have already noted how this is associated with the growing prominence of the market economy and its increasingly pervasive implications for the nature of society. Some interpreters resort to Polanyi's earlier description of such changes as the propensity of the market economy to develop into a market society, aptly described by him as the Great Transformation.[50]

The psychologist James, in his survey of elites in 22 countries, from the USA to China and Russia, focuses that 200-year transformation into this generation and into the development of what he describes as 'selfish capitalism',[51] in words reminiscent of R. H. Tawney's earlier classic tract for the times, *The Acquisitive Society* (1921). The features of this selfish capitalism include judging company success by share price, privatizing utilities, minimum regulation of business and taxing of the rich, and 'the conviction that consumption and market forces can meet human needs of almost every kind'.[52] America is its apotheosis. In the historical analysis of empires and capitalism, this represents the emerging contemporary cycle, for example, Bobbitt's market state.

It is not just the emergence of selfish capitalism which disturbs the psychologist James, it is its embodiment in Fromm's *marketing characters*, deeply scarred by emotional diseases. These 'experience themselves as a commodity, with their value dependent on success, saleability, the approval of others'.[53] It is a society and characters marred by depression and anxiety, profound obstacles to happiness, to Aristotle's good life. And James illustrates these trends and traits with a series of interviews perhaps best typified by the contrasting New York stories of Chet and Sam. Chet, the Nigerian taxi driver, who has an income 1,000 times less than the stockbroker, Sam, is 'contented, optimistic, sexually faithful and religious; he is courteous, friendly and open' with serious health problems, no money or medical insurance. Sam is 'discontented, pessimistic, sex-addicted, and an atheist'.[54] He is 'domineering, unfriendly and healthy', and moves from one home to another in his private jet. The one suffers from the disease of marketing characters, what James calls 'affluenza', the plague of affluence. The other has developed the antidote to it.

These connections are regularly made across the literatures, certainly using different concepts, yet all recognizing the link between unhappiness and contemporary economic and social change, and their contribution to the formation or deformation of personal and communal character. It represents the contemporary embodiment of the philosophical history of happiness in terms of addressing the question of what kind of life and society constitute human well-being. It confirms the evidence from transitions and paradoxes. It generates understandings of the happiness hypothesis as history of histories.

Elaborating the Happiness Hypothesis: Of Genes, Lists and Health

Contextualizing the happiness hypothesis begins to reveal important features of well-being. Yet much necessary detail needs to be added before an adequate picture of contemporary happiness emerges for our consideration in terms of its implications for an enquiry into faith and political economy. One such addition which is of particular importance and crosses a number of disciplines, including Christian social ethics, is the re-emergence of the nature versus nurture argument. Important discoveries in psychology, genetics and neurophysiology raise profound questions that, among other things, focus attention on what can be feasibly undertaken by human endeavour, personally and collectively, to promote greater happiness and, conversely (and quite essentially) attack the causes of unhappiness. Both strategies will be firmly illustrated with reference to health, marriage and inequality.

Nature versus nurture: revisiting and reformulating an old conflict

For much of the twentieth century, most disciplines have emphasized the human ability to transform self and environment. That is and will change significantly, but only as a necessary rebalancing. For example, there is a growing recognition by economists of the implications of research in psychology and neurophysiology for understandings of economic behaviour. This is likely to involve, in conjunction with other findings, including the new awareness of the limitations of economics, as noted above, a reformulation of our interpretations of economics as behaviour and social arrangements. Indeed, these findings have implications across a number of fields including Christian social ethics and philosophy. Both regularly work with understandings of human behaviour increasingly disconnected from new research in the medical sciences. Essentially, the research recognizes the importance of heredity and shared human characteristics, while acknowledging the space for human endeavour. Recent and current emphases on post-modernity as the dominance of difference now need to be complemented by the recognition of shared experiences of being human, including as proximate universals.

In the happiness hypothesis, these understandings are reflected in discussion of a happiness setpoint, determined by inheritance and environment, and which varies little over time, and of the opportunities this presents for changes in personality and social arrangements. So brain studies recognize the importance of the left side of the brain, behind the forehead, as linked to the generation of happiness. This is described and measured by MRI scans, therefore indicating that happiness is not just a subjective state. What you say in relation to happiness surveys clearly now corresponds to levels of activity in different parts of the brain. Genetic advances similarly describe the more determinative features of behaviour. These studies have particularly influenced the discipline of psychology.[55] Using genome research, important findings apply to various aspects of personality, yet even here there are some flexibilities. Genes should be understood not as blueprints specifying a person's structures, but recipes for producing a person over many years.[56] Yet all 'psychological studies of heritability still leave a major role for experience'.[57] That being said, Freud's basic premise, that personality is shaped 'primarily by childhood environment', is still undermined – as are other related premises in other disciplines.[58] It is rather out of the contribution of environment and heredity that a *setpoint* emerges. Essentially this represents each person's characteristic level of happiness – not as a narrow confined fixed point – but as a 'potential range or probability distribution'. Whether you are at the higher or lower side of your potential range is more determined by external factors.[59]

For Seligman's pioneering work, accepting the intensive influence of heredity on personality formation, still allows for the significant impact on happiness of two kinds of externals. First the conditions for your life, which include the facts of your life which you cannot change, for example race, gender, age, disability. However, some facts you can change, for example, your wealth and your mental state through meditation. Yet conditions are frequently constant over time, therefore representing what we have to adapt to. But second, there are voluntary activities which you can choose to do. These 'offer much greater promise for increasing happiness while avoiding adaptation effects' of the conditions for your life.[60]

It is out of this research that there emerges what Lyubomirsky, Sheldon, Schkade and Seligman call 'the happiness formula':

$$H = S + C + V$$

H is happiness, S is the setpoint, C is the conditions of your life which can be changed to some extent. V is voluntary activity, which is a major opportunity for change. One of the tasks of positive psychology is 'to use the scientific method to find out exactly what kinds of C and V can push H up to the top of your potential range'.[61]

Interestingly, two economists provide creative interpretations of these two perspectives of setpoint and conditions/volunteering. For Adam Smith, in his *Theory of Moral Sentiments*, on the former, he notes: 'In every permanent situation, where there is no expectation of change, the mind of every man, in a longer or shorter time, *returns to its* natural state of tranquillity. In prosperity, after a certain time, it falls back to that state; in adversity, after a certain time, it rises up to it.'[62] Sen usefully addresses the importance of not accepting life as determined solely by setpoint. For him, a person in poverty is disadvantaged whatever they think about it: 'can we possibly believe that he is doing well just because he is happy and satisfied? Can the living standard of a person be high if the life he or she leads is full of deprivation?'[63] Both economists illustrate the potential for the discipline's constructive engagement with the happiness literatures.

'I have a little list': classifications of constituents of happiness and well-being

Lists of categories are always contested. In the hands of the elect they lead to their petrifaction. Popularization by the world results in their dilution. Yet as Haidt has acknowledged with regard to Peterson and Seligman's table of 24 principal character strengths, classifications are useful because they can point 'to specific means of growth toward widely valued ends without insisting that any one is mandatory for all people at all times'.[64] They can help diagnose our different strengths and assist us to cultivate excellence.

Like Koko, the Lord High Executioner in the *Mikado*, there is a 'little list', in this case of the main factors which promote happiness, which become particularly significant once basic incomes are achieved. The list I will use is drawn from the economist Layard's Big Seven. It is based on the US General Social Survey, which enables the first five to be put in order. The survey asks how happy people are in general, and how satisfied they are with particular dimensions of life. Additional detail is provided by the invaluable World Values Survey, taken on four occasions from 1981, interviewing 90,000 people from 46 countries. Importantly, the Seven fill out the 'conditions' and 'volunteering' features noted in Seligman's 'happiness formula' above – in terms of what can be done to increase happiness.[65]

First, Layard lists *family relationships,* because differences in them profoundly affect happiness for good or bad. Repeated throughout the research, and across disciplines is the performance of marriage as the most effective form of family life in terms of its association with happiness. In other words 'people generally become happier as a result of marriage'.[66] Equally, other forms of familial relationship are not as effective, including cohabitation, with single parent families scoring lower, and people living alone, even lower. The break-up of relationships has a *severe* impact on happiness. Divorce causes it to fall by 5 points on the happiness scale (from 10 to 100). Measured in financial terms it is 'more than double the effect of losing a third of one's income'.[67] Separation is even worse, as is widowhood. Such fractured relationships have a cumulative effect on a nation's happiness. The benefits of marriage relate to the quality of relationships as the heart of mutuality, reciprocity and gifting – the paradigm and metaphor of love. Layard's language (and indeed, reverberating across the research) profoundly resonates with Christian literature: 'We need other people, and we need to be needed. Increasingly research confirms the dominating importance of love.'[68] People who are married, and then others in other forms of *stable* relationship, are healthier and live longer. They are happier.

Second is *income.* We have already repeatedly noted its significance for well-being, particularly as a key factor in the transitions, and especially from the profound restrictions of absolute poverty to affluence and relative deprivation. We have also noted the financial quantification of that transit point with regard to the happiness literatures. More specifically, a fall in income by a third causes a fall in happiness of 2 points on the happiness scale – quite modest, compared with other factors, as we are beginning to see.[69]

Third, work, as main provider of income, of necessary relationships outside family and essential opportunity to contribute to wider society, has historically and contemporarily been a formatively broad basis of happiness and general well-being. It has, and can be, a significant means of creativity, and an opening to self-realization, self-worth and even self-transcendence (we will seek these characteristics in the following note on organization and development theory). It has also always been associated with alienation and oppression. These damaging consequences for happiness in modern societies are particularly associated with unemployment. For Layard, it is a major disaster because it severely affects self-respect, social relationships and that opportunity to contribute to the wider processes and benefits of society. To lose one's job therefore affects one's happiness far more than the loss of income. Yet the kind of work one does, particularly lack of opportunity to participate in it, also has a damaging effect on health and wider well-being, including as a major embodiment of inequality.[70] All will be noted later, with reference to ILO and WCC conversations on 'decent work'.

Fourth, community and friends play a major part in happiness as well as social capital. They represent close personal networks and the wider support of neighbourhoods and their associations. Friendships can be formed in early life, particularly in school, and survive gracefully throughout it. They are a bedrock of good health, with family – as is the trust which undergirds them, spilling out into good safe neighbourhoods. Their well-being quality is measured, as we have seen, by the extent of trust, voluntary bodies and volunteering: 'living where you can trust others makes a clear difference to your happiness'.[71]

Fifth, health. Although health is not the lead contributor to happiness, its absence as ill-health both corrodes well-being and is a key indicator of it, particularly in conjunction with inequality. Physical limitations can be adapted to much more so than mental disorder. Emotional distress is a major feature of communal as well as personal unhappiness. James's study of affluenza, and its corollary selfish capitalism, is a stark and varied illustration of this. More on health will follow.

Sixth, personal freedom. This relates to the opportunity to participate in society, in those aspects of life which exercise so much influence over us, from government to work, assembly and views of life. It therefore corresponds to three dimensions of freedom, personal, political and economic. This also links to the factor of community, and the strength of voluntary bodies and volunteering. Churches and other faith communities deeply inform this and most of the other factors. It also connects with forms of political and economic arrangements. Economic democracy will be addressed later, as will political democracy, but the latter is particularly used in this factor. On the one hand, the remarkable levels of unhappiness in Communist societies also point to the taken-for-granted freedoms of the West. On the other hand, these are strikingly confirmed by Swiss democracy. People are happier in those cantons with more rights to referenda.[72] War and other forms of insecurity also cause great ill-being.

Seventh, personal values and philosophy of life. The subjective dimension of well-being, say as happiness, is clearly related to the inner person.

Although we are now realizing that it has powerful objectively verifiable features, say through brain studies and epidemiology, we are equally increasingly aware of our resources and potentials for personal transformation. Throughout the first part of this enquiry, the contribution of values, norms, sanctions, virtues and philosophies of life was firmly evident. They were not in any way restricted to, but were clearly embodied in the religious field and social capital. That *spectrum of presences* is also reflected in and confirmed by the nature of these seven factors of happiness in general, and by this particular one, as personal values and philosophy of life. To read Layard the economist and Haidt the psychologist is a most powerful endorsement of this judgement. The sudden injection of the spirituality of love, religiously connected, into the endpiece of the neo-Marxists Hardt and Negri's *Empire*, is but one surprising confirmation of the significance of an emerging connecting of happiness and political economy as actual and potential account of human well-being which embodies what I will describe as a *nexus* of philosophy of life and its virtues, ethics and economics, and the religious field. They are relatively autonomous yet equally profoundly interacting. All these features are present in relation to these Big Seven factors when they are read in conjunction with other contributions on happiness from other disciplines. As it is, Layard firmly develops the importance of philosophy of life for well-being in terms of its inner character, its potential for change through meditation, Buddhism, self-help groups like Alcoholics Anonymous, cognitive therapy and drugs. It relates powerfully to what he calls finding 'comfort from within', to connecting with a power or reality greater than oneself – so some 'call this source of comfort "divine"'. Not surprisingly, although most commentators don't really know what to do with it, 'one of the most robust findings of happiness research' is 'that people who believe in God are happier'.[73]

It is a remarkable list, but only because it summarizes the findings of so much of the research, not least because there are such correspondences with other lists relating to well-being, including from different perspectives and disciplines. I will note these briefly, accepting they warrant further work of elaboration and correction.

First, from my own work. For a William Temple Foundation Council meeting, I noted how William Temple's classic of Christian social ethics, *Christianity and Social Order* (1942), is in a continuing dialogue with the happiness list, including Layard's. Temple's concluding six points for a way forward for society (essentially middle axioms) suggest:[74] concern for children (major emphasis today on contribution of first three years of a child's life to its well-being, including emotional); concern for the family (central part in happiness and social capital, including the dominant role of marriage); education (for Offer and Layard, key indices of the virtues of self-control and prudence for engaging affluence; with schools and colleges as locations for the teaching of ethics); work and, conversely, opposition to unemployment (like Temple, rejecting unemployment and again emphasizing employee participation in the workplace, and Layard's welfare to work programmes); leisure (current focus on work–life balance, and Nussbaum and James on the importance of play);[75] and human rights (on democracy, political liberties and welfare–dignity–contentment as wellbeing).

In my *Through the Eye of a Needle*,[76] I also noted the well-being links between, on the one hand, Layard and Halpern on happiness and life satisfaction and, on the other hand, Sen, Nussbaum and Alkire (and Finnis) on human capabilities. The former have been summarized under Layard's Big Seven, the latter are: bodily life (health, vigour, safety); skilful performance in work and play; friendship or sociability (between persons in various forms and strength, including marriage and neighbours); knowledge (of reality, including aesthetic), and practical reasonableness (harmony between one's feelings and judgements); and transcendence, religion (harmony with the widest reaches and most 'ultimate sources of all reality including meaning and value').[77]

Second, as Layard observes, his Big Seven are similar to Sen's personal capabilities, including 'economic facilities, social opportunities, protective security, political freedom and transparency guarantees'. Nussbaum, like Sen, working with a reformulated Aristotelian framework, has a more complex list including: 'life; bodily health; bodily freedom; senses, imagination and thought; emotions; practical reason; affiliation; relations with other species; and control of one's environment'.[78]

Third, I have also observed a strong potential conversation between the happiness list and the classification systems of organization and development theory. For example, Maslow's hierarchy of needs is related to the workplace, an important part of Layard's list. Yet it also resonates with Layard's philosophy of life. The hierarchy of needs identifies levels of human need, which, once satisfied, and only then, move on to other higher needs. He therefore begins with the basic level of needs, the physiological requirements of food, shelter and nurture, followed by the needs for security, shelter and a sense of belonging and community. Then come the higher levels of need, moving more on to the dimensions of aesthetics, learning and discovery, esteem and self-respect, and self-actualization. Only then can a further level be progressed to, as transcendence, with its strong spiritual connotations. It is a well-developed account, tested in working organizations, which acknowledges that humans require satisfaction and stimulation at deeper levels if they are to realize their full potential.[79] These arguments relate increasingly to the recognition of new forms of co-operation and networking through the development of new communication technologies – as noted in Part 1, and in the works of Hardt and Negri, Fukuyama, and now by Wilkinson, and not least, as the evolving forms of institutional capital.[80] Modem 2002 identified the importance of releasing 'spiritual energy among managers and groups within an organization', acknowledging 'the deep bonds occurring when people share common values, principles and a sense of purpose greater than themselves'.[81] It is a conclusion confirmed by the work of Merchant and Gilbert from a very different perspective, namely social work, mental health and spirituality, that 'the concept of "meaning" in the workplace (analogous to what we might call "spirituality") began to make a marked appearance'.[82]

Fourth, and more speculatively, the constituents of identity developed by Huntington offer rich comparison with the above classifications, not least because of the contribution of identity to bonding social capital, and its community and associational forms. Again, it links back into Part 1, particularly to civilizations as an alternative mode of organizing to empires, and therefore to the religious field. Huntington's list, drawn from a variety of sources of identity, includes: ascriptive (age, ancestry, kin, ethnicity, race); cultural (tribe, family, way of life – religion, language, civilization); territorial (neighbourhood, city, nation); political (interest group, movement, ideology); economic (job, work group, class); and social (friends, colleagues, leisure group, social status).[83]

Measuring happiness impacts: health, marriage and inequality

The task of describing and elaborating understandings of happiness becomes more manageable for the writer and accessible to the reader when its actual outcomes are identified, measured and examined. That process is facilitated by the research operation because it is expressed on a spectrum or continuum moving from happiness to unhappiness, life-satisfaction to dissatisfaction, and well-being to ill-being. The negative end of the continuum is particularly stark in its statistics and stories. It is especially focused on deprivation and marginalization processes. The poor are therefore more likely to suffer from unemployment, inadequate incomes, broken or impoverished relationships, unsafe and low-trust neighbourhoods, ill-health and earlier death, lower political participation and lower church attendance.

The Religious Contribution: A Complex in Complexities

Three areas will briefly illustrate these impacts of the happiness spectrum: health, marriage and inequality. All three reflect a growing consensus that social and relational arrangements regularly influence economic growth rather than economic growth fuelling welfare improvements.[84] The link between economy and well-being remains strong; it is the weight and direction of the flow between them that is becoming more apparent. It is an important provisional conclusion: that economic factors are not as important as social factors in the promotion of well-being in a post-scarcity epoch; and that economic growth is then more likely to be fuelled by welfare improvements than vice versa. If, as is the case from a BBC national opinion poll, 80% agreed that 'A government's prime objective should be to achieve the greatest happiness of the people, not the greatest wealth', then that judgement both confirms and elaborates that opinion poll.[85]

Health

We have already observed, in the previous chapter on social capital, how the latter impacts on physical and mental health in terms of preventing ill-health and aiding in the recovery from it. The material on faithful capital confirmed and extended that well-researched judgement, in this case with regard to the added dimension of religion in general and spiritual capital in particular. A brief note on the happiness output on health therefore assumes and draws on all these contributions.

Two aspects warrant further attention. First, the disturbing significant increase in mental health problems in the era of the Great Disruption, and in advanced economies, has highlighted the happiness paradox most fiercely. James's study of elites uses a WHO survey of rates of emotional distress in 15 different nations, including the USA, New Zealand, Mexico, Japan, China (Shanghai) and Nigeria. It paints a picture of disturbing proportions and persistence in terms of emotional distress (as depression, anxiety, substance abuse and impulsivity–aggression).[86] It represents an epidemic of mental disorders and therapies, the greatest public health problem in the world after heart disease. There is also considerable agreement that there exists a strong correlation between emotional distress and income growth and inequality (as the double effect paradox of prosperity).[87] The figures for Britain are striking, with 25% suffering serious emotional distress, and another 25% on the verge. 'Put bluntly, half of us are in a bad way.'[88] Singapore, after a relentless drive, inspired by Lee Kuan Yew, father of the nation, in pursuit of selfish capitalism, became the seventh in the global league table of per capita average incomes. By 1998,

16.6% suffered from minor depression and anxiety rates.[89] Denmark, in contrast, pursued what James describes as the route of unselfish capitalism. Promoting a more socially and economically egalitarian society, expressed in the absence of hierarchies in 'families, schools, and organisations', with strong support for women and men and child-rearing, and high taxes on the rich, the results suggest 'that the splendours of its social system have been converted into lower rates of emotional distress'. It is one of the very few developed nations whose happiness ratings have increased since 1950. Its major depression rate (in the previous two weeks) was half the European average.[90]

The second aspect continues this theme of the close relationship between ill-health and income inequality. Wilkinson's figures on health inequalities are stark and disturbing. Comparing black and white men and women from 23 rich and poor areas in the USA: the difference in life expectancy between rich whites and poor blacks was 'close to sixteen years'.[91] More significantly, it is not just a comparison between top and bottom in income and health. It is rather one that runs *throughout* society: 'the health gradient runs through all classes from top to bottom of society to the extent that, even if we managed to remove all the health problems associated with poverty, the greater part of health inequalities would remain untouched.' Your health chances 'are graded by socioeconomic status'.[92] For Wilkinson, such contrived and *condoned* injustices, even to the extent of reducing lives by seven years, are 'a fundamental issue of social justice'.[93] Examinations of health, social relationships and therefore of happiness and well-being are profoundly stories about society and behaviour, about social life and the persons who constitute it.

Marriage

Marriage remains the basis of family relationships and their future in terms of their deep influence on childhood development. For James and Wilkinson, their research particularly confirms the importance of child-rearing for present and future happiness and for the economy of well-being. It is an economy which stretches increasingly beyond income. In Becker's *Treatise on the Family*,[94] mating and parenthood are modelled 'in terms of the preferences of the rational, self-seeking, maximising consumer'.[95] What this omits of course, is 'emotion overriding calculation' as both the empowerment of sexuality and embodiment of deep friendship.[96] Marriage, therefore, as the combining of relationship and economy in covenant and contract is a 'superior state'.[97] According to conventional measurements of well-being it is the preferred family state. Compared with other forms of close relationship, it promotes better physical and mental health, life expectation, sex life, happiness, and children (raised by their own married parents they 'do better in almost every respect').[98] Yet after 1960, despite these decisive advantages, family breakdown has increased significantly with detrimental consequences for parents and children, and for their happiness. By now, only half of American 15-year-olds 'live with their biological father'.[99] In Britain, the figure is two in three. The major increase in divorce and cohabitation ensures that one third of children are born outside marriage (despite unmarried couples being twice as likely to split up as married parents).[100] And remember, divorce is the second major source of unhappiness after unemployment. For Offer, these trends represent 'the retreat from commitment',[101] affecting now the majority of family relationships and most starkly epitomized by the rise in teenage pregnancies.[102] For Wilkinson, like violence among young men, they are 'among the clearest statistical indicators of the social damage of inequality and low social status'. 'Girls who have had a stressful early life are likely to reach sexual maturity at a younger age'; if brought up without a father, they are also 'likely to become sexually active and become pregnant earlier'.[103] When joined with deprived young men from equally deprived, stressful and broken families, the effect is to 'to increase risk taking among young men'.[104] The result, among other things, is teenage pregnancies in situations marked by inequality, ill-health and life-dissatisfaction.

In an important critique of the happiness hypothesis, Ormerod and Johns confirmed one of my own observations on this research material, and particularly its impacts on relationships. Like them, I observe that it does suggest 'a conservative paternalism' with regard to family life, marriage, divorce and children. Yet the proponents of happiness are rarely heard *actually promoting* 'marriage and religious faith'. It does appear that the modern liberals of the academy and government do not find 'such models' attractive. The contrast between research findings and policy implications is stark. The economist Oswald surveyed 93 academic papers on happiness and marriage. The benefits of marriage in terms of avoiding psychological illness, longevity, health and happiness are clear *and*, equally, 'confined to those who are married rather than cohabiting'. And the benefit difference is '*large*'.[105] If the BBC national opinion poll is an accurate reflection of public views on happiness, then the government's 'prime objective should be to achieve the greatest happiness of the people, not the greatest wealth'.[106] Bridging that gap between prioritizing in research findings and their public avoidance is one of the tasks of this enquiry.

Inequality

Again, so much material has already emerged with regard to the connection between happiness and inequality, particularly with regard to the impacts of the happiness hypothesis as traced on the well-being–ill-being continuum. The material especially connects societies on a spectrum from more unequal to less unequal societies. Wilkinson notably argues that inequality and health impacts spread across the complete income spread. Yet that is no novel judgement. In his observation on American democracy in mid nineteenth-century America, de Tocqueville firmly concluded that the strength of its associational life was connected to what he called 'the equality of conditions', and how this informs the 'workings of society', its 'political mores', 'sentiments' and 'customs'.[107] It was a recognition that the closer you are in social conditions, the easier it is to practise reciprocity, to see yourselves through the other person's eyes.

For Putnam, using the same kinds of understandings, but in the contemporary context, and as constituents of social capital today, 'Equality is an essential feature of the civic community'.[108] Participation in community life is therefore much stronger where income differences are smaller. Not surprisingly, Sweden is more equal, healthier and has high trust in contrast to the more unequal, high crime, and less healthy USA.

That positive relationship between more equal societies and greater happiness is confirmed by its converse – the clear and damaging consequences of greater inequality. Whether measured in terms of crime, tracing the firm relationship between inequality and homicide, or democracy with smaller proportions bothering to vote, or death rates as lower in relation 'to narrower income differences', the accumulating evidence is that inequality is bad for your happiness and society's.[109] Yet Wilkinson's survey of the statistical evidence suggests even more, that the relationship between health and inequality is essentially a '*causal* pathway'.[110] It is a warning to all who reflect on the social capital and happiness literatures 'to recognise the extent to which increases in social capital (and happiness) are dependent on greater equality'.[111] It is a recall, issued by the early Christian socialists to 'a fuller realization of our inherent sociality'.[112] The happiness hypothesis, in all its intricacy of material, across many accumulating disciplines, confirms, elaborates and measures the adequacy of that judgement.

Matters Arising: An Emerging Agenda for Ethical Religion and Ethical Economics

Developing the field of religion in this enquiry has begun to demonstrate its importance both in itself and in interaction with other fields and experiences. These matters arising will now reflect on how the happiness hypothesis develops these understandings further. What emerges is essentially a continuum from ethics to religion, and vice versa, but also from market mechanisms to an economy of regard, again and vice versa. Both recognize the contribution of religion to the ethical task and thereby to other fields. That interactive relationship between religion and ethics, including their relationship with say economics, is of renewed importance. Effective engagements with global poverty and environmental crisis will increasingly require that collaboration.

The contribution of religion to both continuums highlights their emerging importance for clarifying the nature of that contribution. It will, for example, become evident that although there is a distinction to be drawn between ethics and religion, drawing a line between them is unhelpful if not impossible. Describing the contribution of ethics and religion is therefore best done through continuums. For example, if we locate ethics and economics at one end of a spectrum (as the 'secular') and religion at the other, there are two main ways in which they relate to each other. At one end are the profound *overlaps* between the secular and the religious. These can take the practical form of partnerships say on poverty reduction. Academically they suggest multidisciplinary and interdisciplinary collaborations. At the other end is the religious contribution as *difference*, as more *distinctively* religious in its embodiment, in contrast to the shared valuing in partnerships. Both ends of the spectrum, and how they shade from one to the other, will be illustrated with practical examples of the religious contribution in the following section.

In this reflection on the implications of the happiness hypothesis for understanding this religious contribution, two routes will be followed. First, an examination of the importance and role of ethics in the hypothesis and how this connects with the religious role. Second, an exploration of how the hypothesis includes both a recognition of mainstream economics, as market mechanisms, and an example of a different way of organizing economic life, as an economy of regard. Both routes describe these relationships as continuums. Both help to develop an understanding of religion's role in relationship to political economy as *faithful economics*: as faithful economies, where faith and ethics and economy overlap, and as theological economy where the difference factor is more obvious and influential. In other words, these two matters arising perform an important role in the following chapter, and in the third part of this enquiry.

The ethics and religion of happiness

Morality is of profound importance in the happiness literatures, and major contributors from different disciplines including economics and psychology also recognize the role of religion both in happiness formation in general, and in an interactive relationship with the ethics of happiness.

To begin with ethics. A number of the sources dedicate sections in their books to ethics: for example, the Kennys' chapter 9 is on 'Happiness and Morality'.[113] As with the philosophical history of happiness, there is no overriding consensus on an ethics of happiness. Most do recognize the contribution of religion: the Kennys' survey noted the work of Augustine and Aquinas as religious developments of Aristotle's views, and Scotus's decisive break with them by incorporating happiness into a wider framework of divine and natural law which came to include justice and the common good. These combinations continue to be of great importance, including informing secular ethics through Sen and Nussbaum's work on capabilities, and the wider role of human rights.[114] Reformulated interpretations of natural law also reflect these continuities. To focus on a particular ethical tradition, utilitarianism, as Layard does, is best located correctionally in such a wider context. That task is certainly emphasized by the psychologist Haidt, witness the subtitle of his book, 'Putting Ancient Wisdom and Philosophy to the Test of Modern Science'. His focus on three historic and contemporary zones of religion and ethics demonstrates his work with a continuum from ethics to religion (the three are: Indian – Hinduism, Buddhism; Chinese – Confucian; Mediterranean – Jewish, Christian, Greco-Roman, Islam).[115]

The features of this brief survey are reflected in the variety of contributions to the ethics–religion continuum already noted in this enquiry. They include:

- in the happiness hypothesis: philosophy of life, personal values, religion (Layard, Haidt, Kenny) and ethical social arrangements (Wilkinson, James);
- in the related social capital literature: norms and sanctions (Halpern), and religious contributions (Putnam, Fukuyama);
- in the religious field: as faithful economics; as the contribution to social capital, empires – as civilizations (Putnam, Huntington, Braudel).

They provide a substantial assumed preliminary to the following reflections.

On morality and happiness

The dimension of morality is critical to the modern interpretations of well-being. The Kennys' usefully note three essential elements in a moral system.[116] First, a *moral community* provides the communal formative function in the development of values, virtues, and sanctions. It is recognition that morality cannot be purely personal. It is rather profoundly social. This strongly links to current ethical debates over the importance of character in the formation of virtues, and their location in particular moral traditioning communities. Haidt rightly emphasizes this development.[117] Second, a set of *moral values* carried out in a framework (or purpose in life) which includes certain behaviours and therefore *sanctions*. The values are *shared* including through participation in particular moral communities. They involve such 'non-material' values as truth, justice and love, which distinguish them from economics. With others, I also argue that such values interact with political economy as *ethical* or *normative* economics.[118] *Third*, is a *moral code*, required by membership of a moral community and society. This suggests, for Kenny, the use of wider moral traditions than utilitarianism. Rape and torture, for example, are intrinsically wrong and not just because of their consequences. This has important implications for the role of dignity, as human rights, in well-being, as well as providing a critique of Bentham and utilitarianism. Bentham was particularly dismissive of the natural law–human rights premises: 'Natural rights is simple nonsense: natural and imprescriptible rights, rhetorical nonsense – nonsense upon stilts.'[119]

The elaboration of morality in the happiness hypothesis develops a number of additional understandings. First, because there is a serious overlap with the social capital literatures, they provide useful clarifications. For example, Halpern's three components of social capital illustrate well these correspondences:[120] his *networks* connect with moral communities; his *social norms* and *sanctions* relate to moral values and codes – and enriched by his use of *habits*: Haidt, in this connection notes how 'ancient texts' emphasize practice and habit rather than factual knowledge in moral development.[121]

Second, most rightly acknowledge morality as bigger than happiness. They talk of the common good – as the pursuit of our own happiness and therefore of others' happiness – as 'an overarching moral principle'.[122]

Third, morality is therefore always moving through and beyond our confined circle of self, family and friends into a wider world (a form of bridging and linking social capital). Kenny usefully describes this as *oikeio-sis*, or the Stoics' home-making – of making ourselves at home in the world and others at home with us – spreading outwards to embrace world and universe.[123] This universalizing feature of relationships is central to the moral systems of most major faiths (see Palmer later).

Fourth, morality as wider than happiness, and generating a common good, emphasizes the importance and role of justice.[124] It is present in most cultures, and figures prominently in the founder of modern economics: for Adam Smith, more than self-love was required for socially moral adequacy – 'In the race for wealth, for honors, and preferments, he may run as hard as he can . . . But if he should justle, or throw down any of them . . . it is a violation of fair play.'[125] Justice was a basis of society, 'to constrain greed and self-love' – it was also a criticism of the adequacy of welfare economic utility, since individuals motivated by their own desires in the free market do not always contribute to the fulfilment of all.[126] Indeed, for Layard, the sense of fairness, of right and wrong is so universal that it is 'likely to have a genetic element that is amplified through learning'.[127] The nature–nurture balance of the happiness research has very significant implications, therefore, for ethics.

Fifth, being moral in the literature is distanced not simply from features in utilitarianism, but also from Kant's deontological ethics. For Kant, doing good should give you no pleasure. MRI scans show differently. Doing good contributes to happiness; it gives pleasure.[128]

The happiness material is also useful because it provides an essential ethical dimension to the cases for poverty reduction and more co-operative ways of working.

Poverty reduction programmes include promoting pro poor economic growth. For Layard, 'the principle of Greatest Happiness is inherently pro poor'.[129] It therefore gives morally practical focus to the general moral case. For the Kennys an additional dollar in rich economies adds nothing to happiness. Yet that same dollar would contribute to well-being in poor economies in terms of vaccinations say against measles. It is therefore 'difficult to understand the moral case against moving that dollar'.[130] That pro poor bias is also supported by the use of a reformulated Rawlsian difference principle, that 'to the extent social institutions create social or economic inequalities, they must be designed to the maximum benefit to those at the bottom of these inequalities'.[131] The examples of the effects of health inequalities noted above underwrite the value of such a corrective ethical principle.

The development of more cooperative ways of working, particularly in economics, is given further support by Haidt's reflections on reciprocity, an important part of the happiness and social capital literatures. The golden rule of love as reciprocity crosses faiths and moral systems, powerfully binding people to one another. Haidt traces its origins to the 'genetics of kin altruism' and its generating of sociable species.[132] Living in co-operative communities is a preferred way of operating because both individual and society benefit from it. Faced by the threat of scarcity (including in hunter-gatherer societies), the co-operative strategy is not zero sum limited but rather the expansion of the pie through collaborative endeavours.[133] Such a more egalitarian social order has already been identified with greater health and social well-being as unselfish capitalism. And it provides an additional ethical argument for the following economy of regard.

On morality interacting with religion

The literatures are mostly clear and persuaded over the important role of religion in happiness, but chiefly in terms of a reciprocal flow from ethics to religion. Haidt gives more thought to the religious component. There are again substantial overlaps with the social capital literatures particularly on the practical benefits of religion for social well-being.

It is perhaps not surprising that the author of the Protestant work ethic should be especially critical of the politics of happiness as 'flabby eudaimonism'. Rather we should 'cultivate and support what appears to us *valuable* in man: his personal responsibility, his deep drive towards higher things, towards the spiritual and moral values of mankind . . .'.[134] Identifying the contribution of the ethics–religion continuum roughly follows Weber's menu in terms of foundational norms rooted in religions, religious tools for happiness, the promotion of character and virtues, and then a transition into transcendence including as 'ethic of divinity'.[135]

First, on the basis of much research across religious and moral systems, Haidt, and Seligman before him, highlight a number of findings. One is the presence of 'a small set of innate moral intuitions' which 'guide and constrain the world's many moralities'. One such example is the view that 'the body is a temple housing a soul within'.[136] Another such is the principle of reciprocity so foundational for social capital and happiness, and for moral systems. As the golden rule, for Confucius, it meant 'What you do not wish for yourself, do not do to others', for Rabbi Hillel, 'That which is hateful to you, do not do to your fellow'; in the New Testament, 'love your neighbour as yourself, and do as you would be done by'.[137] Among other things, it informs understanding of co-operation, as we have noted.

Second, is the valuing of religious tools to promote happiness and overcome personal ill-being. These focus on meditation, and draw from various faiths. The Buddhist tradition provides a rich source for this dimension of building religio-moral capacity: like the Dalai Lama, the 'aim of life is happiness and the avoidance of suffering' – and that means replacing negative thoughts with positive ones.[138] Like other religious traditions, we will always have anger inside us. The task is to manage it so it does not dominate us, and that can be achieved partly by reflecting on positive good feelings towards self and others. For the Dalai Lama, 'I feel from my own experience that when I practise compassion there is an immediate direct benefit to myself . . . I get 100% benefit, while the benefit to others may be 50%.'[139] To develop such positive thinking and living, Buddhists use the technique of meditation in order to develop inner calm. Only thus can the emotions be addressed. And the good is through and beyond self-realization to 'a harmonious relation to the world about us'.[140] An equivalent function is performed by the Christian tradition of spirituality, including use of St Ignatius Loyola's *Spiritual Exercises*, and other similar vehicles.[141] Again, a key contribution to the pursuit of spiritual wholeness, holistic living and holiness is the cultivation of thankfulness and the transcendence of self, including through the service of God and therefore his creation. Other similar systems include Alcoholics Anonymous with a way of working which is profoundly moral *and* religious, giving people 'a sense of purpose and hope'. It is essentially a way of accepting self in and through a mutual sharing with others.[142]

Third, the importance for happiness of the promotion of virtue, and therefore of the character that provokes and sustains them. Here, Haidt shows a strong preference for the emerging argument in philosophy and ethics against quandary or dilemma ethics, ethics as facing problems, and for the development of character from which flows those virtues necessary for facing up to life, including its problems.[143] Supporting such character and virtue formation is the essential contribution of moral and religious traditions, and their location, in turn, in faith and moral communities. It constitutes a profound revisiting and reformulation of the Greek tradition of happiness as 'an activity of the soul in conformity with excellence or virtue'.[144] That redrafting of virtues has been undertaken in the contemporary context by Peterson and Seligman. On the basis of a survey of lists of virtues from religions to organizations like the Boy Scouts, six families of virtues emerged, having been present on nearly every list: wisdom, courage, humanity, justice, temperance and transcendence ('the ability to forge connections larger than the self').[145] These are then elaborated into 26 principal character strengths – for example, temperance links to self-control, prudence and humility. For them, the pursuit of such virtues in living 'engages you fully, draws on your strengths, and allows you to lose self-consciousness and immerse yourself in what you are doing'. Haidt's conclusion is that 'The virtue hypothesis is alive and well, firmly ensconced in positive psychology'.[146]

Fourth, is the firm recognition of hints of realities and experiences greater than self – the glimpse of a transcendent, the elevation of the human spirit. As a 'third dimension' (beyond ethics of autonomy and community) or 'ethic of divinity' this both takes us into the heart of religion and retains a purchase on wider spiritual experiences.[147] It is a perception of sacredness as human need, recounted, for example, in Eliade's *The Sacred and The Profane* (1959/57)[148] and embodied in religious places (temples, churches), times (holy days, seasons) and activities (prayer, special dancing). These enable human encounters with the divine, providing 'intimations of sacredness'. For Haidt, through his study of religious experiences, this includes recognition of 'uplift', of the elevation of the human spirit.[149] That engagement with the vertical can come through worship; for Christians, through a Pentecost–Holy Spirit experience. Sacred writings are full of such encounters: the *Bhagavad Gita* describes how Arjuna says 'Things never before seen have I seen, and ecstatic is my joy; yet fear-and-trembling perturb my mind.'[150] The Christian account of the transfiguration of Jesus relates a similar experience, and will figure large in the final part of this enquiry. It is important to note, however, that these experiences are not restricted to the professing religious. Layard talks of the need for 'the sense of an overall purpose wider than oneself'.[151] In Tawney's *The Attack*, he writes of Beatrice Webb's diligent work on the Commission on the Poor Laws. She was both severe rationalist and reluctant mystic. After a difficult session of the Commission she went to St Paul's to pray – 'I find it best to live as if the soul of men were in communion with a superhuman force which makes for righteousness'.[152] Haidt supports this wider understanding of transcendence experience with reference to Maslow's *Religions, Values and Peak Experiences* (1964). In it, the great organization and development theorist writes of 'peak experiences', those 'extraordinary self-transcendent moments' that feel qualitatively different from ordinary life' – in fact, he lists 25 of them, and they are linked to ultimate work experiences.[153]

What these commentators are arguing for is the overlapping of profoundly religious and profoundly human experiences: 'Morality and religion both occur in some form in all human cultures and are almost always both intertwined with the values, identity and daily life of the culture.'[154] Any full account of human nature must now take account of that continuum of 'morality to religion'. It is quite unacceptable *not* to recognize that religious dimension as most clearly expressing that human experience of sacredness. In other words, 'the scientific community should accept religiosity as a normal and healthy aspect of human nature – an aspect that is as deep, important and interesting as sexuality or language (which we study intensely)'.[155]

The happiness economy: from market mechanisms to economy of regard

Translating from one language to another is always a complex matter given differences of context. To translate the happiness hypothesis, including as the ethics–religion spectrum, into political economy is equally challenging and equally essential for human well-being in a post-scarcity, post-absolute poverty generation. What is beginning to emerge for this exploration at this point is another paradigm. This certainly builds on the continuum from ethics to religion, and is indeed informed by it in terms of interacting complementarities. The paradigm itself is therefore not surprisingly evolving as a continuum of market mechanism and behaviour interacting with economy of regard. It becomes more obtrusively linked to the previous religio-ethical continuum when that concept of regard economy is also described as an ethic of reciprocity and even more so when that is linked to Tanner's economy of theological grace in Part 3.[156]

These languages illustrate very firmly: that this moral economy spectrum embraces key findings from Part 1, namely, capitalism, market mechanism, the religious field and social capital; that this is now evolving into happiness hypothesis literature complexities and what they are now suggesting in ethics, religion and political economy; and that, in turn, is leading into Part 3 with its thesis of the transfiguring of capitalism. This continuum is therefore of triple significance. It is a contribution to well-being from the happiness hypothesis; it bridges the major parts of this enquiry; and, in this part, as a form of faithful economics, it illustrates the different facets of faith contributions to global change.

The shape of this developing paradigm interacts two emerging findings for political economy from the happiness hypothesis. First is the importance of market mechanisms and behaviour, and their reformulation through interaction with other disciplines. Second, the economy of regard is developed as an integral part of a comprehensive political economy, and including a subset as forms of economic democracy.

Informing both is the critical dialogue between them, and their drawing from wider research fields through the happiness hypothesis. This capitalizes on the *correspondence* between a constructive critical engagement with economics from social capital, the happiness hypothesis and ethics perspectives, and important developments within that discipline.[157] That same correspondence technique is also used to equal advantage in Part 3, promoting resonances between contemporary economics and a theological economy of grace.

The two aspects of the continuum can also usefully be related to Wilkinson's two strategies for addressing scarcity, with their roots in pre-history and present throughout history. On the one hand, the strategy of dominance relates to the influence of the strong and powerful over the allocation of scarce resources. On the other hand, the co-operative or affiliative strategy aims 'to constrain dominance behaviour and replace it with more social systems of allocation'.[158] *Both* are practised in varying degrees in all societies. What Wilkinson detects is the centre of balance moving more from dominance to affiliative in a post-scarcity context. It is a change expressly recognized in the happiness hypothesis, as the growing significance of social relationships and the increasing limitations of economics including as income. It is a movement which does not discount the economic influence, but it does move the balance more towards, in this case, an economy of regard and the greater prominence of reciprocity in social arrangements.

The paradoxes of market mechanisms and behaviour

There is a striking convergence across the literatures and disciplines which is very critical of the current operating of market economies in terms of their negative impacts on well-being. The contributions of increasing incomes do not bring greater fulfilment, and, as economic and social inequalities, they have decisive and demonstrable negative consequences for health, relationships, crime and education. These impacts are also connected to the behaviours often associated with more affluent societies, and are arguably rooted in the market economy and economics themselves. These criticisms vary in intensity from James's condemnation of selfish capitalism and its associated disease of affluenza, to the more economically sensitive judgements of Layard.

Yet what is also very clearly and firmly evident is the acknowledgement that the market plays a central part in the debate over well-being and has an indispensable part to play in the future, howbeit an evolving and reformulated one. For Layard, economics is a 'sophisticated tool' with the market as a 'terrific' framework.[159] For Wilkinson, 'a major role for the market in our lives is still an inescapable necessity'.[160]

Much of this recognition centres on the role of the market mechanism, with the price system matching supply and demand, offering for modern complex societies an indispensable information co-ordinating function and signalling system for the allocation of relatively scarce resources. It therefore organizes the voluntary exchange of consumers and producers in the market, it drives efficiency to eliminate waste through competition, and its cost benefit analysis system questions policies where costs exceed benefits. Its achievements in contributing to the increase in wealth, so central to overcoming absolute scarcity and to increasing well-being has been unparalleled in human history. Wilkinson rightly talks of 'the unprecedented extent to which our modern material interdependence on each other is organized through the market'.[161]

The combination of these limitations and necessities represents the paradox of the modern market. Yet there are important arguments drawn from the happiness literatures in economics, psychology and epidemiology which suggest that the market's defects can be addressed. For example, the substantial differences between nations with regard to income inequalities, happiness and trust indicate the capacity for improvements.[162] Illustrations drawn from current experience confirm that judgement. A 1993 World Bank report on eight South East Asian economies noted the contribution to economic growth of government policies, and more egalitarian strategies to increase public support for change. Similarly, in Britain in World War Two, more equal sharing of the burden of conflict generated public co-operation in the war effort.[163] Other economic studies of inequality have produced much information on the feasibility of reducing it, including the examples of Costa Rica and the state of Kerala in India, interestingly concluding that 'the commonplace opposition between globalization and egalitarianism may be overdrawn.'[164] That key role of government in reducing inequality is also acknowledged by the eminent economist Arrow who considers 'the redistributive role (of government) as of the greatest importance, potentially and *ethically*, and much of the government expenditure in all countries is devoted to that end'.[165]

The role of such policies as progressive taxation, welfare, education, health and minimum wage do allow Wilkinson to conclude rightly that 'although the market will continue to coordinate many areas of life, we can at least partially liberate ourselves from its clutches by reducing the power of inequality that both fuels it and makes it such an irksome taskmaster'.[166] Yet economic and psychological perspectives also point to the need to reformulate understandings of economic behaviour in economic processes. The weight of evidence on such behaviour, norms, morals and their role in well-being and economic growth leads Layard to identify features of human nature which the happiness hypothesis confirms as central to a more adequately functioning economics.[167] These include the recognition of external effects in relation to economic transactions (for example, encouraging economic growth through greater population mobility is detrimental to social capital); it also acknowledges how values and norms are changing in response to external influences – say family life through divorce – and that more altruistic behaviour leads to greater happiness. Both challenge those economists who overemphasize self-interest. Layard therefore concludes that the 'substantive' findings of psychology need to be implanted 'into the framework of economics' and especially the new findings on 'external effects and the formation of values'.[168] That finding is confirmed by Haidt and the psychological evidence that 'Human rationality depends critically on sophisticated emotionality'; that 'It is only because our emotional brain works so well that out reasoning can work at all'.[169] It constitutes a much more scientific view of behaviour than the crude rationality theory of many economists. That is further confirmed by other research from the 1990s, that the processing system in the mind is twofold, controlled and automatic: for example, of the hundreds of operations occurring in the mind in each second, only one is not done automatically.[170] Our overidentification with conscious verbal thinking, as rationality, clearly needs reformulating. Given such evidence, Layard rightly concludes that the market mechanism of economics is necessary for well-being, 'What is wrong is the theory of human nature'.[171] The possibility of reformulating understandings of economic behaviour in order to promote well-being and reducing the obstacles to it, begins to confirm the feasibility of constructing a political economy more happiness friendly. The work on an economy of regard confirms and extends that possibility.

An economy of regard: affirming reciprocity and grace

Promoting more co-operative ways of living, working and structuring society has a long and complex history, including as prehistory and genetic features. Layard argues that when the human emerged out of Africa, 'We survived because our genes gave us the ability to cooperate.'[172] Offer notes Adam Smith's recognition of sympathy of and for others as central to well-being, and how this desire for regard is 'hard-wired into our psyches'. Both recognize that this is 'a more credible and a more ethical basis for policy'. Co-operative ways of living and working offer that.[173] For this is both historical and contemporary argument. The happiness hypothesis gives some support to that significance, for example, in its affirmation of reciprocity and a more egalitarian society as central to well-being. The obstacles to that, namely, ill-health, crime and political apathy are equally acknow-

ledged. It is profoundly rooted in moral behaviour, including the formation of character, virtues, norms and sanctions. In particular, it is central to
all religions, including Christian. The latter linked co-operation and belief
operationally through the work, for example, of the Christian socialists in
the later nineteenth century.[174]

The modern beginnings of the movement beyond scarcity and absolute
poverty accentuate and embody such co-operative developments and
possibilities. The marked increase in life expectancy, health, education,
income, human rights, and democracy confirm that general trend to more
egalitarian ways of operating societies. Alongside such trends is the
supportive persistence of non-market centres of human activity and
production. In other words, Polanyi's memorable argument in his *The
Great Transformation*, that Britain underwent a dramatic change in the
eighteenth century 'from socially embedded reciprocity to impersonal
price–drive market-exchange' was not as widespread as he and others have
argued.[175] For example, it did not replace trust and gift exchange and their
contribution to economics in reducing the transaction costs of compliance
and enforcement. As important, the family and household continued to
exert great influence on life and happiness in general and on economic
activities in particular – what Offer has called 'an economy of regard'. The
family's focus on reciprocity as non-market exchange constitutes 'the well-
spring of regard'.[176] It is a fundamental deployment of capital, on the one
hand as economic, for example through the major growth of global remittances, but particularly through the contribution of family businesses, so
powerful in say the emerging economies of Asia. It is equally significant, on
the other hand, as social capital, as the gift economy, as, for example, the
contribution of women in the home, including caring for the sick, the
elderly and children. Estimates of its economic value vary between one
quarter to over one third of national product. It is profoundly labour intensive and, for Offer, a 'superior good'.[177] Since the 1960s, it has been calculated that in 20 countries nearly 80% of 'the time available [to people] was
spent *outside* paid work, in various forms of social interaction, in domestic work, or alone'. Parental care, so essential for young children and their
future happiness, particularly constitutes an 'unmeasured but vital input
into human capital, and determines the ability to participate in the economy and society'.[178] The monetary value of caring for the sick and elderly
by the unpaid has been calculated at £39.1 billion in 1992 (7.5% of national income), four times as much as 'joint private and public expenditure for
long-term care'. Yet this economy of regard stretches beyond the household and into the formal economy.[179] This is illustrated by the growing
importance of team working and networking, reinforced by the accelerat-

ing impact of information technologies, and flowing into the knowledge-driven economy. Hardt and Negri also deploy these resources as integral parts of their 'multitude' countermovement to global capitalism.[180] As a determining factor in the informal economy, and its deep inroads into the formal economy, such regard, such co-operation and collaboration, is 'a good in its own right, quite apart from its instrumental value'.[181]

Economists have similarly argued for an understanding of economic life that registers the importance of broader definitions of behaviour and its economic and social implications. Falk and Fischbacher, in their exploration of 'the economics of reciprocity: evidence and theory', add another related conceptual interpretation of economic organization, working with a critique of economic behaviour as 'rational and selfish' and registering reciprocity as 'a powerful determinant of human behaviour'.[182] But it is Wilkinson who develops this most, through his reflections on economic democracy, essentially as a subset of the economy of regard. Extending people's ability to have a greater say over their lives to include the workplace is, indeed, one of Layard's Big Seven, as 'personal freedom',[183] and it figures large in studies of the impacts of inequality on health and well-being. It has also played a prominent role in social Christianity. In England, for example, the Church Socialist League's deep involvement in Guild Socialism was a creative development of workers' control which needs to be run alongside the Christian creation of producer co-operatives and their important contribution to consumer co-operatives.[184] William Temple brings that tradition into contemporary political economy with his commitment to every citizen having 'a voice in the conduct of the business or industry which is carried on by means of his labour'.[185] Similarly, in America in the same period, Walter Rauschenbusch, the leader of the Social Gospel before 1914, argued powerfully against such robber barons as the Rockefellers and for the Christianizing of the social order, particularly through the extension of democracy into the economy.[186]

Against this backcloth, Wilkinson's exploration of participation in economic life is particularly pertinent. His detailed empirical analysis of the causal relationship of ill-health and inequality is persuasive because it includes studies of the middle classes and not just the extremes of inequality. So a study of 17,000 men in government offices in London demonstrated that death rates from heart disease in the lowest ranks were four times as high as among senior administrators in the same offices. Ill-health was powerfully related to hierarchy and the lack of control over one's life at work.[187] What Wilkinson therefore proposes is to attack that problem by extending employee share ownership from being a means to give employees more financial incentives and commitment to the company, to the point where they own over 50% of the shares and so control the enterprise. It represents 'a more democratic and egalitarian way of controlling business' which can be deployed to give all employees clear and tangible means to have a decisive say in their lives and wider relationships.[188] And he is particularly concerned with its feasibility. He therefore notes that there are already 10,000 firms with 10 million employees with an average employee share ownership of 15–20% in the USA. In Britain, in 1998, share ownership schemes included 22% of all employees and nearly 15% of companies. Conyon and Freeman's (2001) survey of such firms found that they were 'associated with substantial improvements in productivity'.[189]

In terms of what a majority employee stake in the company would look like, contemporary examples of full co-operatives provide important evidence for the economic benefits of employee (share) ownership. The John Lewis Partnership in Britain is a very successful commercial enterprise in a very competitive sector. In Spain, Mondragon is even more impressive. Founded by a priest in the mid twentieth century, another illustration of the religious influence in economics of regard, it has developed into 120 employee-owned co-operatives, with 40,000 worker owners, with sales of $4.8 billion per annum. They are 'twice as profitable as other Spanish firms and have the highest labor productivity' in Spain.[190]

Such modest incremental change from within and from below constitutes an important complement to government-driven strategies to modify the market mechanisms as top-down measures. What is more important is that 'such democratic systems are perfectly compatible with the need to maintain a large element of the market in the coordination of economic activity'.[191] It is that ability to promote a more social and relational form of economy and economic activity which addresses significantly the lessons of the happiness hypothesis. In conjunction with modifying the market mechanisms and economic behaviour, they constitute, as a continuum from market mechanism to economy of regard, a more ethically adequate economy and economics judged by the contribution to human well-being. And because of that powerful ethical dimension, and its interaction with religion, it is equally a contribution to faithful economics.

7

Mapping Faith-based Contributions to Well-being

In the total global picture the religious contribution is both essential and prominent, yet in no way exclusive. It has always to be considered in relation to other fields. Indeed, its interaction with other interests is both a fact of life and, it will be argued, an increasingly preferred strategy. Yet that contribution is also a discrete entity or field, and so has to be explored in its own right. Such work has already begun in Part 1 and continued through the examination of the happiness hypothesis. The enquiry now needs to focus on aspects of that faith contribution in itself, essentially as a mapping exercise reflectively considered. It will certainly exhibit significant continuities with the earlier material, in terms of *issues addressed*, for example, globalization, labour, poverty, finance and health. It will also reflect *how* that engagement actually occurs both as a variety of religious types of response, from resurgent religion to liberal Western religion, and as a variety of *ways* of operating, best expressed as a spectrum. This will deploy the typology fashioned in the *Through the Eye of a Needle* exercise, moving from 'overlapping consensuses' to 'promoting understandings and practices in economic affairs which are distinctively different from the mainstream' in economics and politics.[192] The role of this final chapter of Part 2 is therefore to focus on the faith-based contribution itself, from the perspective of religion operating as religion.

Such a mapping takes for granted the foundation of the faith contribution, in the Christian case, in the lives of churches and Christians in their normal routines, including their continuing involvements in all sectors of society as government, business and voluntary, and at all levels from local to national and international. Through the daily lives of individuals in their families, friendships, neighbourhoods and associations they are a fundamental resource in the daily and historic task of developing human well-being.

The following review will rather concentrate on the more organized aspects of religious or faith-based contributions, drawing on selected

145

sources representing that interdependence of economy and social which is emerging as a particularly prominent part of this enquiry and its findings. There are, of course, a great array of such studies, including accounts of the multitude of community initiatives consequent on the *Faith in the City* (1985) report and its Church Urban Fund.[193] To widen such an exercise into the literatures of other faiths would present an even more daunting, if not overwhelming task. The following mini case studies are therefore representative samples as provocation to others to amplify the material and correct the lessons it draws. But any enquiry, attempting any degree of adequacy, has necessarily to include such an account. It matches the importance of any other chapter in this survey.

The material is arranged into four sections. The first takes account of the ways in which faith contributions are always part of wider relationships and social fabrics, to a greater or lesser extent. The mapping exercise of the NWRDA's two reports on '*the contribution made by faith communities to civil society in the region*', and the study of their actual economic value, is a graphic illustration of that profound interaction between faith and its localities. I summarize such a reading of faith contributions as partnerships, often unintentional or 'natural', and increasingly intentional. A brief reflection on partnerships is therefore of some importance. And because these are often engaged with 'poverty reduction', and so eroding unhappiness, this will also feature in this first section.[194] There is a formidable literature on such partnership involvements with local, national and international practical strategies for the reduction of deprivation and marginalization. Faith communities are often at the forefront of such initiatives, particularly in their local communities, and driven by very clear faith beliefs.

The next two sections essentially form two sides of the same coin – the actual mapping of various faith-based contributions to social well-being. They embody a number of important features: they engage with issues like globalization, health, poverty, finance and environment, as a continuing agenda from Part 1; they interact with the happiness hypothesis, and its main premise, that adequate income is essential for well-being, but beyond that, non-economic factors are more significant; they illustrate a spectrum, operating from overlapping to distinctively different; and finally, although drawn principally from the Christian tradition, they include important examples from Muslim and Buddhist traditions, and, most usefully, partnerships between faiths. As a result, section two concentrates on faith-based examples of more partnership working. Section three places a greater emphasis on the difference or added value character in the case studies.

The fourth section pursues the latter through three brief examples of faith providing what is claimed to be distinctive faithful economics. These claims will be examined in critical conversation with an economist in order to tease out a little further this important dimension of faith contributions.

Of Partnerships and Pro Poor Strategies

In the Christian tradition in Britain engagement with and in partnerships has become of increasing importance in recent history, and particularly in addressing poverty and marginalization. Five years ago, my work focused on Christianity in Britain.[195] That more domestic emphasis has now to be located in much wider global contexts, and to include other faiths. The two, partnerships and poverty reduction, warrant separate examination even though it is their interaction which is of prime importance.

Partnerships

The churches' involvement in partnerships in Britain is understood as the institutional or individual member's participation in organized relationships with the public sector, as national and local government, the business community, and the voluntary sector as civil society. It can involve combinations of one or more. They are regularly focused on addressing relative deprivation and social exclusion in both urban and rural areas, but principally the former in terms of demographic weight. Much impetus was provided by the seminal report, *Faith in the City* (1985). Through the William Temple Foundation, a consultant body in that process, I produced the first draft of the section on the Church, with its commitment to a 'local' 'outward looking' and 'participating' Church, so partnerships were central to that, both with other denominations and with secular bodies – indeed, it roundly declared 'the idea of partnership as a guiding principle in urban regeneration is one we welcome.'[196] That intent, fleshed out through numerous projects, often pump-primed financially by the Church Urban Fund (CUF), was further encouraged by the subsequent report *Faithful Cities* (2006), on the twentieth anniversary of *Faith in the City*, and its section 'Partnerships with each other', including different Christian denominations and other faiths, and with government. Recommendation six is on partnerships. It is awash with practical examples, including the Bradford Mentoring scheme for under-achievers, the Health for local families, and the Lichfield Savings scheme.[197] These all engage precisely with key aspects of the happiness hypothesis. Behind this upsurge lies the increasing commitment of government to this, particularly under New Labour. Prime Minister Blair acknowledged the contribution of faith-based organizations, in terms of their values and members, in strong language: 'In carrying out this mission you have developed some of the most effective voluntary and community organisations in the country'.[198] There is currently much government interest in extending this work into more central welfare and health delivery. Undergirding all this is my theological reflection describing the emerging age as of partnership and reconciliation. It includes a more detailed examination of partnerships, and their strengths and limitations in local, national and international contexts.[199]

The justification of partnerships reflects the important role of religions in them, and their wider significance, and again drawing from a variety of sources.

First, there is a growing recognition that the increasingly global nature of the major problems we now face are so complex, and cross so many boundaries whether political, cultural or religious, that no one standpoint, however substantial or sophisticated, can hope to engage them adequately. World poverty is powerfully historic and powerfully intransigent to date, and particularly as inequalities. The rapidly evolving environmental crisis represents an even greater and quite awesome challenge in terms of the sustainability of the planet itself. Partnerships, as the collaboration of many disciplines, seen a little in the happiness hypothesis, are increasingly demanded for the adequate analysis of such problematics, and partnerships as practical collaborations between sectors are needed to address them effectively.[200] In *Public Theology for Changing Times* (2000), I concluded that 'Partnership is the recognition that we cannot go it alone in terms of understanding and praxis, nor should we desire to . . . The alternative is the way of global death.'[201]

Second, Marshall rightly reminds us that much has been achieved in poverty reduction since 1945, not least through the many projects she describes in her *Fight against Poverty*.[202] It has resulted in the major erosion of absolute poverty in China and India and in the worldwide increases in literacy and life expectancy. This tells us that such problems are created significantly by social constructs, and can be changed for the good accordingly. The serious erosion of absolute scarcity and poverty represents, as we have seen, one of the historic moments for human well-being.

Third, the religious contribution to partnerships is beginning to be acknowledged in terms of its quantifiable actual and potential resources, its distinctive dimensions, and both as individual faiths and as dialogues between them. Beginning with the depth and breadth of religious resources available for partnerships, for Kimball, 'religion is arguably the most pervasive and powerful force on earth'. For Marshall, it is 'pivotal in the daily lives of most of the world's people'. It is one of the world's principal providers of health and education, with its strengths being particularly at local level where the impact of delivery is totally decisive. Health systems without health delivery to actual people are useless. Faith-based organizations with their 'broadly and deeply established roots' are indeed sometimes 'sole providers of services and community enablers'.[203] Palmer puts even more organizational and economic weight on the religious resource. For the President of the World Bank, the 11 major faiths in the Alliance of Religions and Conservation (ARC) constitute two-thirds of the world's population, own 7% of the habitable surface of the planet, have a role in 54% of schools, and have an institutional share of the investment market of 6–8%.[204] Clearly such resources are a strategic prerequisite for the formation of faith contributions, which are undeliverable without them, and are the necessary material embodiments of faith. Yet equally important are the less tangible dimensions of faith-based organizations in terms of their traditions, values and spiritualities. It is the latter which are particularly driving the secular acknowledgement that 'the links between faith and development have become much more apparent', and especially when there is a growing awareness of the 'multifaceted and complex processes [which] underlie economic and social change', and the recognition of faith and development's ultimate concern with holistic well-being.[205] It is at this point that the wisdom and experience of faith traditions become so indispensable. For at the heart of faith is a lived experience of reciprocity between divine and human, between humans, and between human and environment. Finally, there is a growing awareness of the 'common values' that link many if not most cultures,[206] often with deep roots in religious teachings and traditions – exemplified, for example, by the prevalence of forms of the Golden Rule of ethical behaviour in all the great faiths. Such commonalities support and encourage the growing and increasingly necessary interfaith dialogue and collaborations. These are epitomized by the World Faiths Development Dialogue (WFDD) and its promotion of constructive conversations between great faiths and global institutions like the World Bank, on poverty relief and its removal. The WFDD has worked to encourage interfaith alliances in the most difficult contexts, including in Guatemala (decades of civil war and inequality), Ethiopia (war and famine) and Tanzania (HIV/AIDS).[207] Their work has involved creating dialogue between faiths, governments, NGOs and the World Bank, 'to explore common interests and competing priorities among faith traditions and development partners, especially the World Bank'.[208]

Given such justifications for partnerships, there is a remaining and important question concerning the choice of partners, which Malcolm Brown usefully addresses. Clearly, for religious traditions, not every partnership is acceptable – 'some beliefs and practices (fascism, racism, sexism, apartheid) are beyond the liberal pale'. Traditions should therefore develop criteria 'for deciding with whom, and on what terms, it is proposed to enter dialogue'. His criteria include: 'a commitment to objective truth at some level; commitment to the possibility of new knowledge rather than treating any particular state of human understanding as complete for all time, and commitment to seek improvement in world affairs'.[209] Although the agenda emerges out of a Christian post-liberal tradition, it gives some idea of the tasks facing faiths when they enter partnerships.

Poverty reduction

Are the poor always going to be with us?[210] Opinion has been divided through history into the present. From psychology we know that dreams should be taken very seriously. When people also dream of a world without want, a world flowing with milk and honey, it is profoundly a world of abundance. Indeed, some theologians reject mainstream economics because they premise such a world as reflecting God's being.[211] Is it only a dream? If we mean a world beyond the scourge of absolute poverty, that is clearly achievable, and is occurring as we speak. The earlier transition arguments assume a post-scarcity as post-absolute poverty, with all the possibilities for good health and a new problem of affluence which presents new challenges to health and well-being. But these are post-absolute poverty problems. That transition is a reality for an increasing number of people post-1945, yet it is equally clear that that represents the beginnings of a journey, because a billion people, one in six of the world, are still living lives of absolute poverty, defined as $1 a day. If a broader definition of poverty is used, and much opinion supports that, then we are talking about 'The continuing suffering of almost half of the people alive in the world today – who live daily with poverty, disease, and hunger, who have few opportunities, little access to the most basic services, and muffled hope for a better future.'[212] The Millennium Development Goals, set by world leaders in 2000 as targets for 2015, actually reveal as much the nature and extent of the poverty problem as they do aspiration. Besides the goal of reducing absolute poverty ($1 a day) by half, they included universal primary education for boys and girls (particularly overcoming discrimination against the latter), reducing under-five-year-old mortality rate by two-thirds and maternal mortality by three-quarters, to reverse the spread of HIV/AIDS and malaria, and to halve the proportion without sustainable access to safe drinking water and basic sanitation.[213] It is a most disturbing audit of threats to human well-being. When the constant challenge of war, particularly as civil conflict, and violence as threat to neighbourhood security, is added to those of famine and disease, then the three spectres of the Malthusian nightmare continue to be ever-present realities in our world.

Taken together, these spectres constitute both religious and moral challenge, in addition to the obstacles they present to well-being, which have already been elaborated, particularly in the examination of social capital and happiness. For example, religiously, the great faiths have a 'strong common thread' which links them in 'compassion and concern for those who suffer'.[214] The poverty question is a condition of the world question for many of their leaders, theologians and local members. It is a concern deeply rooted in the sacred writings and traditions of the world faiths. For example, in sacred books, the Sikh Gurus stood by the 'low' and the 'poor' as a matter of compassion and justice. So the Guru Nanak said: 'There are the lowest men among the low castes. Nanak, I shall go to them. What have I got to do with the great? God's eye of mercy falls on those who take care of the lowly.'[215]

In terms of religious tradition today, liberation theologies, which cross faiths, are focused on the Divine bias to the poor, or the preferential option for the poor, all reflecting the Divine's, and therefore the disciples', deep concern for the vulnerable, for the marginalized. R. H. Tawney, Christian and ethical socialist, usefully links such religious accents to the moral case against poverty. In his memorable statement, he observed that there is 'no touchstone, except the treatment of childhood, which reveals the true character of a social philosophy more clearly than the spirit in which it regards the misfortunes of those of its members who fall by the way'.[216] That ethical dimension, such a foundational part of our spectrum of ethics to religion, was most powerfully expressed by the Kennys' philosopher–economist contribution to the well-being debate: when we know that the impact of a dollar in a wealthy country is virtually nil, and we know what the great value of a dollar is for the poorest (one billion on one dollar a day) – in terms of preventing death through starvation or disease – then 'it is difficult to understand the moral case against moving that dollar'.[217]

What the happiness research has also confirmed is that the poor are integral parts of society, and that society as a whole is infected by problems of say inequality, with immense consequences for *all* its members. Remember that that threat to well-being assumes new forms in affluent societies, and is nonetheless a deep threat to happiness. It is in order to capture that commitment to the whole, to wholeness – to the holistic and holiness – that some understanding of some kind of common good needs to be revisited (in Part 3). It is what the happiness research calls a philosophy of life and the common good. But this does not exclude a commitment to the poor, as we have seen, but rather recognizes it in and through that commitment to the common good of all. For it is that which therefore drives us to be particularly concerned for the most vulnerable, the poorest, the marginalized. And, again connecting to the happiness findings, this allows us to work with the market mechanism, as economic growth, for the good of the whole (and so beyond absolute poverty and scarcity) and equally for *social* well-being. (The effects of this equilibrium on economic policies will be discussed next.)

It is this understanding of what I call a bias for inclusivity, for the whole, and therefore for each vulnerable part, which is strongly rooted in religious tradition, and which I will illustrate through the Christian tradition.[218] This formative argument draws on St Paul's teaching in the New Testament, on the image of the Church as the Body of Christ, a body made up of many different parts, each with a particular contribution to make. As Forrester observes, Paul has taken 'an idea common in the culture of his day' but then he 'reshapes it *radically* to make it serve a new purpose'. For the Greeks routinely used the image to suggest some parts were intrinsically superior to others. In contrast, Paul recognizes that 'Diversity of gifts and functions does not lead to diversity of worth, esteem or status': different individual gifts and needs, confirmed by Sen's arguments for our different capabilities to function in life, are all fully and equally members of his one body.[219] Most importantly, Paul then goes on to argue that the least powerful were of particular importance for the body's health – as Tawney recognized 1900 years later – for 'those parts of the body that seem weaker are indispensable' (1 Corinthians 12.22). It is a model for being Church as Christ's body, and as Christ's followers, and it is therefore increasingly seen as a model for human living. For 'Humans are intended to live in community with one another, a form of living that is modeled, albeit imperfectly, by the Christian Church.'[220] It is a most powerful social modelling of social arrangements, divinely inspired, and informed by the happiness–social capital literatures – that we are meant to live in a reciprocating way in a political economy of regard or reciprocity.

Such claims are based on both biblical and wider Christian tradition sources, drawn also from many of the great world faiths, and from the secular evidence of the well-being literatures. And, most importantly, they can be and are being embedded in contemporary policy-making. These programmes are both multidimensional – from local government, through national and into global governance – and multifaceted, covering economic, political and social aspects of living.

They initially centre on the commitment to economic growth and market mechanisms as essential for human well-being. Even the more radical New Economics Foundation accepts that 'There is in the current climate, no real alternative to economic growth that doesn't involve the risk of even greater hardships for the most vulnerable in our society.'[221] Yet they equally recognize that those processes *alone* will not deliver sufficient well-being for the poorest – in terms of the paradox of prosperity as the creation of affluence and inequality, and the fact that most of the Millennium Development Goals will not be achieved by 2015. Economic growth has therefore to be *bent* to address the needs of the poorest, what the literatures describe as pro poor economic growth – as the bias for inclusivity translated into political economy.

This programme importantly operates at a number of different societal levels. Initially, the initiative was taken by the UN Development Programme (UNDP), and its recognition that the poor are unlikely to receive a fair and necessary share of economic growth if they are not empowered economically and politically. Such pro poor economic growth policies therefore include working with markets by encouraging growth in sectors where the poor are concentrated (agriculture, small-scale enterprises, including family businesses), expanding programmes with high impacts on the poor's capabilities (health care, education, micro-finance), and eroding gross inequalities since the greater the inequalities the higher the growth rate needed to reduce poverty. A UNHDR study published its report in 1996 demonstrating that

> since 1960, no country has been able to follow a course of lopsided development – where economic growth is not matched by human development or vice versa – for more than a decade without falling into crisis. During the past three decades every country that was able to combine and sustain rapid growth did so by investing first in schools, skills and health while keeping the income gap from growing too wide. [222]

It is such pro poor economic growth which has been developed at *national* levels by China's President Hu Jintao's '"scientific development" (meaning pro-poor and pro-environment)'. In Britain, it is illustrated by the Scottish Executive's Closing the Gap programmes, and by such local authorities as Sheffield's closing the gap policies – both seeking to erode the gulf between richest and poorest people and areas.[223]

In trade policies, so essential for raising the poorest nations and peoples out of poverty, as India and China have recently demonstrated, that again means developing pro poor programmes. For example, the World Trade

Organization's (WTO) Doha Development Agenda included a commitment to try to negotiate a Special and Differential Treatment (SDT) 'for developing nations as a tool for addressing some of the inequalities in trade'.[224] The following fourth section of this chapter includes a brief note on fair trade, which is an NGO/business/faith-based organizations partnership engaged with this aspect of pro poor economic growth.

The extension of the pro poor economic growth model into fields already identified as central to human well-being is therefore of particular relevance to this enquiry.[225] The argument for *pro participation* (or democracy) economic growth acknowledges the link between economic growth and human rights, encouraged by partnerships, including faith-based organizations, to generate more equal and effective human capabilities. (The madrasas in the next section do this with regard to women.) This also links strongly to wider commitments to erode inequalities for the greater well-being: 'the responsiveness of income poverty to growth increases significantly as inequality is lowered' and so more equal societies grow faster. Therefore, for example, 'greater gender equity and equity in general endowments and assets, has a double impact on poverty reduction because in more egalitarian societies the impact of the growth rate is greater and the growth rate will itself prove to be higher' (World Bank 2000–1). In other words, 'justice is good for the economy',[226] or, in Sen's words 'The market economy flourishes on the foundation of such development.'[227]

Given the unravelling environmental crisis, a third bias has been developed, pro environment sustainable economic growth – as 'a process of change in which the exploitation of resources, the orientation of investments, the paths of technological development and institutional change, are in accordance with current and future needs' (*Our Common Future*, 1987).[228] The programmes of ARC in providing sustainable growth through environmental schemes, and in partnerships with faiths, governments and civil society, will therefore figure significantly in the next two sections – as fishing and forest projects particularly.

The enquiry into happiness has also demonstrated the need to add a new bias, namely, a pro-happiness economic growth. The achievements of economic growth in raising many incomes significantly above the absolute poverty level, began, as we have seen, to generate situations in which increasing incomes are not commensurate with increasing happiness. The weight of concern rather shifts to incorporate a social-relational quality of life agenda. It also became clear from this research that the problems of inequality and unhappiness ran throughout society and were not the exclusive problem of the poor at all. Rather, the happiness agenda relates to individuals, communities and nations, to the whole of society, to the common good of all. Like all the other diseases, it requires partnership, both as multifaceted analysis, and as practical collaboration of faith-based organizations, government, business and civil society. Poverty reduction therefore performs the important task of confirming the essential role of partnerships in the contemporary context, and the nature of much of their agenda, with religion being integral to both.

Faith-based Organizations in Partnerships

This section and the following should be treated as two sides of the same coin. This section is concerned more with faith-based organizations working in partnerships, the next with the more distinctive added value of faith involvements in society. In some ways this is a more forced classification. The issue of added value is clearly part of this section, for example, in the Ugandan clinics and the East African pre-school madrasas. As a preferred way of working, partnerships also occur in the next section, in environmental and community regeneration schemes. What therefore emerges could be more accurately and graphically described as a continuum, moving from faith-based as partnership-oriented to more distinctively belief-oriented – almost a gradation of intensities. That spectrum is also reflected in other differences of emphasis. This section particularly addresses some of the key social issues identified in Part 1 and in the happiness hypothesis – for example, globalization, work, finance, health, education and environment. Yet it does this as faith-based involvements always deeply informed by spiritual capital, as the motivation and resources of beliefs, worship and virtues – all as part of the body of faith, as faith communities and traditions as unique sites of character formation. The greater focus on partnerships in this section typifies bridging social capital, in this case as *faithful capital*, linking faith and community, government, and NGOs in common ventures. The next section also contains such an emphasis, but also includes examples of bonding faithful capital, acting as actual or potential sources for the bridging function.

Much attention in the West has been concentrated on acknowledging the Great Disruption, and particularly its damaging consequences for the social capital of individuals, communities and nations, but also in seeking ways to rebuild that capital capacity. Putnam's *Better Together* documents some of the latter intentions.[229] Use will be made of this material in the next section to illustrate faith-based as more bonding faithful capital with its bridging implications. Yet the increasing weight and energy of religious activity is focused more and more in the South, including as resurgent religion. An account of faith-based contributions to well-being which did not therefore acknowledge this changing balance of power would be seriously inaccurate. The stories which follow, in both sections, reflect this changing equilibrium. Most are drawn from the poor South. They consequently represent a variety of faiths, sometimes working in partnership, and paying particular attention to Islam and Christianity, but also Buddhism.

Although the mini case studies represent very different situations and faiths, there are certain underlying similarities which suggest some guiding insights for future activities.

First, the value of partnerships between faiths, governments and NGOs is reaffirmed, at national and local levels. They are particularly needed to co-ordinate initiatives to overcome wasteful duplication of scarce resources and to maximize synergy. In a number of countries, in East Africa, Latin America and Asia, partnerships between faiths are beginning to emerge as both necessary and preferred routes for interventions, not least to prevent clashes of civilizations and the destructive potential of religions.

Second, the most decisive interventions are often, indeed invariably, locally based. The output of partnerships around faith-based activities has to be judged by better health, education and communities, by better lives, and particularly of people in their relationships. Smaller is often better, not least because building up trust and reciprocity, the bedrocks of good societies by virtually every measurement of the complex of constituents which make up human well-being, takes time. Political and economic programmes rarely understand this, which is why they are routinely inefficient.

Third, this enquiry has been strongly weighted towards political economy, and it has been increasingly evident that the religious field plays an actual and potential role in it, not least through its connections with the ethical dimension of human living. That said, what these case studies reveal is that civil society and faith communities have 'relatively low comfort with economic language'. This is compounded by 'a tendency for hard-nosed economists to discount language that summarizes concepts in terms other then theirs'.[230] Yet economics is an integral part of well-being in that, as we have seen, it both provides indispensable resources for well-being as income, and for health and education, and also contributes formidably to the obstacles to well-being. That broad span of economic impacts is reflected in all these case studies. In some, it is particularly focused, for example in the Inter-American Development Bank initiative, and in the International Interfaith Investment Group. This enquiry is dedicated, among other things, to developing this relationship between faith and economics, including increasing comfort with 'economic language'.

The Religious Contribution: A Complex in Complexities

Dialoguing the contests over globalization: the Fez Colloquium[231]

The annual colloquium held in Fez in Morocco seeks to provide hospitality to two major perspectives, the yearly World Economic Forum, held in Davos in Switzerland, and the World Social Forum, which moves around the globe. The Colloquium therefore represents the contest over globalization, in terms of its proponents as alliance of governments, multinational institutions like the WB, IMF and WTO, and transnational companies and financial organizations, and in terms of its opponents, as the increasing coalescing of very disparate groups functioning as anti-globalization, anti-capitalism and anti-American.

Fez's founding genius was Faouzi Skali, a Moroccan scholar, anthropologist and entrepreneur. Its guiding theme is 'giving soul to globalisation' by fostering conversations between the deeply divided opinions on and experiences of global processes. Its participants are drawn from these opposing world-views, therefore rightly acknowledging that such contrasting standpoints can learn from each other without detracting from their distinctive integrities. In that promotion of partnerships, the potential for overlapping consensuses is exploited while acknowledging the profound importance of and necessity for difference. The Colloquium therefore seeks to perform a classic bridge-building function reminiscent of Tillich's '*on the boundaries*' construct as of the essence of faith and its encounter with otherness and not its assimilation.[232] The use in this enquiry of *correspondences* between contrasting fields performs a similar function – of identifying points of actual and potential connection which are open to exploitation through their interaction. This often leads to a process of reformulation *within* integrities, and often to their mutual benefit. MacIntyre and others have noted the opportunity this provides for the reformulation of tradition, including religious, through comparable interactions with outside influences and contexts.[233] The Fez Colloquium works in a similar way by bringing together very different perspectives with the potential for generating new reflections on globalization.

Fez also promotes a dynamic confrontation not simply between opposing forces of globalization, but also between modern and ancient cultures and their histories. In all these agendas religion plays a key role, initially in terms of Muslim, Jewish and Christian traditions, but increasingly including other faiths. Particular use is made of music and art as an integral part of its wider concern of 'giving soul to globalization'. It therefore has 'a global vision of a multicultural world where differing cultures and perspectives all find a place'. Indeed, the rich variety of musical traditions is a major draw to the Festival. The 2003 programme included Gilberto Gil

(Brazil), Mohamed Reza Shajarian (Iran), Yungchen Llamo (Tibet), Doudo N'Diaye Rose (Senegal), the Whirling Dervishes (Syria) and the Anointed Jackson Sisters (USA). It represents a multifaceted engagement with globalization 'extending well beyond simple facts and values to the world of the spirit, to work towards a richer menu of options for the future'.[234]

Furthering ethical economics: the Inter-American Development Bank Initiative[235]

Latin America is a prime location of resurgent religion, especially as Roman Catholicism. It is the site of recent violent conflicts, profound economic instabilities, grave inequalities and deprivation, and of religious reaction to them as liberation theology. It therefore provides a potentially important context for faith involvement in partnerships in relation to the promotion of ethical economics. An early attempt to do this has been provided by the Inter-American Development Bank's exploration of 'social capital, ethics and development'.[236]

At the height of the social, political and theological conflicts in 1988, the bank sought to develop relationships with major faiths to promote well-being through an economic development which acknowledged the importance of social relationships and ethics as central to those processes. It committed itself to merge ethical dimensions into its deliberations on development as an integral part of a multidimensional approach to policy-making. In 1999–2000 it therefore launched its 'Initiative on Social Capital, Ethics and Development', overseen by an advisory board of religious leaders, economists and former heads of state.[237] Priority in bank and economic development processes was given to such concerns as: which values should inform development strategies and policies, how should regional leaders react to issues with strong ethical dimensions (to sharp inequalities, poverty and discrimination), what ethical codes should key groups adopt, and how could solidarity ethics be practised? Through a series of seminars across the continent, and by developing networks of support, its underlying objective was to create 'propitious conditions for developing the basic components of social capital, such as association and cooperative capacity, interpersonal trust, and civic conscience'.[238] Importantly, this project, supported by faith communities, was an acknowledge-ment, in Sen's words, that we need to 're-examine old issues (for example, the role of the market) in new light' and also 'address new issues that have been brought to prominence by the interactive world in which we live (including the demands of an un-segmented global ethics)'.[239] Sen then acknowledged the role of the project in furthering such an agenda by successfully encouraging a great number of people 'to think about development ethics and consider ways and means of advancing the use of ethical thinking and normative behaviour in the cause of economic, social and political progress'. Such initiatives have also broadened 'the intellectual horizon of economists and other social scientists some of whom tend to presume that the hard work of development demands only canniness and prudence – not ideals of commitments or morals'.[240]

Promoting decent work: conversations between the ILO and WCC[241]

Work has played a central part not just in the happiness hypothesis and social capital, but also as a strategic foundation of global capitalism. A constructive organized conversation over time between the premier global institution concerned with working life, the International Labour Organization (ILO), and the premier global Christian ecumenical movement, the World Council of Churches (WCC), clearly has the potential to be of major importance for human well-being. So many criticisms, for example, of globalization, relate to its damaging consequences for jobs themselves (in advanced economies), but also for their quality (driving down standards of working life through unfair competition). Some of these matters have already been addressed, but this partnership dialogue brings into the debate a spiritual dimension through the involvement of faiths (the WCC ensured other religions participated in the process). That connection of spirituality and work, its nature and organization, has already been noted, including in the work of Merchant and Gilbert.[242] This dialogue both confirms and extends that knowledge.

The conversations between the ILO and the WCC began in 2002, and were inspired by the priest Dominique Peccoud, advisor to the director-general of the ILO. They focused on the useful concept of decent work (which could also be called ethical work). By this was meant not simply fair wages, equality in work places, and social protection but also 'the spiritual foundations that have, from time immemorial, made work central to human society'.[243]

The project then recognized that the development of legal instruments for informing and promoting decent work globally (now increasingly essential for human well-being) regularly engaged the question 'how far it is possible to design international legal instruments around *a set of values* that we agree are common to human existence, or are differences of culture so deep, and so intense, that a "clash of civilization" is inevitable?' It is the Hollenbach question about reconciling universals and locals, recast in a work context. The dialogue then proceeded to agree that 'a people-centered approach that encompasses humans' material and spiritual aspirations' acknowledges the importance of work in that conviction, and that work was therefore 'more important' than economic systems, including 'capitalism', and 'constitutes the source of dignity, family stability and peace'.[244] The possibility of a shared set of values around such an estimating of work's nature and significance was highlighted by the religious contribution's locating of it in a divine context: 'that God or the Creator is the archetypal worker, and that human work is an extension of that divine activity' (for Muslims, since God is transcendent, man's work cannot be a continuation of God's). It is a multidimensional understanding of work, firmly involving a spiritual perspective, always going beyond, although powerfully including, work as meeting material needs. It therefore links with organization and development theory, and the progression of human well-being beyond income satisfaction and into meeting social, psychological and spiritual needs. 'Only work that enables an individual's growth can be called decent.'[245]

That commitment to spiritual work necessarily includes a commitment to ethical work. This understanding from the dialogue includes the recognition of the legitimacy of collective action, the condemnation of compulsory labour, the rejection of child labour, and opposition to discrimination in occupation and employment.[246] The connecting of spiritual and ethical as formative principles of decent work also constitutes an important contribution to the emerging understandings of both faithful economics and ethical economics – and of the interactive relationship between them, and their location on a continuum.

Respecting and utilizing the different integrities of partners: Uganda's fight against HIV/AIDS[247]

The HIV/AIDS pandemic has devastated sub-Saharan Africa, already the poorest region on earth. As the focal point of a remarkably resurgent religion, both Christian and Muslim, its fight against the disease presents particular problems for partnerships involving religion and government. For HIV/AIDS focuses on the 'most intimate of human behaviours' always generating strong premises of religious belief, behaviour and sanctions.[248] Yet what could be the obstacles of religion to well-being progress in reversing the disease's spread (a Millennium Development Goal), also present opportunities, given the need for local and personal involvements in that campaign. The Ugandan experience of partnerships between faiths, government and NGOs is a remarkable testimony to the potential of this ambivalence of religion. For what has emerged is a way of respecting differences in addressing sexual matters yet equally a commitment to share goals. The result has been a campaign conducted mosque by mosque, church by church, increasingly *'a new dynamic mosaic of partnerships'*.[249]

The story is even more remarkable given Uganda's history. Having gained its independence only in 1962, from 1971 until 1986 it experienced political and economic crises, and civil war. And on top of such calamities, HIV/AIDS struck in 1982, or SLIM as it was known (because the disease made you slim). With the active support of President Museveni (including his public recognition of the disease, highly unusual for African leaders), there gradually emerged what became the Ugandan AIDS Commission. This included the religious leaders of the three major faith traditions in Uganda – Catholic, Protestant and Muslim – with each chairing the Commission in turn. The cornerstone of its strategy was based on ABC, private abstinence (especially directed at young people), being faithful (particularly in marriage), and the use of condoms (with a dramatic increase in them). ABC was then located in wider strategies, emphasizing local health clinics and the care of orphans.

The thorough involvement of the three faiths in these programmes was essential for their success, since 'Religion is inextricably woven into every aspect of life in Uganda ... in their sense of personal identity, their thought patterns, their moral judgements and their perceptions of the disease' (Kaleeba, 2000).[250] The degree and extent of the religious involvement in these programmes was unusually thorough: the Roman Catholics, with 25% of the health-care infrastructure, including local clinics, ensured each of the 19 dioceses had a senior HIV/AIDS coordinator; the Anglicans mobilized health workers at local parish level in a *holistic* caring of services, personal hygiene, reproductive health, HIV prevention, care and support; the Islamic Medical Association of Uganda developed a contribution recognized as best practice by the UN with prevention programmes using local imams, each with a male and female assistant – with therefore 8,000 religious leaders and community volunteers supporting over 100,000 households. Women's participation was particularly recognized.

What emerged was a most significant understanding and interpretation of partnerships. While most faith communities opposed condom use in principle, few openly opposed the government's distribution programme. The government in turn was sensitive to the position of the faiths, and so avoided overly aggressive promotion. 'Each and every element has been vital to Uganda's success in reversing HIV/AIDS trends.'[251] In terms of religious participation in partnerships, it constitutes a lesson in facing up to the Hollenbach question by developing shared overall programmes which respect differences and integrities.

Promoting equity in education: madrasas in East Africa[252]

The Madrasa Early Childhood Program in East Africa is supported by the Aga Khan Foundation and operates in Kenya, Tanzania and Uganda. It began with small initiatives in the 1980s which recognized 'communities' concerns that their children understand their local culture and religion while also improving their chances for access to and success in formal education'.[253] The well-being literatures' findings strongly corroborate such an emphasis on early childhood development as of formative significance for personal and communal growth. The recognition of and the capitalizing on religious traditions and experiences also reflected the programme's correspondence with these wider research findings.

The project initially emerged when Muslim community leaders expressed their concern to the Aga Khan that more children should succeed at university-level education. That longer-term aim was rightly seen as dependent on developing the commitments and skills of young people at an early pre-school age. To do this, the programme worked with local communities and families, and most importantly, built on the local organization and traditional Islamic educational institution, the madrasas. It was particularly committed to developing the education of girls, and so placed great weight on the involvement of women as teachers and organizers in the localities. Its strategy of recruiting local women for pre-school training and operating the local organization was given early high priority. The curriculum was developed with communities and their religious leaders 'The resulting "integrated" preschool curriculum combined local Swahili culture (language, songs and stories), key values and teachings from Islam, and contemporary methodology and content.'[254]

By the end of 2002, the Madrasas Resource Centres (MRCs), formed to institutionalize the programme in each country, were working with 185 communities in East Africa. Non-Muslim children were accepted on a modest basis, normally in proportion to their numbers in the locality. Parents chose it as the best and most affordable in the area, and it was seen to enrich their own religious beliefs.

An evaluation of the scheme identified five keys to its success. First, its community development and mobilization processes, using a community development officer locally. It is this community ownership which is 'the critical difference between MRC preschool and other preschool initiatives'.[255] Second, the local management of each school reflects a strong commitment to self-help, in terms of the selection and training of members of committees. Women were well represented in them, as required by the MRC. Third, funding is provided by the Aga Khan Foundation as pump-priming, to stimulate local fund-raising and local financial management. Fourth, the programme is implemented flexibly, using local feedback and evaluation processes. Again, the commitment is to gradual change, step by step, with the rejection of any overextension of the project. Fifth, strong administration at regional and national levels was undertaken by highly committed people.

As a partnership with local people and religious institutions, the MRC has also influenced governments in Africa as a model for expanding local education, particularly of women, again a Millennium Development Goal, and confirmed by wider research as the indispensable contribution of women to economic development in the poorest nations.[256] Achieving such well-being objectives requires the effective partnership with local religious institutions and people, respecting their religious traditions alongside accepting the modern educational understandings of curriculum and learning techniques. It represents another contribution to understanding the distinctive, added value, of religion's role in the development of people and communities. It represents the interaction of the difference of local traditions with more universal experiences and commitments. It is in that context that delivering greater equity for women can often have the greatest opportunity for success.

Rescuing identity and environment: the Mongolian Sacred Sites Initiative[257]

In 1999 the World Bank, the World Wide Fund for Nature (WWF) and the Alliance of Religions and Conservation (ARC) formed a partnership to support the Religions in Biodiversity project with particular reference to Asia. Its task was to develop links between religious values and sustainable development. It represented a bias for inclusivity which enlarged pro poor economic growth to incorporate pro environment and pro participation growth: 'The project reflects a growing conviction among development institutions that religions can exert a material impact on the environmental debate at the grassroots level, not only by teaching facts about the natural world but also by providing leadership and taking direct action on conservation projects.' That practical religious output included Buddhist monks in Thailand promoting forest conservation, a Christian environmental education and retreat centre in Papua New Guinea, and using the Islamic traditions of *harim* (protected lands) to defend national parks.[258]

A particularly useful example of the project is the Mongolian Sacred Sites Initiative, illustrating 'the intersection between religious and cultural values within an unusually short time'. The acknowledgement of religion's added value, as difference factor, recurs through these projects particularly, and provides links into the next section, which will examine this added value dimension more thoroughly.

Mongolia's national and cultural identity has been strongly associated with the reverence for nature through much of its history. From shamanism's beliefs and rituals to Buddhism from the twelfth century it led to a Mongolian belief 'that the fate of humanity and nature are inextricably interwoven [which] complemented Buddhist support for compassion for all life'. It was powerfully embodied in legends and sacred writings and profoundly focused on the significance of forests and waters. All that changed dramatically with Communist dictatorship from the late 1930s, when all but one of 746 Buddhist monasteries were destroyed, and 17,000 out of 110,000 monks were executed. As the religious tradition faded, so did support for nature, with dire consequences in 'degraded land, polluted water, and decimated animal populations'.[259]

With the fall of Communism in 1990, the task was to revive religion and its cultural values, 'to restore and protect the environment in tandem with growth and development'.[260] The project contributed to this process by collecting hundreds of parchments in order to discover the 280 legends once codified in historic holy Buddhist texts called sutras. The Buddhist Gandan monasteries in Ulaanbataar played a major role in this revival, including the Boyd Khan Sacred Mountain. This rediscovery of sacred texts linked to environmental projects was vital for the success of the initiative, and involved the partnership of local monasteries and communities. The latter was particularly important, demonstrated by the fact that 'Communities at every sacred site have expressed gratitude for efforts to combine conservation and tradition.'[261] The cumulative effect was also to reinforce and enrich Mongolian identity. It has confirmed the importance of 'the religious and cultural approach to development', through in this case, environmental sustainability. It joins other examples in this section on health education, work, finance and globalization. For Dr Sukhbaatar, author of *Sacred Sites of Mongolia*,

In Mongolia, venerating, fearing and obeying the deities of the mountains, waters, and land was a very important form of environmental protection. The religious ritual both protected nature and instilled overall respect into the people. As such, these stories and the traditions behind the names may yet turn out to be one of the greatest gifts of Mongolia's past to her present.[262]

This modest and selective collection of glimpses of faith-based partnership working seeks only to begin to illustrate their actual and potential significance for economic development and environment. Behind such effort lies capacities as motivating forces and resources. With faith-based organization (FBOs), their characters are formed by and in faith communities and traditions. The actual outputs often overlap with those of other bodes but they can assume more distinctive forms. This enquiry has continued to demonstrate the significance of such character and forms, each part contributing further understandings of them. It is not surprising that from this section and from the next two, additional relevant material will emerge. For example, with faith-based partnerships this information relates particularly to models of activity, to measuring faith's added value, and as guidelines for further involvements.

Differing models of FBO relationships with partnerships

The weight of evidence from these projects is generally supportive of partnerships because of their ability to bring together different experiences and resources. There is *no* evidence that any one perspective or tradition, including religious, can 'go it alone'. There is simply too much variety with too much substance as quantity and quality, and the problems are too complex to either suggest that *or* allow for that. Yet within that partnership-working, religions play an indispensable part, and clearly should do more *and* be encouraged to do more by other partners. Welcome signs, evidenced by World Bank reports, are beginning to suggest this may be happening, particularly with the Bank and IMF's movement from the 'one model fits all' approach.[263]

Yet beside that fundamental premise there are clear signs that FBOs are developing ways of operating which cannot simply be fitted comfortably into the partnership model. These can be rather provisionally summarized, at this stage of their development, as a critique of and alternative to mainstream partnership modelling. Both relate to the fundamental character of the religious field which requires and informs its existence as an autonomous field, even though it also clearly interacts with other fields, including in partnerships. In other words, faith groups, for Marshall, 'apply different concepts of time, space, welfare, and commitment to development that we might also call heart and soul'.[264] (She does not take into account how theory or theology, including as reasoning, is also a basis of and indispensable to that faith contribution, as we will see in the remaining sections and in Part 3.) FBOs always therefore contain the potential for critique of other partners, and for developing alternatives to them, including to mainstreams in political economy.

First, as critique. The different values of FBOs can include rejecting government views, for example on contraception. The Ugandan account of the programmes to combat HIV/AIDS shows how this difference factor can still be accommodated in wider commitments, but that outcome was dependent on *both* partners being prepared to contribute to that valued wider objective and to take the appropriate steps to enable that to happen in terms of modifying their approaches accordingly. The involvement of FBOs in Poverty Reduction Strategy Programmes (PRSPs) also reflects a strong recognition that economics, and government and secular bodies alone, are not sufficient for adequate economic development. Ensuring that a more multidimensional approach shapes thinking and practice on poverty reduction is and will be a continuing struggle, and indeed, is always likely to remain a continuing and necessary critical perspective.

Second, as alternatives. The underlying character of FBOs can move beyond criticism to begin to embody what can sometimes have the essence of an alternative to mainstream thinking and practising. For example, promoting dialogue between contesting partners can begin to suggest new ways of thinking and working. There are signs of that in the Fez Colloquium in more general terms. The madrasas illustrate how FBOs can set up effective parallel systems, but normally also working in tandem, and partnerships, with other systems, for example, run by governments. The three case studies in the final section of the chapter will test these critique and alternative models further, including with reference to Muslim Interest Free Banking.

Measuring the added value of FBOs

Given the recognition of the distinctive character and features of the religious field, and consequently of FBOs, there is growing interest in developing ways of measuring such added value contributed by FBOs, and particularly as alternative models. Ugandan health clinics and East African pre-school madrasas have both undergone such evaluations, and both illustrate the *clear* and empirically verifiable nature of the *differences* FBOs bring to economic development, essentially, as the added value of faith. This will be explored briefly at the beginning of the next section.

Emerging guidelines for future faith-based partnership working

Although these suggestions are tentative, particularly because they need much wider testing, certain valued ways of working are emerging. First, there is growing evidence of the importance of creative partnerships and alliances that include a faith-based presence. Indeed, there is an increasing need for them, given the daunting nature of the problems they face, and the failure or unacceptable dilatoriness of present endeavours to address them. Second, besides partnerships between FBOs and other fields of influence, partnerships *between* faiths should also be given increasing weight. In Ethiopia, for example, PRSPs demonstrated the importance of the national coordination of faith-based initiatives. Similarly in Central America, in the struggles against conflict and violence through peace-building initiatives. The Ugandan example on HIV/AIDS shows the possibility and value of such collaboration.

Third, spotting the possibilities for what Marshall calls 'unconventional dialogue' can attract 'different perspectives' and break down 'barriers'.[265] The Fez Colloquium used multicultural public displays to do this, deeply informed by various religious traditions with their skills and experience in embodying values and beliefs in music, story and art forms.

Faith-Based Organizations as Difference: Addressing Added Value

Pursuing the nature and extent of the distinctive features of faith-based organizations (FBOs) is important in itself, but also because it contributes to building up knowledge of the religious field. The accounts of projects deployed to illustrate this emphasis in FBOs as the difference factor, including as added value, are drawn from studies of faith-based involvements in economic development, environment, civil society, urban regeneration and social capital. They indicate the continuing importance of partnerships and faith-based participation in them – for example, projects on trees and community regeneration, and drawing on new research in Manchester.

The previous section's greater emphasis on bridging social capital is continued in this section, but also with greater recognition of the function of bonding social capital, including its potential for developing into bridging social capital. Examples are drawn from community development in Egypt and Poland, fishing in Zanzibar and American mega churches.

Again many of the projects do address global issues, as in the previous section, but perhaps a little less prominently. The following argument is arranged into three parts, a brief note on measuring added value, a longer account of projects and a concluding list of factors contributing to religious difference.

Measuring added value

Measuring is a matter of recurring importance throughout this enquiry, not least because of its intentional focus on political economy, and the influence, in turn, of political economy in the current global context. And economics, and its interaction with welfare and the happiness hypothesis, ensure that both include estimating their *impacts* on human well-being. Not surprisingly, there is much resistance to justifying this approach where the subjects for measuring interact most closely with more non-material values and practices, and particularly religious involvements. Yet the happiness hypothesis clearly requires and benefits from research methods that use quantitative and qualitative methods of measurement. There is no reason to treat FBOs differently. Indeed, they can form part of the arguments supporting FBOs as critique of and alternative to the mainstream, including as political economy. Two examples illustrate such possibilities, and more importantly, provide empirical evidence of the actual added value of some faith-based initiatives. This is also a response to Marshall's call 'for measurement of the material results' of 'faith and development partnerships' as they gain 'a higher profile'.[266]

First, from Uganda's experience of faith-based provision of primary health-care services, there emerged a report *Working for God: Cost-Benefit Reflections on Faith-Run Clinics in Uganda*, by the economists Reinikka and Svensson.[267] This research examined the contribution of faith-based not-for-profit (NFP) organizations in providing health-care facilities (compared to equivalent secular NFP and government services). The government provided a grant of $1,650 to each dispensary in 1999–2000. The conclusion of the research identified that faith-based NFP services 'could not be explained under a profit-maximisation framework' – that they hired qualified staff for under the minimum wage; were more likely to provide 'pro-poor services with a public goods dimension, such as outreach and training of community health workers'; the services were of higher quality than government dispensaries; they charged lower prices than the private sector; and, if given government financial aid, they increased 'laboratory testing for malaria and intestinal worms and lowered their prices for outpatient consultations'.[268]

In other words, it illustrates that 'the value of faith can be rigorously analyzed and quantified', and can demonstrate the added value of faith. Yet, as the report concludes 'faith will still be a complex and ultimately unknowable "orienting life force" first, and a value to subject to measure only second'.[269]

The second example is provided by the pre-school madrasas of East Africa, generating another parallel system to the secular. The evaluation used an adapted version of 'Harm and Clifford's early childhood environmental rating scale', which assesses the quality of the learning environment. Comparing the madrasas with non-madrasas, the evaluation revealed that with the former 'the difference is statistically significant in 8 of the dimensions', and scoring higher in 9 of the 11 dimensions.[270]

Both studies therefore suggest that the importance of FBOs, running parallel programmes to the secular, can generate greater value – as added value therefore, including reference to a distinctive or difference character which can be both critique and embodiment of alternative ways of working to the mainstream.

Accounting for the difference factor: case studies of more distinctive FBOs

These accounts are brief summaries only, the sources are referenced for more detailed follow-ups. They are roughly divided into two lists: first, the most distinctively different and separate from the mainstream, including some more illustrative of bonding social capital (or faithful capital) – for example, of the Zanzibar fisherman and the Egyptian mosques. These can also include empowerment processes capable of supporting or transitioning into bridging faithful capital: for example, the Saddleback megachurch and the Polish Madonna. The second list consists of projects which combine both distinctively different and partnership factors. They include yew trees and churchyards in Britain, two case studies from Manchester, and the Valley Interfaith programme in the USA. The spiritual currency programme could be located in either list, but it is located in the first.

Projects more distinctively different from the mainstream

Muslim fishing in Zanzibar[271]

Fishing off the Tanzanian coast, from such islands as Zanzibar and Masali, is a centuries-old tradition and profession. Undertaken by mainly poor communities, they began to use dynamite, which killed the fish but had catastrophic impacts on fragile coral reefs and the wider ecosystems. Scientific surveys persuaded the government to adopt the usual tactic of banning the practice, which, of course, continued. A joint venture, including the ARC and the Islamic Foundation for Ecology and Environmental Science, realized that these Muslim communities needed to see the religious significance of the environment, and therefore how using dynamite contradicted this. Working with the local sheikhs, using the Qur'an and stories about the Prophet's denunciation of waste, the fishermen were helped to see the importance of sustainable fishing. For example, they used such Quranic texts as 'O children of Adam! . . . eat and drink: but waste not by excess for Allah loveth not the wasters' (Surah 7.31). 'What government laws and the threats of violence failed to do, Islam in partnership with the environmental insights of conservation bodies managed to achieve' because 'it made sense within the people's culture and world view, and it drew not just upon ecological information but on a profound understanding of human nature in the sacred texts.'[272]

Social Islam in Egypt[273]

Emerging from the slums of Cairo, the Community Association of Esbet Zein created a wide-ranging welfare and economic development provision, based around mosques and covering urban and rural areas. The centres extended

> the scope of traditional Islamic societies (such as Qur'an memorization, religious publication and burial of the dead . . .) into new areas of social service provision . . . Typically, they provide a range of services including basic medical care at a fraction of the cost elsewhere, child day care, remedial education, religious instruction and vocational training – often sewing for women, carpentry and mechanics for men . . . Such developments have given local mosques a new importance as a centre of community life, renewing and extending their traditional functions. They have also enabled religious leaders to extend their leadership roles in local communities.[274]

It is a comprehensive service paralleling the state's, religiously based, and providing high quality outputs with demonstrable added value. When I first read this account I was struck by the remarkable similarities to community-based church projects say in Britain's *Faith in the City* and *Faithful Cities*, and as already noted in the USA. These cases are more clearly religiously based and so more distinctively separate from mainstream secular types.

Religious statues and creating national identity: the Black Madonna to Bodhisattva of Compassion

Once again, I was much struck by the similarities between two differently sourced case studies. These illustrate the major impact a unique distinctively religious artefact can have on religious and national identity which secular resources could never provide. The Polish example, in addition, indicates the use of religious symbols as radical critique of secular mainstream, leading to an alternative government emerging. From 1957 until 1980 a copy of the icon of the Black Madonna was taken around every parish, spending a night in each place. It was a profoundly symbolic event manifesting Polish history and culture, and therefore religiously expressed, and which 'strengthened social integration on both local and national levels and rejuvenated the religiosity of the Poles'.[275] In addition, it created networks of and for potential and actual resistance to Communist rule, resulting in the Roman Catholic Church's fundamental role in the revolution which overthrew Communism in 1989–90.

In a similar vein, Palmer recounts 'the extraordinary story of the rebuilding of the statue of Avalokitesvara in Mongolia', symbol of national identity and Bodhisattva of Compassion. Destroyed by atheistic Communism in the 1930s, under Stalin's orders, it was resurrected with the overthrow of Communism in 1989. Faced by widespread poverty and unemployment, the new minister of education was presented with much expert advice for the country's reconstruction. He decided that the first task was to ignore these recommendations and to do something totally different. He set about making a new statue of the Protector of Mongolia, Avalokitesvara, financed by the people themselves. 'The statue changed everything. It also changed the worldview of not a few aid agencies with respect to what it is that helps people make sense of the world and thus change it.'[276]

Spiritual currency: the '3iG'

The year 2000 witnessed a historic meeting between major faith representatives and the environment and development worlds in Kathmandu. They
agreed to encourage the creation of an international interfaith investment
group, or 3iG, and the ARC was asked to organize it in the light of a growing awareness of the economic assets of faith communities. The ARC had
begun such an audit of major faiths in 1999. It quickly acknowledged the
staggering sums and outputs involved (already noted in the *England's
Northwest* survey of faith-based economic impacts on communities). For
example, Palmer relates how the United Methodist Church, the fourth
largest denomination in the USA, had $70 billion total investments, with
the Church of England worth nearly a hundred times more. The Roman
Catholic Church, with one billion members, has 20 million staff (priest,
monks, nuns, teachers, youth workers, etc.) with enormous building
assets.[277]

The ARC also recognized that most faiths had investment policies in
terms of what not to invest in, including tobacco businesses, alcohol firms,
armaments, distilleries and gambling organizations. What ARC did was to
develop that understanding of ethical economics much further by encouraging faith investment in ventures and companies with clear beneficial
social and environmental impacts. Supported by good research, the finance
officers from different faiths set up the 3iG in 2002, as an independent
body to which faith financial departments could relate. The management
group was advised by religious and secular experts. One of the strategies
was to focus on 'cluster groups' in key areas for creative ethical investment,
including alternative energy. Another related strategy was the 'cascade
effect' through each faith agreeing to pass on information on ethical
investment to its members, including individuals, to invest their assets in
socially responsible ways.[278] So the United Methodist Church in the USA
has a pension fund of $12 billion, yet their congregations include five to
seven million families with likely investment savings (pensions, equities,
etc.) of $250–500 billion. The 3iG model also recognizes the integrity of
each faith including pursuing its own ethical economics, yet that shared
agenda embraces the differences. It constitutes another response to the
Hollenbach question of how to hold together universals and differences. It
represents 'one of the most dramatic examples of the interaction between
religious worlds and secular worlds'.[279]

The Religious Contribution: A Complex in Complexities

Brave social capital

Ann Morisy's reflections on church contributions to social well-being suggest another form of social capital, brave social capital, in addition to bonding, bridging and linking social capital. Brave social capital is the 'willingness to provide support to those who are likely to be perceived as carrying some kind of threat or menace'.[280] Her accounts illustrate the concern for hospitality and kindness which can 'unleash' what she calls 'the cascade of grace from which an unknowable range of people and situations benefit' (the concept of 'cascade' has also just been used by Palmer to describe 3iG strategy). This cascade of grace is 'uncontrollable, unpredictable and virtuous' as signs of God's kingdom.[281] So a Mothers' Union group in a Kent village met three Mothers' Union workers from Zimbabwe, and agreed to collect old sewing machines to help in the Zimbabwean villages. And they then decided to take them themselves. These British women were all over 60, and they therefore chose this route of 'venturesome love', resulting in an amazing cascade of grace impacting on local families, communities and organizations, a powerfully transforming experience.[282]

Mega-church: from crowds to congregation[283]

Putnam's account of the Saddleback mega church in Lake Forest, California, exemplifies the possibilities of a reversal of the Great Disruption of the late twentieth century in advanced economies. Religion has traditionally played a key role in American great awakenings from the early eighteenth century.

Beginning from a meeting of seven local people in Rick Warren's living room in 1980, the group decided to canvas 15,000 homes in a classic American suburb of houses and shopping malls. Two hundred turned up for an Easter service in the local high school. Now 45,000 see Saddleback Church as their church, a church set in 79 acres, with acres of parking space, with a large convention centre type church, religiously distinguishable only by its modest cross. In so many ways it is quite unlike a typical Western church in terms of dress, worship and architecture: in spirit, it is closer to the resurgent religion of the South. Its mission statement within the entrance hall, is 'Magnification, Membership, Maturity, Ministry, Mission'.[284] Using techniques of globalization, it shapes its ways of worship and discipleship according to global consumer, information technology, capitalist formats. Yet it is clearly so much more than that in terms of the message such media embody – that God is directly involved in every life, that 'God has a plan for you', and that means responding to God's invitation, through his grace, using the inerrant Bible as the complete guide to Christian discipleship.[285] It offers complete certainty in an ambiguous uncertain world, attracting numbers far in excess of liberal equivalents with their recognition of the ambiguities of faith and life (for example, the successful All Saints Episcopal Church, Pasadena).[286]

Faced with such a massive congregation, Saddleback Church has chosen to work with small groups or cells of up to 16 people in which people spend time together to know and be known to one another. It reminds me of Ted Wickham's use of such cells in Sheffield's steel works in the 1950s, modelled partly on early Methodism's use of such cells. The church also uses groups for

> every conceivable need and talent: couples groups, singles groups, a group for single parents of teenage children and one for mothers of preschoolers, Women to Women ministering, men's morning Bible study, deaf Bible study, a group combining volleyball and Bible study, groups for women with breast cancer, a group for 'teens-in-temptation', one for families with incarcerated loved ones, groups for separated men and separated women, a group for sufferers of chronic pain or chronic illness, and a 'Geeks for God Ministry' for Cisco-certified networking professionals, among many other.[287]

Eight thousand people are in such groups at any one time. It is in such locations that people learn to become members one of another, as the body of Christ, where the virtues of trust and reciprocity are learned and enhanced. It represents a journey from the anonymity of mass membership to the effectiveness of a congregation of congregations, a grouping of groups. As such it also represents the development of bonding social capital, with the clear possibility of development into wider bridging and linking social capital, a route followed by early British Methodists in the late eighteenth and early nineteenth centuries.[288]

Projects with distinctive religious components in wider partnerships

Churchyards, yew trees and the Millennium Dome

In the 1980s, the 'Living Churchyard' scheme in Britain exploited the sacred places of religion which have often existed for many centuries. Local Anglican parish churches, surrounded by churchyards, had the potential to provide 'sanctuary for species whose living space had been so cut back' through urbanization. Now, 6,500 churches run 'their little plots of land as "sacred ecosystems", without pesticides, and mowing the grass only once a year – ensuring that a number of species of birds, reptiles, insects and bats can thrive'.[289] From clear distinct views of the sacred, linked so often to space, as continuity of presence and source of the spirit's refreshments, there emerges a tool for conscientizing children, families and communities in pro environment thinking and practice. John Reader's *Local Theology* contains a useful case study of this type of the utilization of local space as sustainability FBO.[290] In a similar way, Sikh temples now hand out 10 million saplings every year instead of sticky sweets as part of their new 300-year 'Cycle of Creation'.[291]

That religious commitment to the long term was particularly widened in the Millennium Project in 2000 to plant 8,000 yew tree saplings in church yards to celebrate Christ's birth using cuttings from trees alive at the time of Christ. The saplings were distributed at packed churches for the blessing of the trees. In 1,000 years' time, one in twenty could still be alive, a 'memorial to the local enthusiasm for both nature and the sacred', in stark contrast to the government's absurd Millennium Dome. It illustrates 'the difference between putting on a show that a government decided was good for the people and creating a story that others can share. One was a project literally without roots that was afraid to be honest about the reason for the celebration – the birth of Christ.' It is a typical example of the bankruptcy of the Western secularization thesis. In contrast, there was a scheme which 'chose one of the most powerful sacred trees of ancient Britain – and said let's celebrate through it'.[292]

Valley Interfaith: churches and community regeneration[293]

Valley Interfaith represented a coalition of 45 churches to improve the performance of schools in the Rio Grande area – a poor set of communities, close to the Mexican border. Using the Alinsky method of community advocacy to mobilize marginalized communities, the project capitalized on the strong network of local churches led by local people, clergy and nuns. Like Saddleback Church, the key was to work through small groups of intimate high trust relationships, of bonding social capital, but also able to bridge communities through networks, and to develop substantial connections (linking social capital) with political representatives, acting as classic pressure groups to achieve improvements in education, housing and environment. For one organizer, inadvertently linking such FBOs to global capitalism, 'There are two sources of power, organized money and organized people. We don't have organized money, but we have the people.'[294]

Two Manchester case studies on churches and urban regeneration[295]

On the basis of a three-year William Temple Foundation research project 'Faith in Action' into church relationships to urban regeneration in some of the poorest areas in England, Chris Baker has developed two case studies of FBOs. The Eden Harpurhey Youth Project works under the umbrella of the evangelical Message Trust. It is committed to working with young people in poor communities, and has developed a series of creative involvements with youngsters in Harpurhey, working with a variety of partners from schools to police. In particular, it has created the Matrix Mentoring Programme for individual young people, linking them with caring experienced adults. In terms of rebuilding social capital, Putnam also points to similar work in the USA.[296] The Eden Project's 'Entry to Enterprise' also helps young people to build up entrepreneurial skills.

The second study examined the Community Pride Initiative, created by Church Action on Poverty, a national pressure group which I helped to found in the early 1980s, and by local churches. Its task was to develop local community empowerment, for example by using a liberation theology methodology as a participatory budgeting scheme, involving local people in local authority budget setting.

Both case studies revealed how the work was 'underpinned by a moral and spiritual vision of transformation and hope'. So although both work with other partners in shared objectives of community regeneration, they also stress 'the unique Christian base from which its values and motivations spring and this has expressed itself in going beyond the accepted boundaries of secular-based interventions by consciously living out the principles of "going the extra mile", open acceptance and unconditional love'. This normative base also involves them in critiquing 'accepted norms, values and methodologies if these go against the fundamental value of human dignity and worth made in the image of God'.[297] The Eden project also emphasizes the incarnational character of Christianity through a '"unique operating policy" of locating its staff residentially within the Harpurhey neighbourhood'.[298] In both cases, the mixture of distinctively Christian and partnership with others ensures the projects retain a clear Christian character which can act as critique of mainstream policies where appropriate, and developing projects offering alternatives to mainstream policies.

The Religious Contribution: A Complex in Complexities

Factors informing religious difference

As these mini case studies unfold they reveal a number of lessons for further faith-based involvement in society. For example, small groups often play a central role in building up trust and reciprocity, and can shape the moral adequacy and effectiveness of large groups and organizations. Yet it is the contribution of the faith community and tradition to informing the distinctive nature of the faith-based contribution to well-being which is most relevant in this section, not least as the basis of faith's added value. Palmer is particularly clear that, although religious organizations fail (and sometimes catastrophically), their long history and, more recently, their survival (longer than any empire or economic system) means that 'Somewhere along the line the main faiths have discovered a few basic truths about how the world and humanity behave and why – and this has been the core of their success.'[299] His list of such factors is useful because, although it emerges out of his survey of religious involvements in environmental projects, it also resonates with other economically oriented projects and sources used in this survey.

First, telling stories. All faiths are full of stories encompassing a variety of types and experiences. Their value in the development of faith traditions and communities is immense, and particularly in character formation. Most importantly, they reflect how rationality-based understandings *must* be complemented by pre and post rationality discourses in which feelings, for example, can play a central part. This has important connections with earlier reflections on human behaviour in economics as inclusive of yet going beyond, human rationality. For some, like Iris Young, narratives are also a way of ensuring the marginalized, among whom story-telling is traditionally significant, can develop means of combating the rationality-bound discourses of the powerful.[300] The example of the Zanzibar fishermen illustrated the power of religious stories to change behaviour for the good, in this case to more environmentally sustainable fishing.

Second, the importance of images and beauty. Embodying great religious and moral truths in art forms is again integral to human history and experience. The Orthodox Church's tradition of using icons is particularly significant as a means of fostering worship and enriching personal and communal spiritual development. For Palmer, they are 'physical embodiments of the Church's teaching that it is only through material things that God's beauty can be appreciated'. For St John of Damascus, 'I shall not cease reverencing matter, by means of which my salvation has been achieved' (*On Holy Images*, 1.16).[301] They are a reminder that, although poverty reduction is centrally concerned with improving the material conditions of life, culture for the poor is equally important. The project *Art for the World*, criticized for wasting money on art exhibitions, argues that their partners in the poor South reply that 'as everyone knows, [humanity] does not live by bread alone'. As a recent World Bank survey indicated, 'culture, even for people living in extreme poverty, is no luxury. In fact, in many respects it is central to their lives.'[302] The stories of the religious statues in Poland and Mongolia illustrate their strategic value in promoting well-being, including for faith as resourcing resistances and alternatives to mainstream systems.

Third, sacred places also have a recurring value for the human spirit as locations for encountering the divine, as embodying the intimations of that which is beyond human experience. Davie writes persuasively of the renewed interest in sacred spaces in the secularized West, despite the decline of mainstream churches. For her, pilgrimage churches represent 'stories that are told in stone, in art, in music, and in literature' – embodying 'aesthetic or symbolic memory'. She particularly connects them with pilgrimages, including as the spiritual journey of life itself.[303] The choice of the mosque as centre for reconstituting community and well-being in East Africa and Egypt, and of churchyards as focal points for environmental regeneration, are examples from this survey which also indicate the relevance of this factor.

Fourth, the importance of 'cycles and celebration' for sustaining human living through turbulent contexts is a recognition that the human spirit needs both repentance and celebration. All the 'major faiths have . . . structured annual cycles that help carry people through the year, making the monotony of everyday life manageable and celebrating the changes of the natural seasons' – whether Ramadan/Eid, Lent/Easter, Pansa/Wesak, Rosh Hashanah/Yom Kippur, Ashwin/Divali. For Palmer, these present a stark contrast to secular agencies in the poverty reduction field. These 'present a consistently gloomy picture of the world in the hope that shock tactics will produce compassion or repentance. They usually don't.'[304] It is rather faiths and traditions, rooted in the immediate, and enfolded in the long term of long history, but set in the context of eternity, which can and do offer ways and means for making sense of life, and for changing it for the better. The story of the yew trees in Britain illustrates that capacity in simple and meaning-rich ways. Stories, pictures, places and cycles all contribute to that potential for transformation. Yet this survey has also revealed that such spiritual realities are not the exclusive property of any one faith, but are shared across faiths, and experienced beyond faiths. The distinctively religious, the resources behind the added value of FBOs are both peculiar to faiths and shared beyond them. They also become part of the human itself. The Polish Madonna inspired more than the faith community, although it certainly did that. It was also a powerful resource for the Solidarity movement. The brave social capital of the Kent Mothers' Union cascaded across networks wider than the faith-based, although powerfully inspired by it. It is almost as though when we reach the most distinctive heart of the difference factor in religion, which we can, we also reach beyond it into the very nature of being human as the pursuit of human well-being or fulfilment. It is both powerfully religious and thereby also powerfully human. It is that continuum again, but here in relation to the distinctively religious, which warrants further detailed and critical examination which will be the objective of the next and final section.

Explorations into Faith's Added Value

To subject the distinctively religious to further scrutiny, I have chosen three topics. Although only a brief examination, it has a significance for this enquiry beyond its size. Each topic is firmly connected to ethical economics, but also to the development of faithful economics. All three have roots in medieval religion's engagement with economic affairs, as the search for a just price and wage, and in the condemnation of usury or interest. Long describes his preferred religious tradition for addressing economics as *residual*, following Raymond Williams's use of the concept, as 'effectively formed in the past (the Thomism of the middle ages) but is still active in the cultural processes, not as an element of the past, but as an effective element of the present'.[305] It is that suggestion of the recurring concern for the ethical dimension of economics which has persisted for 800 years in Europe, which may well be undergoing a process of rediscovery and reformulation. The organized concern for equity in trade, which includes fair wages and prices, for liberation from national debt, and for alternative financing in Islam, should be considered as important features of this religio-ethical resurgence in political economy and wider society.

Although all three topics can be described as residual tradition, our interest is in their contemporary development. They all occur in that historic post-1945 generation, and particularly in the last 20 years. It is no coincidence that this same period witnessed the rapid expansion of globalization, and an outburst of virulent neo-liberalism in political economy under Thatcher in Britain and Reagan–Bush in the USA. It also therefore includes the rise of the countermovements of anti-globalization, anti-capitalism and anti-Americanism.

The three topics also reflect a continuum moving from fair trade, through debt release, to Muslim interest-free banking. It is a journey from more partnership FBO to FBO as separate, as alternative system to mainstream economics. In some regards, debt release as the Jubilee 2000 campaign, stands in between fair trade and Muslim banking. It is strongly informed by sacred texts and traditions, yet also undertaken through partnerships with secular agencies. The final topic, Muslim interest-free banking is particularly interesting, not simply because it represents a clear critical religiously-based alternative to modern economics and economic policy. It was also the basis of a two-year research project in Manchester, which brought Christians and Muslims together to explore the relationships between faiths and finance. An essential part of that project was the contribution of a senior academic economist, Professor Ian Steedman. His sharp questions on religion's engagement with economics in general (in his chapter 'On not traducing economics' in *Through the Eye of a Needle*), but in particular with the religious rejection of interest in the report *Faiths and Finance*, will be used to illustrate the problems as well as possibilities of a religious-ethical approach to economics. That conversation is also an important part of the fair trade consideration.

Fair trade: the pursuit of equity in economics; problems and possibilities

The dramatic increase in world trade since 1945 is both indicator of the take-off of economic growth, including as globalization, and a principal driver of such processes. The latter includes the major contribution to poverty reduction achieved say by China and India, by opening up their economies to world trade. Yet the picture is not one of progress alone at all. It includes the persistence of one billion people living in absolute poverty, growing inequality between the richest and the poorest in the world population, and the stubborn refusal of advanced economies, through agricultural tariffs and subsidies, to practise the free trade they proclaim. The task, already firmly recognized in this enquiry, is to hold on to the progress made in economic development and well-being, in terms of health, education and income, but equally to engage vigorously in poverty reduction – for example through pro economic growth policies. Fair trade should be located in relation to the latter. For example, it can be usefully connected to the earlier note on the Special and Differential Treatment proposals in current trade negotiations and to Bhagwati's proposals to promote the interests of the poorest and most marginalized nations. Central to all such programmes is a profoundly ethical dimension. Fair trade epitomizes that, because it is essentially the informing of trade, as economic processes, with moral purposes as economic objective and means. It is a recognition that trade must be just, particularly with regard to the poor and marginalized, and that will involve bending economic mechanisms to further that primary commitment. It therefore represents ethical interference in positive economics. Or does it? So much of this enquiry to date has demonstrated that the moral, and indeed the religious, are inextricably part of the human project, biologically, historically and contemporarily, and that includes the economic dimension of that project. We are now working with continuums on which different emphases are located and therefore always connected. The days when political economy could be isolated from wider processes are rapidly disappearing. But equally, the necessary persistence of the valued contribution of economics to well-being in terms of its resourcing and as mechanism, continues to occupy a foundational part of this enquiry. That balance, already acknowledged in the happiness hypothesis section, and earlier in Part 1, is also sharply presented by fair trade – that is, how to reconcile market functions and socio-ethical realities.

Fair trade embodies these predicaments as an interaction of economics as trade and ethics as justice. Hira and Ferrie define fair trade as 'a movement to integrate ethical principles in consumer decision-making'.[306] But it is more than that. It is also significantly informed by religious commitments, including historically. Moore rightly traces its present form to such bodies as the Mennonite Central Committee trading with poor communities in the South in the 1940s,[307] and to the recent impact of religiously inspired companies such as Tradecraft in Britain (created by Christians from St Johns College Durham initially in the 1970s), and the growing involvement of churches, for example as fair trade dioceses.[308] Yet its origins are also deep in Christian history, in the medieval commitments by Church and society to a just price and wage, two essential features of the contemporary fair trade movement. The latter requires the rich North to pay a fair price (not the market price) for products, often food or drink, from poor South producers. This allows the payment of fair wages (not set by the market) to the workers in the South, along with the provision of resources for improving health care and education. It therefore both represents critique of existing economic system and offers possible alternatives to it. Both critique and alternative inform the continuum used by Moore, and by Hira and Ferrie. They develop two versions of fair trade. On the one hand, there is the reformist type, which uses fair trade to promote more equitable trade within existing structures. It does this by contracting with producer partners by ensuring the price given for the commodity

covers the cost of production, offering a social premium for local development projects, and providing partial advance payments to avoid small
producers going into debt. There is much argument over the extension of
fair trade into the mainstream of retailing in the West, concern whether
this will dilute the principles of fair trade, and discussion over more effective certification procedures. On the other hand, the radical strategy can
seek to develop fair trade as an alternative to current world trading systems, dominated by the WTO and by global capitalism. This includes the
development of Alternative Trading Organizations (ATOs).[309] Christians
are involved in both strategies, with such bodies as Christian Aid and
Tradecraft being reformist, and theologians like Michael Northcott using
the model of the body of Christ as religious basis for developing fair trade
as an ethical alternative to the WTO. Long's *Divine Economy* supports
this perspective through commitments to a just price and wage.[310] Using
fair trade as a critique of and alternative to mainstream economics is also
reflected in the co-operative model present in fair trade producer practice.
This too has strong historical roots, for example in Christian socialism or
social reformism. F. D. Maurice conducted early practical experiments in
producer co-operatives in the 1850s in Britain, working from the theological premise that the fatherhood of God required the brotherhood of man.
When combined with the understanding of God as Creator–Producer, then
a direct theology moved from such theological principles to the promotion
of producer co-operatives.[311] Yet the major weight was placed by other
Christian socialists like Neale on consumer co-operatives. Both led the
early Christian socialists to play a lead role in the passing of the Industrial
and Provident Societies Act in 1852, which gave some legal security to co-
operatives. One of their expert witnesses in Parliament was the leading
proponent of classical economics (and 'economic man') J. S. Mill. The
consumer emphasis was later continued by the Christian Social Union, and
its use of the consumer voice to campaign for businesses paying a fair wage
and against those which did not. Again, this led to legislative action as the
Trade Board Act of 1909.[312] It provides an important source of current
minimum wage legislation.

Fair trade as a contemporary movement grew in significance from the
1990s, and has been usefully described by Moore, using FINE's work, as

> a trading partnership, based on dialogue, transparency and respect,
> which seeks greater equity in international trade. It contributes to sus-
> tainable development by offering better trading conditions to, and secur-
> ing the rights of, marginalized producers and workers – especially in the
> South. Fair trade organizations (backed by consumers) are engaged

actively in supporting producers, awareness raising and in campaigning for changes in the rules and practice of conventional international trade. (FINE, 2001)[313]

As such, fair trade is therefore committed to consumers paying modestly higher prices for products. This is then used to pay higher wages and provide improved local welfare provision for fair trade producers, preferably organized in co-operatives. Coffee has been a major commodity used by fair trade, but it is expanding into other areas, including crafts and clothing. The movement also performs another function, acting as conscientizing instrument in campaigns to change the unfair rules and practices of the current global trading system, particularly with regard to EU and US agricultural protectionism. These two functions of fair trade represent two sides of the same coin, continually interacting. The latter occurs, for example, with the development of the commitment to ethics in economics among consumers in affluent advanced economies. This informs both consumer behaviour and pressure groups on world trade. There is growing evidence for such a growth in ethical awareness in economic behaviour. Surveys of consumers who might purchase fair trade goods divided them into ethical consumers (23%), semi-ethical (56%) and selfish (17%). Both ethical and semi-ethical were increasing at the expense of the selfish. Drawing on a range of surveys in 1997, Nicholls notes that 'Ethically sensitive consumers are no longer a small, if vocal, pressure group: rather, a third of the public now see themselves as "strongly ethical".'[314] It is such evidence which now needs to be connected to the happiness hypothesis research in terms of the importance of reciprocity in human behaviour, and how giving reinforces the well-being of both donor and recipient. It also links to the wider debates over the harmful effects of inequality on well-being, and therefore the strategic importance of its erosion.

Yet none of this evidence rules out the continuing importance for well-being of economic growth and the contribution to it of the market economy and mechanism. What has emerged from this enquiry is the growing evidence from within economics and in related disciplines for the reformulation of market economy and mechanism. These findings are developed further by the critical discussion of fair trade by economists, raising questions which religious opinion should engage with.

For example, the market mechanism's value includes using the price mechanism, operating in a market open to competition, as a signalling function of the pressures of supply and demand. To override that critical coordinating function by paying prices and wages according to the fairness principle is likely to have not just unforeseen, but foreseeable consequences.

These include: the likely oversupply of commodities, resulting in reducing prices in the non-fair trade sector; delaying the move into higher value added production because producers are subsidized to remain in poorly profitable and price-volatile sectors; reinforcing dependency; and disadvantaging further those not in the producer co-operatives – since most workers are not. Hira and Ferrie suggest a way of addressing some of these issues. Since the minimum price guarantees of fair trade goes against the basic sense of economics – that price must act as a signal of supply and demand – they support agreeing a minimal percentage of the final price for farmers 'thus preserving the efficiency and flexibility of the price signal to reflect market supply and demand conditions'.[315] This corresponds to Bhagwati's financial and training support for those harmed by globalization processes as preferable to undue interference with the market mechanism. What is not being proposed is the abandonment of pro poor economic growth, but a more careful design.

A more complex problem is presented by general economics and the happiness hypothesis, that achieving greater economic growth and prosperity results in the proportion of income spent on food diminishing (Engel's law). This therefore supports the need for low income economies to develop more diversified economies, and to move away from overdependence on increasingly vulnerable primary commodities. Fair trade is too closely associated with promoting the latter.

It is such problems which confirm the judgement that fair trade cannot 'resolve the bigger problems of unfair trade related to agricultural and other forms of subsidization and protection that the North utilizes to the great detriment of the South'.[316] Nor can it, or should it, stop the move to increasing prosperity with its consequences for food production. Yet what fair trade does offer is a necessary contribution to a wider task, 'to hold Northern and Southern governments accountable, to diversify developing economies, including to ensure minimum decent living conditions and access to health and education'.[317] Fair trade can only be part of such wider struggles, like the promotion of decent work noted earlier. Despite its recent growth, it remains 'relatively small in trading terms'. In 2003, Tesco's turnover was $45 billion, 90 times the world turnover of fair trade.[318]

And yet, fair trade can open doors 'to more wide-ranging changes and claims for principled justice and norms to re-shape the world economy'.[319] Despite his strong criticisms of the medieval commitments, in religion and ethics, to a just price and wage, the economist Galbraith also recognizes the recurring importance of such religious ethics. For him, 'The concept of the just price survives . . . in the everyday reference to what is fair, reasonable or decent in a price as established in individual negotiation and by implication in the condemnation of the profiteer, predator, exploiter or unduly grasping seller or buyer.' So although the market economy and mechanism has come to dominate our understandings and practices,

> Yet, if exiguously, the notion of a higher order of justice than that of the market has also survived. A legislated minimum wage is seen as a necessary manifestation of such justice. . . . All these, in one established modern view, are greatly at odds with the efficiency of the market. They remain, nonetheless, as a distant – perhaps very distant – echo of the teachings of the Schoolmen.[320]

Fair trade brings that echo into the present where it joins substantial evidence from the well-being and happiness literatures, that economics is undergoing a major reformulation.

Religious ethics and the liberation from debt: Jubilee 2000 as paradigm for added value's potential

The massive rise in indebtedness of poorer nations from the 1980s was closely connected to the increased liberalizing of financial markets, the availability of finance including from oil price rises, and the willingness of banks and multilateral financial institutions to lend money to poor nations. The willingness of the latter to borrow, often for ill-advised projects and for the illegal private bank accounts of corrupt governing elites, gravely compounded the problem. Changing interest rates, and greater financial stringency, drove many into deeper and deeper debt. Paying the interest alone exacerbated the problems of such nations, with dire consequences for the poor. Government resources, modest as they were, were diverted to debt repayment and away from the basic health care and education which are so central to human well-being: 'In Tanzania, for example, one child in six dies before the age of 5, but the government spends more on servicing its debt than on primary health care. Money needed for health and education programs goes instead to rich international creditors whose billions have often propped up crooked local elites' (Ann Pettifor, Jubilee 2000 organizer).[321] Debt and poverty reduction were quickly and inextricably bound together, becoming one of the Millennium Development Goals in 2000.

The Jubilee 2000 campaign addressed that highly complex and multidimensional agenda by focusing on the debt forgiveness of the most heavily indebted poorest nations. Repayment of the debt was impossible given the low incomes of such countries and the demands on them to provide basic well-being programmes. In response, the mainstream global financial institutions, including the IMF and World Bank, the rich nations, and the major banks argued for the recycling of debt to preserve the integrity of the financial and credit systems, and for their own self-interest.

What Jubilee 2000 proposed was the opposite to such conventional economic wisdom. It argued for the debt relief of the poorest nations by a process of forgiveness. It therefore represented a radical critique of mainstream economic theory and practice, and proposed an alternative, and did so inspired and informed by the principles of the Jewish–Christian traditions. Its subsequent effectiveness related to its use of classic pressure group tactics, and to the ability to develop partnerships often with unlikely institutions and groups. The journey of debt relief which has followed has proved to be long and arduous given the obstacles of governments and international institutions and the complexities of the problems associated with such objectives and processes. But it has begun, and is having demonstrable benefits for the well-being of some of the poorest people on earth. The limitations of Jubilee 2000 are clear, and are essentially associated with its lack of economic and political capacity particularly when confronting the complexity of national and international economics and finance. This is only exacerbated by the intractability of vested interests routinely opposed to debt relief as the transfer of resources from the richest to the poorest. The issue of the gross misuse of resources by elites in the poorest nations, an integral part of the wider issue of government transparency, efficiency and accountability, substantially compounds the problems of debt and poverty. It also thereby erodes the effectiveness of the case for poverty reduction.

Jubilee 2000 began in the minds, hearts and souls of a British government official Bill Peters and an academic Martin Dent. Both were retired and in their seventies. They 'first developed the idea of linking debt relief to the faith-based concept of jubilee and the new millennium in the early 1990s'. I know because I had some supportive correspondence with them. Their arguments represented the ethics–religion continuum: ethically, because 'wealthy creditors had an ethical responsibility to devise a sustainable solution to excessive debt among the world's poorest countries'; religiously, because they were inspired and provoked by the biblical concept of jubilee, of liberation from slavery and debt, and its connection to the approaching millennium year of 2000, a 'year of biblical jubilee, when creditors would forgive all the debts and developing countries could begin again'.[322] For so it was recounted in the Hebrew scriptures, 'And you shall hallow the fiftieth year, and proclaim liberty throughout the land to all its inhabitants; it shall be a Jubilee for you' (Leviticus 25.10). Using these Jewish scriptures, shared by Christians and Muslims, the seven yearly, and seven times seven year cycle of the liberation of the Jews from slavery and debt was astonishingly and successfully translated from an agrarian society over two millennia ago into a worldwide campaign to liberate the poorest nations from unrepayable debt in a highly complex global economy increasingly informed by financial systems and power. In other words, 'The scriptural roots of debt forgiveness provided a broad-based appeal on which the Jubilee network constructed its campaign.'[323] By 1999 Jubilee South, based in the developing economies, was also a significant partner. Eventually, the whole campaign covered 60 countries and collected 24 million signatures supporting its case. Its effectiveness, as a campaign, evolved through stages from heavy conditionality for debt release to a greater priority to the debt relief itself. The first Heavily Indebted Poor Countries (HIPC) initiative in 1996 therefore linked debt relief with progress on economic reform, and made slow progress. In the first three years, 14 nations were eligible according to the strict criteria, yet only 4 received debt relief (Uganda, Bolivia, Mozambique and Guyana). Jubilee 2000 persisted with its criticisms and its vision for greater debt forgiveness. Eventually, the World Bank agreed to move 20 countries into the HIPC and PRSP process by the end of 2000.

Jubilee 2000 was therefore essentially an ethical-religious campaign broadly based and drawing on 'moral imperatives inherent in Christianity and Judaism as well as other world religions'. As a campaign, it attracted unlikely partners from Democrats and Republicans in the USA, trade unions and development agencies like Oxfam, Christian Aid and CAFOD in Britain, to trade unionists from Mozambique, priests from Zambia and economists from Ecuador. It was probably the most effective 'global social movement' including the anti-globalization, capitalism and American countermovements.[324]

It is appropriate to acknowledge its location in relation to such movements, because it involved strong criticism of the world financial systems, including the World Bank, and particularly the IMF with its 'one-size-fits-all strategy' imposed on developing economies. The link between debt relief and poverty reduction became increasingly significant, and connects directly with the happiness–well-being research. For example, the resources released by debt relief were particularly moved into health care and education where modest sums produce major outcomes in terms of increasing human well-being. The transfer of resources from rich to poor nations was similarly relevant to the happiness findings: it represented a *reversal* of 'indebtedness as a transfer of wealth from poor to rich countries that cripples their development prospects'.[325] Given the significance of inequality and the consequent requirement for prioritizing responses to it, the debt forgiveness process represents an important redistribution which clearly benefits the poor. The happiness findings argue that it also benefits the rich.

In terms of religious added value through the partnerships of Jubilee 2000, a World Bank official judged that it 'undoubtedly helped inspire rapid implementation of the enhanced HIPC process'.[326] As a contribution to faithful economics it also illustrates the *potential* of sacred writings and traditions to engage directly with the most complex and intractable areas of the global economy in the form of its financial systems – and to do so as FBOs with the critique of and alternative to mainstream economics and finance. Yet the commitment to human liberation from enslaving systems and ideas is both deeply embedded in religious tradition and a *shared human* aspiration. As embracing continuums from ethics to religion, and from partnerships to faith-based as difference, Jubilee 2000 therefore represents an important contribution to both ethical and faithful economics. Its engagement with global financial capitalism as an increasingly dominant global problematic is continued in quite different ways by Muslim interest-free banking, where economic questions are more strongly raised about religious and ethical economics.

Muslim interest-free banking: testing the religious alternative economics to the limit

As a Christian, exploring other faith understandings of economics is one of my emerging priorities. I am only at the beginning of such a journey, particularly with Islamic economics and finance. The first steps I took are recorded in my *Marginalization* with a section on Muslim interest-free banking.[327] The second occurred when I oversaw the process leading to the book, *Through the Eye of a Needle*, with its contribution from Zahid Hussain, 'Contours of an Islamic Political Economy'. The most recent step involved a small research project in Manchester which brought together Christians and Muslims to share their faith understandings of economics. It produced the publication *Faiths and Finance. A Place for Faith-Based Economics (a preliminary statement from Muslims and Christians in Manchester)* (2006). An essential part of this process was the challenging perspective of an academic economist. His wider criticism of the moral and religious engagement with economics took the form of a contribution to

Through the Eye of a Needle, 'On Not Traducing Economics'. His critique in the Manchester report, of the mainstream Islamic condemnation of interest is particularly important for this enquiry. It is also relevant to similar mainstream Christian positions on usury up to the end of the Middle Ages, and to a renewed current interest in it, particularly the Christian Council for Monetary Justice, and theologically in the work of such radical orthodoxy exponents as Long and Goodchild.[328] In addition it also resonates with economic criticisms of the just price and wage, for example in Galbraith's work quoted earlier. It has therefore a strategic value for this enquiry, and particularly for this section on faith-based contributions to political economy.

The mainstream Muslim condemnation of usury or interest (and therefore of contemporary mainstream neoclassical economics, and of global capitalism, especially its financial systems) is but one side of the coin. The other side is the growing practice of Muslim interest-free banking (MIFB).

The religious condemnation of usury links the Abrahamic faiths. From the Torah comes the basic Deuteronomic obligation, 'You shall not lend upon interest to your brother' (Deut. 23.19f.). The Christian version expanded the commitment to include all people, and not just Jews or Christians, 'Lend expecting nothing in return' (Luke 6.35). For Muslims, 'O believers! Do not live on usury (compound interest) which is compounded over and over again. Have fear of Allah so that you may prosper' (The Holy Qur'an 3.130).[329]

In the Middle Ages that connection was reinforced by the Christian rediscovery of Aristotle's work through Muslim translation, and its condemnation of usury for making money out of money. There is a considerable literature in this field including Preston, Wilson, Buckley and Chapra.[330]

What is particularly striking about MIFB is its emergence in the 1970s, alongside the growing prominence of resurgent religion in Islam in the Middle East and the South. In 1977, the International Association of Islamic Banks was formed to promote interest-free banking through partnership schemes. In 1975 the Dubai Islamic Bank was founded, and in 1977 the Kuwait Finance House, and in 1981 the Saudi Bank in London: 'These operate parallel to traditional Western banking systems, but standing as a financial paradigm for facing up to marginalization from an Islamic perspective, a reminder that "Social goals are understood to form an inseparable element of the Islamic banking system that cannot be dispensed with or neglected."' Interestingly, for one commentator, it suggested: 'A puritan and scripturalist world religion does not seem necessarily doomed to erosion by modern conditions. It may on the contrary be favoured by them.'[331]

The condemnation of *riba* or usury was based on the teachings of the Qur'an and the Shari'ah, the divine law governing private and public life. Usury was regarded as exploitation of the poor, and so contrary to the integrity of the religious community, in conflict with *ummah*. Incorporating this religious condemnation into the banking system therefore reflected the wider Islamic understanding of a community concerned to protect the poor and to promote productive partnerships. The latter was achieved through a variety of financial instruments often corresponding to those developed by Christian theologians in the Middle Ages. Generally, these schemes use money deposited in banks, which is then lent to clients – say to purchase a house or for personal loans, or to build a factory.[332] With the latter, therefore, the industrialist pays a specific percentage of the profits for a designated period, which is passed on to the depositors by the bank; losses are similarly shared. 'Trade-oriented activities therefore replace credit activities and interest: "interest-bearing loans are replaced by profit-seeking investments."'[333]

The growth of MIFB affects not just the banks dedicated simply to it. Western-based secular mainstream banks are rapidly developing Shari'ah-compliant services, including HSBC, Lloyds TSB and Citibank. Part of this movement is due to the growing significance of the migrant in origin Muslim population in the West, and especially the request for Shari'ah-compliant mortgages. In 2005, in terms of British financial markets, Datamonitor reported 'demand for sharia-compliant mortgages was strong, and could yield up to £4.5 billion in advances by 2006'. In 1998, there were 176 Islamic banks or financial institutions operating in 38 countries: 'These institutions had total assets of $148 billion, paid up capital of $7.3 billion, and generated $1.2 billion in aggregate net profits in the latest year of operation' (International Association of Islamic Banks).[334] Yet although Islamic banking has grown strongly, it still only comprises a 'small percentage of the global banking system'. For Zahid Hussain, 'Islamic finance and banking (still) provide a fairer and more ethical way to handle financial affairs, it promotes entrepreneurship and risk sharing and doesn't exploit the poor. Islamic financial systems will also enable clients to choose financial instruments that suit their business needs as well as their social values and religious beliefs.'[335]

An economist appraising such a significant faith-based financial system addresses both the practice of borrowing and lending in general, and then the particular issue of interest-free banking. In the borrowing and lending process, for example, once stripped of its embodiment in power relationships, it is then seen to serve both the interests of lender and of borrower, with each party free to enter into the transaction. 'Although lending and borrowing normally takes place in terms of money, of course, normal people are not interested in acquiring money for its own sake; it is a means for buying the things they are interested in.'[336] Interest is the agreed price paid for that loan. The lender of money at interest does not get 'something for nothing' – the basis of Aristotle's and the medieval Christian criticism of usury – because 'the borrower may put a *higher* value on the commodity purchased now (with the money borrowed) than on what could have been purchased a year hence (with the money repaid including interest)'. People care when goods are available to them, and when money is.[337]

In other words, 'borrowing and lending at a positive real rate of interest can *benefit both* the lender and the borrower, whilst harming nobody' – even though clearly this mechanism, when related to the abuses of wealth and power, distorts that process.[338]

With regard to interest-free banking, Steedman observes that the current mainstream Muslim view on usury is not the only Muslim interpretation. All agree that the Holy Qur'an prohibits *riba*. The argument, for some, is what that means. Does it include the banning of lending and borrowing at interest? What is condemned, and rightly, was the practice of doubling a debt if not paid on time, and doubling it again if not paid by the new date. But that is not the same as lending and borrowing at interest. So a leading centre of Sunni thinking, the theological research institute of the Al-Azhar in Egypt, ruled in 2002 that 'fixed interest rate lending is permissible'.[339]

The economist, Steedman, then addresses arguments used by Muslims (and Christians) to defend the religious and ethical condemnation of interest.

First, the argument that interest destroys brotherhood and friendship – or, in well-being language, trust and reciprocity. If 'interest' is understood as the debt-doubling condemned by the Qur'an, then that is clearly right. Yet that is not an acceptable argument if extended to condemn 'lending and borrowing, at relatively low real rates of interest, via "the Halifax" for example'. Lenders are not always rich, or borrowers poor. Second, the argument that 'the possibility of lending at interest must destroy the incentive to work' is empirically inaccurate. Some do live off interest, and do not work, but millions do not. Most who lend and borrow are not rich.[340]

Third, while Islam has a very positive attitude to business, including its financing, the objection is to the loan financing (fixed interest rate financing) of business. It is an acceptable form of finance if lender and borrower *share* the risks of profit and loss, as already noted. Its condemnation of loan financing is because it is regarded as placing all the risk on the borrower. Again, empirically, this is not the case. Lenders are damaged if the enterprise files for bankruptcy. In addition, it is unclear why risk sharing should be treated as ethically superior (in the way F. D. Maurice presumed producer co-operatives were ethically superior to consumer co-operatives). 'The business borrower may well be better informed about the business and its risks than are potential providers of finance.'

In other words, for Steedman, 'the opposition to interest is, then, both scripturally suspect and weak in reasoned support: which is why some Muslims reject that opposition.' Is MIFB practice more effective? Many Muslim authors argue that 'the practice is as disappointing as the theory'. For example, Islamic financial institutions have largely abandoned their profit-and-loss-sharing on the basis of their systems. Many banks are understood to put major sums of money into fixed-interest accounts with Western banks. In practice 'a major activity of Islamic banks is now murabaha financing, which is not fully Shari'ah compliant'. As with medieval instruments in the Church, when examined in detail how they actually operate 'it is found that very often [they differ] from straight-forward loan financing at fixed interest only by verbal subterfuge that creates an "Islamic" facade'. The fact that some Western secular banks now operate Muslim-compliant sections is essentially to tap a new market 'whilst making no significant changes to their conventional' non-Muslim Banking practices.[341]

The criticisms by economists of interest-free banking clearly carries serious weight, particularly when the justification for the condemnation of interest uses arguments which contain serious empirical inaccuracies. The weightier case relates to the increasing inappropriateness of doctrines, for example against usury, given the rapidly changing context of the early modern period in Europe. By the sixteenth century, therefore, theologians sought to find ways of morally justifying the financing of new commercial and industrial transactions. These were of value both to general well-being and to the benefit of business and financiers. Such arguments increased in nature and extent with the rise of modern economics and industry in the late eighteenth century. Yet throughout this long history and into the present, important questions, powerfully ethically and religiously charged, have persisted or reappeared. For example, with regard to the latter, Jubilee 2000 burst on the contemporary scene as a powerful re-embodi-ment of basic biblical principles, illustrating that they can be transposed from very different pre-modern contexts into a post-modern and global-ized one. That argument could be similarly used to justify interest-free banking. The persistence of the religio-ethical challenge throughout history resides in the high priority given to matters of justice or fairness, and particularly with regard to the poor. Since financial systems have regularly played a prominent part in exploiting the vulnerable, it is therefore not surprising that the commitment to justice also regularly takes the form of using economic processes fashioned to protect the poor and condemn the powerful. In Parts 1 and 2 this interpretation of economics was related to fields of power and influence. Social or faithful capital cannot be divorced from such powerful relationships within which they are clearly embedded. Yet equally clearly, we have recognized that the nature of financial mechanisms and transactions can and should be also considered apart from such relationships, including as ideal forms. Yet the operating of them rarely if ever can be so separated from context and realities. And that makes the contributions of FBOs, and faith-based finance and economics, a legitimate and necessary contributor to such debates. And this will apply both in terms of their addressing the positive and negative effects of economic relationships on people's lives and communities but also the economic processes themselves. So from within economics, and certainly from related disciplines other than economics, there is, as this enquiry has demonstrated, a growing interest in addressing the deficiencies of economics, including as the reformulation of economic behaviours and mechanisms. What was discussed in Parts 1 and 2 was how this could be done, including by exploiting the correspondence between such external concerns and concerns internal to the disciplines. This will also be revisited in Part 3, through the work of Tanner on her economy of grace.

It is the case, therefore, that fair trade, Jubilee 2000 and MIFB can and should be subject to economic criticism, and particularly where empirically inaccurate claims are made. Yet they also contain profound practical and theoretical understandings if not examples where criticism of mainstream economics is justifiable, and where the development of alternatives to mainstream practice could also contain insights for well-being worthy of further economic development. Hira and Ferrie's judgement on the limitations and possibilities of fair trade is also relevant to debt forgiveness and interest-free finance: 'Ultimately, we hope that once these problems are ironed out, fair trade principles will become like worker safety and environmental regulations in the North – minimal standards that are a given for all international production, and not just a niche market.'[342] It is, in other words, a matter of *mainstreaming* into the field of political economy substantial religious-ethical convictions. The survey of faith-based contributions to society, including as the three concluding examples and as the religious-ethical dimension in the happiness hypothesis, suggests the feasibility of such a mainstreaming process.

Part 3

Religion and the Transfiguration of Capitalism: Continuing Agendas

Introduction

It is very easy to say what Part 3 is *not*. It is *not* a conclusion with definitive answers to questions posed in the previous sections of the argument. It is *not* a *synthesis* generated out of the dialectical interaction between the context of Part 1 and the faith-based activities of Part 2. It is *not* the proverbial cream on the pudding or the rabbit pulled out of a hat. It is a point reached at the end of this particular enquiry, which in itself is a continuing process of work therefore still in progress. That will certainly be my intention. For example, I am now involved in a university research contract exploring the nature and possibilities of religious contributions to the happiness hypothesis, including estimating their added value. I hope too that others will test these very provisional frameworks. They need to be questioned, amended and maybe jettisoned. Because the enquiry has turned out to be broad in its extent, covering many detailed areas, my contribution is based on very limited sources. The opportunities this presents for others far better equipped is therefore great.

As matters arising it certainly represents a firm development of insights or issues which I judge to have emerged out of Parts 1 and 2. There are others, obviously, because the rest of the book is where the *major* substance of the whole project is to be found (not least in terms of the size!). There really is a great deal of material covering a broad group of issues and disciplines. If there are any jewels in this work, they are there. This final part is therefore truly a series of matters or agendas arising from that major part of the enquiry.

'Matters arising' are not incidental to an agenda; they are not of minor importance to a programme. For many years I have prepared agendas and chaired meetings. Indeed, I taught such procedures for the Workers Education Association (WEA) and the Trade Union Congress (TUC) training sessions for shop stewards in the 1970s. Matters arising are therefore those matters of tactical if not strategic importance which have emerged or arisen from previous agendas. They are matters which need to be *progressed*, and so they form important parts of agendas for further work until the tasks are completed. The agenda items in Part 3 are like that. They emerge from the previous agendas developing in Parts 1 and 2, because they are of continuing significance and so require further work. In each item, particular sources will be used which I have found especially informative. The perspectives are all faith-based in order to illustrate the contribution of this dimension to human well-being. For example, in Chapter 9 on ethics, I have used Cowley's work on personalist ethics and a related interpretation of the common good.[1] These connect with the earlier happiness investigation, its lists on characteristics of human fulfilment and recognition of the importance of a social philosophy of life as common good. But also, her work on global finance goes to the heart of the global capitalism of Part 1.

The agenda that shapes the following matters arising consists of the following items. First, anthropology, reflecting the recurring concern over what it means to be human, and linking critical analysis of economic behaviour and the well-being literatures (Chapter 8). The second item, the ethics to religion continuum, reflects on personal ethics and virtues and their interrelationship with reformulated understandings of the common good. As philosophy of life in the happiness hypothesis and formative influence on faith based contributions to society, it constitutes a major ground of this enquiry (Chapter 9). The third area of interest focuses on the significance of multidisciplinary perspectives and interdisciplinary procedures, including on partnerships, but here extended into ecumenical ethics and the increasing relevance of interfaith ethics for the religious task (Chapter 10). The survey of FBOs in Part 2 has begun to reveal the actual and potential contributions such collaborations can and should make. The fourth item contains two reflections; on the one hand, it summarizes the implications of this research for a reformulated typology of Christian social ethics engaging with political economy; on the other hand, it locates this project in the tradition in British Christian social ethics that traces the evolving relationship between religion and capitalism (Chapter 11). This enquiry claims to be its latest stage. Fifthly, these items all influence a further consideration of ethical and religious economics, with implications for policy directions (Chapter 12). As with other items, this constitutes a more faith-based dimension to earlier discoveries. This leads into a final item, a reflective consideration of, and meditation on, the transfiguration of Christ (Chapter 13). Essentially, it is a summary of the other five items which in turn represent the rest of the book's findings. It can thereby also become a model for the transforming of capitalism. It is the paradigmatic gift of the religious contribution to global change.

Since every Part has begun with a story, what follows is the story of the transfiguration as recounted in the earliest Gospel, St Mark's:

Religion and the Transfiguration of Capitalism

And after six days Jesus took with him Peter and James and John, and led them up a high mountain apart by themselves; and he was transfigured before them, and his garments became glistening, intensely white as no fuller on earth could bleach them. And there appeared to them Elijah with Moses; and they were talking to Jesus. And Peter said to Jesus, 'Master, it is well that we are here; let us make three booths, one for you and one for Moses and one for Elijah.' For he did not know what to say, for they were exceedingly afraid. And a cloud overshadowed them, and a voice came out of the cloud, 'This is my beloved Son; listen to him.' And suddenly looking around they no longer saw any one with them but Jesus only.

And as they were coming down the mountain, he charged them to tell no one what they had seen, until the Son of man should have risen from the dead. (Mark 9.2–9)

Whitby is one of the great sacred places in England, with its awesome ruined abbey on top of the cliffs, home to the formidable St Hilda, and the Synod of Whitby in 664 which determined the Roman as against Celtic character of the English Church. I once led a retreat in the nearby convent and ended by reading this account of the transfiguration. When I had finished, I asked the people how many water mills were there in England in 1086, as recorded in the Domesday Book. They sat there like startled rabbits, not least because they kept the rule of silence! The answer was 5,624, an astonishing 1 for every 50 households.[2] The reason for the question is that in Mark's account of the transfiguration, quoted above, he describes how Jesus' garments became 'glistening, intensely white, as no fuller on earth could bleach them'. It is that reference to *fulling* (only in the Revised Standard Version, sadly) that interests me, because that treatment of cloth was often done mechanically, in water-driven mills. And that concerns technology, and technology is a principal driving force of industrialization, and of globalization today. As economic growth it undergirds the transition from absolute scarcity and poverty which has proved to be so seminal for improving well-being today and for the paradox of prosperity and happiness. It represents the profoundly essential materiality of life on earth. Yet another feature of the transfiguration story centres on the importance of tradition, including its religious form – shaped by faith communities, and an integral part of character and virtue formation, and therefore of faithful (and social) capital, and human well-being. For on the sacred mountain, Jesus, the new covenant of Christianity, meets with Moses, the law-giver, and Elijah, the prophet, the heart of the Jewish tradition, and foundations of Islamic tradition. But then there is a third critical dimension in the story, the encounter with the totally Other, the transcendent God, who declares to the fear-stricken disciples, 'This is my beloved Son; listen to him.' Again, we have seen the central importance of that transcendence dimension of human experience in resurgent religion in Part 1 and in the happiness literature in Part 2 – as powerfully located in religious tradition, but also experienced beyond it. It is these three components, materiality, tradition and transcendence which will resonate through this final part of the enquiry, as they have through the rest. That is why transfiguration is a legitimate matter arising, and why this book will end with a reflection on it, as symbol of the transformation of capitalism.

8

Faith-based Contributions to Post-scarcity Anthropology
Developing a Theological Anthropology

The pursuit of human well-being is an agenda which increasingly raised questions suggesting, and indeed requiring, a reformulated anthropology. Explorations of market economy and mechanism have regularly evolved into critical conversations over their understanding of human behaviour. From Adam Smith's *Theory of Moral Sentiments* in 1759 to contemporary work on the happiness hypothesis broader interpretations of the human have repeatedly emerged from within economics, but also confirmed and elaborated by other related disciplines, particularly psychology, anthropology, sociology and philosophy. All the sources have also acknowledged the value of ethics to this discourse, and most have touched on the role of religions in the formation of tradition, cultures, value systems. Sometimes under the guise of a philosophy of life, and then on a side road wandering into the field of religion, declaring that people who believe in God are happier, there is a clear and explicit recognition of religion's contribution to well-being.[3] Occasionally, some academics have forsaken their disciplines and moved into more powerfully moral interpretations which stop short of noting their normal and expected religious connotation or source. Hardt and Negri's *Empire* goes further and astonishingly ends with references to St Francis.[4] Much firmer acknowledgement of the importance for well-being of religion as faith traditions and communities is found in the work, published by the World Bank, of Marshall and Palmer.[5] When this rich variety of material is confirmed and enlarged with references to understandings from the religious field, then a substantial part of the discourses on well-being emerges. Much of this material can be described as a contribution to what scholars have usefully called a theological anthropology. In other words, if the search for well-being in general, and for what it means for human fulfilment in particular, is *multidimensional* then the faith-based contribution should be considered at least as one such dimension.

Clearly, any consideration of a theological anthropology is a vast area of endeavour, and of growing interest. In the field of Christian social ethics, for example, research into the beginning and end of life, and of the associated medical and genetic interventions, is a rapidly expanding area of interest. Some of that work will be used to engage with the well-being literatures and their interaction with political economy.[6] These reflections on the contribution of Christian social ethics to views of the human that are relevant to the happiness hypothesis and economic change are therefore necessarily very selective. The key features of such a theological anthropology are consequently considerations of matters arising, from Parts 1 and 2, for the tradition of Christian social ethics. They are therefore modest in size and scope, yet nonetheless an important jigsaw piece in the total enquiry. In terms of supportive material, I am fascinated to once again see, for example, the connections between modern reflections on human dignity and say the contributions of sixteenth-century Spanish Dominicans and the conflicts over the rights of indigenous people in Central America under Spanish rule![7] Similarly, the connection between the importance of stories in faith traditions, identified in reflections on Pentecostalism in Part 1, and for Zanzibar fishermen in Part 2, is confirmed as a vital and indispensable dimension in faith's added value, but this time, to an evolving faith-based anthropology.

The argument itself will be in four stages, after an initial reflection on lessons for these thoughts from the idea of a post-scarcity anthropology already such an important part of the enquiry. Each is a contribution to a theological anthropology. The first considers Browning's pre-moral goods,[8] and including their references to lists of characteristics of human well-being already identified. As a multidimensional phenomenon, these are connected to the faith dimension itself, the distinctive, the difference factor, including as potential added value, to wider discourses. This is elaborated as the second section, with reference to the contribution of faith narratives and beliefs. The third briefly explores the nature of that distinctive function, in terms of essentialism or environment (in happiness language), using current material on eugenics and the mentally disabled, and Spanish Dominican work in the sixteenth century on rights. Finally, again a brief note on how these different dimensions, as pre-moral goods and focused distinctively faith perspectives, are linked, including using a variant of the correspondence theory already deployed. In other words, the religious dimension of well-being is itself a series of dimensions which need to be identified and interacted. What is proposed is therefore similar to Elaine Graham's objective, namely, to develop 'a normative framework for articulating a system of values, priorities, and criteria by which the proper *ends of humanity* might be adjudicated'. It is a recognition, of the different dimensions in such an understanding of humanity, that they also constitute, because of its faith-based character, an 'alternative horizon by which human value is located as transcending human utility or objectification and restored to a deeper irreducibility'.[9]

The earlier discussion of transitions included the recognition of the movement beyond scarcity and absolute poverty, particularly in the later twentieth century in some developing economies. The achievements this represented in terms of better health, in the form of improved life expectancy, and better education, in the form of increased proportions in school, when accompanied by income growth, constituted major developments in human well-being. Yet the even greater progress in advanced economies, particularly in income per capita, was also increasingly accompanied by no commensurate growth in happiness. That paradox of prosperity therefore presented particular challenges to life satisfaction. The acceleration of choice in post-industrial societies, when combined with significantly higher levels of emotional ill-health, began to present new challenges to people. This was summarized by Wilkinson, very precisely, as the emergence of a *'postscarcity anthropology'* – its possibilities and its limitations.[10] It is in relation to such a context and conclusion, that the actual and potential role of faith-based anthropology should be considered.

Pre-Moral Goods: Beyond 'the little lists'

When considering the key features of well-being in general and happiness in particular, some are firmly connected to the functioning of the economy. In Layard's Big Seven, income and work are directly linked to it, with the resourcing of health and security more tangentially related. Although more and more evidence is accumulating suggesting that well-being and human fulfilment now require more than material resources – a classic phenomenon of post-scarcity contexts – it would be unacceptable to underestimate their continuing central contribution to human well-being. This is the case when considering the multidimensional nature of well-being, and the anthropologies associated with it: 'What it means to be human, and what is happening to the material world, are not matters that divert us from the true task of spiritual reflection and Christian living, but their very preconditions.'[11]

It is that affirmation of the role of such pre-conditions for human fulfilment which is most usefully developed by the concept of pre-moral goods, and their function in both post-scarcity and theological anthropologies.

They link very firmly to the lists of the characteristics of happiness, and they lead into the wider role of the more distinctively theological dimension.

For Browning pre-moral goods are 'experiences and objects that are considered pleasant, fulfilling, agreeable, healthy, or in some way enhancing to human life'. Yet they are not 'directly or fully moral goods'.[12] For example, they include education and health – both key parts of well-being, and in measuring economic development through the Human Development Index. These are pre-moral goods, but they only become fully moral goods when guided by 'just purposes and consider the needs of others'. Reconciling inevitable conflicts between them is a 'distinctively moral task'.[13] They are therefore an essential part of the multidimensional nature of the human, and much defined by such secular disciplines as sociology, economics and evolutionary psychology. They have not figured prominently in theology, although Christian social ethics is directing more attention to them, for example, our current research project on the happiness hypothesis and religion.

It is these pre-moral goods which Browning rightly locates in a larger five-fold 'view of the multidimensional nature of the human', and they are also integral to moral thinking: first, a *visional dimension* of reflection' generated by narratives and metaphors 'about the ultimate context of experience' – as for example, 'the nature of being' (very reminiscent of the happiness literature, and James's affluenza arguing for countering this 'disease' by promoting being rather than having); second, an *obligational dimension* – guided by moral principles, for example, the Golden Rule, or Layard's utilitarian principle of the greatest happiness of the greatest number; third, a *pre-moral goods dimension*, including those necessary for human survival and well-being, including income, work, health, etc.; fourth, a *ruling societal and ecological order dimension* – whether gravity, weather, modern urbanization or feudalism – all shaping our needs; fifth, a *practices and rules or habits dimension*, shaped by the other dimensions, and including training to be a teacher, driving cars, etc.[14]

Browning then notes how major current secular anthropologies focus on particular dimensions, whether modern psychologies, like Maslow's self-actualization theory, or rational choice economics.[15] Most importantly, he recognizes that these secular disciplines correspond much more closely to theology than they assume. Both secular and religious anthropologies are 'morally and metaphorically freighted', it is just that 'theological anthropology takes responsibility for its moral and metaphysical judgements while many other contemporary anthropologies do not'.[16]

Returning to the lists of necessary characteristics for well-being in the earlier happiness discussion, Browning refers particularly to Finnis and Nussbaum's research on essential goods. For Finnis, a natural law scholar, his list includes 'life, knowledge, play, aesthetic experience, sociability (friendship), practical reasonableness and religion'. They are all essential for moral judgements, but require 'a theory of obligation to morally take into account the basic goods of others', by treating them as ends.[17] For Nussbaum, a neo-Aristotelian polymath, ethics needs to actualize 'within a moral framework the premoral goods of life'. Her list is similar to Finnis's, and works with capabilities, like Sen. It includes 'life; health; bodily integrity; senses, imagination, thought; emotions; practical reason; affiliation; other species; play; and control over one's environment'.[18]

The resonances and differences between these lists, religious and non-religious, are remarkable. For example, all acknowledge the importance of health and relationships. They also recognize the human spirit's dependence on play or aesthetic experiences. Yet what they lack is even more important. Compared to the religious list, they do not have 'an explicit narrative envelope for their list of basic goods and capabilities'.[19] And this is of decisive significance for well-being and happiness, as this enquiry has begun to demonstrate in terms of the contribution of faith communities and traditions as distinctively religious, or as added value.

Spiritual Capital: The Indispensable Difference Dimension

What has become clear in and from this enquiry is not just the relative autonomy and integrity of the religious field, which therefore locate it in relation to other fields like the capitalist economy and the political arena. Any competent engagement with the contemporary context that does not take that substantially into account is inefficient, inaccurate and indeed incompetent. What has also become apparent, and this makes that judgement even more forceful, is the distinctive nature of that religious contribution, what I have also described as the additionality factor and the added value dimension of faith-based contributions to society, of faith itself. That is both a qualitative character but also a quantitative one. It can be, and is being, measured, as we observed in the case studies in Part 2. In the earlier reflection on faithful capital in Part 1, use was made particularly of the William Temple Foundation's (WTF) valuable distinction between religious capital as the output of faith communities, and spiritual capital as motivating force. It is the latter which now requires further examination. Indeed, the WTF's definition provides a useful starting point in itself for exploring the distinctively faith-based dimension of what it means to be human, and not just as a link with previous arguments. Its research suggests that spiritual capital 'refers to the values, ethics, beliefs and vision which faith communities bring to civil society at the global and local level. It also refers to the holistic vision for change held within an individual person's set of beliefs.'[20] Using the sources I have found particularly relevant for this task, three dimensions of spiritual capital emerge as of particular importance in themselves for understanding a faith tradition's distinctive energy (in this case Christian, although with clear equivalents in the 11 major faith statements on environment collected by Palmer).[21] They are also highly relevant to this enquiry. The first reflects on the central role in faiths of the religious narrative: the second explores the nature of God and its direct implications for a theological anthropology as theory and practice; the third notes now such a view of the human necessarily includes a dimension which Woodhead has carefully described as apophatic anthropology, the dimension which is beyond reason and experience.[22]

The story of stories: the nature and role of narrative in spiritual capital

At certain points of this enquiry, the contribution of narratives has been carefully noted. For example, they play a powerful, and indeed decisive, part in the resurgent religion of Pentecostalism as sacred narrative enacted in the daily lives of Christians and their faith communities. For Martin, 'Christian faith is about an "express image" and the story of the loving purposes of God in Christ. The text is woven into action, Word into words, both now and in the circumstances of its original production within the lived experiences of the first communities of faith.'[23] For Palmer, surveying the rich tapestry of religious contributions to environmental and economic sustainability, 'all religions pass on their messages and their ethos by telling stories'.[24] The decisive function of faith communities and their traditions in character and therefore virtue formation, was clearly visible in these accounts of the added values of faith contributions to social capital.

I will illustrate the nature and significance of faith narratives with reference to two examples listing central features of Christian narratives and the role they play in the formation of a theological anthropology; the first is from Soulen and Woodhead's study, *God and Human Dignity*, identifying the direct implication of belief for a Christian view of the human which very clearly and decisively establishes its *difference* dimension. The second is used by Browning as an indispensable contribution to locating pre-moral goods within a necessary wider framework of moral-theological meaning.

Soulen and Woodhead's reflections on 18 impressive contributions to a collaborative study identify three recurring features of the distinctively Christian context, each relating to a central feature of the divine works, all elaborated in the foundational narratives of the Christian faith, embodied in tradition and sacred writing. What emerges is a theological anthropology, a narrative of God and humanity, which 'In its theocentricity . . . is anthropocentric'.[25]

The first is God's work of creation, including the fashioning of humankind as a whole. For Lactantius (d.320) God created humanity as a 'sacred animal', therefore confirming its dignity, and conversely, prohibiting its killing. The central and classic biblical text is in Genesis (1.26), with God declaring 'let us make man after our image and likeness'. That divinizing of man becomes the religious foundation of the human rights project, again in that post-1945 generation.[26]

The second divine work is God's redemption in Christ as a basis for human dignity, and its appropriation through the practice of Christian virtue as Christian discipleship. It profoundly focused on the great theme of being in Christ, generating a foundational sense of equal dignity. For St Clement (d.215), the root of all dignity is 'the greatness of the dignity of God . . .' for 'the living creature which is of high value, is made sacred by that which is worth all, or rather which has no equivalent, in virtue of the exceeding sanctity of the latter'.[27]

The third Christian context is 'God's consummation as the eschatological goal of creation' – that all existence, including human, is journeying to a *telos* or goal, in God, and that 'the divine likeness itself is only "reached in the end", having been "reserved for the consummation"'.[28]

From these foundational narratives of the divine works, Soulen and Woodhead draw three lessons for a theological anthropology. First, 'human dignity is conferred by God. It is not a self-grounded possession enjoyed apart from relationship to the Creator, Redeemer and Sanctifier.'[29]

Second, 'its measure and norm is (therefore) to be discovered not in social convention but in God' and in the ways of God's relationships to the world. Human dignity is therefore located not 'so much in self-possession as in dispossession' – of caring for others. It is the basis of that reciprocity, that brave social capital in Parts 1 and 2. In a powerful concept, Soulen and Woodhead rightly talk of Christ's 'transvaluation of dignity' – within and outside the Church – again as we have regularly experienced in this enquiry.[30]

Third, its indispensable context is the Church, conferring the communal rather than individual character of the human. Again, in another striking phrase, so deeply relevant to the happiness hypothesis and other findings,

'Human beings are not whole, but part of a larger whole' – namely the body of Christ, which we have already described as model of Church and paradigm for society as partial reality and promised destiny.[31]

It is the cumulative effect of these divine works and their intimate implications for theological anthropology which should be thus summarized: 'In its theocentricity it is anthropocentric.'[32]

Browning's foundational narratives do overlap with Soulen and Woodhead's, but are more geared to the task of Christian social ethics in developing a theological anthropology. He therefore takes the pre-moral goods, so central to human well-being, and argues, justifiably, that to be operational they need to be located in a wider narrative framework which alone could provide the motivation for moral action, and the ontological grounding through story-bound motifs. Only with and in such a context can the moral life be practised: for 'The moral life is more than a matter of actualizing premoral values in ways that show justice and respect to one's neighbour. It entails believing the moral life is worthwhile to begin with, that one's neighbour is worth respecting, that one should persist when one is failing, and that one should have hope in the face of discouragement.'[33]

The Christian story, for Browning, provides such a narrative framework. At its heart is what he describes as: 'the inner core of Christian ethics . . . Loving your neighbour as yourself means . . . doing *good* to your neighbour as you would have them to do *good* unto you.'[34] That formulation of the Golden Rule is described by Janssens later as a love ethic of 'equal regard'. The Golden Rule has appeared strongly in the rest of the enquiry, and the concept of regard, here religiously grounded at the centre of Christian ethics, is the basic regulating principle of the concept of an *economy of regard* – and that flows naturally and logically into Tanner's *economy* of grace, to be discussed later.

Browning's narrative structures follow Reinhold Niebuhr's, using basic story metaphors. The first is the metaphor of God the Creator, the ontological status of goodness in all the created world: 'God saw everything that he had made, and indeed, it was very good' (Genesis 1.31). It is in that divine context that pre-moral goods are imbued with a 'sacred valence', and must therefore be treated as such.[35] Second, the metaphor of God the Creator gives unique status to human beings as made in God's image. It is this which necessitates respect – or rather *regard* – for the *imago Dei* – for both other and self – as of intrinsic value, as ends and never means. The third metaphor, again of God the Creator, informs our understanding of love as 'equal regard about the limits of life'.[36] We are infinitely finite, as is our planet. It is that profound sense of finitude, of the limits of being human, which ensures human hopes, including as pre-moral goods, can never be totally realized. There are always more goods to seek than can be actualized. It is a basis of modern economics itself through the context of scarcity, and therefore of the conflict over goods and their allocation. For Robbins, therefore, economics is 'The science which studies human behaviour as a relationship between ends and scarce means which have alternative uses'.[37] Philosophers and economists, for example Nussbaum, do *not* take account of this narrative, and the tragedies inevitably associated with it, and how therefore to cope with it, including narrative-wise. The creation narrative does precisely that: it tells us 'that we must have our theories of the goods of life, but none can be absolutized and all must be subservient to the principle (or kingdom) of love as equal regard among all humans'. Fourth, the metaphor of God the moral Governor, in Christian narratives, is demanded by the presence of sin as well as finitude. Finitude generates conflict over goods, but that becomes evil only through human misuse. Again, this reinforces 'the inner core of Christian obligation, namely an ethic of equal regard defined as justly respecting both self and other while also working for the good of both self and other'. The fifth metaphor, or rather metaphors, are the Christian narratives of sin, grace and forgiveness, which allow the human to counterbalance pressures from 'inordinate self-interest' and selfishness.[38] It is that understanding of God's freely given grace, never earned, which assures Christians that 'they are justified before God even if they fall short'. Fifth, the Christian narrative of the cross 'adds an element of supererogation to the love ethic of equal regard' – as the sinless, heedless, self-sacrificial, sin-bearing love of the cross. Here is the totally different dimension of the religious narrative, of the totally added value. The utilitarianism of Layard, and the deontological theory of Finnis and Nussbaum, with their love ethic of equal regard – none can 'address the disruptions of sin and evil'. To do that means sacrifice – 'in renewing the core ethic of mutuality and equal regard'. The disruptions of sin will always require and indeed demand that. Always. Narratives of cross and forgiveness address precisely 'how just love for the good of the other and self is sustained in the light of sin and brokenness'.[39]

It is the contention of such understandings of the religious narratives, and their indispensable contribution to the religious dimension of the anthropological question, which allow Browning, and Soulen and Woodhead, to take 'tentative' but I believe firm steps towards a 'new Christian humanism' – firm,[40] because the evidence in this enquiry from other secular sources – say in the happiness hypothesis – confirms that possibility, that need. Their work demonstrates that, in narrative detail.

Lessons from the nature of God for what it means to be human

Understandings of the nature of God include, as we have seen, the use of metaphors which also illuminate understandings of the human. Two further themes recur in the theological literatures which relate directly to the development of a theological anthropology – the social nature of God and the concept of partnership in God.

The first draws powerfully on trinitarian understandings of God. For example, Zizioulas rightly distinguishes between individual and person, with the latter dominating Christian theology and experience in worship and in the Eucharist. As a 'relational ontological category', the particular person's identity is not found inside us – as soul or private existence – existing before we then encounter the outside world. The trinitarian persons of and as God is the ultimate demonstration of 'the way in which we are all constitutive of one another. The personhood of each human is the work of all people in the whole history of the world.' In other words, this 'divinely created personhood, echoes God's own life in "communion"'.[41] To treat the person as isolated individual contradicts that understanding. It is a 'lie', in the way in which F. D. Maurice considered untrammelled competition between individuals as a 'lie', because it, too, was diametrically opposed to God's creation of persons-in-community, in co-operation.[42] The human task is therefore to replicate that social reality of reciprocity by 'mirroring and joining in God's loving, participatory, personal existence' (Zizioulas).[43]

In the Trinity, the three 'persons' are such because of their difference from and in relation to each other. As with God, we too are therefore persons in and through our relationships with others. We are 'members of one another' (Ephesians 4.23), and so our difference as unique persons is only unique when 'we are *for* others'. Once again, it is a confirmation of regard, and so of the importance of an economy of regard.[44]

It is this Trinitarian making sense of difference through relationships which ensures persons are woven into the lives of others: 'They participate in one another's lives, whether they realize it or not.' This is no abstract universal human nature eroding difference, but divinely given ontological reality which generates what Spivak calls 'a strategic essentialism', a commitment to human solidarity: 'Not only does all human life and history take place within the divine economy, which is definitive of what it is to be and act humanly, but our human solidarity is constituted *relationally*, both in relationship to God and to one another.'[45] It is both recognition of a fundamental utilizing of what is shared in God as human and which is also inclusive of the profound uniqueness as the difference of each person. The equal regard is from difference to difference in and through an essential overlapping solidarity.

The second theme follows from the first, and reflects on the concept of the human participation in God, powerfully embedded in Patristic and Eastern Orthodox traditions, and in Anglican tradition, through the work of Allchin. In the latter, it is liturgically expressed in the collect for the first Sunday after Christmas: 'Almighty God, who wonderfully created us in your own image and yet more wonderfully restored us through your son Jesus Christ; grant that, as he came to share in our humanity, so we may share the life of his divinity.'[46] It is this belief in a participating God which focuses on Christ's participation in the human through the incarnation which in turn invites and resources (through the Holy Spirit) the human's participation in the Godhead. For Elaine Graham, exploring the anthropological implications of new technologies, 'An understanding of *human* creativity as participation in *divine* creativity affirms the goodness of our inventive abilities.'[47] That theme of participation is strongly present in this enquiry in various forms – from Wilkinson's arguments for a more cooperative way of organizing work to the development of pro participation economic growth as integral part of poverty reduction programmes. Here, that theme is located in the nature of God and therefore in theological anthropology and discipleship as model and metaphor, as source, inspiration and pattern.

Apophatic anthropology: continuing notes for human pretensions

Participation in a participating God has many implications for theological anthropology, one of which is particularly challenging to attempts to try to understand everything on earth. That is a prime reason why we have progressed into a post-scarcity context for an increasing proportion of the world's population. Yet to participate anthropologically in the divine nature as image of God is also to participate in the profoundly unknowable, 'that the divine lies beyond words, concepts and understanding', and therefore there is that in the human which is equally beyond understanding. In other words, for Woodhead, 'we are pointed toward the necessity of an apophatic approach in anthropology as well as in theology'.[48] As such it is a recognition of finitude, the essential limits of living, including understanding, and including in relationships. So much of our closest relationships include the unknowable of the given. Yet it is equally a reflection of the human model itself, made in the image of God, and therefore not containing their essence in themselves but in and through the God 'into

whose image they are to grow. They become human by becoming divine –
which means growing into something we do not know or control rather
than something we already possess.'[49] There is something in the human
which is therefore beyond what we do, beyond moral agency. That is the
story of Kelly, so vividly told and analysed by Reinders. Kelly was diag-
nosed from birth as micro-encephalic. Since a significant part of her brain
was missing she was what some call a 'vegetable'. What does it mean to
define her as a human? Reinders argues that her essential humanness is like
ours, in God. It is 'why divine agency – not human agency – is the primary
concept of theological anthropology'.[50] It is beyond our understanding.

For Woodhead, such 'An apophatic anthropology requires that we open
ourselves to the unknown in order to become more than we can possibly
know. It is much safer and easier to choose a route that has already been
clearly mapped out – but that is not the same as entering into Life.'[51] It is
an essential creatively cautionary note to the most well-meaning of human
ambitions to elaborate more adequate anthropologies, because it locates
them even more in a necessary context of finitude without in *any* way
diminishing the importance of the human project in pursuit of greater
human well-being. And that includes measuring it in appropriate ways.

The Penultimacy of Proximate Concerns for Human Flourishing

The multidimensionality of a theological anthropology includes the great
themes of creation, redemption and eschatology, yet it also contains what
Browning has called 'a proximate concern for human flourishing'.[52] That
is not to demean or reduce the significance of pursuing well-being. It is
rather to locate and relativize it within the divine economy. A cluster of
arguments develop the nature of that 'proximate' character of the human
task and reinforce its importance in Christian social ethics in terms of what
Bonhoeffer described as penultimacy.[53] The first reflects further on the
strategic essentialism used by Spivak. While understanding that postcolonial theory argues for a 'decentred, free-floating "postmodern self"', he
acknowledges that the commitment to human liberation against a variety
of oppressions, including the various forms of marginalization, requires
'the adoption of an essentialist stance'. It is that commitment to 'a universal human solidarity',[54] which in no way overrides the importance of difference, which is also another version of Hollenbach's question of how to
hold together the commitment to universal justice and rights, and the
acknowledgement of our local traditions and customs.

Haidt's work on shared moral understandings, including basic virtues, also underwrites that commitment to explore the basic nature of the human, including its religious character, while at the same time allowing for the human capacity and freedom to influence the context as environment.[55] Browning's deployment of an 'inner core of Christian ethics' also represents an attempt to deepen the ontological, including as moral, character of the *proximate* nature of the human task.[56] These reflections should also be linked to the renewed focus on the nature or nurture argument in the happiness-psychology research findings in Part 2 and its rejection of the dominance of difference which can pervade post-modernity. Its use of brain studies and genetics, and the happiness setpoint, constrain the space for human contributions to change but do not remove it. Woodhead's apophatic anthropology similarly acknowledges dimensions of human experience in a theological anthropology including areas beyond human understanding and therefore significantly beyond human influence.

Several stories confirm that strategic essentialism of human dignity including its modification by difference and its resulting proximate character. For example, Soulen's examination of the new eugenics and its potential deployment to determine the new kinds of persons for the future by using genetic knowledge to shape the next generation is highly relevant. Although this can promote well-being by avoiding disease, it can also be used to confer advantages – not to make people better, but to make better and more fortunate people. It can contradict the theological principle of equal regard. As with earlier eugenic selection, which so blatantly transgressed that notion of equal regard, it assumes 'as a matter of course that the weak have little or nothing to contribute to the well-being of the strong'. Yet the Christian narratives regularly reflect God's choice of the 'least likely: from Moses the stutterer, or David, the youngest of eight brothers, or the Suffering Servant without form or comeliness'.[57] We have already noted in the bias for inclusivity, how, in the body of Christ, the least important are central to the well-being of all. The story of Kelly confirms and extends that strategic essentialist understanding of human dignity – that human beings are dignified by a divine act of communion regardless of their status or condition, *or their capacity as moral agents*. The full status of the human is primarily the result of divine agency. Strategic essentialism is profoundly divine gift.

I came across the final story from a study of sixteenth-century Dominican work on human rights. For, as today, human rights presuppose a Christian anthropology rather than explicitly stating it. Yet that dual nature of human rights was a profoundly liberating tool in sixteenth-century Spanish jurisprudence. Had the conquered Indians of Central and South American any rights? Were they conferred through conversion by the Church, and therefore one of the benefits of conquest? All classic arguments of the religious complicity in the imperialism of Part 1 of this enquiry. Yet in this story, the great lawyer Vitoria argued that Indians had rights *before* the Spanish invasion *because* they were created in God's image. They had rights by nature, by natural law, not grace (as Wyclif argued). Like Aquinas, it reflects a commitment to the social nature of human rights, rooted in an objective moral wider, as the profound obligation of the human to others. Vitoria and the Spanish Dominicans' work represents a theological stance against the operations of global empires and for a theological anthropology which includes dimensions *transcending* local cultures and differences.[58] It confirms the penultimacy of the proximate value of the pursuit of human fulfilment.

Connecting the Dimensions of Theological and Secular Anthropologies

The multidimensional nature of emerging secular and theological anthropologies presents both possibility and challenge. The undoubted richness and yet empirical accuracy of the development of multidisciplinary understandings of well-being are becoming more self-evident. This first chapter of Part 3 of the Enquiry is hopefully indicating a similar benefit from the study of theological anthropology. To enhance that reality and potential further does require developing the connections and interactions between the dimensions, and indeed between the different anthropologies. Various hints appear in the literatures which can be exploited to achieve such goals. First, the Christian narratives, evidenced in the work of St Irenaeus, distinguish between the *image* of God in which we find ourselves, and the *likeness* of God into which we are to grow and achieve in end time. Between the two is the journey itself, the space created for the development of pre-moral goals and the penultimacy of proximate concerns, a space also identified by the happiness hypothesis for the contribution of human agency to well-being.[59] It represents, as the image of God, potential to be realized. It is these interim activities which can be appropriately measured. Interim work is a profoundly theological understanding and can be usefully appropriated.

A second insight comes from Browning's work, where he develops a narrative-based framework within which to locate pre-moral goals and other dimensions of a theological anthropology. What he then advocates is interesting – that other traditions, including in other faiths, should undertake a similar exercise. On that basis of shared enterprises, 'each tradition should enter a *correlational dialogue* with other traditions and with the human sciences to develop heuristic models of what human beings require to live well and flourish'.[60] This links with my earlier use of pursuing creative correspondences between reformulations of economic behaviour and work on behaviour in other related disciplines. Tanner's work on an economy of grace similarly engages in a correlative dialogue with mainstream economics. Again, in a later section on interfaith-ecumenical work, the use of parallel hermeneutics performs a similar function.[61] All these procedures can be deployed to promote connections between anthropologies and within them, to their mutual benefit. Although this chapter has rightly been used to develop a theological anthropology, its connections to other anthropologies, and to the wider sources and materials in this enquiry, have consistently acknowledged the multidisciplinary and multidimensional character of the pursuit of human well-being, and of the distinctive nature of the religious understanding of the human. Reflection on a Christian view of the human confirms and enlarges that judgement.

9

Personalist Ethics and the Common Good

The Search for Moral Wholeness

The increasing significance of the religious and ethical dimensions pervades this whole project certainly as the cumulative effects of their interpenetration of every single part of it, including what at first sight appears to be the most secular. Capitalism, empires and globalization are inextricably bound up with the most profound moral and religious questions.[62] Indeed, it may be that the whole is more than the sum total of the parts. Moral economies and globalization are integral parts of a transcending common good of and for all. Certain sections of the Enquiry indeed argue for that. Layard asks quite explicitly 'Can we pursue a common good?'[63] That is not a surprising development given the regular acknowledgment in these literatures of the vital need for a philosophy of life, for an overview within which to locate both personal and societal endeavours. These are inevitably interpenetrated with strong moral dimensions. And all ethical theories, and certainly those assumed by economics, presuppose an anthropology. There is, in so many ways, a natural progression through the different chapters of this final part of the enquiry. That is particularly evident in the connections between the previous chapter on anthropology and this, with its focus on ethics particularly from a theological (or Christian) perspective.

In terms of the principal sources used, they are almost self-selecting. From my overview vantage point of the whole project, I have been regularly surprised how literatures from quite different disciplines and perspectives feed into what have become major emphases in the research – for example, the issue of non-moral (premoral) and moral goods, and their role in promoting well-being. I have therefore found Cowley's work to be the main foundation for this section, not least because of her knowledge and my ignorance. Her study of *The Value of Money: Ethics and the World of Finance* addresses directly the global financial market from the perspective of Christian social ethics. Her knowledge of personalist ethics and natural law traditions of moral discoursing overlaps profoundly with the matters arising from this enquiry. In some ways, she represents the real potential of a reformulated tradition of moral theology which is likely to play an increasingly important part in the engagement by religious traditions of increasingly global questions. Other sources delight by their contribution, particularly Morisy on spirituality and Himmelfarb on virtues and Jewish communities in nineteenth-century London's East End.[64] Like Cowley, I will divide the argument into two parts, on personalist ethics and on the common good. This should not be allowed to detract from the necessary and inevitable continuous flows between them. They unequivocally constitute two sides of the same coin.

Developing a Moral Anthropology: The Utility of Personalist Ethics

In so many ways, my respect for the market economy and mechanism remains undiminished. My judgement in *Christianity and the Market* still stands, that they are the least harmful ways of operating increasingly complex modern economies.[65] Recognizing their relative importance to human well-being both confirms that enduring value but also locates them in wider, including moral, contexts. These underwrite that significance, but also subject it to critical appraisal. For example, with regard to the latter, when ethics are combined with religion, psychology, sociology, philosophy and epidemiology then the results can be a serious questioning of market economics. There is growing evidence from all these sources (and from within economics) that neoclassical economics fails to account for actual behaviour, making unrealistic assumptions of human motivation. Developing adequate anthropologies cannot therefore be achieved simply from within the neoclassical free market frameworks. For Einstein 'No problem can be solved from within the consciousness which created it. We must learn to see the world anew.'[66] For example, the problem with economics is that, like every system, it has an ethics, and 'Every ethics is based on an image of the human, on an anthropology.' In the case of modern economics, the utilitarian view of the person, which informs it and is revisited and reinforced by Layard, is based 'essentially on a person's desires' understood as 'a set'.[67] It is the aggregating of these individual desires which informs its view of society, as the greatest happiness of the greatest number.

To develop a more adequate view of the person and ethics as a personalist ethics, Cowley uses Janssens' work – even though it is drawn from the field of biomedical and sexual ethics. What is interesting for me is how closely this connects to the characteristics or dimensions of what it means to be human theologically, in the previous section. Because Cowley's work on financial markets is so close to my own work on political economy, her choice is likely to be particularly relevant to my task. For example, she recognizes that 'a moral anthropology' is necessarily, broader than, although inclusive of, the search for human dignity (as Kelly's story reminded us).[68] It is ever-expanding, like Sen's work on human capabilities, and, crucially, multidimensional. The moral acts flow from the moral person, including in its relationships, and therefore as informing the shape of social arrangements. Although Kelly's story has rightly reminded us that theological anthropology is broader than moral anthropology, the latter plays a foundational part in it in terms of influencing the *space* available for human endeavour already identified. Promoting human well-being flows naturally from that.

The person as our focus in this part of the chapter is rightly understood as 'a unity' of the recognized dimensions of the human: 'there is no separate "I" which *has* these dimensions. I *am* these dimensions. There is no priority of dimensions, only the unity of the person.'[69]

In that wider context, Janssens' eight fundamental dimensions of the person are: first, as a subject, 'called to be conscious', and acting according to conscience, freely and responsibly. As a subject, a person cannot be treated as a means; second, as the wholeness of embodied spirit, with both material and spirit absolutely essential for human functioning; third, as intrinsically bound up with the material in creation; fourth, as interrelational with other persons; there is no Buberian I without a Thou; fifth, as interdependent social being, living with others, including in social institutions and structures (these are often omitted, wrongly, from such lists); sixth, persons are called 'to know and worship God – open to the experience of transcendence', seventh, historical (we have already noted the importance of this dimension, particularly in Part I); eighth, as equal but unique – we all share 'the same human nature and condition', enjoy dignity and are worthy of respect. Such 'Fundamental equality explains why some moral obligations apply to all'.[70]

The combination of these dimensions generates criteria for morally evaluating an action: it is therefore morally right 'if it is beneficial to the person adequately considered in himself or herself (that is, as a unique, embodied subject) and in his or her relations (that is, openness to others, to social structures, to the material world and to God)'.[71]

This understanding of the human is clearly 'not culturally specific', and rightly so.[72] Our relational and embodiment dimensions, for example, require reasonable stable structures for the upbringing of children. The happiness/well-being literatures are *uniformly* committed to this. Yet what is not argued for is the particular form that commitment to family should take. This constitutes an important way of holding together universal and difference, both of which are increasingly recognized by the research.

Two dimensions of such personalist ethics, relationality and transcendence, are relevant to the task of addressing political economy.

First, *relationality*. Most modern ethical theories, including that which underlies economics today, assume human life is profoundly and essentially concerned with individuals. They are, in other words, 'counter-factual' because we are rather profoundly and essentially socially organized individuals in our very nature. It is this foundational relationship with others which the rational-individualist model of economics omits: 'Economic rationality provides too thin an understanding of what it is to be human and prevents reflection on the ways in which self-interest and other interest interact and *modify our choices and decisions*.'[73] In my *Marginalization*, I found the work of Iris Young particularly helpful; like other feminist writers she was very critical of 'abstract atomistic individualism' as a 'patriarchal construct' and therefore of the ahistorical assumptions behind economic man, and its potent inaccuracy according to, for example, the well-being literatures, and the conclusions of the previous section on anthropology.[74]

Second, *transcendence*. The primacy of individual choice in economic theory contradicts the classic integration of the dimensions of the person as its grounded moral identity. It is that which is formed in traditioning communities as moral character and virtue. Like the psychologist Haidt in the happiness studies there is therefore a strong recognition of the inadequacies of the normal 'quandary' approach to ethics.[75] Like modern economics' *thin* view of the human, this too is profoundly *reductionist*, reducing ethics to 'specific actions viewed from the minimalist perspective of being right or wrong'.[76] The formation of character as the basis of virtue-living, in and through traditioning communities, represents a far richer understanding of ethics. Like the personalist interpretation of ethics, it generates a more accurate and *thicker* understanding of life.

That locating of person and ethics in contexts always transcending the individual is reinforced by Janssens' sixth dimension, 'Called to know God and worship God – open to the experience of transcendence'.[77] It is the multidimensionality of the person, and that perspective which points to reality greater than ourselves, present in all the lists of human characteristics surveyed, which can only be adequately made sense of by being grounded in some understanding of the divine. That understanding is confirmed by the experience of all the major world faiths.[78] It is this inter-action between God and person, Creator and created which is the basis of lived relationships and therefore of the moral dimension within them. Interpreting Aquinas's understanding of that relationship, 'The moral life is seen in terms of the person's multiple relationships with God, self, neighbour and the world.'[79]

At this point, I want to summarize this work on personalist ethics using several stories to illustrate the importance for ethics of character and virtue, and then of transcendence as spirituality.

The communal formation of character and virtue

The first story concerns the Financial Services Authority (FSA). I once gave a lecture on religion and capitalism in its beautiful and hubristic head-quarters in Canary Wharf! One of the FSA's regulatory requirements for an approved financial enterprise is the criteria for an Approved Person. This relates to (i) honesty, integrity and reputation; (ii) competence and capability; (iii) financial soundness.[80] What is very clear, as Adam Smith knew only too well, is that virtuous living as honesty, integrity and reputa-tion is not formed primarily within the economic system, within work, but outside, in families and traditioning communities. It therefore follows that 'what the FSA in particular has legislated for is impossible if the only con-text is that of its sphere of work and influence'.[81] In other words 'It is always within some particular community with its own specific forms that we learn or fail to learn to exercise the virtues.' And these virtues and their communal formation, can be deeply critical of the life of mainstream societies, practices and theories where the latter are seen as contradicting virtue. For MacIntyre, it is where 'forms of social and political life in which the practice of the virtues is at revolutionary odds with those forms, so that one can only be virtuous by being in systematic conflict with the established order'.[82] The existence of standpoints in the FBOs surveyed in Part 2 which were sometimes critical of and developed as alternatives to mainstream practices and theories profoundly illustrates this reality and potential of virtuous living.

The location of the second story moves from today's FSA's Canary Wharf to the nearby East End of London in the later nineteenth century. In her splendid study of the *De-moralization of Society* the historian Himmelfarb compares the accumulating social capital of Britain before 1900 with its dismantling after 1960, what Fukuyama has referred to as the Great Disruption. A key location for the nurturing of character and virtues was the family and the neighbourhood as family of families, and generator of voluntary bodies: 'The working class family is now shown as the repository of the conventional Victorian values: respectability, hard work, self-help, obedience, cleanliness, orderliness.'[83] The promotion of virtue was necessarily accompanied by the imposition of sanctions. The recent distaste for the latter as well as the former contradicts Himmelfarb's analysis, but *also* the studies by Kenny of moral systems, already noted, and Halpern's sociological survey of social capital. What is equally important, and again routinely ignored today, is that Victorian governments also assumed 'that every proposal for alleviation (of poverty) should produce moral as well as material benefits'.[84] That dimension of a *moral audit* is a profoundly important addition to the multidimensionality of moral anthropology.

In an interesting case study, Himmelfarb illustrates these interpretations through the story of the Jewish community in the East End of London, using Beatrice Webb's work. Closely knit, governed by self-governing religio-social institutions and conventions, but above all by family ties, its system of charity closely followed Himmelfarb's wider analysis. For example, it preferred financial support for self-help enterprises, 'to enable recipients to become self-supporting' (today's micro-loans for poor women in Asia).[85] Even more interesting was Webb's description of the immigrant Jewish ethos, as self-help, as a Jewish version of Weber's Protestant work ethic. For her, the immigrant Jew 'seems to justify by his existence those strange assumptions which figured for *man* in the political economy of Ricardo – an *Always Enlightened Selfishness*, seeking employment or profit with an absolute mobility of body and mind, without pride, without preference, without interests outside the struggle for the existence and welfare of the individual and the family'.[86] It would be foolish to judge such ethics as seriously deficient because of their focus on self-help. For Himmelfarb, this ethic of 'Always Enlightened Selfishness' was profoundly mundane because it 'takes people as they are as they always have been, as human beings capable of being enlightened as well as self-interested – enlightened precisely because their "self" (or "better self" for T. H. Green) naturally embraces family and community, economic interests and moral values'.[87] It would be easy to be nostalgic faced with such stories from the past, but they are replayed today in Jewish, Muslim and Christian families. An important task is how to reinforce such character-forming locations and to enlarge their implications through *corresponding* contemporary and more secular locations as well as religious. Here I think of Baker's interesting use of *micropublics*, places in cities today like parks and public squares where people from very different backgrounds and traditions *have* to encounter each other for dialogue and negotiation.[88] It is the cumulative effect of all these character-forming locations which can and should contribute to developing a sense of sharing and solidarity.

A story of transcendence and spirituality

Ann Morisy's work is full of good stories. We have already referred to her brave social capital. Here, confirming the work on happiness of the psychologist Haidt, she reflects on the significance of the sense of transcendence, including as integral part of contemporary experiences of spirituality. She therefore notes that the majority of British adults claim to have had experience that is 'not everyday', involving a 'presence or power' in their lives as 'patterns associated with religious experience'. The research, particularly by Hay, is increasingly robust, suggesting that the persistence of religious experience indicates 'a biological capacity for such perceptions'.[89] It is these transcendence encounters, a key Janssens' dimension of the person, which also have important ethical implications and connections. So often 'the person who has had a religious experience reports that as a result they have become more thoughtful and more moral in their dealings with others'. As the 'relational consciousness',[90] also so central to Christian social ethics, it leads on a naturally to consideration of its indispensable social ramifications as the common good.

Promoting a Moral Society: Developing the Common Good

The overriding societal concept in Christian social ethics in the modern period has been, and still is, the common good, with all its strengths and limitations. It has particularly figured prominently and impressively in modern Roman Catholic social teaching. For example it has been a recurring feature of the long tradition of papal social encyclicals from 1891 (*Rerum Novarum*) to the present (*Centesimus Annus* 1991). In 1996, in national developments, the Conference of Catholic Bishops of England and Wales produced *The Common Good* 'designed to summarize and mobilize the tradition of catholic social teaching'.[91] Its implied critique of Thatcherite economic and social philosophies, with their focus on a possessive individualism, certainly contributed to that moral shift in public opinion which then informed the Labour landslide in 1997. Two Roman Catholic Jesuit scholars of real eminence have also carefully and critically reappraised the nature and role of the common good, Patrick Riordan's *A*

Politics of the Common Good and David Hollenbach's *The Common Good and Christian Ethics*.[92] In Anglican social ethics, Ronald Preston was also a strong advocate of its value. In my own work, despite strong criticism of it in *Public Theology for Changing Times* (2000), I began its reformulation in *Marginalization* (2003) and more recently *Through the Eye of a Needle* (2007). In the light of this research project that process of re-evaluation continues, given the regular focus on the balance between universal and local (in the Hollenbach question), and between nature and nurture in the happiness hypothesis, and in the reformulation of anthropology as personal in constant interaction with social.

This chapter on ethics has likewise balanced personal and social, with each informing the other. As person and common good, both are essential for well-being, and for the religious contribution. Both are continually interacting in 'fruitful tension'.[93] Again, what follows draws heavily on Cowley's work including its implications for economics.

As in the reflections on the person, the common good similarly provides a constructive critique of market economics and mechanisms. Their value is firmly acknowledged, as we will soon see through papal social encyclicals. Their limitations again focus on inadequate views of the human in its relationships. For example, revealed-preference theory 'fails to recognize and value *common* interests and interdependence' falsely polarizing self and other interests.[94]

The concept of the common good itself assumes the partial capacity of human reason to understand the good including in its communal form – not least because so many goods and experiences are shared and make essential contributions to human well-being. A useful revised definition was provided by the great Second Vatican Council, recognizing 'the common good embraces the sum total of all those conditions of social life which enable individuals, families and organisations to achieve complete and efficacious fulfilment'.[95] Most importantly, there is now a clear recognition that there is no final definition of the common good. It is continually evolving, not least in relation to changing contexts. Yet not withstanding this contextualizing, the focus on the centrality of moral social arrangements to the human task remains constant. That is the case because it is always grounded in what it means to be human, including as and for the benefit of us all, for human well-being as a whole. The theologian Grisez has usefully developed such a linkage between human fulfilment and the common good through a list of 'basic human goods which fulfil persons'. The added value of this is that it continues the theme of work done on lists of human characteristics or dimensions for different but related objectives – as here. The connection *between* them is particularly important for their creative potential in constructing multilayered understandings of human well-being. Grisez's list includes (1) self-integration as harmony between all the parts of the human and generating freely chosen action; (2) practical reasonableness as the harmony of moral reflection, free choices and their execution; (3) justice and friendship as aspects of 'the interpersonal communion of good persons'; (4) religion or holiness, as harmony with God – later expanded to include the 'non-theistic but more-than-human source of meaning and value'; (5) life as health, safety and pro-creation; (6) 'knowledge of various forms of truth and appreciation of various forms of beauty or excellence', (7) skilful work and play which enrich us.[96]

Grisez rightly notes that these constitute only 'a reasonable approximation in our time of what contributes to human flourishing'.[97] Throughout this reflection on the common good there is a continual effort to recognize both the continuing value of the common good (as universal) and its recurring reformulation (in particular contexts and cultures). This helps my earlier unease with its pretensions to a universalism, inevitably time and location-bound, and invariably with a propensity to authoritarian tendencies. Rigali usefully describes these tensions and ways of rightly and necessarily accommodating them in terms of: 'the inculturation of these universal values in the shared meanings, values, and institutions of a particular culture (that) constitutes the universality-in-particularity of morality'.[98]

Grisez's list of basic human goods or rather intrinsic characteristics of what it means to be human, including ethically and religiously, are 'aspects of the person'. They are not to be confused with such extrinsic goods as property. These vary significantly in form across cultures and histories: 'the concept of the common good is (therefore) grounded in an anthropology found across cultures'.[99] It is this cross-cultural character that can be more effectively deployed to engage a global context, including globalization processes, than 'the individualistic, western model of self-interested rationality'. As Cowley rightly observes, this concept of the common good overlaps greatly with the traditions of the major world religions, including Islamic and Eastern cultures. Palmer's collection of the faiths' statements on environment powerfully confirm this judgement. For example, in Japan, the Canon Company used the term *kyosei*, translated as 'living and working for the common good', to inform the corporate ethos and its connection with national identity. The potential of the concept is that it could therefore facilitate 'cross-cultural dialogue on what constitutes the good life and the good society'.[100] This could include reference to the debate over global ethics or global ethic, to be briefly referenced in the following section on interfaith – ecumenical social ethics.

Central to this emerging understanding of the common good is the foundational understanding of the person-in-relationships, including community and society. It is the opposite of Mrs Thatcher's supposed declaration that there is no such thing as society. Instead, there is no such thing as the isolated individual. And that relates to understandings of basic human goods which must often 'be pursued with others in a social context'.[101] This view is very critical of Rawls's contractarianism with its analysis of individuals as an understanding of society as means for negotiated private ends. For Cowley, this represents a 'false assessment of how we achieve many of the goods we seek'. So often these goods, for example as 'outcomes based on frankness and equality . . . presuppose a certain culture, a certain society which gives these goods meaning'.[102] It is a profound recognition that so often such goods are socially and culturally embedded in themselves, like the understanding that the person can only be concerned and engaged as embedded in relationality. For Taylor,

> If these things are goods, then other things being equal so is the culture that makes them possible. If I want to maximise these goods, then I must want to preserve and strengthen this culture. But the culture as a good, or more cautiously as the locus of some goods (for there might be much that is reprehensible as well), is not an individual good.[103]

The goods therefore become common goods.

In order to illustrate further the multidimensional character of the common good, its two features, subsidiarity and solidarity, will be examined. They allow greater elaboration of the concept, and also provide further checks on any movement towards more authoritarian or paternalist interpretations or applications.

Subsidiarity

The classic definition of subsidiarity was developed by the great social encyclical *Quadragesimo Anno* in 1931. As a protection against the totalitarianism of interwar Fascism and Stalinism, it argued that it is 'an injustice and at the same time a grave evil and a disturbance of right order to assign to a greater and higher association what lesser and subordinate organisations can do'.[104]

Two particular functions are derived from this, which also promote greater participation in decision-making (already identified as major contribution to happiness and poverty reduction). The first is that it encourages decentralized decision-making, encouraging the decisive involvement of people in their local groupings, including as family. The in-built tendency of the modern state, including as regional entity like the European Union, is to take more power to itself to the detriment of the proper integrity of the local. The second complements and enriches this decentralizing function by encouraging the building up of local networks and associations as a renewed institutional framework. As civil society, through its voluntary bodies and intermediate associations, these constitute those thick forms of social relationships within which character and virtues, like trust and reciprocity, are formed. Faith-based contributions to the common good are deeply embedded in such institutional dimensions. Grisez unusually and yet wisely includes then in his list above of those 'basic human goods' which constitute the properly functioning moral person.

Solidarity

The common good is rooted in our shared humanity. It is therefore essentially inclusive or nothing at all. That is why the bias for inclusivity is such a preferred strategy for achieving well-being and therefore pursuing poverty reduction. It arises from, indeed is demanded by, the nature of God in its interaction with human formation. The virtues of solidarity cannot be reduced to a warm feeling of comradeship for and with others particularly in the struggles against oppressions. It is strongly generating of trust and in turn dependent on it. Its commitment to freedom is far more than the absence of restraint. This is illustrated by the role of freedom as an important theme in contemporary economic philosophy. Interestingly, Milton Friedman and Amartya Sen, both Nobel prizewinners in economics, and representing two ends of the spectrum of mainstream neo-classical economics, focus on the importance of freedom for human well-being. It also features in Layard's Big Seven of happiness construction. For Friedman, in his *Free to Choose*, the freedom to choose provided by the mechanism of an autonomous free market is in stark contrast to a state-controlled economy (so criticized by his mentor, and Mrs Thatcher's, Hayek's *The Road to Selfdom*). For Sen, in his *Development as Freedom*, freedom is rather the goal of development, requiring the provision and encouragement of basic capabilities, like health, education and income, for human functioning in terms of enabling people to pursue their self-chosen purposes.[105] Yet for Christian belief, and for Christian social ethics therefore, these necessary features of what it means to be human, to pursue human fulfilment effectively, through the common good, although rightly related intrinsically to the pursuit of freedom, are located intrinsically and inextricably to the pursuit of the good in God. For Cowley, 'What safeguards the common good is the conviction that the final good of every person – that is, God – transcends any good that can be achieved politically, economically or culturally.'[106] It is this contextualized understanding of freedom which therefore attains its fulfilment in the worship and service of God. In itself, it is both gift and obligation, a paradox captured beautifully in the second collect for peace, in Anglican Morning Prayer, which prays that God 'who art the author of peace and lover of concord, in knowledge of whom standeth our eternal life, whose *service is perfect freedom* . . .'[107]

The common good therefore performs important functions in the Christian schema. First, 'it gives *appropriate* weight to society', avoiding the problems of collectivism and individualism: for example, the latter, as the utilitarianism of economics is more concerned with the aggregate good which can and does conceal those grave inequalities which are so damaging to well-being.[108]

Second, it provides a richer framework for discussing the ends of economic processes and values, like efficiency.

Third, its thick understanding of human fulfilment generates 'many cross-cultural values', of increasing significance when facing increasingly global questions.[109]

Fourth, it strongly advocates greater inclusion, not least by working against the exclusion of the marginalized.

Fifth, by relativizing economics it allows a more careful reformulation of economic understandings. As a totally essential means to the end as common good, it has an essentially instrumental function. For *Gaudium et Spes*:

> The ultimate and basic purpose of economic production does not consist in the increase of goods produced, nor in profit nor in prestige; it is directed to the service of man, that is of man in his totality, taking into account his material needs and the requirements of his intellectual, moral, spiritual and religious life. Economic activity is to be carried out according to its own methods and laws, within the limits of the moral order, so that God's design for mankind may be fulfilled.[110]

By so relativizing the economic order, it is more creatively open to interaction with other dimensions. Through the overarching principle of the common good, a more adequate anthropology erodes the reductionist view of the human as economic man, and challenges the supremacy of the market by enriching the social dimension. It also challenges, through its bias for inclusivity, 'the reality of asymmetrical power which is ignored both in the neoclassical economic paradigm and in utilitarianism, where each individual counts as one and only one'.[111] The direct engagement with inequality, such a profound distortion of personal and social well-being, is therefore given a place of central importance in the political economy of the common good. The essential but more modest role for economic activity is therefore an accurate reflection of both what the common good requires and what the well-being research profiles for life-satisfaction in a post-scarcity era.

10

Collaborative Working
From Ecumenical to Interfaith Social Ethics

The importance of collaborative working has both inspired and informed this research. Particular projects, partly set up to feed into this enquiry, have also contributed to this way of operating which becomes process and product. For example, the Manchester Christian–Muslim conversations on finance were concerned with interfaith economics developed through the cooperation of experienced practitioners and theoreticians. Another project was the process leading to the publication, *Through the Eye of a Needle*, which also had a modest multifaith character. What began as 11 individuals agreeing to contribute to a process developing religious perspectives on political economy emerged as a strongly collaborative venture. The individual contributions remained the core of the project and publication, but it was transformed by a co-operative effort, including a residential meeting in which each contributor discussed his or her paper with the group, including a shared conclusion. Everything was constructively amended as a result. It was at this point that the project's findings for the nature and purpose of collaboration moved 'from being rather a mundane task to being rather strategic (for the development of Christian social ethics and its contributions to Church and society)'.[112] Importantly, a key part of its conclusion was also recognition of the importance of 'extending social ethics from ecumenical to interfaith collaboration'. It therefore noted and welcomed the emergence of forms of collaborative working which moved '*from* work within Christian churches and denominations *to* ecumenical working, and now also *to* interfaith working'.[113] Importantly, this way of co-operating was seen as a *continuing* process which recognized the integrity of each part. These include the different traditions represented by different Christian denominations, whether Roman Catholic or Methodist, the development of collaboration between them as ecumenical working, and finally the engagement with other faiths as interfaith working. This finding has been significantly endorsed by this research project in a variety of ways. First, the principle itself of collaborative working strongly informs the detailed areas of the enquiry, and their interaction. Each field of influence, whether capitalism or religion, has been developed and indeed enriched by the acknowledgement of a multitude of different perspectives – as multidisciplinary tasking. Each field has always been interpreted as a relatively autonomous reality – that is, always including its interaction with other fields as empirical reality and as actually and potentially profoundly creative. Second, when an important issue emerged as requiring more detailed analysis, for example, as anthropology in this final part, then it became increasingly necessary to engage it as a multidimensional phenomenon, including as religious and ethical, and again requiring multidisciplinary work. Third, it has also become very evident that collaborative ways of working developed in different forms. Practically, this has taken the form of partnerships. Given the complexity of contemporary problems, and that no one discipline or experience alone had sufficient acceptable authority to engage them effectively, then collaboration emerged as a practical reality and preferred mode of operating. The survey of faith-based organizations included partnerships with governments from Africa to Britain.

Theoretically, such collaborative working has taken an interdisciplinary form, of agreed sharing of insights to generate a complex multidimensional interpretation. The happiness hypothesis is beginning to emerge as this, and our Manchester University research programme will fill out its religious dimension in greater detail.[114] The various lists of anthropological and ethical factors are also ripe for such development. Fourth, partnership and interdisciplinary working is also informing interfaith collaboration, as we have noted, for example in Ethiopia and Central America.

It is in the light of this brief summary of ways of collaborative working identified in this enquiry, that this particular section will be developed as a matter arising with a distinctive contribution to make to the research. Although it does not represent a strong area of personal expertise, especially in knowledge of other faiths (than Christian), it has become increasingly evident that it will play an essential role in emerging research agendas as interfaith social ethics. Indeed, the focus on political economy requires such a development into interfaith working. The very roots of the words economics and ecumenical are shared. The Greek word for stewardship, *oikonomia*, used in the New Testament, is deployed to describe managing the household, from which our word economics emerges. The Anglo-Saxons took that meaning deliciously further: stewardship for them became sty-wards, or keeping the pigs, a key part of the economics of the household. The other use of the Greek word was to the whole inhabited world, from which our word ecumenical is derived. Although appropriated by Christians to describe co-operation between different Christian denominations as the ecumenical movement, it originally had a much broader remit which relates directly to the contemporary global context and to the collaboration of faith.[115]

These two features will form the basis of this chapter, as ecumenical working between Christian denominations interacting with a new dimension, with other faiths, which are then deployed to engage the global economy. The material will therefore be arranged in two parts. The first begins with the Christian ecumenical movement and the particular contribution it has made to a way of working between faiths. Its value is confirmed by reference to other comparable methodologies. The second then illustrates the potential value of bringing different faith perspectives together to focus on two shared agendas, the environment and the global economy. A brief note will be added with reference to the debate over a global ethic, using material from the Faculty of Theology of Uppsala University.

The Ecumenical Contribution to Interfaith Collaboration

When William Temple, in 1942, described the ecumenical movement as the 'great new fact of our era', it was no exaggeration.[116] The nineteenth century was deformed by the internecine warfare between the different denominations, even over burial places. To bring them together was no mean achievement and, indeed, became a paradigm for what now, in our new global context, has to emerge as interfaith working. The threat of Huntington's clash of civilizations and Jenkins's identification of sites for conflict between Islam and Christianity makes that preferred way of working into an absolute necessity. As Küng has declared there will be no peace on earth without peace between religions.[117]

It is in this context that the ecumenical movement's contribution to this project and to social ethics can be seen as particularly fruitful. For example, the Life and Work Conference at Oxford in 1937, produced important criticisms of capitalism, which retain their relevance. Even more important was the WCC's development of a tradition for engaging the whole of society, from the Evanston Conference's theme of a responsible society through the just, participatory and sustainable society, to the current justice, peace and the integrity of creation.[118] The growing influence of liberation theologies reflected the shift of power from the old churches of the West to the resurgent religions of the South confronting endemic and extensive poverty and injustice. Yet, as a recent and valuable WCC interdisciplinary research project on globalization has noted, these earlier ideals have increasingly become disconnected from churches and contexts. It accepted, refreshingly, that the ecumenical ethical enterprise was in a 'crisis of self-understanding. Ideals that once seemed compelling now fail to address the human condition'. Rather than refurbishing old images, it addressed the basic question of 'How should ecumenical social ethics be understood in order better to address the crisis of meaning and purpose besetting humankind in today's "globalised" world?'[119] It is that locating of the ecumenical in wider contexts, and how they addressed it, which provides an important contribution to this part of the enquiry. What they did was to develop a collaborative way of working which extended the ecumenical into interfaith arenas. First, given the conflict between liberal and liberationalist positions, they recognized that they could agree on their location on a spectrum, and needed to discover ways of fostering dialogue between them. Second, that methodology was developed by addressing the much wider agenda of how to discover ways of collaborating between the three great Abrahamic faiths with their past and present history of conflict. Out of that could come a 'moral witness . . . against economic and political aggrandizement', what would essentially be an interfaith public theology. Mudge's proposal constitutes a '"way" in which these covenantal traditions can covenant together in a "parallel hermeneutics" of the public world designed to foster global frameworks of human life-together in which the "minds" of our societies can be redirected towards paths of peace'.[120] It is a process and objective quite critical to this enquiry. It provides a way of connecting faiths, and the secular, to agendas relating to well-being and economics and also illustrates the added value of faiths to these processes.

Mudge achieves this by developing the understanding of covenant, including as the central human qualities of interaction, by initially locating it in the Abrahamic story of covenant. Strategically this is significant because it connects the three Abrahamic traditions. 'Narratives with covenantal implications for the entire human race are interwoven throughout the complexly interrelated scriptures of Judaism, Christianity and Islam' as a covenantal coherence. The latter is provided by, for example, 'the story of the gift of children to Abraham and Sarah' in whom they rejoice and for whom they must be responsible if the covenantal gift is to continue. The three traditions developed different stories of this narrative which also gave 'a certain interfaith coherence to this material'.[121] For at this point, Abraham is neither Jewish, Christian or Muslim. The Abrahamic covenant provides a foundation for all three faiths, *even* if interpreted differently. The fulcrum passage is Genesis 12.1–3:

Now the Lord said to Abram, 'Go from your country and your kindred and your father's house to the land that I will show you. And I will make of you a great nation, and I will bless you and make your name great, so that you will be a blessing . . . and by you, all the families of the earth shall bless themselves.'

The task is to find 'a hermeneutic of all three versions of the Abrahamic tradition that not only takes account of such hazards and others like them, but also aims at resistance to totalization and the reconstruction of frameworks for abundant life'. The tool Mudge develops is *'parallel hermeneutics'*.[122] Its added value is that it complements other related or similar tools emerging in this enquiry. For example, the use of the correspondence method for developing a conversation between economics and other disciplines has already been noted, and will be used again in the later section on faithful economics. The procedure used in the Manchester Christian–Muslim conversation over finance, and the method used in the *Through the Eye of a Needle* project all sought to identify overlapping insights or agendas out of very different traditions, the continuing integrity of which was always fundamental for the collaborative way of working.

Parallel hermeneutics is a fine example of this process. For example, it is a way of proceeding which means 'that Jews, Christians, Muslims – together [importantly] with the "secular" partners in struggle whose solidarity we solicit – should all continue *to interpret their sources*, their historic traditions of shared life, with the fullest independence and integrity, but now begin to do so walking *next* to one another on a *common* path'. It is therefore not concerned to promote common belief systems, or a doctrinal merger. It rather involves pursuing a 'parallel relationship' with one another each asking questions in their own way within their traditions, acknowledging that others alongside are doing it in their ways too.[123] And, as Schweiker has observed, by living in an increasingly shared space, it is one in which 'cultures or civilizations (or religions) act back upon themselves with respect to information coming from other cultures and civilizations'.[124] We regularly interact, as we have already noted, with other fields. MacIntyre regarded such interaction as a critical part of the reformulation of tradition, including religions.[125] How we respond to such interactions affects both theory and practice, including in interfaith projects. 'In short, however different from each other we may be, we bear hermeneutical responsibilities toward one another: to hear accurately and to reply fairly. We are responsible also for the *practical* consequences of our interpretative work in the worlds we share. All these are reasons for using the word "parallel".'[126]

What is interesting in Mudge's work is that he rightly extends the process of a parallel hermeneutic from religious partners to secular ones – recognizing that their religious roots assist this process as does the presence of religious fragments (a concept also used by Forrester) in contemporary secular experience and discourse.[127] Capitalizing on these *resonances* acts as a bridging function between the different traditions and fields.

Such fragments or resonances include covenantal qualities of human interaction, which we have already identified in the explorations of social capital, faithful capital, the happiness hypothesis and the religions–ethics continuum. They connect the use of parallel hermeneutics with the Abrahamic faiths to these wider debates and arenas. They also further illustrate the added value of faith as an essential and distinctive dimension in the pursuit of human well-being. And, as promise-keeping, rightly noted by Arendt as the basis for all human institutions, it is 'the payoff in secular terms of what the scriptures understand in religious terms'. What she also recognizes is that keeping covenant promises needs to also be connected to 'patterns of promises behind our accepted social habits' – and here, she mentions the covenant God finally makes with Abraham. In other words, 'Human promise-keeping, for its very salvation, has to be taken up and included in the promises of blessing inherent in God's purposes for the human race.'[128]

This connection between human secular and religious fields is explored further through three examples of the covenantal qualities of human inter-actions, namely trust, solidarity and responsibility. All three have been greatly enriched by the work of a variety of secular disciplines like psy-chology, sociology and economics, in ways remarkably reminiscent of the happiness research. All also belong deep in faith traditions as well as being located in the public world, even though with different meanings. Each reveals different patterns of human promise-keeping.

As these three move from the religious and through the secular world Mudge traces their erosion through stages from this 'thick' to 'thin', and suggests how the contribution of faiths, using a parallel hermeneutic, and so in conversations with the secular, can contribute to their revival.[129] The first stage traces the original clear and formative influence of religious covenantal narratives. The second notes their 'deterioration in the social potency' as they move further from that religious connection and into the secular field.[130] This is evidenced by two complementary trends, on the one hand, a decline in the quality and extent of good social relations, and on the other hand, for Habermas, the increasing colonization of society and its lifeworld by an ever-intrusive state and market.[131] The third stage is an acknowledgement that they can be revived, not least by reconnecting the secular with the religious narratives. From the vantage point of this enquiry, it is a journey demonstrating the added value of faith through a methodological tool, and a journey paralleling Putnam's charting of the decline of social capital in *Bowling Alone* to attempts to rebuild it in *Better Together*. These developments through stages are then usefully illustrated through the three covenantal examples, trust, solidarity and responsibility. Again, they resonate strongly with the emerging findings of this Enquiry.

'Fostering conditions of trust'[132]

Strongly rooted in religious covenantal narratives and resourced for many centuries by dominant faith communities and traditions, trust began to be disconnected from a religious root in Europe in the eighteenth century with the rise of Deism and rationalism. In many ways, Adam Smith's life and thought embody that transition, and particularly through his successors. Rational choice theory, rooted in economics, therefore becomes a calculating method in social and political life. 'Social thinking becomes the calculus of how a relentless pursuit of private interests, even in highly regulated environments, will lead ourselves and our competitors to behave.'[133] The Great Disruption from 1960 to 2000 in the West, so carefully charted by sociologists and historians, described the grave erosion of social trust and its disturbing consequences in crime and family breakdowns. It is in the rebuilding of that trust, so central to the very possibility of cohesive associations and communities, which will rely on 'new associational relationships capable of moderating purely economic forces'.[134] To that end, an important contribution would be 'the redeployment of covenantal visions living in conscious parallelism with one another in the global public sphere' – essentially a 'mutual inquiry' between faiths, traditions and the secular, into 'what it is in our respective traditioned self-understandings that makes us trustworthy'. And that is the Abraham question – that promises will be kept because 'the Promise in which we believe entrusts that responsibility to us'.

The contribution of faith communities and traditions to that process of the parallel hermeneutics of promise-keeping thus becomes a basis of trust today by fostering the 'formation of trust-based frameworks or institutions'.[135]

'Acting in solidarity'[136]

Already identified as an important part of the common good, like trust, solidarity is another 'publicly accessible conceptual derivative of covenanting or promise-keeping'.[137] Strongly related to communal living, originally often religiously inspired, it reflects a unity of interests, sympathies or aspirations. Its secular journey through nineteenth-century revolutionary commitments and into the twentieth century's deep divisions between conflicting ideologies eroded its ability to hold together the varying ways in which people stood against the increasingly dominant powers of Hardt and Negri's 'empire' of global capitalism. Yet whatever their countervailing power of the *Multitude* has, it does not persuade on the solidarity count. Their hint of the importance and appropriateness of a religious narrative (the references to St Francis in the final pages) offers the opportunity to enrich and extend that potential for a solidarity in promoting the well-being of all through critical dialogue with covenantal communities. It would be seeking 'to articulate concretely God's prevenient will to solidarity with the human race'.[138] It would be reaching out in solidarity with the Other in need not as investment but as act of communion.

Taking responsibility[139]

Like solidarity, responsibility is a relatively recent addition to our language. The experience itself is again deeply rooted in the biblical narratives. For Brueggemann, 'Abraham and his family are a responding community that takes responsibility for the world'.[140] Religious and secular traditions still acknowledge that responsibility for the world, particularly to the poorest. The well-being and happiness literatures are full of the argument for that commitment to human fulfilment. The rediscovery of the faith contribution to human wholeness therefore now relocates it as an indispensable dimension in a post-scarcity anthropology. And that includes the rebuilding of responsibility (and, indeed, of trust and solidarity). Such a reconstruction is likely to acknowledge three senses of being responsible to some kind of promise, to oneself, to others and to the ultimate ends of community 'implied by one's philosophical or religious tradition'[141] (the faith dimension – again, this is paralleling so clearly the dimensions identified in the reconstruction of a moral anthropology, personalist ethics and common good, Layard's Big Seven and so on!).

In addition to its illumination of the religious contribution to well-being, the contribution of a parallel hermeneutic also confirms the strategic importance of methodology, including the value of pursuing what I have earlier referred to as overlapping consensuses. The hermeneutic recognizes that it is possible to get inside others' thoughts and traditions, to pursue the connections between them and so to begin to generate reciprocal understandings and practices. For Mudge, this understanding is a *thicker* version of Rawls' overlapping consensuses. The latter he judges to be 'a passive, rather blurry "overlap" of traditions judged "reasonable" if they support the philosopher's theory'. It is too much concerned with individuals and rationality. The pursuit of the necessary thicker overlapping consensuses are between 'independent tradition-based, interpretations of the public world',[142] involving religious and secular traditions. That requires the down-to-earth negotiations between different cultures and faiths to try to find ways of living and working together on certain matters, like environment and economic development, where some overlap is feasible. These collaborative methodologies, involving interfaith and secular, are means to that end.

Multifaith Contributions to Environment, Global Economy and Global Ethics: Journeying into Interfaith Collaborations

This survey reflects the limited sources available for describing strong examples of clear interfaith work on economic affairs. There is certainly evidence that corresponds to the earlier stages of parallel hermeneutics, of developing different faith accounts on environmental and global economy agendas as part of the same collaborative ventures. Some effort has also been deployed to begin to identify overlaps. The Manchester Muslim–Christian project on finance did both, including agreeing a final section of the report, 'What Christians and Muslims and Economists share, how they differ, and what they can do together'.[143] Similar attempts to identify convergences are made in the two sources principally used in this section. At certain points I have taken those reflections further in order to test out the possibilities and potential shape of such overlaps. The following material is divided into two sections, the first working from multifaith contributions on the environment, the second on the global economy. It ends with a brief addendum on the problem and possibilities of a global ethic to which religions contribute.

Faith in conversation: multifaith reflections on the environment

The environment figures increasingly prominently in economic affairs particularly as the pursuit of sustainable development. We have already noted the importance of pro environment economic growth. It is a primary objective in the UN's Millennium Development Goals, and informs the character of moral growth, as we will shortly see. The Brundtland Commission report, *Our Common Future* (1987) defined it as 'development that meets the needs of the present without compromising the ability of future generations to meet their own needs'. It is an agenda central to human well-being, and is thereby powerfully ethical. The Brundtland report ends thus: 'The issues we have raised in this report are inevitably of far-reaching importance to the quality of life on earth – indeed, to life itself. We have tried to show how human survival and well-being could depend on success in elevating sustainable development to a global ethic.'[144] What this brief section does is to fill out that ethical dimension into a religious one by promoting the statements on environment by the world faiths and reflecting on their convergences. It will concentrate on the faith narratives, recognizing that their practical implications are traced in Part 2.

The Alliance of Religions and Conservation (ARC) continued a process begun in 1986 which has resulted in the 11 major world faiths each producing a statement which 'summarized its relationship with and beliefs about the environment'.[145] These are usefully included in Palmer and Finlay's *Faith in Conservation*. The word limit was 2,000 and, most importantly, where possible, each was produced by major institutions within each faith. For example, Islam's was the work of the Muslim World League, Judaism's of the World Jewish Congress, and Christianity of the Franciscans and WCC. The next section on the global economy is the work of individuals from the faiths and so does not carry the same weight. The statements have also acted as 'a catalyst for a real participation of faiths in ecology', but they have in addition 'opened a window into the beliefs, into the very soul of each faith'. They each reflect 'something of the approach and attitude of the faith to both the notion of the written word and the notion of what is central to that faith'.[146] They constitute a real first stage in that parallel hermeneutic process.

To take that process further, in this case by identifying certain themes that recur in the statements, begins to illustrate their potential for generating thick overlapping consensuses – thick because they reflect the strong distinctive integrities of particular faith traditions and their collaborative potential as interfaith working. I have chosen three because of their prominence in the statements and because they engage directly with the emerging agendas of this enquiry.

- *Stewardship of the earth.* We have observed already how this concept links economics and ecumenical, and now environment, as sustainable development. All the faiths begin with the fundamental premise that the earth is God's. It is not a biocentric or anthropocentric view of nature. It is essentially and profoundly theocentric. For Muslims, 'To Him belong all things in the heavens and on earth. And enough is Allah as a Disposer of affairs' (004.171). Only then is man's role defined in relation to Allah 'Behold thy Lord said to the angels: "I will create a vice regent on earth"' (002.030), as steward of God.[147] There can be no absolute claim to private property. Equally, possessive individualism is rejected – the core of James's contemporary disease of affluenza, of the endless pursuit of material possessions and position, of having rather than being. The faiths invariably require us to 'enjoy without possessing, and mutually benefit each other without manipulation' (Buddhist).[148]
- *The interconnectedness of all in God.* For Muslims, the Oneness of Allah, or Tawheed, is the first and ultimate Islamic principle. It is 'the primordial testimony of the unity of all creation and the interlocking grid of the natural order of which humanity is intrinsically a part'.[149] It is the interconnectedness of all, cascading out from person to family, community, nation, world and universe, which recurs in the statements. And this connects strongly with the earlier discussion of the body of Christ metaphor. For Buddhists likewise, 'The health of the whole is inseparably linked with the health of the parts', and vice versa. The Vietnamese monk Venerable Thich Nhat Hanh sees this as 'the reality of the interconnectedness of human beings, society and Nature'.[150]
- All these beliefs are always inextricably linked to *faithful living* as predominantly promoting co-operation and reciprocity, trust and compassion. All flow from God's love and the embodying of that love in and for the human. The virtue of *compassion* is therefore dominant in these literatures, a reminder that Christian social ethics should not unduly focus on justice. Forrester usefully begins that relocating process of the primacy of love in relation to justice.[151] Again, justice is also acknowledged as a central influence on religious, personal and social behaviour. For Muslims, 'O ye who believe! stand out firmly for justice as witnesses to Allah even as against yourselves or your parents or your kin and whether it be (against) rich or poor: for Allah can best protect both' (004.135).[152]

Religious perspectives on the global economy: unfinished business

This work on a multifaith evaluation of the global economy is the result of a collaborative research project commissioned by the Boston Research Center for the 21st Century (BRC). Inspired by the Club of Rome's *Limits to Growth*, it represents a religiously based dialogic approach to global problems. It seeks to do this by examining 'the role of the world's religious traditions in finding ways to conquer human greed and transform the global economy, which too often leads to the victimization and exploitation of the vulnerable'.[153] The title of the resulting publication, *Subverting Greed*, reflects that priority, and indeed bias. It is not a careful analysis of the discipline of political economy, too easily assuming the global economy is a neo-liberal project. It therefore too easily coincides self-interest and greed. The detailed analysis of both values in relation to economic life is much better accomplished by Patrick Riordan's 'Common Good or Selfish Greed' in *Through the Eye of a Needle*. In addition, the individual contributions by scholars from seven religious traditions, African Igbo, Hindu, Buddhist, Confucianist, Jewish, Christian and Muslim, are not representative of their faiths, but nonetheless do provide valuable faith perspectives on the shared agenda of the global economy. For example, although it begins as an ethical exercise, it is rightly assumed that the dialogue will lead 'to explicitly religious conversation because religious ethics are rooted in religious beliefs'.[154] It therefore begins a journey of ethically based religious narratives running alongside each other, asking the same question, and so beginning a process of parallel hermeneutics. What I have done is to note possible convergences.

The strength of the research, as with the *Through the Eye of a Needle* process, lies in the individual perspectives. For example, the commentary on the Igbo people in Africa represents an unusual religious tradition in such collaborative ventures. As one of the primal religions of world history, it reflects on the influence of the conflict between matriarchy and patriarchy in the development of political economy. The value of the former, through the contribution of the household, and its consequent influence on market exchanges, provides an informative conversation partner with this enquiry's economy of regard. The Hindu contribution usefully warns us of the tendency of institutional religions, in this case, India's caste system, to accommodate to the powerful, and in turn to be exploited by them. The Buddhist tradition reminds us that, like most religious, Buddha 'does not endorse any one economic system', yet equally acknowledges that 'no economic system can be divorced from values'.[155] Some faiths, like Judaism and Islam, translate these basic regulatory principles into legal systems (reminiscent of the medieval Church's teaching and religious laws governing economic living, including as a just price and wage, and condemnation of interest).

Knitter, an editor of the project's publication, interestingly asks the question, after surveying these different faith perspectives, can they 'sing together', can they produce a common stance on the global economy, and particularly its damaging consequences?[156] He is clear that they cannot sing the same tune, not least because that would obliterate the distinctive significances of the different traditions. But they could sing in harmony together in the polyphonic form of relatively autonomous parts – essentially a varying yet harmonizing message. Sedgwick deploys that concept of polyphonic to describe the task of Christian social ethics in a post-modern and post-industrial society in *Through the Eye of a Needle*.[157] It is then also used to illustrate the hybrid type of Christian social ethics as an interaction of types. It could therefore provide a useful way of describing shared understandings which emerge out of the parallel hermeneutic process.

Reflecting on the different faith perspectives in *Subverting Greed*, I can detect five such recurring features which could be developed polyphonically, reflecting the multidimensionality of the traditions' perspectives. There are strong resonances with those emerging from the environment and faiths project.

- All is God's, so our stewardship is primarily accountable to God. For Hindus, the first mantra of the *Isa Upanishad* declared 'All that is there in the universe belongs to God, Enjoy it sacrificially, Greed not. After all whose wealth is it?'[158]

- The interdependence of life, locates the human contribution in a series of connectivities from local to universe. The Confucian perspective, so important in a China entering deeply into the global economy, understands the person as a moral agent in the self-unfolding process of cosmic order, stretching 'from the near to the far, from oneself to the family, kin, community, state, world and beyond'.[159] Tanner's economy of grace uses such religious understandings as offering a 'correspondence' opportunity for constructively engaging with globalization processes.

- The well-being of all is prioritized to inform critiques of the present global economy and to suggest alternative ways of operating it. For the Hindus, the Vedas teach that the whole creation, including the human, originates with God. The Vedic ideal of Vasudhaiva Kutumbakan seeing 'the whole of the human species as an extended family, insists on prioritizing the needs of the poor and the powerless'.[160] It therefore becomes a critique of greed, gross inequalities and the atrophy of community, and a proponent of the bias for inclusivity, and therefore for the poor and marginalized.

- All the faiths are seen as condemning the greed so associated with what James called selfish capitalism. This is reminiscent of the 1937 Oxford conference[161] of the ecumenical movement, and its four classic criticisms of laissez-faire capitalism – one of them condemns its production of acquisitiveness. This brings to mind R. H. Tawney's *The Acquisitive Society* in 1921 and James's *Affluenza* in 2007, which span the twentieth century, and which reject its growing absorption with the spirit of having rather than being. Yet most of the faiths recognize that greed cannot be 'subverted'. As desire, it forms an important function in human behaviour. The religious task is to balance it, so that it is less likely to develop into greed. Compassion and the pursuit of justice are seen as performing that vital equilibrium function.[162] James's study of the spread of affluenza among elites in increasingly prosperous advanced economies argues the same, but from a secular stance. The use of meditation and positive psychology perform a similar function in the happiness literatures.

- An important strategy for promoting well-being and attacking the obstacles to it, is the virtuous and vicious circles model. 'The ethical task, from a Hindus perspective, is to enable and enlarge the potential for good and to minimize the scope for evil and exploitation.'[163] This will again figure prominently in the faithful economics section. This illustrates how these specific but general imperatives emerging from the religious tradition can enter into constructive dialogue with many of the matters arising from the work on economic affairs and human well-being which figure so large in this enquiry. The detailed implications of these imperatives are found in the particular accounts in the report *Subverting Greed*. It is the potential for developing them through parallel hermeneutics which is more relevant to this particular section of my enquiry.

An addendum on global ethic or ethics

The earlier brief reflection on sustainable economic development, including its connection with pro environment or sustainable economic growth, leads into the debate over the potential and problems of a global ethic. It is a debate of increasing importance in an increasingly global context facing problems requiring global action, and therefore the theories, including ethical, to support it. Such theories and practice will and do involve a religious dimension. The role of interfaith social ethics would be highly relevant to that contribution. The most useful contribution to these rapidly emerging debates is provided by the report *Sustainable Development and Global Ethics* from Uppsala University, Sweden, the edited papers from an international Nordic conference. One of the key areas of concern is the discussion over a global ethic or global ethics. The latter, global ethics can refer to 'a theoretical and critical reflection on moral issues concerning development, environment and international relations'.[164] This is both a necessary and a desirable practice, given the recognition of the multidimensional reality of the human task today, and the centrality of ethics to it. Engagement with poverty reduction and the happiness hypothesis cannot be conducted adequately without it. The former, the pursuit of a global ethic, assumes sets of values and principles can and should be universally accepted – that they are common to all human beings. It suggests 'a universal consensus on some moral ideals – such as peace, welfare, sustainability and social justice – which is shared by all human beings irrespective of their social and cultural contexts'.[165] For the best expositor of such a global ethic, Nigel Dower, such a set of values and norms are 'global in *content*' or '*accepted*' across the world as a matter of fact.[166]

Hans Küng, the great Roman Catholic theologian, has worked assiduously to develop such a universalistic model of a global ethic. He has been particularly identified with encouraging the world religions to contribute to a universal ethic through inter-religious dialogue – including its engagement with the global economy. His *A Global Ethic for Global Politics and Economics* (1997) describes his procedures and judgements.

Grenholm, and many others, are deeply critical of such universalism because it fails to engage 'cultural diversity and ethical pluralism',[167] it seriously underestimates the feasibility of achieving such consensus from such incommensurables as the differing and competing faiths and ideologies in our world, and it often 'presupposes a view of humans that is too universalistic'. A much more accurate response by religious ethics is what Grenholm argues for as an 'ethical contextualism according to which our moral conceptions are formed within particular social and cultural contexts'.[168] This certainly accepts the necessity and possibility of developing global ethics as 'critical reflection upon global moral issues'.[169] Consensus, including as global ethic, is not essential, although critical dialogue across boundaries is achievable.

What this enquiry has identified both enlarges that latter understanding and maybe questions it. It develops it, for example, through the parallel hermeneutic, and other related processes, as both achieving constructive dialogue between different faiths and the secular, and attempting to deliver some overlapping consensus substantially thicker than Rawls's. What the critique of universalism does not necessarily account for is the growing recognition that certain agreed commitments, say to the common good on human welfare, are invariably required to be translated into and embodied in local cultures, including religions. In addition, the lists relating to the common characteristics of what it means to be human and moral are also increasingly relevant to transcontextual understandings contextually located and formulated. That understanding is reinforced from the happiness research, but also from wider sources, that the human condition contains shared features reinforced by genetic and neurophysiological research. The debate is no longer between nature and nurture. Any adequate account of the human *and* its social arrangements, has now to take account of both. The title of the contribution to the Uppsala project by Christien van den Anker, 'What is Global Ethics? Bridging the gap between Universal and Contextual Theories',[170] describes this concluding judgement – that interfaith social ethics is a worthwhile and feasible task and that may well include shared understandings between religions, and between religious and the secular. Both global ethic and ethics need to be part of the emerging agenda of religious ethics.

Of Typologies and Traditions
Refurbishing Tools of Christian Social Ethics

Like all disciplines, Christian social ethics has developed a repertoire of skills and tools, a variety of traditions, and strong arguments over most of that repertoire. Because it is concerned with practical outputs as well as theory, it has been likened to a craft. That centrality of practice in Christian social ethics has persisted through its long history, with interesting resonances between movements. For example, there is a connection between medieval theory and practice with regard to economic life, as the ban on usury and the commitment to a just price and wage, and today's liberation theology locating praxis (as theory informed practice) at the centre of its way of doing theology. Both are traditions, both are committed to personal and corporate living informed by Christian convictions, both therefore place great emphasis on economic affairs as integral to any adequate understanding of Christianity. The differences between them are also great, reflecting the contested nature of Christian social ethics. Liberation theology's distinctive methodology begins with praxis and only then reflects theologically on it. Medieval catholic social teaching, like most subsequent and previous traditions, began with understandings of God and then what this involved for the practice of living.

The concern for practice has been reinforced by contemporary Western Christian social ethics as the commitment to *practical* theology, and the associated recognition that it should be *performative*.[171] Both features have recurred throughout this enquiry. For example, they can be seen in the central role played by the accounts of the practical outputs of faith-based organizations (FBOs) from Africa and Asia in the South to Europe and the USA in the North. The concern to demonstrate their added value, and the critical conversations over the appropriateness and form of measurement, illustrate the importance of the performance, and its marking, of FBOs.

To discuss now tools of Christian social ethics also fits comfortably with the understanding of the discipline as *craft*. It is certainly part of the meaning of moral theology as developed by Dunstan in his thought-provoking study, *The Artifice of Ethics*.[172] His detailed understanding of law and ethics, particularly in the then emerging field of medical ethics, has continued to be an important contribution to the craft of Christian social ethics. It appears, for example through Cowley's use of Janssens' experience to inform her construction of a personalist anthropology and ethics. She deploys this as part of her engagement with the intricacies of global financial markets, probably one of the most complex problematics facing the social moralist today.

There are two tools which have occupied prominent places in the repertoire of the craft. The first, typologies, was particularly used and elaborated in Richard Niebuhr's classic text of Christian social ethics, *Christ and Culture*. The second, identifying and analysing traditions in Christian social thought and practice, was reinforced by Troeltsch's magisterial *The Social Teachings of the Christian Churches*.[173] Both tools have already figured large in this enquiry. For example, they appear as continuums in Parts 1 and 2, and as the recurring recognition of the significance of histories in Part 1 and as traditions in relation to faith communities throughout this work. As matters arising they therefore justify further attention, particularly in terms of using the research findings to develop them further.

Typologies to Continuums

The danger presented by too simple taxonomies particularly relates to their arbitrary restrictive function and effect. The use of ideal types or models in economics, for example in terms of economic man, illustrates such limitations. Yet as identifying patterns and interactions in human experience, and as hypotheses emerging for testing further in practice, they have provided valuable tools for understanding and predicting human behaviour. As a discipline, Christian social ethics, overlapping with secular disciplines, like sociology and economics, which regularly deploy them, has found a similar use for them. The *Through the Eye of a Needle* research process, as feeder into this project, identified such a typology as a useful way to describe the variety of different and competing understandings emerging from the work of its 11 contributors. It was agreed that such a mapping exercise would enable us 'to see what is going on in the broad, in terms of the clustering of traditions, in the differences and possible collaborations, and in what is new'.[174] It is therefore also a contribution to an emerging agenda in this research, of identifying points and ways of collaborating which also recognize the continuing and necessary value and integrity of different contributions. Usefully, *Through the Eye of a Needle* also recognized the strong and important connection between typologies for Christian social ethics and for ecclesiologies, for what it means to be Church. It is a link with which we are very familiar in this research, as the recurring relationship between faith traditions and faith communities. In an important editorial of an edition of *Crucible* dedicated to ecumenical social ethics, Stephen Platten illustrated how the Anglican tradition of moral theology forged significant connections with Anglican ecclesiology from the seventeenth century to the present. The latter includes the Anglican and Roman Catholic bilateral agreed ecumenical statement on morals, *Life in Christ: Morals, Communion and the Church.*[175] This evidence therefore locates these findings in the centre of ecumenical understandings and ethics, already identified above as essential feeder into interfaith ethics.

The above typology for Christian social ethics engaging political economy identified two clusters representing two ends of a continuum or spectrum: on the one hand, the overlapping consensus as practical co-operation of faiths in partnerships with government and other secular sectors and bodies; and on the other hand, the distinctively different from the mainstream understanding and practice, including as critique and alternative. Both have featured regularly in this research as appropriate tools for interpreting material. A third, hybrid type, representing the continuing interaction of the two ends of the spectrum, was described as 'more flowing, fluid and blurring', creatively referred to as 'polyphonic, yet nonetheless significantly cohesive as to warrant definition as additional type'.[176] That concept of polyphonic was used above by Knitter to describe the possible shared contributions of faiths to engaging the global economy.

Reflecting on the material in this research therefore has implications for the interpretation of this typology which justify a little elaboration, essentially as a testing out of the earlier research model, including its likely reformulation.

Concerning the *Through the Eye of a Needle* typology itself, the concept of a *continuum*, in addition to that of a typology, seems to be useful for describing the theory and practice of Christian social ethics addressing global change, and the classifications which flow from it. The continuum indicates shadings of *emphasis* from one end of the spectrum, as overlapping consensuses, to the other as distinctively different from mainstreams. The varying emphases represent *styles* or *modes* of operating often as complexes of emphases, as multidimensional. For example, faith is the principal determinant of the mode or style, including as FBO activity. The particular style or mode of the faith based operation determines its point of location on the continuum; if there is greater procedural mode to the operation, it can be better characterized as a formal type. The use of a continuum rather than typology is more useful in this regard, because it suggests a better flowing movement across a continuum rather than a series of fixed types. The concept of flows also corresponds to its regular use in the literatures to describe globalization in general, and the impact of new communication technologies in particular.[177] However, an overemphasis on flows to describe the continuum is unwise. Flows and blurring of edges are characteristic of the hybrid type interacting between overlapping consensus and distinctively different. It does not necessarily generate the same stability and continuity of structure necessary for strong communities and trust. As Baker's classic study of hybridity observes, commenting on Sandercock's powerful arguments for hybrid cities, 'A depressing feature of her case studies of practical experiments in multiracial and multi-ethnic coalitions is that they are almost all short lived.'[178]

Given these conceptual adjustments, the three types or modes of operating in *Through the Eye of a* Needle are confirmed by the research, particularly the value of the two ends of the continuum. The overlapping with the secular of FBOs' style and mode has been especially confirmed, whether as partnership or interdisciplinary working. The parallel hermeneutic methodology rightly included the secular as part of the interaction. It is an important acknowledgement that operating in a global context cannot be achieved by resurgent religion or capitalism alone. Both religion and secular are required for adequate engagement; an undue concentration on one or the other is likely to be detrimental to human well-being. The multi-dimensional nature of problems and responses demands that. For example, the propensity for religion to develop into unrighteousness, reminiscent of Reinhold Niebuhr's supposed quip that there is nothing more unrighteous than the righteous man, only confirms the profound inadequacy of a theocratic model.[179] The failure of the spiritual to take the material seriously, including as secular, has been confirmed by the research as mutually detrimental. Yet although these limitations of religion do suggest the corrective and counterbalancing value of partnerships, the role of religion in them is also profoundly beneficial. For example, the integrity of the overlapping consensuses style and mode of operating includes a distinctive dimension of the religious contribution both as values (spiritual capital) and also as informing the outcomes (as religious capital). The two Manchester projects, described earlier by Baker, and the Ugandan HIV/AIDS work of FBOs, illustrate that multidimensional character of the overlap. The distinctive contribution of religion to the virtue of toleration in liberal societies, argued for by Brown in his 'Christian Ethics and Economics after Liberalism', also reinforces the view that the distinctively difference of faith is *not* restricted to the distinctively different type but is also regular and valuable feature of overlapping consensuses.[180]

The distinctively different mode and style of operating constitutes, in the continuum, a more focused emphasis on and prioritizing of the unique features of religious traditions. It is more clearly associated, for example, with the added value of FBOs. Jubilee 2000's justification of debt forgiveness, and Muslim interest-free banking illustrate this type, including its propensity to act as both critique of and alternative to mainstream secular practices and theories, including in economic affairs. Its more frequent reference to and deployment of the transcendence dimension in developing its contributions to society also reflect its more distinctive character.

In the development of both the overlapping and distinctive types, an important contribution is made by the nature of the relationship to the secular (including as material world) as converging or diverging. It plays a similar role in Niebuhr's typology in *Christ and Culture*, with culture, as the other field to religion, informing the relationship that determines the religious type. In this enquiry too, culture, including as materiality, represents a way of doing things which is not specifically or necessarily religious in motivation or output. This secular or material reality assumes new significance with the emergence of modern urban industrial societies in terms, for example, of the growing prominence of technologies. These are more than technique or artefact or artifice. For Elaine Graham it means seeing '*techne* as spiritually and theologically worthwhile, and to affirm that a quintessential aspect of our very humanity is realized in and through our relationships with our tools and technologies'.[181] It is this aspect of a social construct which relates to but is also beyond the person which includes a critically important dimension of economics. Summarized as the positive or engineering dimension as against the normative or ethical dimension of economics, it includes the market mechanism and basic 'laws' of economics.[182] Although rightly castigated for its claims to be value-free and 'scientific', it does incorporate elements that cross particular cultures and time frames and which are of major importance for human living. Being a Muslim or Christian does not mean transcending the laws of supply and demand with impunity. To do so, results in major damage to both. Both overlapping and distinctively religious types are profoundly informed by culture as secular and material. Yet their interaction with it then constitutes on irreplaceable prerequisite for the process of transfiguration to be described later.

The evidence from the research for hybridity, the third mode or style of operating, is less substantial, although proponents of it could well interpret the evidence differently. Hybridity is a reminder of a way of working that interacts overlapping and distinctive to varying degrees of intensity. It therefore occupies a place which cannot principally be located under one or the other, and yet is clearly dependent on them, normally to a greater or lesser degree on one or the other. As a mixture of the two, Baker illustrates it with reference to Rushdie's 'our mongrel selves', and especially to Sandercock's *Mongrel City* (2003). Linked particularly to a post-colonial, post-modern culture, it reflects the tendency to greater fluidity, to more networking forms, to liquid rather than more structured organizational forms.[183] It is a form of operating with much blurring of the edges and of interactions between particular traditions and understandings, epitomized in John Reader's imaginative study *Blurred Encounters: A Reasoned Practice of Faith* (2005).[184] Because it is so linked to post-contexts it may lack the strength or solidity to become a more permanent type. The classic liberal All Saints Church in Pasadena, California, has experienced growth in recent years, and epitomizes the commitment to hybridity as the ambiguities of life styles and faith. Yet although successful, it pales into significance compared to the size of impact of the Saddleback mega Church. Comparing the two, Putnam concludes 'certainty has a wider appeal than ambiguity'.[185] Yet despite lacking that wider appeal and organizational strength, hybridity is a necessary reminder and embodiment, typologically, that many modes and styles of operating will not be necessarily predominantly overlapping or distinctively different. In that crucial sense, like the two ends of the continuum, it possesses a distinctive and valued character. In some ways, it connects with the debate which has recurred through the enquiry over Hollenbach's question of how to hold together, if it is possible, commitments to the universal value of basic human dignity and the essential contribution of more local differences. For example, the happiness hypothesis has utilized new evidence from the medical sciences, particularly genetics and neurophysiology, to confirm the significance of the shared characteristics of what it means to be human. Yet it also recognized the space left for the particular and culture-constrained contributions of human endeavours to well-being. What is generated by that interaction, and it is invariably an interaction between inherited and environmentally produced, could be described as a hybridity. The same applies to the contest, in the search for global ethic or ethics, between universalist and contextualist. It is suggesting that there is a distinct and necessary integrity in the interaction itself. And that also thereby confirms the essential importance of the two ends of the continuum.

The Religion and Capitalism Debate: A Tradition in British Christian Social Ethics

It was this debate which first inspired me to embark on this research project. Given the greatly changing context, particularly evident from the 1990s, Ronald Preston's seminal contribution to the relationship between religion and economics needed to be taken further forward. The third stage of the debate, his *Religion and the Persistence of Capitalism* (1979),[186] no longer captured the rapidly changing secular and religious situations. Globalization was transforming late twentieth-century economic systems and processes, and western Christianity, essentially Preston's setpoint for interpreting religion, was increasingly marginalized by the resurgent religion of the South. This research began as a response to that predicament. The intention was to produce the next, fourth, stage of the debate as religion and the transcendence of capitalism. What has emerged is rather different from that narrowly focused conception. As a much more broadly based enquiry into the contribution of faith to global change it has ventured into terrains sometimes unfamiliar to Preston, indeed, to which he would not always have been sympathetic. He would certainly have raised a disapproving eyebrow over developing distinctively faith-based economic outputs. Yet this wider programme has now returned to that original debate, and will end with a reflection on religion and the transfiguring of capitalism. Thus has the world gone full circle!

The journey in terms of that debate in British Christian social ethics is therefore worth recounting a little, but now particularly in the light of the material emerging from the enquiry. This should add new perspectives through a conversation with the debates' chief proponents.

The debate to date covers Hobsbawm's 'short twentieth century', from just after the end of the First World War to the collapse of communism in 1990.[187] Two of its stages relate to the Great Disruption of post-1945, with its major decline of social capital and the freezing of happiness in the west. Because the debate begins outside Britain, with the work of Max Weber, it is best to begin there. It was his initial treatise, *The Protestant Ethic and the Spirit of Capitalism*, which provoked the British response. Beginning life as a series of articles in 1904–6, it appeared in book form in 1930, translated by Talcott Parsons, and with a foreword by R. H. Tawney. The splendidly informative footnotes cover a third of the book! To briefly summarize this, and the first two stages of the debate, the works of Tawney and Demant, I will use Preston's (the third stage) comments on them as my entry point, developing them through dialogue with material from my enquiry.[188]

For Preston, Weber's thesis assumed some kind of connection between capitalism and Protestantism (particularly as Calvinism). That proposed linkage continues to be highly contested, yet never erased, not least because of its repeated reappearance – for example, in Pentecostalism in Latin America today. That wider context was also recognized by Weber, and his studies of religion in India and China (remarkably prescient, given the current newly arrived dominance of emerging economies led by China and India!).[189] This gave added force to his focus on an aspect of Calvinism that appeared to be particularly congruent with the emergence of the capitalist spirit (especially the disciplined, acquisitive and ascetic behaviour as a way of cementing one's calling and election). In other words, he identified religion as an independent variable or source of insight which did not merely, in Marxist terms, reflect the material context, and indeed could challenge it. 'Subsequently, however, those elements in the religious insight which are particularly relevant to believers in their particular situation are picked out and stressed by a process of what he called "elective affinity".'[190] Later industrial capitalism particularly reinforced these elements.

What is especially interesting in this interpretation is the recognition of religion as an independent variable, emerging from what I have referred to as a relatively autonomous field of influence and power. The focus on Puritanism, and especially as Calvinism, similarly resonates with my research, for example in the growing prominence of resurgent religion, and how this can link with the generating of ways of living compatible with economic growth.

The British debate begins as a constructive, critical response to this Weber hypothesis. It is in three stages, which almost suggest a dialectical progression, the final Preston synthesis stage emerging out of the interaction of the first two, Tawney and Demant.

The first stage, R. H. Tawney's *Religion and the Rise of Capitalism*, is the most memorable and continues to have an impact on research (not least because it is still in print; most publications in Christian social ethics, including mine, are rapidly out of print!). Tawney carefully tested Weber's thesis in relation to British Puritanism in the sixteenth and seventeenth centuries – what became known, given the path-finding nature of his research, as Tawney's century. For Guscott, given Weber's thesis that the Calvinist attitude to predestination 'revolutionised protestant trade', Tawney's work rather suggested that it 'merely confirmed existing business values'.[191] What Guscott does is to illuminate that thesis further in a new study of Humphrey Chetham, Puritan merchant, capitalist and philanthropist in early seventeenth-century Manchester. He epitomizes 'the myriad of ties between the godly and the mainstream . . . Religion was a complex product of trade networks, kinship, friendship and personal belief.'[192] It is the latter which Weber argues, was of particular significance. What is interesting is what that belief and combination produced – essentially an interaction of distinctively religious and overlapping consensus. Chetham's fortune, when he died in 1653, aged 72, was valued at the massive sum of £13,897 1s. 2d. His will ensured the setting up of a school for 40 poor boys (now Chetham's School of Music), and a library, the first major public library outside Oxford and Cambridge.[193] The Feoffees, or trustees, were carefully selected to represent parliamentarian and ex-Royalist interests, and quickly collected an astonishing jewel with books from all over Europe and beyond, including Catholic as well as Protestant interests. It was here that Marx and Engels met and studied, providing source material for Engels *The Condition of the Working Class in England* (1845) and their *Communist Manifesto* (1848). And that links into the recognition of the great influence of fields of power in shaping individual and communal lives.

To return to Tawney's work more directly. Preston interpreted Tawney's major concern to be the seismic change in Christian social thought. In the sixteenth and seventeenth centuries he detected a transformation from a corporative to an individualist understanding, essentially reflecting the creeping secularization of life. Human affairs became self-contained, no longer part of a hierarchy of values with religion constituting the apex. This had three consequences. First, Christianity no longer provided the basis of civilization. Christendom was increasingly replaced by a secular society. Jenkins's study of resurgent religion today is intriguingly titled *The Next Christendom: The Coming of Global Christianity*. Second, Christianity also developed a sharp antithesis between personal and corporate morality, which persists to this day, despite all the efforts of churches and Christian social ethics. Cowley's work on ethics and the world of finance today tries to bridge that gap, as do my earlier reflections on the interaction between personalist ethics and the common good. Third, the churches abandoned the confirmation of any particular social ethic or economic system, including as an endorsement of membership. Duchrow's efforts today to do so, with regard to a confessional condemnation of global capitalism, represent a whistling in the wind.[194]

In many ways, these three consequences of a marginalizing of religion from public life inspired Tawney to promote a strong Christian critique of capitalism and the search for alternatives, including religion's contribution to them. For him, 'Compromise is as impossible between the Church of Christ and the idolatry of wealth, which is the practical religion of capitalist societies, as it was between the Church and the State idolatry of the

Roman Empire.'[195] It is almost exactly a religious version of James's secular critique of selfish capitalism in his recent study *Affluenza*.

Yet, as my doctoral research into Tawney's papers in the LSE also revealed, his ethics were a complex mixture of radical and pragmatist, almost like Humphrey Chetham's progressive Puritanism. Indeed, MacRae described Tawney as a 'medieval schoolman', struggling to develop a new and more relevant social ethic for corporate and personal living.[196] It was almost as though, at times, he was trying to rectify his great judgement against the eighteenth-century Church that 'The social teaching of the Church had ceased to count, because the Church itself had ceased to count.'[197] That struggle in Tawney between change and stability, present in Chetham as epitome of Weber's progressive Calvinist capitalist, is captured in Tawney's understanding of religion as inspiring change for the better through the security of faith. In his *Commonplace Book* entry for 3 November 1912, he writes: 'This is the supreme *paradox* of religion that it sets men changing the world for the better who believe that from eternity to eternity all is well, that it sets in the forefront of revolutions those who believe that one great revolution has freed men once and for ever . . .'[198] It is as though the paradox of prosperity of the happiness hypothesis can be most appropriately engaged by the supreme 'paradox of religion'. The problem of the relationship between religion and capitalism may well include the seeds of its solution, as my transfiguring of capitalism but here also in Tawney's first stage of the debate.

V. A. Demant's *Religion and the Decline of Capitalism* appeared in 1952, in the post-war Britain of the Labour landslide victory in the 1945 general election, with its promise of radical socialist reform in a context of the triumphal global surge of communism. Capitalism, to all intents and purposes, looked to be an increasingly marginalized cause. Against that backcloth, Preston interprets Demant's work as a further reflection on Tawney's emphasis on the growing secularization and autonomy of economic life in Britain. Working in a more broadly cultural way, Demant acknowledged that the economic individualism of the market economy did make some contribution to a personalism congruent with the Christian view of the human. Yet the market more disturbingly eroded 'the non-economic foundation of society', the 'complex net of non-contractual moral, legal and religious bonds which capitalism both assumed and at the same time undermined'.[199] It is an impressive argument, from a man, Demant, who I met at the end of his long illustrious academic life. Yet Preston, like his friend the economist Munby, was deeply critical of Demant's history and work, on three counts. First, Demant assumes, and prefers, a Christendom framework, epitomized in the work of his friend,

T. S. Eliot's *The Idea of a Christian Society* (1939). Second, his weak doctrine of the state, a corporate reality so increasingly significant as the twentieth century evolved, owed more to his medieval longing than a mastery of contemporary history. Linked to that deep deficiency, third, he never understood the workings of the modern economic system and economics. Preston, as an economist, regarded his strong support for the Major Douglas Social Credit scheme as a disaster.[200]

Yet in the light of my enquiry, Preston's judgements need to be revisited. The significance of the religious contributions to global change in both South and North, cannot any longer be satisfactorily addressed simply from within a 'secular society' thesis as propounded by Preston's colleague, Munby.[201] The development of faith-based organizations, including their distinctive, added value character, now significantly challenges Preston's deep earlier hostility to Demant's 'Christendom' approach, without in any way subscribing to a reinvented Christendom. An increasingly plural context makes that both empirically impossible to achieve as well as equally undesirable given the continuums of faith and secular emerging in this enquiry. There are therefore three aspects of Demant's work which are now very relevant to the outcomes of this research. First, the commitment to those values and networks supportive of strong personal and social relationships is an essential part of any adequate market economy but the damage the latter does to them has to be actively resisted and counterbalanced. Second, and closely connected to the first, Demant was critical of an overemphasis on the state as dominant deliverer of welfare. Like Bishop Hunter of Sheffield, pioneer supporter of post-war industrial mission, he rather advocated a greater commitment to voluntary bodies, to what we would now call civil society.[202] In these, the churches played a central role. Interestingly, in 2007, the present Labour government has been encouraging faith-based organizations to make bigger contributions to welfare delivery. The report of the NWRDA, *Faith in England's Northwest: The contribution made by faith communities to civil society in the region* (2003) has already identified some of the existing work of FBOs in society. Third, Demant's leadership role in the Christendom group from the 1920s until the early post-war period complemented his practical commitment to religiously based contributions to society with the theoretical search for what it described as a distinctively Christian sociology. That search continues to this day. For example, Preston regarded Milbank's *Theology and Social Theory* (1990) as the best exposition of the Christendom stance he had come across. The radical orthodoxy 'group' epitomizes a particularly 'thick' version of the distinctively Christian type I have described. Again, the discoveries of the second stage of the debate, when viewed through the work of Demant, contains features of renewed interest to the contemporary context. Preston would not have been amused!

The third stage is, in fact, Preston's own work, *Religion and the Persistence of Capitalism* (1979). Rather than dying, as Demant assumed and desired, the blessed animal capitalism kept recovering, and indeed flourishing. The post-war period represented its greatest achievement in economic growth, including per capita. The post-scarcity thesis supports that judgement. Yet Preston's acknowledgement of its strengths was clearly balanced by a clear recognition of its limitations. His later book, *Religion and the Ambiguities of Capitalism* (1991),[203] epitomizes that carefully judged interpretation. Trained in economics at the LSE, he was one of the very few theologians really familiar with that discipline. He therefore had a very economically sound understanding of the market mechanism and its essential role in the delivery of human welfare in heavily populated modern societies. He acknowledged, too, the great superiority of the market economy over the only feasible alternative, the command, or state run, economy. Its collapse in 1989 confirmed that judgement. His chapter on 'Understanding Economics and its Limits', in *Religion and the Ambiguities of Capitalism* remains the best exposition by a theologian of market economics. It is a pity most have not read it, or more likely, not understood it. The multifaith contributors to *Subverting Greed*, noted above, would particularly benefit from a copy. Yet Preston was equally aware of the market economy's limitations, particularly its consequences for inequality. These should be addressed by government, and particularly a democratic socialist one. What he would not easily understand, and certainly not sympathize with, is the growing significance of FBOs, and the renewed interest in the distinctively religious function in society as both critique of and alternative too, mainstream economies and economics. His rejection of the arguments against usury in the medieval Church illustrate this conviction. In this his views coincide with the economist, Ian Steedman's judgement in the Manchester Christian–Muslim *Statement on Finance*, and in *Through the Eye of a Needle*.[204] I am unsure, too, whether he would appreciate the limitations as well as the strengths of ambiguity and paradox. The increasing influence of resurgent religion, in contrast, would have deeply disturbed him, particularly its views on sexuality and the Scriptures. Moving *directly* from Scriptures, doctrine or natural law to detailed judgements on complex contemporary problems, he regarded as methodologically unsound and its judgements equally suspect.[205]

The fourth stage of the debate is this enquiry. The greatly changing context at the beginning of this new century represents both secular and religious change. Reflecting on this allows new insights to engage with the first three stages of the British debate on the relationship between religion and capitalism, revealing its strengths and limitations. Learning from them should allow a more adequate reformulation of the religious contribution in its engagement with capitalism. I describe that as religion and the transfiguration of capitalism.

12

Faithful Economics

From Moral Economy to Economy of Grace, and Putting them to Work

Two areas of interacting interest particularly drove this enquiry, Christian social ethics and political economy. The journey of the project greatly broadened that original focus into accounts of resurgent religion and faith-based contributions to globally dispersed societies, and into a complex of debates around happiness and well-being. Any exploration of matters arising from that research should revisit that interaction of Christianity and political economy, described as Christian political economy in my earlier study, *Marginalization*. What emerges is a new way of formulating that religious contribution to global change, which I will describe as faithful economics. This is both compatible with the use of faithful capital in Part 1, and the recurring reference to faith communities and faith traditions. It is particularly conceptually suited to the development of interfaith-based social ethics.

Although these reflections on faithful economics have connections with my use of Christian political economy in *Marginalization*, and its four components (ethical economics, measurement systems, distinctively religious economics, and heteroclitical or heretical traditions),[206] I worked from new material, using new sources, including some specifically chosen for this section. Here I refer to Henderson and Pisciotta's *Faithful Economics: The Moral Worlds of a Neutral Science* and Tanner's *Economy of Grace*.[207] Although randomly selected, like many of the resources used earlier, I have once again been struck by the remarkable overlaps between them, along with their new perspectives.

The choice of the concept, faithful economics, was confirmed by my very late introduction to the book *Faithful Economics*. It did, in fact, emerge from the first part of the enquiry, in the reflections on the religious field and social capital. Because of the recurring significance of continuums for my work, and particularly as ethics to religion, and moral to theological anthropologies, I found that the continuum from ethical to theological economics can be usefully described as faithful economics. The continuum also arises from the use of the concept of fields of influence and power to describe the autonomy of say capitalist economies and religion in Part 1, always also a relative autonomy because of their necessary and inevitable interactions. That interrelationship between economy and religion can be appropriately embodied in the concept of ethical economics, operating essentially as a bridge between them. It identifies important correspondences to be vigorously exploited as such.

The discussion of faithful economics will therefore begin with a brief reflection on ethical economics, including as moral growth, ethical globalization, and an economy of regard, all identified earlier. It constitutes a dimension in economics reinforced by the different faith perspectives on the global economy, and plays an integral part in the happiness and well-being agendas. The other end of the spectrum of faithful economics concentrates on a theological economy. The problem with my earlier recognition in *Marginalization* of the distinctively Christian economics as Jubilee 2000, and in this enquiry, is that it conveys a piecemeal and restricted approach to a theological economics. I have therefore rather concentrated on developing this type much further, using Tanner's economy of grace as example. Normally, when theologians attempt such a project they routinely produce an account totally at variance with contemporary economics and economies. Meeks's *God the Cooperator*, Peters's *In Search of the Good Life*, and Moe-Lobeda's *Healing a Broken World*, fall into this trap.[208] What is particularly significant in Tanner's economy of grace is that it contains a number of key features which avoid these dangers and feed centrally into this enquiry. For example, she develops a totally theological account of economics which is quite at variance with secular economics. Yet it is constructed as a field of influence which also therefore interacts with the existing field of the capitalist economy. Where such correspondence between the two fields occurs, for example as the interdependence of the global economy and globalization processes, these can be exploited to promote the transformation of the market economy. The economy of grace therefore provides a theological basis for a critique of and developing alternatives to the existing mainstream economic system. I will then use these interconnections in the final section as the basis for sketching policy areas emerging from ethical and theological economics, but supplemented by material drawn from the well-being literatures. It is an intentional illustration and demonstration of the overlapping consensus principle and type and the formative contribution to it of the very distinctively religious economy of grace, with the latter located also in relation to the distinctively religious type. It is a further example of the potential added value of faith but also of the whole complex of faithful economics, including the role of ethical economics. It also thereby illustrates the multi-dimensional character of the faith contribution itself, and its essential role in well-being, including as a more morally and theologically adequate political economy for the early twenty-first century.

Ethical Economics and Moral Economies

At the heart of modern mainstream neoclassical economics is a view of human behaviour originally shaped by the particular context of a mid to late nineteenth-century Europe rapidly undergoing an urban-industrial revolution. It strongly emphasized the human as isolated individual, rationally motivated to pursue and maximize its self-interest in a capitalist free market. Through a variety of mechanisms and philosophical understandings, particularly utilitarianism, it would also thereby work for the benefit of society as a whole.

A changing context has begun to challenge that foundational understanding. The epic post-1945 era of the beginnings of a serious transition from scarcity and absolute poverty into the problems of the paradox of prosperity, has contributed to a growing awareness that the original pursuit of economic well-being now needs to be broadened or extended. The nature and significance of the human-in-relationships (as social capital and as what we now call the happiness hypothesis) is a matter of profound economic concern in terms of more accurate understandings of human behaviour in economic pursuits. That concern is reinforced by the foreseeable (never mind unforeseeable) damaging consequences of economic actions and understandings for the contemporary more adequate interpretation of the human.

Much of this debate over the nature of economics has been expressed as an argument over the legitimacy of and comparative weight to be given to the positive and normative dimensions of economics. Sen usefully describes them as engineering and ethical economics.[209] It is a long-standing debate, certainly occurring among the early Christian political economists at the beginning of the emergence of the modern discipline of political economy.[210] The positive or engineering dimension, as we will see, refers to the more technical, scientific, hard side of the discipline. The ethical I could define, adapting Waterman's description of Christian political economy, as 'a label for the intellectual enterprise of combining neo-classical political economy with normative social theory'.[211] To develop these understandings further, I will explore, briefly, three issues: first, revisiting the positive–normative debate, using new material published since my *Marginalization*; second, to note the use of such concepts as moral economy, and the implications of measuring it; third, connecting the debate over ethical economics into interfaith ethics.

The positive–normative debate in economics

An editor of *Faithful Economics* has not inaccurately described modern economics as essentially 'functional atheism', although economists have acknowledged 'the place of values and ethics in economic discourse' throughout the twentieth century, from Schumpeter to Arrow.[212] Such a concern, however, was increasingly marginalized by a 'dominant tradition',[213] epitomized by the Chicago school, which was predominantly secularized in terms of displacing the normative from any serious influence. Its focus was the neoclassical paradigm of rational choice, with its assumption of rational behaviour as primary motivator for economic action, particularly as the maximizing of self-interest. It represents a very focused, narrow, scientific value-free interpretation of economics. It emphasizes the factual and predictive properties of the discipline, divorced from the normative, and therefore claiming to be as scientific as the physical sciences. For Hayek, it was no more sensible to discuss the morality of the market than to discuss the morality of climate.[214] Economics is 'fundamentally a *positive* social science',[215] and so for Milton Friedman, is therefore 'independent of every value proposition or of every ethical position. Its utility is not to describe "what ought to be the case" but "what is the case" . . . In short, positive economics is, or can be, an "objective" science in precisely the same way as any of the physical sciences.'[216] That is a judgement rife in economics, from Ricardo in the earlier nineteenth century, through Walras at the end of it, to Robbins in the middle of the twentieth century to Friedman towards its end. It dominates economic textbooks and economic policy. Ethical or normative economics is ostensibly not part of the economic discipline. Robbins in Britain illustrates this well, and is interestingly connected to various parts of this enquiry. For example, he taught Preston at the LSE, and the lecture series named after him was recently used by Layard the economist to launch his new science of happiness. Robbins's definition of economics remains central to the discipline: 'The science which studies human behaviour as a relationship between ends and scarce means which have alternative uses.' This interpretation clearly informs his divorcing such positive economics from the normative: 'Unfortunately it does not seem logically possible to associate the two studies in any form but mere juxtaposition. Economics deals with ascertainable facts, ethics with values and obligations. The two *fields* of enquiry are not on the same plane of discourse.'[217] Friedman takes that further. For him, the normative is quite dependent on the positive. For example, policy conclusions 'by their very nature, rest on prediction based on positive economics'. The positive is therefore independent of the normative, but the latter is dependent on the positive. 'Any policy conclusions necessarily rest on a prediction about the consequences of doing one thing rather than another, a prediction that must be based – implicitly or explicitly – on positive economics.'[218] The normative is downgraded as subjective in contrast to the hard objective facts of the positive. Yet we now know from the happiness studies that its categorization as subjective well-being can no longer be underestimated in importance because the work of say Layard in economics and Haidt in psychology confirms the empirical character of the happiness research with reference to neurophysiology and robust survey work. These findings are increasingly eroding the polarizing of hard and soft economics as positive and normative. They confirm the importance for economics of the long tradition of ethical economics, in clear interactive relationship with positive economics. It is a tradition stretching from the beginning of modern economics, in the work of Adam Smith, through Malthus, J. S. Mill, Marshall and Keynes to Sen and others today. It is a judgement that human behaviour in economics centrally and rightly includes self-interest, yet always also interacting with more socially informed experiences and understandings of the human. It concludes that the dichotomy between self-interested individual and society is false, that 'Most human action . . . is undertaken somewhere between complete isolation and interaction with everyone else . . . within groups such as family, friends, neighbors, fraternal organizations, or members of the local church, synagogue, or mosque.'[219] It suggests that economics would therefore benefit from 'a more robust inclusion of the concept of social capital in research'.[220]

Adam Smith also certainly understood the importance of individual self-interest in economic behaviour. We do expect our dinner from the butcher's 'self-love' not 'benevolence'. Yet he was equally clear that human behaviour was also informed by rules of conduct: 'Those general rules of conduct, when they have been fixed in our mind by habitual reflection, are of great use in correcting misrepresentation of self-love concerning what is fit and proper to be done in our particular situation.'[221] That recognition of behaviour as broader than, though inclusive of self-interest, also figures prominently in Sen's work today:

The wide use of the extremely narrow assumption of self-interested behaviour . . . has seriously limited the scope of predictive economics . . . the jettisoning of all motivations and valuations other than the extremely narrow one of self-interest is hard to justify on grounds of predictive usefulness, and it also seems to have rather dubious empirical support. To stick to that narrow path does not seem a very good way of going about our business.[222]

These arguments do not, of course, reject the importance and legitimate role of self-interest in human behaviour and in Christian social ethics. For Patrick Riordan (and, interestingly another Jesuit, a generation earlier, Gerard Hughes) self-interest constitutes an important and legitimate Christian value, and even if misused can still be located usefully in the wider framework of the market mechanism's co-ordination function for the human good.[223] This in no way detracts from Offer's judgement that this supposedly rational choice of individuals is frequently myopic, for example as the pursuit of obesity, alcoholism and drug addiction.[224]

All these evidences of a reformulation of understandings of economic behaviour are confirmed by recent research from within the discipline. For example, the 2002 Nobel Prize in Economic Science was shared by Kahneman and Smith, who 'questioned the extreme view of rational behaviour as the basis for economic decision-making'.[225] That recognition is increasingly complemented and supplemented by richer empirically accurate views of human behaviour, including in economic affairs, and including a strong ethical dimension. The behaviour of economists them-selves confirms this judgement, 'If actual behaviour is not influenced by moral-ethical considerations, then economists expend an inordinate amount of effort studying questions dealing with issues such as equity, income distribution, discrimination and access to health care'. Economics is not value-free and it is now 'impossible to be a good economist without knowing something about ethical values' (Machlup).[226]

Of course, this recognition of the ethical dimension of economics in no way overrides the importance of positive economics, as the economist Ian Steedman and the theologian Ronald Preston have reminded us. The con-tribution of self-interest and market mechanism are central to the delivery of human well-being in densely populated and increasingly complex societies. The task is not to override positive economics by asserting the dominance of the ethical, in the way Long's radical orthodoxy would achieve through theology.[227] The task is rather to *reassert* the ethical part of the economics continuum, from positive to normative. A function of the overlap of that continuum with the one moving from ethical to theological economics is to support and enhance that reassertion of the importance of ethical economics to the economic task.

On moral economies

The significance of ethical economics is also reflected in the references to that normative dimension informing the shape of the economic system itself. It is what *Through the Eye of a Needle* referred to as 'the contours of an ethical political economy for the twenty-first century'.[228] Two examples in the enquiry illustrate this trend. First, Robinson's discussion of *'ethical globalization'* – of bending global processes to promote the well-being of all – involves ensuring free trade is not exploited to the greater advantage of the rich economies, particularly in agriculture, but is rather supported by such mechanisms as the Special and Differential Treatment of the WTO to protect the poorest nations.[229] Second, that ethical globalization can then be located in relation to what Stiglitz, Nobel prizewinner in economics, has called *moral growth*:

> In short, the debate should not be centred on whether one is in favour of growth or against it. The question should be, are there policies that can promote what might be called moral growth – growth that is sustainable, that increases living standards not just today but for future generations as well, and that leads to a more tolerant open society? Also what can be done to ensure that the benefits of growth are shared equitably, creating a society with more social justice and solidarity than one with deep rifts and cleavages of the kind that became so apparent in New Orleans in the aftermath of Hurricane Katrina.[230]

It is an understanding of an ethical economic system which now also addresses the issues of sustainable development and the deep inequalities which so distort human well-being and happiness.

Yet alongside that task is the complementary role of developing ways of measuring that ethical contribution as test of moral seriousness and rebuttal of the 'subjective' charge by positive economics. Himmelfarb's earlier reflection on Victorian values noted how social policies addressing the poverty question linked the delivery of material *and* moral well-being.[231] Ways of assessing the moral impact of policies should therefore have a high priority in the promotion of happiness. An 'economic impact assessment' by the government's NWRDA of faiths' contributions to society now needs to be complemented by a moral impact assessment of government's contributions to society.[232] That measurement of added moral as well as religious value with reference to FBOs, discussed in Part 2 above, is confirmed from the economic literature, for example, by Nelson's advocacy of the 'econometric study of the impact of Christian practices – even differing theologies – on societal outcomes'.[233] Extending that mechanism to moral assessments of secular policy-making is of some importance.

That broader evaluative commitment is embedded in early modern economic history. For example, Adam Smith asserted in his *Enquiry into the Wealth of Nations* that

> No society can surely be flourishing and happy, of which the far greater part of members are poor and miserable. It is but equity, besides, that they who feed, cloath and lodge the whole body of the people, should have such a share of the produce of their own labour as to be themselves tolerably well fed, clothed and lodged.[234]

The moral economy seeks to promote that judgement in a globalized context, appropriately assessed and measured.

Faith justifications of ethical economics

In the interfaith study of the global economy two contributions confirm and illustrate the value of ethical economics. The first, from the African Igbo people, emphasizes the relational understanding of economic behaviour and systems (the ideology of *umunne*).[235] In particular, it does this from a matriarchal experience. As a model, it therefore underlines the model of reciprocity and sharing in economic exchange, resonating with the economy of regard. Equally it links to the recent feminist influence on economics, including Christian – for example, in the development of 'economic man' into the 'Imperfectly Rational Somewhat Economical Person'.[236]

The second, from the Buddhist tradition, refuses to separate economics from ethical and spiritual dimensions. Economic laws which do not incorporate them are not acceptable. Distribution always has a spiritual-moral character, and so cannot be left to the market mechanism. Compassion (*dana*) particularly for the needy is a fundamental priority. No economic system can therefore be value-free. Every production and consumption system encourages certain values and discourages others. For Thailand's scholar monk Phra Payutto,

It may be asked how it is possible for economics to be free of values when, in fact, it is rooted in the human mind. The economic process begins with want, continues with choice, and ends with satisfaction, all of which are functions of the mind. Abstract values are thus the beginning, the middle and the end of economics, and so it is impossible for economics to be value-free.[237]

The argument for ethical economics has merged naturally into the contribution of religious economies.

Concluding the Distinctively Religious Pursuit: An Economy of Grace

Two sources come firmly together as problem and solution: the problem is presented by the marginalization or trivialization of religious belief in Western academies in general and by economics in particular; its solution is suggested by the construction of an intellectually proficient theological economy. The problem was identified and debated by the 2002 Conference on Christianity and Economics at Baylor University in the USA. It sought to discover ways to relate Christian beliefs to the academic work of economists in what it judged to be a more profitable environment, not least given the resurgence of religion globally. For Marsden 'There are good prospects that the twenty-first century academia will be more open to perspectives that go beyond the Enlightenment on questions of religious faith.'[238] What he calls 'Faith-Informed Scholarship' identified three possible roles for the Christian economist – as mainstream scholar, policy advocate and philosopher. For example, this faith commitment would influence the research field pursued, including poverty, health care, environment and debt. Each of these could be described as pursuing fragments, or dimensions of faith ethics lodged in the secular. It is very reminiscent of Duncan Forrester's use of fragments which he rightly and necessarily connects to a corpus of wider theological knowledge or belief systems.[239] If the *Faithful Economics* Conference wishes to achieve that Christian contribution to economics it will therefore be helpful if they are able to relate to such a theological corpus. It would allow them to achieve what they call taking 'the intellectual dimensions of their faith seriously'.[240] It would also satisfy other requirements they identify. For example, Yuengert counsels Christians to address economic man as a theological anthropology.[241] It would satisfy, too, the need to locate in wider frameworks the focused interpretations and transplanting of particular insights from the sacred scriptures to economic life. For example, the Baptist Gushee's 'The Economic Ethics of Jesus' contains five biblical themes on money, wealth, poverty and greed which would benefit from such locating.[242] They include: 'possessions are intrinsically insignificant beyond the basic sufficiency provided by a gracious God'; misjudging the value of possessions provokes greed; this encourages lifestyles of luxury, self-indulgence and 'lack of generosity'; wealth's deceptive allure can choke the soul; Jesus identifies 'with the poor and promises abundance and justice in a coming "great reversal"'.[243] Similar material from this enquiry confirms that judgement. Jubilee 2000, and fair trade's promotion of just price and wage, also move directly from Scripture and tradition to contemporary economic affairs. As valued piecemeal approaches they too would benefit from location within a wider theological framework. I have noted that deficiency in Christian contributions to interfaith work on economics. Compared to Muslim and Jewish work, they lack an overall theological economy within which particular perspectives can be placed. Meeting that need for such a theological economy is the role of this section, not least as essential function on the continuum from ethical behaviour and moral economy to theological economy.

To perform such a complex task, I have found the concept of an *economy of grace*[244] more than meets these and other requirements. Again, I came across it late in the research process, and realized it resonated powerfully with a number of my key findings. At first, I was anxious that Tanner's study would be yet another theological account, strong on criticism of contemporary economics and market economies and generating radically different alternatives quite incapable of any serious prolonged conversation with economic life today. What I discovered was the opposite. The economy of grace is certainly predominantly embedded in the fundamentals of the distinctive theological discourse, but it equally then seeks to engage with the discourse of economics. I had found *exactly* what this particular and important part of the enquiry needed. That judgement is based on the fact that Tanner's economy of grace achieves three objectives which my own research had identified as essential for *theological economy*. First, the human enterprise is divided into a series of distinct fields, firmly autonomous, with their own structures, relations of power and influence, disciplines, theories and customs. Following Bourdieu, although rightly critically, she recognizes that each field defines its own distinctive interests and ends.[245] Economic capitalism is one such field but equally so is religion. The latter is a way of telling the Christian story and its vision of economy that will also bring out its contrast, among other things with the economic field's principles. For Tanner, the preferred entry point into that distinctive character of the religious field can be usefully expressed and defined by the concept of God's grace.[246] It certainly exhibits the unique character of the nature of God and God's relationship to the human. It incorporates the focused value of grace as saving, as the personal encounter between divine and human, but also what Niebuhr called common grace, as God's sustaining power communicated to the human through the structures and structuring of life.[247] It was a concept used by recent major exponents of Christian social ethics, to connect theology and economics, with reference to the unearned character of grace.[248] It relates firmly into the role played by faith traditions and communities, as expositors and channels of grace, and in the formation of character and nature. It also enables Tanner to elaborate God's nature and relationship with the human in ways which clearly engage economic debates.

Second, each field is also relatively autonomous, therefore also interacting with other fields. To supplement this important feature, Tanner develops the correspondence method to identify and elaborate the connections between the economy of grace and the capitalist market economy. The structural analysis across fields ensures relations between fields are then brought into 'correspondence'.[249] This is made possible by discerning intimations of graceful economics within the secular economic field, what she describes as using them as 'hook' and eyes, as 'points allowing an opening for theological economy' to engage with economics. It is remarkably similar to Ted Wickham's use of the secular in order to engage theology in the heavy manufacturing industrial context of post-war Sheffield.[250]

Third, this understanding of the religious field's distinctive economic character allows her to enter into dialogue with the field of the capitalist market economy as both critique and alternative, including an *overhaul* of the existing economic system so that it is more compatible with God's purposes. What she does *not* do, and this is of high importance in terms of complementing the findings of this enquiry, is to require the complete replacement of the existing economic order. Nor does she promote a retreat into relatively autonomous local economies, as advocated by Cobb and Daly, and, more recently, by Peters.[251] Rather, for her, 'a theological economy, no matter how oppositional, is always formed in response to, in a kind of vis-à-vis with, the economy it contests'. In other words, it 'does not linger on the outskirts of the economy, waiting for it to die a natural death, but works from within it, to turn or convert it to *different principles of operation*'.[252]

What are those 'different principles' which constitute the distinctive relative autonomy of this religious field's theological economy? For these determine its discrete identity and thereby the means for identifying and engaging with the corresponding intimations within the field of the capitalist market economy. The principles all emerge from the basic Christian story, again already identified as playing a foundational role in faith tradition and community formation. It has also formed the basis of the parallel hermeneutic.

The Christian story of God and the world is about 'God as the highest good, a God constituted by exchange among the persons of the Trinity, a God who aims, in creating and saving the world, to distribute to it the good of God's own life to the greatest degree possible'.[253] It is the Christian story of creation, fall and redemption, and God's consummation as the eschatological goal of creation, all the fundamental features of the Christian narrative informing the theological anthropology earlier.

For Tanner, God's grace is the distinctive and supreme emblematic of that nature of God, and God's relationships with human beings and creation. It is in and through that, that the well-being of all is pursued. What Tanner has done is to carefully select a fundamental feature of the Christian narrative. Others could and have been chosen, including the Trinity.[254] That is why I describe her economy of grace as *a* theological economy, as illustration and demonstration of what theology can and *must* do, given the implications of this enquiry, not least its role in an adequate faithful economics continuum.

What an economy shaped by grace achieves is very informative for the interacting of religious and economic fields. For example, God's grace is offered free to all, not biased to the rich or powerful. In its distribution, therefore, the 'distinctions of status make no difference'. It is also never reward for effort. It stands against those key features generating the modern disease of 'affluenza' or ill-being, with their focus on status and material acquisitions. In other words, 'The whole Christian story, from top to bottom, can be viewed as an account of the production of value and the distribution of goods, following this peculiar non-competitive shape.'[255] It reflects the dynamic character of God's world through and in God's nature. For Aquinas it is a world 'in which one perfects oneself in imitation of the self-diffusing goodness of God by perfecting others'.[256] It is giving without depletion or loss, developing the Other as God's gift of love. Our response is to build up others, and therefore and thereby ourselves. It is an account of graceful economy which engages, through correspondence with the market economy. But equally, it likewise engages with the central findings on relationships of the earlier reflection on happiness and well-being.

There are three further characteristics which define the central character of the economy of grace. First, unconditional giving. Such is the nature of God's freely given gift to us, that the only adequate response is to give to others in order to extend its benefits: 'God's purpose in giving is to benefit creatures, and therefore the proper return for God's giving is not so much directed back to God as directed to those creatures.'[257] Because it therefore extends beyond kin, it informs the shape and character of social relationships and structures. Well-being is not accordingly dependent on individual performance alone. There are clearly strong connections between these features of an economy of grace, an economy of regard, a moral economy, and ethical economics. Second, universal giving. God's unconditional giving implies its absolute inclusiveness. It requires giving without restriction to the benefit of all, including the stranger and the poor. Grace is therefore our shared or common possession, to which all in consequence have a right. All have access to those pre-moral goods as the resource basis of well-being. A community of concern as wide as God's always generates poverty reduction programmes, including as critique of exclusive absolute private property. As shared grace it represents a universal feature of a theological anthropology. Third, non-competition in a community of mutual benefit. God's gift-giving generates a giving in human relations which strives to meet the needs of all. This in turn shapes a community of mutual fulfilment, including its economic dimension, and so relieves the strain on individual moral performance. Such giving to others is neither at our or their expense, it remains as enhancement of both. It is profoundly a matter of reciprocity, of the well-being of each and therefore all. To so perfect ourselves by making others perfect is also one of the key lessons from the happiness research, that giving by the rich for the benefit of the poor, and thereby the erosion of that inequality which so contributes to ill-health and ill-being, benefits the rich as well. It is reminder of the importance of participation in well-being and in the nature of God and God's relationships with the human: 'Our lives participate in that divine mission and thereby realize the shape of God's own economy by giving that follows the same principle: self-sharing for the good of others.'[258] It is an economy of grace.

Putting Faithful Economics to Work

It is striking that the need to operationalize findings and principles crosses the happiness and well-being research and this Enquiry as a whole, including this section on faithful economics. One of the main attractions of Tanner's economy of grace is that she rightly sees the need to test her theological principles in practice. Interaction between the fields of religion and capitalist economies is integral to the nature of fields and, as Tanner has demonstrated, is further required by the distinctive character of the two fields: religion has the form of an organized economy, as the production and distribution of distinct goods, including grace; and economics makes deeply religious claims. Regarding the latter, Nelson, a 'conventionally trained economist', and not a Christian, finds within his profession the fundamental elements of a religion. Adapting words of J. M. Keynes, Henderson asserts that Nelson's version would be 'Contemporary economists, who believe themselves to be quite exempt from any religious influences in their work, are the slaves of the implicit religion of their discipline.'[259]

Promoting the correspondence between the two fields, Tanner's task is to overhaul the capitalist market economy so that it is more aligned with the principles of the economy of grace. She illustrates that possibility with reference to prominent policy areas from economic interdependence to non-marketable goods. Without these features of an economy of grace, it would appear vague and impractical. The operationalizing of principles is therefore essential for the integrity and credibility of the theological engagement with political economy. It is tests of whether religion really wants to take the world seriously, and thereby becomes significant example of a practical and performative theology.

To expand Tanner's process, I will deploy *corresponding* policy material from across the happiness and well-being literatures, including the main disciplines and perspectives. Again, the convergences between and within these literatures are striking, although there are some subtle and marked differences. For example, the provision and quality of work itself is a high priority for well-being yet absent from Tanner. Similarly she does not focus on the profoundly pervasive damaging consequences of inequality, and omits reference to the deep implications for economic and human functioning of social and political relationships and associations. These omissions will be corrected. Refurbishing democratic participation and promoting happiness are matters which cannot now be addressed effectively apart from economics. Yet unless economics changes through wider conversations, progress on the great post-scarcity agenda will not be achieved.

Tanner's chapter, 'Putting a theological economy to work', is therefore a springboard for sketching the practical operationalizing of a theological economy.[260] This includes her valuable identifying of points where theological principles can be elaborated from within economics and developed in sensitive conversations with it. Yet the policy implications of the promotion of happiness also make formative and unique contributions to theological economics, as well as representing some overlap with Tanner's work. This section is therefore concerned to illustrate how to put faithful economics to work by covering the spectrum of ethical economics to a theological economy, in this case as economy of grace. The ultimate objective can be appropriately described using Tanner's words, that this exploration of faithful economics 'enters into the present configuration of global capitalism to transform it at those points where the two fields cross each other in conflict'.[261] It is, in the language now of this enquiry, an exercise in the transfiguration of capitalism.

As Tanner rightly recognizes, the interaction of fields, and a proper exploration of it, is suggestive of operational possibilities. And it is an exercise in feasibility, that profound economic change can be achieved, not least because of events in recent economic history. For example, the deregulation of financial markets in the 1970s was an important contribution to the growing dominance of global financial markets both in and then increasingly of, the global economy. It is an important illustration of the role and power of governments, because what they deregulated, they could reregulate. The very different models of capitalism, from the USA to Sweden, also indicate the significant space which exists for the feasible development of contrasting economic models. Governments do influence the distribution of private and public sector employment, wage flexibility, levels of government funding, the priorities and extent of taxation, the balance between export or domestic markets, the choice between inflation or job growth, the crucial contribution of education training and health care, and public support for research and development. 'In short, there is always some room to maneuver within capitalism, different options that it is possible to pursue.'[262]

Facing the complexities of global change, fatalism is a routine response much favoured by those in power. It is always routinely wrong. They can always be addressed to promote greater human well-being in its ecological context. Faithful economics is one illustration how that can be achieved, not least because it interacts ethical economics and a theological economy, encompassing within itself the principle of partnership with others.

Before sketching these main policy areas two basic understandings inform their shape and direction. First, all recognize the overall aim of pursuing greater well-being, and that has to include getting to grips with economics but now in a necessarily wider series of interactions. Second, all accept the significance in that programme of the market economy and mechanism, and of economic growth. Equally, all recognize the market's intrinsic defects and deficiencies. Engaging that agenda involves promoting virtuous circles to achieve that aim, and opposing the vicious circles which obstruct it. A moral and theological economy has an important part to play in that whole process.

I have chosen six policy areas to explore covering: the global economy, work and income, welfare, public goods, inequality, and democracy and social capital. The first, third and fourth are lead areas for Tanner, so her theological linkage with economics will be included in them. All will identify issues for general policy themes, if not policy suggestions. They are selected primarily to give a flavour of the much greater detail provided in the various sources from across these literatures.

The global economy: economic interdependence, non-competitiveness and mutually beneficial spirals

These subheadings are separate principles in Tanner's work, but I have drawn them together because they all engage directly with an economic agenda. I have located her 'fictitious capitalism' of global financial markets in this collection for the same reason.

Economic interdependence

A theological economy is primarily a 'universally inclusive system for the increase and distribution of goods, one dedicated to the well-being of all its members and organized to ensure that what benefits one benefits all'.[263] It therefore has the strongest interest in the emerging interconnectivity of both a global economy and globalization processes. That interdependence of individual, family, community, nation, planet and universe, as integral to our participation in God and therefore in God's purposes, is also recurring and fundamental premise of the world's major faiths, as we have seen. In production, through transnational corporations and manufacturing processes, trade between nations, and finance operating freely across national boundaries, a global economic system is beginning to emerge. For Tanner, 'A theological economy has a stake in the expansion of economic concern, so as to break the limits of bounded interests.'[264] What happens in Asia or Africa or Latin America will increasingly affect us, and vice versa. The return to more local self-sufficient communities, already advocated by some theologians, is both nostalgic and a contradiction of the trends of history for at least the last 500 years. Tanner rightly rejects that temptation. The issue, as with market economies and mechanisms, and with economic growth, is who benefits and who loses? To deliver an encompassing global economy therefore means promoting, as we have seen, a bias for inclusivity, including economic growth policies which are pro poor, environment and participation. For Tanner, it means 'One should, whenever possible, promote growth strategies in which the economy grows and poverty is reduced at the same time.'[265] In happiness literatures, it means promoting well-being and overcoming causes of ill-being, linking economic growth and poverty reduction programmes. Free trade is integral to such pressures and principles, standing as radical critique of present practices, particularly by the USA and the EU on agriculture, and supporting the poorest nations in their more gradual entry into global trading processes.

Global production and trade are increasingly overshadowed by what Tanner calls the 'fictitious capital creation of international finance'. By this she means 'capital that increases apart from any increase in the real production of goods and services'. Her argument that these processes are exercising more and more influence in a global economy, and that they can have very damaging consequences, is well supported by economists as well as theologians. The great damage they can do, and have done, say in the East Asian financial crisis of 1997, is unacceptable when the poor bear a disproportionate burden, when 'People without money are thereby further disadvantaged by the capital market.'[266]

There is considerable agreement across secular and theological commentators on proposals for encouraging 'a mutually beneficial spiral' in financial markets, including:[267]

- The possibility of reintroducing fixed exchange rates to discourage financial speculation.
- Taxes on cross-border financial trading (particularly in currencies, although increasingly spiralling into new financial derivatives). For example, the Tobin Tax was developed by the Nobel laureate economist James Tobin, initially to reduce currency speculation – to 'throw sand in the wheels' as he put it. Some also now regard it as a pro poor source for 'the finance of development assistance'.[268]
- Methods to protect developing economies from speculative runs on their currencies. This includes, as Bhagwati and Stiglitz have suggested, the *gradual* introduction of poorer economies into global trading and financial markets. The previous commitment by the Washington consensus to a hasty one-size-fits-all process, favoured by neo-liberal theorists, is roundly rejected.
- The IMF could return to its original brief, to work with developing economies by freeing up financial support for them in economic crises rather than putting the screws on them.
- Encouraging financial schemes geared to the poor, including micro-credit programmes, credit unions and Muslim interest-free banking. The

economic questions relating to them, particularly as elaborated in Part 2 above, should be taken into account, particularly by theologians. Tanner is not unusual in betraying a questionable Aristotelian unease with money 'breeding' in its own right. The growing condemnation of new financial instruments, for example in derivatives and hedge funds, is also symptomatic of an inadequate grasp of the nature and role of finance in a global economy. Cowley's work, *The Value of Money*, is a much more careful and rigorous development of a Christian social ethics' engagement with this crucial aspect of economics.

The principle of non-competitiveness

At first sight there is a major irreconcilable conflict between the principle of non-competitiveness and a competitive capitalist market economy. But as Steedman has rightly reminded us,[269] the Christian inclination to co-operation and against competition, seen in F. D. Maurice's early Christian socialism, is as ill-judged now as it was in 1850. Companies operating in a competitive marketplace, as generator of efficiencies, practise co-operative skills *within* their enterprises. The growth of team-working, linked to new information technologies, is an important part of arguments in Part 1. It is these non-competitive features, built into a capitalist market economy, which Tanner treats as 'the hooks for theological intersection and intervention'. They also include, for example, *the economy of regard* discussed earlier. But she also creatively explores two other features of more mainstream economics. First, what she calls 'the capitalist ideal of a mutually beneficial competitive equilibrium', that competition should always be 'circling around'.[270] For example, Marx's view, in his labour theory of value, was that capitalist profit was always at the expense of the worker, who would therefore endure increasing immerseration (the race to the bottom argument used by critics of globalization today). Yet the employer has increasingly paid the employees more than he gets from them, not least in order to ensure they can purchase commodities and services. 'The theological principles of noncompetition and mutual benefit obviously interact here with the capitalist interest in conditions favouring the possibility of recurrent market equilibrium.' Second, she notes the capitalist interest in 'avoiding mutually destructive economic spirals and in fostering complementary or virtuous ones'[271] (the virtuous and vicious circles argument). This is a recognition that with industrialization, economic growth and decline tend to feed on themselves in cumulative fashion. The task is to get into a pattern of self-sustaining economic growth rather than decline. For example, with regard to the latter, responses to the Great Depression in the

1930s essentially fuelled it. An obverse pattern, particularly applicable to poorer emerging economies with their inadequate domestic markets, is to promote production for export, using labour-intensive industries as a comparative advantage, with increasing diversification. Building up diversified domestic markets and skills is part of that virtuous circle. Challenging that is the asymmetric distribution of power favouring advanced economies, and exploited by them, including to the contrived disadvantage of poorer economies. Addressing trade biases effectively is an essential part of that wider necessary power redistribution, an integral part of the engagement with inequality. As Tanner observes, 'There is an obvious capitalist interest in figuring out what can be done to break vicious spirals of decline, in which each loss feeds every other and everybody goes down together, and to replace them with the opposite sort of spiral, a virtuous spiral of mutual benefit.'[272] Support for that more progressive interpretation comes from the happiness literatures, with their strong argument for redistribution policies, particularly from rich to poor nations, including through increased aid and debt forgiveness. Their argument is that such a bias benefits the rich giver as much as the poor recipient, in terms of happiness delivered. It is a strong endorsement of Tanner's principles of an economy of grace and the mutual benefit to be gained from the gift–giver relationship.

Work and income

Both the nature of work and its organization figure prominently in the well-being literatures. Without a basic income, varying with where economies are on the growth ladder, the opportunities for well-being are severely diminished. The work of Hertzberg and Maslow, noted in the discussion of the happiness hypothesis in Part 2, illustrated this argument. It is an integral part of the achievement of the transition beyond absolute poverty and scarcity. The ability to procure pre-moral goods, discussed above, also relates to this. Yet that same material also indicated that above identifiable levels of income, further increases in income were not linked with a commensurate increase in happiness. Other more non-economic factors, covered in the discussion on social capital in Part 1, and happiness in Chapter 6, then become more significant. Adequate income therefore remains a central but not sufficient part of human flourishing. Work in itself, however, continues to be important for well-being. Unemployment, conversely, is extremely damaging to it. This has an important implication for economic policies, prioritizing full employment as an important goal.

There is a recognition, too, that the quality of work, as outlet for human creativity, and opportunity for self-fulfilment through self-transcendence, is a significant agenda. The WCC–ILO dialogue on decent work, mentioned earlier, is a contribution to that debate, as is the work linking organizational development and spirituality. More particular proposals also emerged from the well-being sources, including:

- The importance of a work–life balance which recognizes the supreme importance of child-rearing for future personal and societal happiness, of leisure itself, and the opportunity to contribute to voluntary activities.
- The use of the tax system to promote that balance and to reduce the emphasis on individual prosperity (which does not produce more happiness) and increase it on public shared goods (which do).
- The proposal to extend employee share ownership as a means to increase co-operative ways of working and organizing, and to resource greater participation in economic decisions. Wilkinson regards this as a bottom-up erosion of inequality, essentially a form of economic democracy. This is an important complement to the later consideration of ways of extending participation as political democracy, again essential for human happiness.

Welfare and unconditional giving

The economy of grace naturally focuses on unconditional giving and mutuality. Welfare is therefore central to it, with commitment to 'welfare provision as a universal entitlement, sensitive only to need' being essential. Access to health care and education based on need and not the ability to pay remains a basis for this understanding. Tanner is deeply critical of global capitalism's deep erosion of welfare (the evidence in *many* countries is the opposite!). But it is her determination to disconnect such a grace-bound interpretation of welfare from the traditional linkage to deserving–undeserving arguments that is most challenging. She therefore contradicts Layard's commitment to welfare to work programmes and the conditionality this implies (yet also its recognition of breaking the dependency of the poor on benefits and of reinforcing the importance of work for well-being). Her argument, derived from her reflections on the nature of grace, suggests that 'While making it (welfare) conditional upon work is incompatible with the theological principle of unconditional giving, welfare provision should, in keeping with a theological stress on a community of mutual fulfilment, be sufficiently far ranging to enable recipients to make contributions to society commensurate with their full potentials.'[273]

Health care and education are designed to enhance that ability to contribute, to give. The happiness material refines this further: health care
needs to give much greater priority to mental health, a major and increasing result of 'the paradox of prosperity' trend; education needs to include,
for Layard, a new and important focus on moral education.

These commitments to welfare play a strategic role in the encounter with
the global economy. They are increasingly regarded as integral to sound
economic growth policies for developing economies, including if they also
are designed to reduce inequalities. The greater the inequalities the higher
the growth rate needed to reduce poverty. For a UNHDR report, in 1996,
the survey of emerging economies revealed that 'During the past three
decades, every country that was able to combine and sustain rapid growth
did so by investing first in schools, skills and health while keeping the
income gap from growing too wide.'[274] Increased welfare does not therefore conflict with economic globalization but 'dovetails with it'. It is consequently essential to support the more flexible working demanded by
global competition in terms of offering essential protection to workers
(rather than protection of jobs). Equally, it is a major resource for generating that social stability and security as both necessary for happiness and for
reducing that social conflict so inconducive to sound businesses: 'Without
welfare provision to lessen the hardships that people face as a result, social
instability is a definite likelihood.'[275]

Public goods: noncompetitive provision and use

Beyond marketization and embodying mutuality, public goods epitomize
the economy of grace. They represent 'states or forms of mutual good
beyond those available by market forces'.[276] They are particularly important because, like the economy of regard, they demonstrate that even in
terms of resource allocation, the normally efficient market mechanism is
not omnicompetent. This is particularly the case where costs and benefits
are not directly monetizable, that is, 'not fully reflected in the prices
charged for goods, and consequently fall outside the bounds of market
transactions': they are, in other words, externalities, and are both good
and bad. The former, as public good, 'cannot exclude anyone from enjoy-
ing once they have been produced'; they therefore are beyond the capacity
of the market's price mechanism.[277] Markets do not therefore find it worth
their while to invest in them – because you cannot get enough people to pay
for them. Since the public use them, and greatly for their mutual benefit,
they are best resourced through taxation. They include a wealth of com-

mon benefits, from lighthouses to parks, museums to policing and defence, from roads to vaccination programmes. All can enjoy them, with no competition since they are neither mine nor yours, yet they are of great benefit to people. More than that, for Tanner, they are emblematic of our common humanity, of our profoundly public life. They therefore draw attention to the public character of all private goods as well. As Sen argues, our productivity, and therefore contribution and reward, is the function of the complete set of our capabilities, as well as the actual effort involved in production. In complex modern economies, 'societies past and present are repositories of knowledge and skills that dictate productivity levels.'[278] And these are the contributions of families, health care and education systems. They are publicly influenced goods. The extension of such goods is therefore a priority for grace economies, representing, as they do, goods 'freely available on noncompetitive terms'.[279]

Negative externalities are represented by the damaging consequences of economic processes for the environment, whether as non-renewable resource depletion or as pollution. There is a real likelihood that the combination will generate an accumulating global environmental crisis. Economically, the task is to develop processes to ensure people and organizations bear the cost of the harm done. This could include, for example, legislative restrictions or carbon trading systems. The objective is to achieve that in relation to sustainable economic development – essentially as pro environment growth. Combining that with pro poor growth possibilities will ensure that the poor do not pay the price of unduly restrictive growth policies proposed by some environmentalists: 'The poverty inflicted there by a no-growth environmental policy can be just as environmentally devastating, moreover, as a policy promoting energy-depleting and polluting growth.'[280] It is, once again, not a matter of growth or not, but of what kind of growth and for whom. And that is why a bias of inclusivity is so important for a faithful economics.

Inequality: the scourge of well-being

God's graceful gift of salvation is to every person and without condition. In that love, all traditional distinctions fall away. All share in that gift, none more than another. In that, all are profoundly equal. The contrast here between an economy of grace and a capitalist market economy is perhaps at its starkest. And, from all the evidences from all the disciplines engaging the happiness hypothesis, we know very clearly that inequalities damage physical and mental health, communities of reciprocity, and relationships across the positionings in society. In contrast, we also know, equally clearly, that a more egalitarian society is very conducive to greater happiness, higher social capital, better health and strong productivity. It is not easy to see why we persist with the one and ignore the other. But that is changing, certainly in the long term, in a post-scarcity world. For Wilkinson, therefore, 'In historical perspective, the trend toward greater social equality seems unstoppable' from the abolition of slavery, the establishment of democracy, the outlawing of discrimination to the 'sharp diminution of some of the more overt signs of class distinctions and deference'.[281] Yet the persistence of grave economic inequalities, and their buttressing of social status which so contributes to emotional ill-being in what James calls selfish capitalism, is a decisive factor in the inability of happiness to rise commensurate with income growth. What is offered as a way of combating this vicious circle crosses a number fields, including religion. For example, economic measures need to be located in the wider strategy of transforming capitalism, but they do also recurringly focus on the following policy areas:

- Taxation: advocating the move from regressive indirect to the more direct progressive taxation. One suggestion is to aim to reduce the ratio between senior manager incomes and the national average to 5:1.[282] That addressing of the higher earners is particularly important. There has been an 'unwritten law' that addressing inequality means raising up the poor. We would do well to heed R. H. Tawney's advice in the midst of his early research on low pay in pre-1914 Britain. For him, the student of poverty should 'start much higher up the stream than the point he wishes to reach; that what thoughtful rich people call the problem of poverty, thoughtful poor people call with equal justice the problem of riches'.[283]

  The happiness literatures also deploy taxation in relation to social relationship enrichment: for example, to encourage a more family friendly work–life balance, and child rearing.
- Welfare: we have already noted the central contribution to welfare *and* more egalitarian societies of strong health care and education programmes. They also play a key role in cushioning more marginal groups in the labour market against the instabilities of a global economy.
- The link between addressing inequalities between as well as within nations has been noted in the first policy area.
- Similarly, Wilkinson's important reflections on extending economic democracy through employee share ownership are also part of this strategy area.

Developing social capital as non-economic contribution to economic well-being

Running through this enquiry is important evidence that a strong market economy depends on a strong social capital, as values, relationships and institutions, including civil society and religion. It represents a fundamental challenge to the market economy both in terms of the damage it inflicts on social capital, and as requiring the reformulation of its understandings of economic behaviour. A moral economy and anthropology, combined with a theological anthropology and economy, have important lessons to teach but using the correspondence method of critical dialogue. There are two more contained areas that the literatures focus on, social capital and democracy. The first recognizes the complex and varied strategies required to refurbish a greatly depleted social capital. On the one hand, the discussion of values and virtues, and their formation, clearly needs to involve, in interdisciplinary and partnership working, the ethics–religion continuum. On the other hand, that task can only be competently undertaken if accompanied by an understanding of the indispensable role played in nourishing characters and virtues by traditioning communities and associations. A modest start has been made by government with regard to acknowledging and supporting the work of faith-based organizations in society.

The second, democracy, is equally complex and essential, reflecting, as it does, the emphasis on participation in our understandings of economic growth and religion. For Dunn, the problem of democracy is its necessary alliance, as representative capitalist democracy, with what he calls the 'order of egotism', essentially the deployment of wealth as economic resources to exercise power far beyond its democratic weight. The value of such representative democracy is that it gives 'real protection for the civil rights of most of the population'.[284] The disadvantage is that it is used by a political-economic class whose main task, in practice, is 'to insulate the rulers as radically as possible from the erratic sympathies and judgements of the citizens at large'. Addressing that problem is therefore as much an economic as a political task. Indeed, Dunn argues that it can only be engaged 'if we come to understand economics well enough to establish some real control over them'.[285] The proposals on employee share ownership, as economic democracy, made by an epidemiologist, complement the policy suggestions on reforming democracy. With regard to the latter, two were noted. The first seek to develop the use of referenda to provoke citizen participation. It is interesting that Halpern's work on social capital highlights the contribution to it particularly in the Swiss cantons which hold them most regularly. Layard also confirms this importance of participation for happiness.[286] The second proposal relates to increasing and improving public access to information. 'The more governments control what their fellow citizens know the less they can claim the authority of those citizens for how they rule.'[287] Both regular referenda and more open societies are emblematic of a commitment to the wider and more fundamental principles of democracy. It suggests that as a way of organizing power, democracy becomes more sustainable when it is fed by an appropriate and complementary way of life. For R. H. Tawney, practising democracy required democratic living.[288] Dunn's two modest proposals for modifying representative democracy need to be located in that wider framework. For that emphasis on a philosophy of life, supportive social, political and economic frameworks, and virtuous living in relationships, is a familiar one. It reverberates through all the well-being literatures and these brief notes on operationalizing a theological economy. All agree, whether promoting happiness or democracy, that reforming economics is essential. Dunn talks of searching for a remedy, 'not merely in moral philosophy or welfare economics, but even in economic organization and political practice'.[289] The contribution of theological economics, interacting, as it does, ethical economics and theological economies, is to that end, of 'a global economy re-organized to avoid crisis by advantaging everyone'.[290]

13

Religion and the Transfiguration of Capitalism

The transfiguration is the story of Jesus' ascent of the mountain 'at the mid-point of his ministry', accompanied by three disciples. His physical appearance is changed, 'metamorphosing into incandescent light', whiter than any fuller on earth could produce. The greatest lawgiver, Moses, and the greatest prophet, Elijah, appear beside him, and talking with him. The disciples are 'overawed at the spectacle', Peter proposing to build three huts for 'Jesus and his celestial guests. At this point a cloud intervenes', and a voice declares Jesus to be the beloved Son. 'Then the miraculous signs recede and Jesus is left alone to descend the mountain with his bemused disciples.'[291] It is a story told in three Gospels (John's is full of allusions to it) and in 2 Peter.

This narrative of the transfiguration introduced the final part of this enquiry. It has proved to be a valuable summary of the matters arising from the enquiry's work in Parts 1 and 2, essentially the nature of the religious contribution to global change. For example, first, the story is profoundly material. The whiteness of Jesus' robe was whiter than any fuller on earth could make, a reference to the technologies of human endeavour. For the translators of the New Testament into English in the sixteenth century, water or fulling mills were an important feature of economic life and well-being. The role of faithful economics is to engage equivalent realities today, including delivering pre-moral goods. In the story, it represented: 'The sheer materiality of the incarnation and the translucence of Jesus' body on the mount of transfiguration, ensures that nature itself is caught up in the deification of human beings.'[292] The material is therefore not an impediment to spiritual growth, but is the very medium of the divine-human encounter. 'Whatever it is, salvation will be an affirmation of the essential finitude of human nature, not an escape from it.'[293]

Second, Jesus' meeting with Moses and Elijah on the mountain becomes an acknowledgement of the importance of the religious traditions of law and prophecy encountering Jesus as the new covenant. The reflections on ethics, and the ecumenical-interfaith concern, were reminder of the role played for human well-being and therefore for economic life, by faith traditions and communities in the formation of character and virtue. The location of economic man in nineteenth-century tradition and context revealed its strength and profound limitations, unless interacting with other traditions.

Third, the discussion of anthropology and ethics consistently included a dimension referred to as the transcendent, the encounter with the Other as greater than oneself. The explorations of the difference or distinctive factor or added value of the religious contribution to society has likewise figured prominently. In theological anthropology, the dimension of the apophatic was a reminder that the human cannot be totally subsumed within measurement systems or by the limitation of human behaviour to rationality. It rather represented the challenge to constantly reformulate such understandings, an important and recurring conclusion of the enquiry. The transfiguration story's account of the heavenly voice out of the cloud, the Hebraic 'Shekinah', declaring Jesus as the beloved Son, reflects the hidden presence always there behind this event, the origin and goal of all that happens.

Importantly, for Lee, these powerful symbols in the transfiguration narrative 'address the world precisely at the points of its disfiguration',[294] and the 'matters arising' in the final part, arising as they do out of the first two parts, demonstrate this – including, for example, as Tanner's 'hooks and eyes' for overhauling market economies. The interactions between the three symbolic groupings embedded in the transfiguration story generate a strong commitment to the transformation of people and society focused on what we have developed as a moral-theological anthropology which can now be seen as a consequence of Jesus' metamorphosis. Again, the narrative reinforces the role of participation in steering economic policies, and its interaction with participation in God. The only account of the transfiguration outside the Gospels is in 2 Peter, with its strong emphasis on human participation in the very nature of God, enabled and promised through the appearing of the Son. It relates to the reality that 'The transfiguration, which embodies symbolically the first coming of Christ, is thus the surety of the participation of believers in the divine life.'[295] It reflects a theology which therefore takes into account 'the interpenetration of the ways of earth and the ways of heaven. A realist theology is precisely that. Christianity working in that way because that is the way it is.' It is 'the kingdom of heaven seeking to enlarge its colonies on earth'.[296] And that combination of disciplines and experiences in collaborative working, which Martin requires as partners in such operationalizing of Christianity, is also a feature of the well-being literatures, and is embedded in the ethics, anthropological and economic chapters of this part of the enquiry.

These interactions within, say faithful economics, also occur with other disciplines and are part of the transfiguration process. Indeed, they are generated from within the narrative itself, which, for example, can be read in two ways. On the one hand, it performs as epiphany of Jesus' identity, not least through the spectacular and singular symbol of the numinous revealing of his heavenly nature; on the other hand, it acts as apocalyptic vision of a new creation through Christ. It is the challenge provoked by being and becoming in the section on theological anthropology, and in our creation in the image of God and our gradual growth into the likeness of God achievable in the eschaton.[297] For Lee, 'Christians are called to live between the appearance of Christ on the holy mountain and his appearance at the end. Living between these two events – which represent the one divine advent – and in full awareness of their truth means that believers are transfigured, participating more and more in the divine nature as revealed in Christ.'[298] It is therefore profoundly concerned with interim ethics, with living in between, as recognition both of our aspirations to well-being and the limitations which circumscribe them. The transition beyond absolute poverty and scarcity is historic representation of that realistic possibility. The features of transfiguration as materiality, tradition and transcendence therefore generate a more comprehensive model or framework, which is both survey of the constitution of well-being and the process for engaging it. It is a connection beautifully captured by the concept of wholeness, an intimate part of the pursuit of well-being, which includes economic life but increasingly its interaction with wider experiences or understandings of what it means to be human in a post-scarcity age. For wholeness is associated in the English language with the word holiness. 'The root of the English word *holy* is the Old English word *halig*, literally meaning *whole*.' So being whole is being 'sound in health, uninjured, restored to health, healed, not broken, undamaged, not broken up or ground, or deprived of any part'.[299] The well-being literatures are full of this search for such health, and particularly critical of mental ill-health, and its links with inequality and economic positioning. This enquiry has therefore given high priority to operationalizing faithful economics, including as the overhaul of market economies. And, if you are married to a Scotswoman, as I am, then you visit Edinburgh regularly, and walk to the bottom of the Royal Mile to Holyrood Abbey and Palace, to the holy cross, the means by which that full wholeness and holiness is achieved, reminder of the cost of the effective pursuit of well-being, and of the truly distinctive and unique contribution to that telos made by the Christian narrative of redemption. Not for nothing is the story of transfiguration the hinge point between the incarnationalism of the Sermon on the Mount and the mount of the cross as our costly redemption.

The story of the transfiguration is therefore both inspiration for the pursuit of well-being and rich seam of materials for modelling well-being. This modelling is not concerned with the architecture of happiness, but rather, for Titmuss, 'to help us to see some order in all the disorder and confusion of facts, systems and choices'. For it was Titmuss's work on the welfare state which so contributed to well-being in Britain in the post-1945 era, but his remarkable study of the efficiency of altruism in the blood-doning system was as important, as a reminder of the central role of virtues in that same well-being.[300] It is this combination of structures and values which generates and requires the supportive framework of a philosophy of life, what the ethics section described as the common good of all.

The value of the contribution of the transfiguration narrative to that wider framework is reinforced by its ability to summarize these interacting factors of Part 3. It particularly enfolds the religious dimensions of well-being in a coherent way of operating. But it also makes another contribution to well-being which is equally important. For it offers a narrative framework *beyond* the religious field to the whole series of interacting fields in Part 1, encapsulating the key features of well-being in the necessary task of transforming the global economy. In many ways, the story therefore becomes *gift* to the secular, because so many of the varied roots of the pursuit of well-being have appeared in the religious narrative of the transfiguration. It is these roots which also correspond to Tanner's hooks and eyes and Forrester's fragments. As the parallel hermeneutics in the ecumenical-interfaith section, it particularly offers opportunity for interacting a core narrative of the religious field with other fields, with the aim of generating greater well-being. It is therefore not gift alone, but also a narrative which can clearly be demonstrated to offer means of interacting with secular fields, particularly the global market economy, with the intention of transforming it.

To illustrate this strategically important capacity of the wider transformative character of the transfiguration narrative, I can think of no more appropriate choice than to pursue that dialogue with the most challenging contemporary narrative I can think of. Tanner has shown how an economy of grace can perform the same task with the global market economy. I will complement that by bringing together in conversation the transfiguration narrative and the narrative of the radical neo-Marxist critique of the *Empire* of global capitalism. That latter concept is essentially the interlocking of three major fields in Part 1, empires, capitalism and globalization. Hardt and Negri's attack on it has been particularly influential in American and British academies, and in anti-globalization, anti-capitalism and anti-American movements. To put the two together is, at first sight, like putting oil and water together. Yet very quickly the language used and its intentions suggest clear resonances with the religious narrative.

It is important to begin this experiment with the shared recognition of the central importance of narratives in the religious and neo-Marxist enterprises. Hardt and Negri talk of narrative's 'real transformative power: the power to confront reality and go beyond the given conditions of existence. The force of these critical concepts, which extends well beyond their ambiguous relations to modern social structures, consists primarily in their being posed as ontological demands.'[301] It is not just this shared commitment to the role of narratives, but the way that recognition is elaborated by Hardt and Negri – the talk of transformative power, of power itself, so central to understanding fields of influence and the relationship within and between them, and the role of critical concepts. It is a description which is relevant to both the religious and secular narratives, and more importantly, to the proposed dialogue and interaction between them.

The process of transformation which Hardt and Negri adopt engages precisely with the process of transfiguration outlined in the introduction to Part 3 – of going into materiality, then through and beyond it as transcendence, but therefore then returning to materiality as transformed – just as Jesus and the disciples always returned to reality from the mountain experience. Transfiguration is that one ongoing and continuous process. Listen to Hardt and Negri: 'Being republican today, then, means first of all struggling *within* and constructing against Empire, on its hybrid, modulating terrains . . . The multitude, in its will to be-against and its desire for liberation, must push through Empire and come out the other side.'[302] The task is to go through global capitalism, so acknowledging its undoubted achievements but then to move beyond it because of its fundamental contradictions. What is totally unacceptable is 'the return philosophy' so loved by radical theologians, for example, radical orthodoxy and the Christendom movements. Hardt and Negri reject any attempt to 're-create the conditions of the past', and gave a further warning that: 'Increasingly, any attempt at isolation or separation will mean only a more brutal kind of domination by the global system, a reduction to powerlessness and poverty.'[303] Constructively critical engagement with global capitalism is the prerequisite of both narratives.

The next stage is therefore to develop ways to achieve that objective of transcending capitalism. Hardt and Negri's approach is remarkably similar to Tanner's use of global interdependence as a transformative hooks and eyes, or Forrester's fragments. They argue, using Deleuze and Guattari, that to resist capital's globalization, 'we have to accelerate the process' by learning 'to think globally and act globally'.[304] This also involves identifying and then exploiting 'ruptures' in that economic system in order to promote the transformative process. So they ask 'where in the transnational networks of production, the circuits of the world market, and the global structures of capitalist rule there is the potential for *rupture* and the *motor* for a future that is not simply doomed to repeat the past cycles of capitalism'.[305] In other words, what is 'the terrain on which contestation and alternatives might emerge', and what are the key pressure points to deploy in and for the transformative process?[306] In my enquiry, the happiness hypothesis and its interaction with surrounding literatures, has provided both constructive critique of market economies and mechanisms, and generated out of that interaction, alternative faith-based understanding of anthropology, ethics and economics. Interestingly, Hardt and Negri's focus on the interconnective potential of new communication technologies 'redefining production processes and economic structures of value' uses languages similar to Tanner's: they talk of 'A regime of production, and above all a regime of the production of *subjectivity* . . . being destroyed and another invented by the enormous accumulation of struggles.'[307] It is that *subjectivity* which is the concept used by the Kennys for happiness, as subjective well-being, potentially implying its lack of objectivity, which we now know is an inaccurate description of the happiness research given the contribution of brain studies and robust survey and measurement systems. Yet the reality and significance of that subjectivity dimension is clear in both narratives, including its decisive contribution to critiques of economic systems and processes, and to their radical reformulation as alternative to current mainstream economics. The objective of both narratives, at this precise point, therefore becomes, using Hardt and Negri's language, 'the transformation of material conditions' and the search for 'the ontological basis of transvaluation'.[308] And then comes their remarkable claim, at the end of *Empire*, for human co-operation to override capitalist competition, for 'the political . . . to yield to love and desire'.[309] And so it is that St Francis is therefore deployed as embodiment of that regenerative process, so that 'This militancy makes resistance into counterpower and makes rebellion into a project of love', and that becomes 'the ontological power of a new society'. Transformation becomes 'biopower and communism, cooperation and revolution (all) remain together, in love, simplicity and also innocence'.[310] But it is precisely at this most intimatory of moments, that Hardt and Negri lose the plot. For *unless* that insightful conclusion is reinforced through being connected to the transfiguration narrative, to the religious-ethical dimension of the religious field, then it simply lacks the spiritual substance to perform the role they correctly ascribe to it. The transfiguration narrative precisely offers that possibility, essentially and profoundly as supreme *gift* to the secular. That very process of giving clearly brings, as this enquiry has demonstrated, the totally necessary added value of faith-based contributions to the Hardt and Negri narrative, so that the recipient is clearly transformed. Yet equally, in that same process, the giver, the transfiguration narrative, is also transformed: for Mudge, developing the very useful parallel hermeneutic as the interaction of narratives, with the possibility of a unique contribution by religious narratives to secular ones,

> The gift is not merely given; it turns out to move more strongly in return. To be in solidarity is to receive a gift, to receive the Promise once again through the Other. To be in covenanted solidarity is to gather around, and share the blessing of those in whose struggles the God of Abraham is perceived to be keeping promises in the world.[311]

Bringing the two narratives together in conversation is a remarkable example of the benefits for a new post-scarcity well-being of a narrative of transfiguration which encompasses new theological anthropology, ethics, interfaith collaboration, tradition and economics, but always in dialogue with and learning from secular processes and theories. It is a remarkable demonstration of the actual and potential nature and extent of the contribution of faith to global change, as the transfiguration of capitalism.

Notes

General Introduction

1. S. P. Huntington, *The Clash of Civilizations and the Remaking of World Order*, Simon & Schuster, 1996, pp. 30, 31.
2. M. Livi-Bacci, *A Concise History of World Population*, Blackwell, 2001. J. Diamond, *Guns, Germs and Steel: A Short History of Everybody for the Last 13,000 Years*, Random House, 1998.
3. Livi-Bacci, *A Concise History of World Population*, p. xv.
4. A. Smith, *An Inquiry into the Nature and Causes of the Wealth of Nations*, Oxford University Press, 1976. A. Smith, *The Theory of Moral Sentiments*, Liberty Fund, 1984.
5. A. Sen, *On Ethics and Economics*, Blackwell, 1999 edition, pp. 2–7.
6. J. Buchan, *Capital of the Mind: How Edinburgh Changed the World*, John Murray, 2004, p. 212.
7. Branko Harvat, 'political economy', in P. Deane and J. Kuper (eds), *A Lexicon of Economics*, Routledge, 1988, p. 299.
8. C. Baker, 'Entry to Enterprise', in J. Atherton and H. Skinner (eds), *Through the Eye of a Needle: Theological Conversations over Political Economy*, Epworth, 2007, p. 191.
9. A. Waterman, *Revolution, Economics and Religion: Christian Political Economy, 1798–1833*, Cambridge University Press, 1991.
10. B. Hilton, *The Age of Atonement: The Influence of Evangelicalism on Social and Economic Thought, 1785–1865*, Clarendon Press, 1988, p. 46.
11. See R. A. Easterlin, *Happiness in Economics*, Edward Elgar Publishing Limited, 2002.
12. A. MacIntyre, *After Virtue: A Study in Moral Theory*, Duckworth, 1981. S. Hauerwas, *The Peaceable Kingdom: A Primer in Christian Ethics*, SCM Press, 1984.
13. J. Haidt, *The Happiness Hypothesis: Putting Ancient Wisdom and Philosophy to the Test of Modern Science*, Heinemann, 2006. A. and C. Kenny, *Life, Liberty and the Pursuit of Utility: Happiness in Philosophical and Economic Thought*, Imprint Academic, 2006.
14. R. T. Peters, *In Search of the Good Life: The Ethics of Globalization*, Continuum, 2004, p. 28. I am indebted to Peters's survey of Christian ethics in her chapter 2.
15. See C. Cowley, *The Value of Money, Ethics and the World of Finance*, T & T Clark, 2006, p. 56.
16. E. Graham, 'Towards a Practical Theology of Embodiment', in P. Ballard and P. Couture (eds), *Globalization and Difference: Practical Theology in a World*

Context, Cardiff Academic Press, 1999, pp. 82–3.

17. C. Baker, *The Hybrid Church in the City: Third Space Thinking*, Ashgate, 2007, pp. 88 and 126.

18. Baker, *The Hybrid Church in the City*, p. 68.

19. R. Niebuhr, *Christ and Culture*, Harper & Row, 1951.

20. Atherton and Skinner, *Through the Eye of a Needle*, pp. 262–3.

21. J. de Santa Ana (ed.), *Beyond Idealism: A Way Ahead for Ecumenical Social Ethics*, Eerdmans, 2006, p. 4.

22. Baker, *The Hybrid Church in the City*, p. 138.

23. de Santa Ana, *Beyond Idealism*, pp. 25, 28, 45.

24. W. Ariarajah in de Santa Ana, *Beyond Idealism*, p. 55.

25. C-H. Grenholm and N. Kamergrauzis, eds, *Sustainable Development and Global Ethics*, Acta Universitatis Upsaliensis, 2007.

26. E. Graham in R. Soulen and L. Woodhead (eds), *God and Human Dignity*, Eerdmans, 2006, p. 277.

27. Baker, *The Hybrid Church in the City*, p. vii.

28. J. W. Henderson and J. Pisciotta (eds), *Faithful Economics: The Moral Worlds of a Neutral Science*, Baylor University Press, 2005, p. 131.

29. R. G. Wilkinson, *The Impact of Inequality: How to Make Sick Societies Healthier*, Routledge, 2005.

30. Diamond, *Guns, Germs and Steel*, p. 111.

31. Diamond, *Guns, Germs and Steel*, p. 285.

32. J. Atherton, *Public Theology for Changing Times*, SPCK, 2000.

Part 1 Introduction

1. M. Hardt and A. Negri, *Empire*, Harvard University Press, 2000.

2. J. Atherton, *Marginalization*, SCM Press, 2003.

3. P. Bourdieu, *The Social Structures of the Economy*, Polity Press, 2005.

4. P. Bourdieu, 'Genesis and Structure of the Religious Field', in *Comparative Social Research*, Volume 13, 1991, pp. 1–44.

5. K. Tanner, *Economy of Grace*, Fortress Press, 2005.

6. P. Bobbitt, *The Shield of Achilles: War, Peace and the Course of History*, Allen Lane, 2002.

7. The importance of historical contextualizing is particularly emphasized by my friend, Wilf Wild, *Crossing the River of Fire: Mark's Gospel and Global Capitalism*, Epworth, 2006.

8. Livi-Bacci, *A Concise History of World Population*; P. Jay, *Road to Riches or the Wealth of Man*, Weidenfeld & Nicolson, 2000; Diamond, *Guns, Germs and Steel*.

9. F. Fukuyama, *The Great Disruption: Human Nature and the Reconstruction of Social Order*, Touchstone, 2000.

10. F. Braudel, *A History of Civilizations*, Penguin, 1995. S. P. Huntington, *The Clash of Civilizations and the Remaking of World Order*, Simon & Schuster, 1996.

11. D. Forrester, 'The Scope of Public Theology', in E. Graham and E. Reed (eds), *The Future of Christian Social Ethics: Essays on the Work of Ronald H. Preston, 1913–2001*, Continuum, 2004, p. 19.

12. See C. Baker and H. Skinner, *Faith in Action: The dynamic connection*

between spiritual and religious capital, William Temple Foundation, Manchester, 2006.

13. See F. A. Hayek, *The Road to Selfdom*, University of Chicago Press, 1972.
14. See Wilkinson, *The Impact of Inequality*.
15. See Haidt, *The Happiness Hypothesis*.

Chapter 1 Empires

16. *Prosperity with a Purpose: Exploring the Ethics of Affluence*, CTBI, 2005.
17. See E. Butler, *Adam Smith – A Primer*, IEA, 2007, pp. 63–72.
18. D. Landes, *The Wealth and Poverty of Nations: Why Some are so Rich and Some are so Poor*, Little, Brown and Company, 1998, p. 422.
19. D. Harvey, *The New Imperialism*, Oxford University Press, 2003, p. 26f.
20. Bobbitt, *The Shield of Achilles*; G. Arrighi, *The Long Twentieth Century: Money, Power and the Origins of our Times*, Verso, 1994; P. Kennedy, *The Rise and Fall of the Great Powers: Economic Change and Military Conflict from 1500 to 2000*, Fontana Press, 1988. F. Fukuyama, *The End of History and the Last Man*, Penguin, 1992.
21. Harvey, *The New Imperialism*, p. 26f.
22. Kennedy, *The Rise and Fall of the Great Powers*, pp. 101–6.
23. R. Ruston, *Human Rights and the Image of God*, SCM Press, 2004.
24. Bobbitt, *The Shield of Achilles*.
25. Bobbitt, *The Shield of Achilles*, p. 570, quoting William Langer.
26. Kennedy, *The Rise and Fall of the Great Powers*, p. xxv.
27. N. Ferguson, *Colossus: The Rise and Fall of the American Empire*, Allen Lane, 2004, p. 262.
28. N. Ferguson, *The Cash Nexus: Money and Power in the Modern World 1700–2000*, Penguin, 2001, p. 391.
29. Kennedy, *The Rise and Fall of the Great Powers*, p. 689.
30. N. Ferguson, *Empire: How Britain Made the Modern World*, Penguin, 2004, p. xi.
31. Kennedy, *The Rise and Fall of the Great Powers*, p. 290f.
32. Ferguson, *Empire*, p. 38.
33. Ferguson, *Empire*, p. xxii.
34. Ferguson, *Empire*, p. xxviii.
35. Diamond, *Guns, Germs and Steel*, p. 69.
36. Ferguson, *Empire*, p. 137.
37. Ferguson, *Empire*, p. 151.
38. Ferguson, *Empire*, p. 139.
39. Harvey, *The New Imperialism*, p. 26f.
40. Ferguson, *Colossus*, p. 16f.
41. J. Stiglitz, *Globalisation and its Discontents*, Allen Lane, 2002, p. 20.
42. On 'soft power', see Ferguson, *Colossus*, p. 20f.
43. Ferguson, *Colossus*, p. 152.
44. Ferguson, *Colossus*, p. 18.
45. Bobbitt, *The Shield of Achilles*, p. 721f.
46. Harvey, *The New Imperialism*, p. 209f.
47. Ferguson, *Colossus*, p. 25f.

Notes

48. Kennedy, *The Rise and Fall of Great Powers*, p. 369.

49. Harvey, *The New Imperialism*, pp. 157, 162.

50. Harvey, *The New Imperialism*, quoting Roy, p. 161.

51. Ferguson, *The Cash Nexus*, p. 418.

52. Huntington, *The Clash of Civilizations*, p. 28.

53. P. Jenkins, *The Next Christendom: The Coming of Global Christianity*, Oxford University Press, 2002.

54. Huntington, *The Clash of Civilizations*, p. 40.

55. Huntington, *The Clash of Civilizations*, p. 39, quoting Braudel.

56. Huntington, *The Clash of Civilizations*, p. 41, quoting Braudel.

57. Huntington, *The Clash of Civilizations*, p. 41, quoting Durkheim and Mauss.

58. F. Braudel, *Civilization and Capitalism 15th–18th Century*, 3 volumes, Collins, 1981–2002.

59. Huntington, *The Clash of Civilizations*, pp. 45–7.

60. Huntington, *The Clash of Civilizations*, p. 54.

61. Huntington, *The Clash of Civilizations*, p. 54, quoting Edward Mortimer.

62. Huntington, *The Clash of Civilizations*, p. 85.

63. Huntington, *The Clash of Civilizations*, p. 92.

64. *The Economist*, 21 January 2006.

65. Huntington, *The Clash of Civilizations*, p. 176.

66. Huntington, *The Clash of Civilizations*, p. 177.

67. Huntington, *The Clash of Civilizations*, p. 196.

68. Diamond, *Guns, Germs and Steel*, p. 92.

69. Wilkinson, *The Impact of Inequality*, chapter 8.

70. Diamond, *Guns, Germs and Steel*, p. 190.

71. J. Dunn, *Setting the People Free. The Story of Democracy*, Atlantic Books, 2005.

72. M. Hardt and A. Negri, *Multitude*, Penguin, 2006.

73. Kenny, *Life, Liberty and the Pursuit of Utility*.

74. Fukuyama, *The End of History*, p. 196.

75. Fukuyama, *The End of History*, p. 48.

76. Fukuyama, *The End of History*, p. 113.

77. Michael Doyle in Fukuyama, *The End of History*, p. 263.

78. Ferguson, *The Cash Nexus*, p. 393.

79. Dunn, *Setting the People Free*, pp. 126–7.

80. Fukuyama, *The End of History*, p. 168.

Chapter 2 Capitalism

81. Jay, *Road to Riches*, pp. 279f.

82. Jay, *Road to Riches*, p. 237, quoting Keynes.

83. Landes, *The Wealth and Poverty of Nations*, p. 236.

84. Landes, *The Wealth and Poverty of Nations*, p. 231.

85. Cowley, *The Value of Money*, p. 31.

86. Cowley, *The Value of Money*, p. 15.

87. Cowley, *The Value of Money*, p. 18.

88. L. Robbins, *The Nature and Significance of Economic Science*, 1934, quoted in P. Donaldson, *Economics of the Real World*, Penguin, 1973, p. 22.

89. Cowley, *The Value of Money*, p. 30, quoting J. K. Galbraith, *A History of Economics*, p. 115.

90. Cowley, *The Value of Money*, p. 28, quoting K. Polanyi, *Origins of our Times: The Great Transformation*, 1945, p. 142.

91. G. Arrighi, *The Long Twentieth Century*, p. 11.

92. Ferguson, *The Cash Nexus*, p. 20, p. 13.

93. M. Novak, *The Spirit of Democratic Capitalism*, Simon & Schuster, 1982. J. Henderson and J. Pisciotta (eds), *Faithful Economics*, p. 141.

94. C. D. Moe-Lobeda, *Healing a Broken World: Globalization and God*, Fortress Press, 2002, p. 1.

95. E. Hobsbawm, *Age of Extremes: The Short Twentieth Century 1914–1991*, Michael Joseph, 1994.

96. Ferguson, *The Cash Nexus*, p. 11.

97. Harvey, *The New Imperialism*, p. 163.

98. P. Kennedy, *Preparing for the Twenty-First Century*, HarperCollins, 1993, p. 193.

99. *The Economist*, 21 January 2006.

100. Jay, *Road to Riches*, p. 14.

101. Jay, *Road to Riches*, pp. 46–50.

102. Harvey, *The New Imperialism*, p. 62.

103. Arrighi, *The Long Twentieth Century*, p. x.

104. Arrighi, *The Long Twentieth Century*, p. xi, quoting Charles Tilly, *Big Structures, Large Processes, Huge Comparisons*, Russell Sage Foundation, 1984.

105. R. H. Tawney, *Religion and the Rise of Capitalism*, Penguin, 1966. V. A. Demant, *Religion and the Decline of Capitalism*, Faber & Faber, 1952. R. H. Preston, *Religion and the Persistence of Capitalism*, SCM Press, 1979.

106. Arrighi, *The Long Twentieth Century*, chapter 1.

107. Kennedy, *Preparing for the Twenty-First Century*, p. 61.

108. Ferguson, *The Cash Nexus*, pp. 281–2.

109. Cowley, *The Value of Money*, p. 92.

110. Bobbitt, *The Shield of Achilles*, pp. 9–10.

111. Fukuyama, *The End of History*, p. 93.

112. Fukuyama, *The End of History*, p. 98.

113. Bobbitt, *The Shield of Achilles*, p. 229.

114. Baker, *The Hybrid Church in the City*, pp. 88, 126.

115. Bobbitt, *The Shield of Achilles*, pp. 668–705.

116. O. James, *Affluenza: How to be Successful and Stay Sane*, Vermillion, 2007; Dunn, *Setting the People Free*.

117. Bobbitt, *The Shield of Achilles*, chapter 12.

118. Bobbitt, *The Shield of Achilles*, p. 221f.

119. Bobbitt, *The Shield of Achilles*, p. 801.

120. Bobbitt, *The Shield of Achilles*, p. 814.

121. Hardt and Negri, *Empire*, p. xi.

122. Hardt and Negri, *Empire*, p. 38.

123. Hardt and Negri, *Empire*, p. 43.

124. Hardt and Negri, *Empire*, p. 46.

125. Hardt and Negri, *Empire*, p. 413.

126. Waterman, *Revolution, Economics and Religion*.

127. Livi-Bacci, *A Concise History of World Population*, p. 29.
128. Livi-Bacci, *A Concise History of World Population*, p. 93f.
129. Livi-Bacci, *A Concise History of World Population*, p. 99.
130. Livi-Bacci, *A Concise History of World Population*, p. 107.
131. Livi-Bacci, *A Concise History of World Population*, pp. 183–90.
132. Livi-Bacci, *A Concise History of World Population*, p. 192f.
133. Livi-Bacci, *A Concise History of World Population*, p. 197.
134. Jay, *Road to Riches*, p. 323.
135. Atherton, *Public Theology for Changing Times*, chapter 4.
136. A. MacFarlane, *The Riddle of the Modern World: Of Liberty, Wealth and Equality*, Palgrave, 2000, p. 182, quoting Lerner.
137. Landes, *The Wealth and Poverty of Nations*, p. 175.
138. Fukuyama, *The End of History*, p. 229.
139. Landes, *The Wealth and Poverty of Nations*, p. 363.
140. Fukuyama, *The End of History*, p. 233.
141. Fukuyama, *The End of History*, p. 227.
142. Landes, *The Wealth and Poverty of Nations*, p. 219, quoting Adam Smith, *Wealth of Nations*.
143. Ferguson, *The Cash Nexus*, p. 366.
144. D. Putnam, *Bowling Alone: The Collapse and Revival of American Community*, Simon & Schuster, 2000.
145. Ferguson, *The Cash Nexus*, p. 366.
146. Ferguson, *The Cash Nexus*, p. 421.
147. James, *Affluenza*, p. 11.

Chapter 3 Globalization

148. M. Wolf, *Why Globalization Works: The Case for the Global Market Economy*, Yale University Press, 2004. V. Gallagher, *The True Cost of Low Prices: The Violence of Globalization*, Orbis, 2006.
149. Tanner, *Economy of Grace*; R. W. Gillett, *The New Globalization: Reclaiming the Lost Ground of our Christian Social Tradition*, Pilgrim Press, 2005.
150. Jay, *Road to Riches*, p. 134, quoting Gunder Frank.
151. Kennedy, *The Rise and Fall of the Great Powers*, p. 35.
152. D. Landes, *The Unbound Prometheus*, Cambridge University Press, 1969, p. 284.
153. Ferguson, *The Cash Nexus*, p. 311.
154. Wolf, *Why Globalization Works*, p. 173, quoting Marx and Engels, *The Communist Manifesto*, 1848.
155. Wolf, *Why Globalization Works*, p. 13.
156. D. Held, 'Becoming Cosmopolitan: The Dimensions and Challenges of Globalization', in P. Heslam (ed.), *Globalization and the Good*, SPCK, 2004.
157. Wolf, *Why Globalization Works*, pp. 48–9, quoting Kenneth Arrow.
158. S. P. Huntington, *Who Are We? America's Great Debate*, Simon & Schuster, 2005, p. 272.
159. Huntington, *Who Are We?* p. 273, quoting Manuel Castells.
160. Huntington, *Who Are We?* p. 271, quoting Adam Smith, *Wealth of Nations*.
161. Wolf, *Why Globalization Works*, p. 52.

162. Held in Heslam, *Globalization and the Good*, p. 8f.

163. Fukuyama, *The End of History*, p. 92.

164. Huntington, *Who Are We?* p. 261. For flows, see Ferguson, *Empire*, p. xx.

165. Wolf, *Why Globalization Works*, p. 97.

166. Wolf, *Why Globalization Works*, p. 96.

167. Huntington, *The Clash of Civilizations*, p. 78, quoting Braudel.

168. Wolf, *Why Globalization Works*, p. 318.

169. D. Hollenbach, *The Common Good and Christian Ethics*, Cambridge University Press, 2002, p. 238.

170. Wolf, *Why Globalization Works*, pp. 86–7.

171. Huntington, *Who Are We?*, pp. 287–8.

172. Ferguson, *Empire*, p. 171.

173. Wolf, *Why Globalization Works*, pp. 50–1.

174. J. Bhagwati, *In Defence of Globalization*, Oxford University Press, 2004.

175. Ferguson, *Colossus*, p. 197.

176. Wolf, *Why Globalization Works*, pp. 29–31.

177. Bhagwati, *In Defence of Globalization*, pp. 36f.

178. J. Keane, *Global Civil Society?*, Cambridge University Press, 2003.

179. Bhagwati, *In Defence of Globalization*, p. 36.

180. Bhagwati, *In Defence of Globalization*, pp. 14, 15.

181. Bhagwati, *In Defence of Globalization*, p. 16.

182. Wolf, *Why Globalization Works*, pp. 4–7.

183. Bhagwati, *In Defence of Globalization*, pp. 4, 30.

184. Atherton and Skinner, *Through the Eye of a Needle*, pp. 233–40.

185. Gillett, *The New Globalization*, p. 104.

186. Gillett, *The New Globalization*, p. 107.

187. Bhagwati, *In Defence of Globalization*, p. 20.

188. Atherton, *Marginalization*, p. 53.

189. Bhagwati, *In Defence of Globalization*, p. 53, quoting Adam Smith, *Wealth of Nations*.

190. Bhagwati, *In Defence of Globalization*, p. 56.

191. Bhagwati, *In Defence of Globalization*, p. 65.

192. Bhagwati, *In Defence of Globalization*, p. 64.

193. Bhagwati, *In Defence of Globalization*, p. 65.

194. Wolf, *Why Globalization Works*, p. 140.

195. Wolf, *Why Globalization Works*, pp. 171–2.

196. Bhagwati, *In Defence of Globalization*, pp. 69–70.

197. Bhagwati, *In Defence of Globalization*, p. 124.

198. Bhagwati, *In Defence of Globalization*, p. 172.

199. Wolf, *Why Globalization Works*, p. 235; p. 238, quoting Theodore Moran.

200. Bhagwati, *In Defence of Globalization*, p. 221.

201. Bhagwati, *In Defence of Globalization*, pp. 221, 222.

202. Bhagwati, *In Defence of Globalization*, pp. 233–9.

203. Bhagwati, *In Defence of Globalization*, p. 254, quoting Adam Smith, *The Wealth of Nations*; quoting J. M. Keynes (emphasis J. Atherton).

204. Bhagwati, *In Defence of Globalization*, p. 265.

Chapter 4 The Resurgent and Reformulating Religious Field

205. Huntington, *Who Are We?*, p. 15. G. Kepel, *The Revenge of God. The Resurgence of Islam, Christianity and Judaism in the Modern World*, Polity Press, 1994.

206. D. Forrester, 'The Scope of Public Theology', in Graham and Reed (eds), *The Future of Christian Social Ethics*, p. 19.

207. P. Berger (ed.), *The Desecularization of the World: Resurgent Religion and World Politics*, Eerdmans, 1999, p. 2.

208. A. McGrath, *The Twilight of Atheism: The Rise and Fall of Disbelief in the Modern World*, Doubleday, 2004.

209. T. Yates (ed.), *Mission and the Next Christendom*, Cliff College Publishing, 2005, p. 49.

210. Jenkins, *The Next Christendom*.

211. Jenkins, *The Next Christendom*, p. 1.

212. Jenkins, *The Next Christendom*, pp. 83–5.

213. G. Davie, *Europe: The Exceptional Case. Parameters of Faith in the Modern World*, Darton, Longman & Todd, 2002, p. 109.

214. MacFarlane, *The Riddle of the Modern World*, p. 256–7, referring to E. Gellner. Davie, *Europe*, p. 161. Huntington, *The Clash of Civilizations*, p. 70f. There is a significant overlap regarding the West as *exceptional*.

215. Jenkins, *The Next Christendom*, p. 1.

216. Jenkins, *The Next Christendom*, p. 3.

217. Jenkins, *The Next Christendom*, p. 10.

218. Jenkins, *The Next Christendom*, p. 2.

219. Jenkins, *The Next Christendom*, p. 7.

220. Jenkins, *The Next Christendom*, pp. 2–3.

221. Huntington, *Who Are We?*, pp. 344–5; Huntington, *The Clash of Civilizations*, p. 96.

222. Huntington, *The Clash of Civilizations*, p. 97.

223. Huntington, *The Clash of Civilizations*, p. 65.

224. Jenkins, *The Next Christendom*, p. 107; Davie, *Europe*, p. 121.

225. Jenkins, *The Next Christendom*, p 128.

226. Jenkins, *The Next Christendom*, p. 215.

227. Jenkins, *The Next Christendom*, p. 219.

228. Jenkins, *The Next Christendom*, p. 107.

229. Jenkins, *The Next Christendom*, p. 216.

230. Davie, *Europe*, p. 23f.

231. Huntington, *The Clash of Civilizations*, p. 94.

232. Davie, *Europe*, p. 159.

233. Hardt and Negri, *Empire*, p. 149.

234. Huntington, *Who Are We?*, pp. 88, 90.

235. Davie, *Europe*, pp. 28–9.

236. Huntington, *Who Are We?*, p. 345.

237. Davie, *Europe*, p. 30.

238. D. Clark, *Breaking the Mould of Christendom: Kingdom, Community, Diaconal Church and the Liberation of the Laity*, Epworth, 2005, p. 249.

239. Huntington, *Who Are We?*, p. 353f. See also J. Dilulio, *Godly Republic: A*

Centrist Blueprint for America's Faith-Based Future, University of California Press, 2007.

240. Huntington, *Who Are We?*, p. 344.
241. Jenkins, *The Next Christendom*, p. 61.
242. Jenkins, *The Next Christendom*, pp. 58–9.
243. Jenkins, *The Next Christendom*, p. 195.
244. Jenkins, *The Next Christendom*, p. 195.
245. Jenkins, *The Next Christendom*, p. 197.
246. Davie, *Europe*, p. 119.
247. Jenkins, *The Next Christendom*, p. 61f.
248. D. Martin, *On Secularization: Towards a Revised General Theory*, Ashgate, 2005, p. 27.
249. Martin, *On Secularization*, pp. 27–8.
250. Jenkins, *The Next Christendom*, pp. 64–5.
251. Jenkins, *The Next Christendom*, pp. 68, 71.
252. Martin, *On Secularization*, pp. 38–9.
253. Martin, *On Secularization*, pp. 141, 142.
254. Martin, *On Secularization*, p. 147.
255. Martin, *On Secularization*, p. 142.
256. *Faiths and Finance: A Place for Faith-Based Economics (A Preliminary Statement from Muslims and Christians in Manchester)*, Manchester Centre for Public Theology, 2006.
257. Huntington, *The Clash of Civilizations*, p. 110.
258. Martin, *On Secularization*, p. 28.
259. B. Lewis, *The Middle East: 2000 Years of History from the Rise of Christianity to the Present Day*, Weidenfeld & Nicolson, 2004, p. 242.
260. Hardt and Negri, *Empire*, p. 147.
261. Huntington, *Who Are We?*, p. 362.
262. Jenkins, *The Next Christendom*, pp. 166–8.
263. Jenkins, *The Next Christendom*, p. 164.
264. Vinoth Ramachandra, 'Religious Globalization and World Christianity', in Yates, *Mission and the Next Christendom*, p. 31, quoting Fred Halliday.
265. Atherton, *Public Theology for Changing Times*, chapter 6.
266. G. Davie, *Religion in Britain since 1945*, Blackwell, 1994, p. 46.
267. A. Hastings, *A History of English Christianity 1920–1990*, SCM Press, 1991, p. 603. J. Atherton, 'Church and Society in the North West, 1760–1997', in C. Ford, M. Powell and T. Wyke (eds), *The Church in Cottonopolis: Essays to mark the 150th Anniversary of the Diocese of Manchester*, The Lancashire and Cheshire Antiquarian Society, 1997, p. 58.
268. Davie, *Europe*, pp. 3–8.
269. McGrath, *The Twilight of Atheism*, pp. 241–2.
270. Davie, *Europe*, p. 5.
271. Davie, *Europe*, p. 19.
272. Davie, *Europe*, pp. 138–9, 147 on church as public utility; pp. 19–20 on vicarious religion.
273. Davie, *Europe*, p. 14. S. Bruce, *From Cathedrals to Cults: Religion in the Modern World*, Oxford University Press, 1996. B. Wilson, *Religion in Sociological Perspective*, Oxford University Press, 1982.

Notes

274. Davie, *Europe*, p. 147.
275. Baker, *The Hybrid Church in the City*, p. 63.
276. Martin, *On Secularization*, p. 24.
277. Martin, *On Secularization*, p. 88.
278. Yates, *Mission and the Next Christendom*, p. 159, quoting D. Tacey, *The Spirituality Revolution – the emergence of contemporary spirituality*, HarperCollins, 2003, p. 78.
279. Martin, *On Secularization*, p. 55.
280. L. Woodhead, G. Davie and P. Heelas (eds), *Predicting Religion: Christian Secular and Alternative Futures*, Ashgate, 2003.
281. McGrath, *The Twilight of Atheism*, p. 263, referring to Harvard Medical School research in 1998, 'Spirituality and Healing in Medicine'.
282. Davie, *Europe*, p. 154.
283. Davie, *Europe*, p. 17 and p. 155, quoting R. Inglehart and W. Baker, 'Modernization, cultural change and the persistence of traditional values' (2000).
284. Davie, *Europe*, p. 156, quoting S. Eisenstadt, 'Multiple Modernities', 2000.

Chapter 5 Social Capital

285. E. Butler, *Adam Smith – A Primer*, pp. 28–9.
286. A. MacFarlane, *The Riddle of the Modern World*, p. 178, quoting de Tocqueville. D. Halpern, *Social Capital*, Polity Press, 2005, p. 5, quoting de Tocqueville.
287. G. Himmelfarb, *The De-moralization of Society: From Victorian Virtues to Modern Values*, IEA Health and Welfare Unit, 1995, p. 57, quoting Burke.
288. W. Temple, *Christianity and Social Order*, SPCK, 1976 edition, pp. 70–3.
289. P. Bourdieu, in J. Richardson (ed.), *Handbook of Theory and Research for the Sociology of Education*, Greenwood Press, 1986. J. S. Coleman, *American Journal of Sociology*, 94 Supplement, 1988, S95–S120. Putnam, *Bowling Alone*, 2000.
290. Fukuyama, *The Great Disruption*, p. 149.
291. Fukuyama, *The Great Disruption*, p. 159.
292. Fukuyama, *The Great Disruption*, p. 27.
293. Putnam, *Bowling Alone*, chapter 23.
294. Himmelfarb, *The De-moralization of Society*.
295. Himmelfarb, *The De-moralization of Society*, pp. 221–2, quoting Carlyle on *Chartism*.
296. Himmelfarb, *The De-moralization of Society*, pp. 224–6.
297. Himmelfarb, *The De-moralization of Society*, p. 242.
298. Fukuyama, *The Great Disruption*, p. 50.
299. Fukuyama, *The Great Disruption*, p. 51.
300. Halpern, *Social Capital*, p. 1, quoting R. Putnam, 'Tuning in, Tuning Out: The Strange Disappearance of Social Capital in America', *Political Science and Politics* Vol. 28, No. 4 (1995), pp. 664–5.
301. Halpern, *Social Capital*, p.1.
302. Halpern, *Social Capital*, p. 4.
303. Halpern, *Social Capital*, pp. 10–13.
304. Halpern, *Social Capital*, pp. 19–22.

305. Halpern, *Social Capital*, pp. 13–19.
306. Halpern, *Social Capital*, p. 29f.
307. Halpern, *Social Capital*, p. 31.
308. Fukuyama, *The Great Disruption*, p. 49.
309. Fukuyama, *The Great Disruption*, p. 50–1.
310. Halpern, *Social Capital*, p. 74, quoting Durkheim, 1897.
311. Halpern, *Social Capital*, p. 80.
312. Halpern, *Social Capital*, p. 93.
313. Halpern, *Social Capital*, p. 151f.
314. A. Offer, *The Challenge of Affluence: Self-Control and Well-Being in the United States and Britain since 1950*, Oxford University Press, 2006.
315. Halpern, *Social Capital*, p. 176, quoting research by S. Knack, 'Social Capital and the Quality of Government: Evidence from the States', *American Journal of Political Science* Vol. 46, No. 4 (2002), pp. 772–85.
316. Halpern, *Social Capital*, p. 185f.
317. Halpern, *Social Capital*, p. 185, quoting Putnam, *Bowling Alone*.
318. Halpern, *Social Capital*, p. 194.
319. P. Bourdieu, *The Social Structures of the Economy*, Polity Press, 2005, p. 193.
320. Bourdieu, *The Social Structures of the Economy*, p. 3.
321. Bourdieu, *The Social Structures of the Economy*, p. 5.
322. Bourdieu, *The Social Structures of the Economy*, p. 193.
323. Bourdieu, *The Social Structures of the Economy*, pp. 197–8.
324. Bourdieu, *The Social Structures of the Economy*, p. 220, quoting Durkheim.
325. Bourdieu, *The Social Structures of the Economy*, p. 215.
326. Bourdieu, *The Social Structures of the Economy*, p. 214.
327. Halpern, *Social Capital*, p. 223, quoting Rothstein.
328. Bourdieu, *The Social Structures of the Economy*, p. 216. See G. S. Becker, *The Economics of Discrimination*, University of Chicago, 1971, and G. S. Becker, *The Economic Approach to Human Behavior*, University of Chicago Press, 1976.
329. Halpern, *Social Capital*, p. 276.
330. Putnam, *Bowling Alone*, p. 294.
331. Bourdieu, *The Social Structures of the Economy*, p. 223f. – 'Postscript: From the National to the International Field'.
332. Halpern, *Social Capital*, p. 236; R. Putnam and L. Feldstein with D. Cohen, *Better Together: Restoring the American Community*, Simon & Schuster, 2004 (henceforth, Putnam, *Better Together*), p. 269f.
333. Putnam, *Better Together*, p. 217 on 'moral economy', and p. 270 on sustainability, a key feature of Stiglitz's moral economy in J. Stiglitz, 'The Ethical Economist' in *Foreign Affairs*, November–December, 2005. This material is developed in Part 3 of my enquiry, on Faithful Economics.
334. Putnam, *Bowling Alone*, p. 66.
335. Both reports are published by the North West Development Agency.
336. Putnam, *Bowling Alone*, p. 67f.
337. Putnam, *Bowling Alone*, pp. 65–6.
338. Atherton, *Marginalization*, p. 41, quoting S. J. D. Green, *Religion in the Age of Decline: Organization and Experience in Industrial Yorkshire 1870–1920*, Cambridge University Press, 1996.

339. Putnam, *Bowling Alone*, p. 66.
340. Putnam, *Bowling Alone*, p. 77.
341. Halpern, *Social Capital*, pp. 178–9, quoting La Porta's research.
342. Putnam, *Bowling Alone*, p. 67, and quoting K. Wald.
343. Putnam, *Bowling Alone*, p. 67.
344. L. Francis and M. Robbins, 'Prayer, Purpose in Life, Personality, and Social Attitudes among Non-Churchgoing 13 to 15 Year Olds in England and Wales', *Research in the Social Scientific Study of Religion*, Volume 17, 2006, pp. 116–17.
345. L. Francis, Y. Katz, Y. Yablon and M. Robbins, 'Religiosity, Personality and Happiness: A Study Among Israeli Male Undergraduates', *Journal of Happiness Studies 5*, 2004, p. 325.
346. Atherton, *Marginalization*, p. 136f., quoting R. Gill, *Churchgoing and Christian Ethics*, Cambridge University Press, 1999.
347. *Faithful Cities: A Call for Celebration, Vision and Justice*, Church House Publishing, 2006, p. v.
348. C. Baker and H. Skinner, *Faith in Action: The dynamic connection between spiritual and religious capital*, William Temple Foundation, Manchester, 2006, p. 9.
349. Gill, *Churchgoing and Christian Ethics*, p. 206f.
350. Baker and Skinner, *Faith in Action*, p. 20.
351. Baker and Skinner, *Faith in Action*, pp. 20–1.
352. Baker and Skinner, *Faith in Action*, p. 46.
353. A. Davey, 'Faithful Cities: Locating Everyday Faithfulness', in *Contact*, 15.2: 'Faithful Cities', pp. 15–17.
354. F. D. Maurice, *The Life of Frederick Denison Maurice*, Vol. 2, Macmillan, 1884, p. 550; E. R. Norman, *Victorian Christian Socialists*, Cambridge University Press, 1987, pp. 31–2.

Part 2 Introduction

1. O. James, *Affluenza*, p. 338.
2. *Faiths and Finance: A Place for Faith-Based Economics (a preliminary statement from Muslims and Christians in Manchester)*, Manchester Centre for Public Theology, 2006.

Chapter 6 The Happiness Hypothesis

3. Atherton, *Marginalization*, p. 76.
4. Kenny, *Life, Liberty and the Pursuit of Utility*, p. 9.
5. Kenny, *Life, Liberty and the Pursuit of Utility*, p. 8.
6. James, *Affluenza*, p. xiv.
7. Haidt, *The Happiness Hypothesis*. R. Layard, *Happiness: Lessons from a New Science*, Allen Lane, 2005.
8. Wilkinson, *The Impact of Inequality*, 2005.
9. Livi-Bacci, *A Concise History of World Population*, p. 93.
10. Livi-Bacci, *A Concise History of World Population*, p. 91.
11. Diamond, *Guns, Germs and Steel*, p. 92.
12. Offer, *The Challenge of Affluence*, p. 36.
13. Layard, *Happiness*, p. 4.
14. J. Atherton, 'Exploring the Paradox of Prosperity: Developing Agendas for

Christian Social Ethics', in Atherton and Skinner, *Through the Eye of a Needle*, pp. 87, 86.

15. Kenny, *Life, Liberty and the Pursuit of Utility*, p. 82.

16. J. Bhagwati, *In Defence of Globalization*, p. 145. Wolf, *Why Globalization Works*, p. 189.

17. Wilkinson, *The Impact of Inequality*, p. 9.

18. Wilkinson, *The Impact of Inequality*, p. 10.

19. James, *Affluenza*, p. 39.

20. Kenny, *Life, Liberty and the Pursuit of Utility*, p. 198.

21. Kenny, *Life, Liberty and the Pursuit of Utility*, p. 191.

22. Wilkinson, *The Impact of Inequality*, p. 244.

23. Wilkinson, *The Impact of Inequality*, p. 248.

24. J. Browne, *Charles Darwin: The Power of Place*, Pimlico, 2003, pp. 276–7.

25. Kenny, *Life, Liberty and the Pursuit of Utility*, p. 187.

26. Layard, *Happiness*, p. 3.

27. Offer, *The Challenge of Affluence*, p. 2.

28. Offer, *The Challenge of Affluence*, p. 286.

29. J. Lomax, 'The Paradox of Prosperity', in *Prosperity with a Purpose: Exploring the Ethics of Affluence*, CTBI, 2005, pp. 30–1, 34.

30. Offer, *The Challenge of Affluence*, p. 16.

31. Atherton, *Marginalization*, p. 165. Measurement issues are more fully discussed in pp. 161–6.

32. Offer, *The Challenge of Affluence*, p. 19.

33. Offer, *The Challenge of Affluence*, pp. 16, 21.

34. Offer, *The Challenge of Affluence*, p. 23.

35. Offer, *The Challenge of Affluence*, p. 28f.

36. Kenny, *Life, Liberty and the Pursuit of Utility*, p. 9.

37. Offer, *The Challenge of Affluence*, p. 35.

38. Layard, *Happiness*, pp. 13–14.

39. See Kenny, *Life, Liberty and the Pursuit of Utility*, chapter 1 for this history.

40. Haidt, *The Happiness Hypothesis*, pp. 156–7.

41. Kenny, *Life, Liberty and the Pursuit of Utility*, p. 24.

42. See R. Easterlin (ed.), *Happiness in Economics*, Edward Elgar, 2002, for economic sources, and Haidt, *The Happiness Hypothesis*, for psychological sources.

43. Kenny, *Life, Liberty and the Pursuit of Utility*, p. 54.

44. Kenny, *Life, Liberty and the Pursuit of Utility*, p. 46, on income; p. 75 on life expectancy. See also R. Fogel, *The Escape from Hunger and Premature Death, 1700–2100*, Cambridge University Press, 2004.

45. Layard, *Happiness*, p. 35.

46. Layard, *Happiness*, pp. 35, 37, 79.

47. Layard, *Happiness*, p. 79.

48. Offer, *The Challenge of Affluence*, p. 8.

49. Layard, *Happiness*, pp. 91–2, Putnam's very title includes this concern, *Bowling Alone: The Collapse and Revival of American Community*.

50. K. Polanyi, *The Great Transformation*, Boston, 1944, in Offer, *The Challenge of Affluence*, p. 75.

51. James, *Affluenza*, p. 11.

52. James, *Affluenza*, p. xiv.

53. James, *Affluenza*, p. 10.
54. James, *Affluenza*, p. 15.
55. Layard, *Happiness*, p. 17f.
56. Haidt, *The Happiness Hypothesis*, p. 32f.
57. Layard, *Happiness*, p. 58.
58. Haidt, *The Happiness Hypothesis*, p. 90.
59. Haidt, *The Happiness Hypothesis*, p. 90.
60. Haidt, *The Happiness Hypothesis*, p. 91.
61. Haidt, *The Happiness Hypothesis*, p. 91.
62. Haidt, *The Happiness Hypothesis*, p. 86, quoting Adam Smith, *The Theory of Moral Sentiments*, 1759.
63. Kenny, *Life, Liberty and the Pursuit of Utility*, p. 170, quoting A. Sen, *The Standard of Living*.
64. Haidt, *The Happiness Hypothesis*, p. 168f.
65. Layard, *Happiness*, chapter 5.
66. Layard, *Happiness*, p. 65.
67. Layard, *Happiness*, p. 65.
68. Layard, *Happiness*, p. 66.
69. Layard, *Happiness*, p. 65.
70. Layard, *Happiness*, pp. 67–8. Wilkinson, *The Impact of Inequality*, pp. 73–4, 163–4.
71. Layard, *Happiness*, p. 69.
72. Layard, *Happiness*, p. 70.
73. Layard, *Happiness*, p. 72.
74. W. Temple, *Christianity and Social Order*, 1942, SPCK, 1976 edition, p. 97.
75. The connections with contemporary well-being sources are referenced in the text. Nussbaum is the exception: see S. Alkire, *Valuing Freedoms, Sen's Capability Approach and Poverty Reduction*, Oxford University Press, 2002, p. 35, referring to M. Nussbaum, *Women and Human Development: The Capabilities Approach*, 2000.
76. Atherton and Skinner, *Through the Eye of a Needle*, pp. 89–90.
77. Alkire, *Valuing Freedoms*, p. 48.
78. Layard, *Happiness*, p. 260, note 4.
79. A. H. Maslow, *Motivation and Personality*, Harper & Row, 1954: see R. Greenwood and H. Burgess, *Power*, SPCK, 2005, p. 44.
80. R. Thorpe, R. Holt, A. Macpherson and L. Puttaway, 'Using knowledge within small and medium-sized firms: a systematic review of evidence', *International Journal of Management Reviews*, Vol. 7, Issue no. 4, December 2005, Blackwell Publishing, p. 272.
81. Greenwood and Burgess, *Power*, p. 52.
82. R. Merchant and P. Gilbert, 'The Modern Workplace: Surfing the Wave or Surviving the Straightjacket?', *Crucible*, January–March 2007, p. 39.
83. S. P. Huntington, *Who Are We?*, p. 27.
84. Kenny, *Life, Liberty and the Pursuit of Utility*, p. 100.
85. James, *Affluenza*, p. 314.
86. James, *Affluenza*, pp. 343–6.
87. James, *Affluenza*, pp. xiv–xv.
88. James, *Affluenza*, p. 35.

89. James, *Affluenza*, pp. 64–5.
90. James, *Affluenza*, pp. 73, 72; unselfish capitalism, p. 328.
91. Wilkinson, *The Impact of Inequality*, p. 15.
92. Wilkinson, *The Impact of Inequality*, p. 16.
93. Wilkinson, *The Impact of Inequality*, p. 18.
94. Layard, *Happiness*, p. 104.
95. Offer, *The Challenge of Affluence*, p. 304.
96. Offer, *The Challenge of Affluence*, p. 307.
97. Offer, *The Challenge of Affluence*, p. 316.
98. Offer, *The Challenge of Affluence*, p. 316.
99. Layard, *Happiness*, pp. 78–9.
100. Layard, *Happiness*, p. 79.
101. Offer, *The Challenge of Affluence*, p. 335f.
102. Offer, *The Challenge of Affluence*, pp. 339–56.
103. Wilkinson, *The Impact of Inequality*, p. 269.
104. Wilkinson, *The Impact of Inequality*, p. 270.
105. P. Ormerod and H. Johns, 'Against Happiness', *Prospect*, April 2007, p. 36.
106. James, *Affluenza*, p. 314.
107. Wilkinson, *The Impact of Inequality*, p. 37, quoting A. de Tocqueville's *Democracy in America*.
108. Wilkinson, *The Impact of Inequality*, p. 44, quoting R. Putnam, *Making Democracy Work: Civic traditions in modern Italy*, 1993.
109. Wilkinson, *The Impact of Inequality*, pp. 50, 52, 104–5.
110. Wilkinson, *The Impact of Inequality*, p. 126.
111. Wilkinson, *The Impact of Inequality*, p. 36.
112. Wilkinson, *The Impact of Inequality*, p. 35.
113. Kenny, *Life, Liberty and the Pursuit of Utility*, p. 135.
114. Atherton in Atherton and Skinner, *Through the Eye of a Needle*, p. 89.
115. Haidt, *The Happiness Hypothesis*, p. x.
116. Kenny, *Life, Liberty and the Pursuit of Utility*, chapter 9.
117. Haidt, *The Happiness Hypothesis*, pp. 166–7, referring to A. MacIntyre, *After Virtue*.
118. Kenny, *Life, Liberty and the Pursuit of Utility*, p. 179.
119. Kenny, *Life, Liberty and the Pursuit of Utility*, p. 181, quoting J. Bentham, *Works*, 1843.
120. Halpern, *Social Capital*, p. 10.
121. Haidt, *The Happiness Hypothesis*, p. 160.
122. Layard, *Happiness*, pp. 95, 125.
123. Kenny, *Life, Liberty and the Pursuit of Utility*, p. 184.
124. Haidt, *The Happiness Hypothesis*, p. 172.
125. Kenny, *Life, Liberty and the Pursuit of Utility*, p. 188, quoting Adam Smith, *Theory of Moral Sentiments*.
126. Kenny, *Life, Liberty and the Pursuit of Utility*, p. 188.
127. Layard, *Happiness*, p. 101. *The Economist*, 6 October 2007.
128. Layard, *Happiness*, p. 101.
129. Layard, *Happiness*, pp. 120–1.
130. Kenny, *Life, Liberty and the Pursuit of Utility*, p. 204.
131. Kenny, *Life, Liberty and the Pursuit of Utility*, p. 202, referring to T. Pogge,

'An Egalitarian Law of Peoples', 1994.

132. Haidt, *The Happiness Hypothesis*, pp. 42, 47. Layard, *Happiness*, p. 117.

133. Haidt, *The Happiness Hypothesis*, pp. 48–52.

134. Kenny, *Life, Liberty and the Pursuit of Utility*, p. 191, quoting Max Weber, in McMahon.

135. Haidt, *The Happiness Hypothesis*, p. 187f.

136. Haidt, *The Happiness Hypothesis*, p. 42.

137. Layard, *Happiness*, p. 117. Haidt, *The Happiness Hypothesis*, p. 45. Matthew 7.12.

138. Layard, *Happiness*, p. 189.

139. Layard, *Happiness*, p. 190.

140. Layard, *Happiness*, p. 192.

141. Layard, *Happiness*, pp. 192–3.

142. Layard, *Happiness*, p. 194.

143. Haidt, *The Happiness Hypothesis*, p. 164.

144. Haidt, *The Happiness Hypothesis*, pp. 156–7.

145. Haidt, *The Happiness Hypothesis*, p. 167.

146. Haidt, *The Happiness Hypothesis*, p. 170.

147. Haidt, *The Happiness Hypothesis*, p. 187.

148. Haidt, *The Happiness Hypothesis*, p. 192.

149. Haidt, *The Happiness Hypothesis*, p. 193.

150. Haidt, *The Happiness Hypothesis*, p. 203.

151. Layard, *Happiness*, p. 234.

152. R. H. Tawney, *The Attack and Other Papers*, Allen & Unwin, 1953, pp. 127–8.

153. Haidt, *The Happiness Hypothesis*, p. 205, quoting A. H. Maslow, *Religions, Values, and Peak-Experiences*, 1964.

154. Haidt, *The Happiness Hypothesis*, p. 230.

155. Haidt, *The Happiness Hypothesis*, p. 211.

156. Tanner, *Economy of Grace*.

157. Layard, *Happiness*, p. 128. Tanner, *Economy of Grace*, p. x. Bourdieu, *The Social Structures of the Economy*, p. 193f., 'Principles of an Economic Anthropology'.

158. Wilkinson, *The Impact of Inequality*, p. 287.

159. Layard, *Happiness*, p. 127.

160. Wilkinson, *The Impact of Inequality*, p. 301.

161. Wilkinson, *The Impact of Inequality*, p. 298.

162. Wilkinson, *The Impact of Inequality*, p. 31.

163. Wilkinson, *The Impact of Inequality*, p. 302.

164. S. Bowles, 'Globalization and Redistribution: Feasible Egalitarianism in a Competitive World', in R. B. Freeman, *Inequality Around the World*, Palgrave Macmillan, 2002, p. 235.

165. K. J. Arrow, 'Distributed Information and the Role of the State in the Economy', in Freeman, *Inequality Around the World*, p. 269.

166. Wilkinson, *The Impact of Inequality*, p. 302.

167. Layard, *Happiness*, pp. 133–5.

168. Layard, *Happiness*, p. 141.

169. Haidt, *The Happiness Hypothesis*, p. 13.

170. Haidt, *The Happiness Hypothesis*, p. 14f.

171. Layard, *Happiness*, pp. 127–8.

172. Layard, *Happiness*, p. 98.

173. Offer, *The Challenge of Affluence*, p. 367.

174. See P. Backstrom, *Christian Socialism and Co-operation in Victorian England*, Croom Helm, 1974.

175. Offer, *The Challenge of Affluence*, p. 75.

176. Offer, *The Challenge of Affluence*, pp. 75, 84.

177. Offer, *The Challenge of Affluence*, pp. 85, 86.

178. Offer, *The Challenge of Affluence*, p. 87.

179. Offer, *The Challenge of Affluence*, p. 89.

180. Hardt and Negri, *Multitude*, p. 79f.

181. Offer, *The Challenge of Affluence*, p. 99.

182. A. Falk and U. Fischbacher, 'The Economics of Reciprocity: Evidence and Theory', in Freeman, *Inequality Around the World*, p. 207f.

183. Layard, *Happiness*, p. 69.

184. Atherton, *Marginalization*, p. 175.

185. W. Temple, *Christianity and Social Order*, p. 97.

186. J. Atherton, *Social Christianity: A Reader*, SPCK, 1994, pp. 27, 181f. (Rauschenbusch on economic democracy).

187. Wilkinson, *The Impact of Inequality*, pp. 15–16.

188. Wilkinson, *The Impact of Inequality*, p. 304.

189. Wilkinson, *The Impact of Inequality*, p. 306.

190. Wilkinson, *The Impact of Inequality*, p. 306.

191. Wilkinson, *The Impact of Inequality*, p. 305.

Chapter 7 Mapping Faith-based Contributions to Well-being

192. Atherton and Skinner, *Through the Eye of a Needle*, pp. 257–8.

193. *Faith in the City*, Church Urban Fund, para. 7.88f., and recommendation 25. The proposal seemed to emerge, almost as a 'rabbit out of a hat' introduced by chairman and secretary (I was there).

194. As principle and strategy required of governments and linked to World Bank financing, see K. Marshall and L. Keogh, *Mind, Heart and Soul in the Fight Against Poverty*, World Bank, 2004 (henceforth, Marshall), pp. 16, 42–3.

195. Atherton, *Marginalization*.

196. *Faith in the City*, pp. 78, 185.

197. *Faithful Cities*, pp. 68, 69, 91, 70, 72, 73.

198. Baker, *The Hybrid Church in the City*, p. 63.

199. Atherton, *Public Theology for Changing Times*, chapters 4–7.

200. Atherton, *Public Theology for Changing Times*, p. 87.

201. Atherton, *Public Theology for Changing Times*, p. 141.

202. Marshall, *Mind, Heart and Soul*.

203. Marshall, *Mind, Heart and Soul*, pp. 1, 2.

204. M. Palmer and V. Finlay, *Faith in Conservation: New Approaches to Religions and the Environment*, World Bank, p. xi (henceforth Palmer).

205. Marshall, *Mind, Heart and Soul*, p. 2.

206. Marshall, *Mind, Heart and Soul*, p. 8.

207. Marshall, *Mind, Heart and Soul*, chapter 2.
208. Marshall, *Mind, Heart and Soul*, p. 208.
209. M. Brown, 'Christian Ethics and Economics after Liberalism', in Atherton and Skinner, *Through the Eye of a Needle*, pp. 63–4.
210. Matthew 26.11 'For you always have the poor with you . . .'.
211. D. S. Long, *Divine Economy, Theology and the Market*, Routledge, 2000, pp. 242–3. See also D. Meeks, *God the Economist. The Doctrine of God and Political Economy*, Fortress, 1989 (also see his use of the concept, 'The Economy of Grace': p. 200); see also 'Desire, Artificial Scarcity and Debt', in his 'The Economy of Grace: Human Dignity in the Market System', in Soulen and Woodhead, *God and Human Dignity*, pp. 205–6.
212. Marshall, *Mind, Heart and Soul*, p. xi.
213. Marshall, *Mind, Heart and Soul*, pp. 5–6.
214. Marshall, *Mind, Heart and Soul*, p. 15.
215. Palmer, *Faith in Conservation*, pp. 137–8.
216. R. H. Tawney, *Religion and the Rise of Capitalism*, Murray, 1926, p. 268.
217. Kenny, *Life, Liberty and the Pursuit of Utility*, p. 204.
218. The bias for inclusivity was elaborated in my *Marginalization*, pp. 117–122.
219. D. Forrester, *On Human Worth: A Christian Vindication of Equality*, SCM Press, 2001, p. 99.
220. D. Hicks, *Inequality and Christian Ethics*, Cambridge University Press, 2000, p. 138.
221. New Economics Foundation, 'Chasing Progress. Beyond Measuring Economic Growth', at www.neweconomics.org, 2004, p. 4. I owe this reference to Professor Ian Steedman's unpublished paper, 'Notes on Income and Well-being', 27 April, 2007.
222. Atherton, *Marginalization*, p. 91.
223. China – see *The Economist*, 13–19 October 2007, p. 27; Atherton, 'The Happiness Hypothesis', *Crucible*, January–March, 2007, p. 32.
224. H. Skinner, 'Trading Life and Death: Reflections on Current Trade Negotiations', *Crucible*, January–March, 2005, p. 6.
225. See Atherton, *Marginalization*, pp. 90–2, 158.
226. Atherton, *Marginalization* p. 158.
227. A. Sen, *On Ethics and Economics*, Blackwell, 1999 edition, p. 259.
228. *Our Common Future*, Brundtland Report, 1987, in Atherton *Marginalization*, p. 158.
229. Putnam, *Better Together*.
230. Marshall, *Mind, Heart and Soul*, p. 29.
231. Marshall, *Mind, Heart and Soul*, chapter 4.
232. P. Tillich, *On the Boundary*, Collins, 1967.
233. Baker, *The Hybrid Church in the City*, pp. 95–6, referring to MacIntyre and the task of reformulating tradition – developed in N. Kamergrauzis, *The Persistence of Christian Realism: A Study of the Social Ethics of Ronald H. Preston*, University of Uppsala, 2001.
234. Marshall, *Mind, Heart and Soul*, pp. 49, 50.
235. Marshall, *Mind, Heart and Soul*, chapter 6.
236. Marshall, *Mind, Heart and Soul*, p. 65.
237. Marshall, *Mind, Heart and Soul*, p. 66.

238. Marshall, *Mind, Heart and Soul*, p. 67.

239. Marshall, *Mind, Heart and Soul*, p. 67, quoting A. Sen 'Ethical Challenges: Old and New', 2003.

240. Marshall, *Mind, Heart and Soul*, p. 70, quoting A. Sen, Speech delivered on Ethics and Development Day, 2004.

241. Marshall, *Mind, Heart and Soul*, chapter 7.

242. R. Merchant and P. Gilbert, 'The Modern Workplace', *Crucible*, January–March 2007, p. 39f.

243. Marshall, *Mind, Heart and Soul*, p. 75.

244. Marshall, *Mind, Heart and Soul*, pp. 77, 78.

245. Marshall, *Mind, Heart and Soul*, pp. 79, 80.

246. Marshall, *Mind, Heart and Soul*, pp. 81–3.

247. Marshall, *Mind, Heart and Soul*, chapter 9.

248. Marshall, *Mind, Heart and Soul*, p. 97.

249. Marshall, *Mind, Heart and Soul*, p. 98.

250. Marshall, *Mind, Heart and Soul*, p. 111.

251. Marshall, *Mind, Heart and Soul*, p. 122.

252. Marshall, *Mind, Heart and Soul*, chapter 15.

253. Marshall, *Mind, Heart and Soul*, p. 184.

254. Marshall, *Mind, Heart and Soul*, p. 184.

255. Marshall, *Mind, Heart and Soul*, p. 186.

256. Atherton, *Marginalization*, p. 82.

257. Marshall, *Mind, Heart and Soul*, chapter 16. See also Palmer, *Faith in Conservation*, pp. 44–6.

258. Marshall, *Mind, Heart and Soul*, p. 196.

259. Marshall, *Mind, Heart and Soul*, pp. 196–7, 197.

260. Marshall, *Mind, Heart and Soul*, p. 198.

261. Marshall, *Mind, Heart and Soul*, p. 199.

262. Marshall, *Mind, Heart and Soul*, p. 200.

263. See especially, Bhagwati, *In Defence of Globalization*, p. 207. Also J. Stiglitz, *Globalization and its Discontents*, Allen Lane, 2002, pp. 128–132, etc. J. Stiglitz, *Making Globalization Work. The Next Steps to Global Justice*, Allen Lane, 2006.

264. Marshall, *Mind, Heart and Soul*, p. 272.

265. Marshall, *Mind, Heart and Soul*, p. 275.

266. Marshall, *Mind, Heart and Soul*, p. 100.

267. Marshall, *Mind, Heart and Soul*, pp. 100–04.

268. Marshall, *Mind, Heart and Soul*, p. 103.

269. Marshall, *Mind, Heart and Soul*, pp. 103–04.

270. Marshall, *Mind, Heart and Soul*, p. 190.

271. Palmer, *Faith in Conservation*, pp. 3–5.

272. Palmer, *Faith in Conservation*, p. 5.

273. D. Herbert, *Religion and Civil Society: Rethinking Religion in the Contemporary World*, Ashgate, 2003, pp. 274–5.

274. Herbert, *Religion and Civil Society*, p. 275.

275. Herbert, *Religion and Civil Society*, p. 201, quoting K. Kubik, *The Power of Symbols Against the Symbols of Power* (1994). See G. Davie, *Religion in Modern Europe*, p. 158.

276. Palmer, *Faith in Conservation*, pp. 11, 12.

Notes

277. Palmer, *Faith in Conservation*, p. 39.

278. Palmer, *Faith in Conservation*, pp. 42, 43.

279. Palmer, *Faith in Conservation*, p. 43.

280. A. Morisy, *Journeying Out: A New Approach to Christian Mission*, Continuum, 2004, p. 237.

281. Morisy, *Journeying Out*, p. 61.

282. Morisy, *Journeying Out*, p. 62.

283. Putnam, *Better Together*, chapter 6.

284. Putnam, *Better Together*, p. 121.

285. Putnam, *Better Together*, p. 31.

286. On All Saints, Pasadena, Putnam, *Better Together*, pp. 135–41.

287. Putnam, *Better Together*, p. 129. See E. R. Wickham, *Church and People in an Industrial City*, Lutterworth Press, 1957, p. 223 ('Wesley had insisted that every member of the Society should be in a class of known membership'); p. 253 – on mission 'cells'.

288. H. Rack, *Reasonable Enthusiast: John Wesley and the Rise of Methodism*, Epworth Press, 1992, p. 241f.

289. Palmer, *Faith in Conservation*, p. 30.

290. J. Reader, *Local Theology: Church and Community in Dialogue*, SPCK, 1994, chapter 5. 'Friends of Hopesay Meadow Environmental Project'.

291. Palmer, *Faith in Conservation*, pp. 30–1.

292. Palmer, *Faith in Conservation*, p. 63.

293. Baker, *The Hybrid Church in the City*, pp. 120–2. Putnam, *Better Together*, chapter 1.

294. Putnam, *Better Together*, p. 31.

295. Baker, 'Entry to Enterprise: Constructing Local Political Economies in Manchester', in Atherton and Skinner, *Through the Eye of a Needle*.

296. Baker, 'Entry to Enterprise', p. 195. Putnam, *Better Together*, chapter 9 'Experience Corps: "Old Heads" to the Schools'.

297. Baker, 'Entry to Enterprise', p. 200.

298. Baker, 'Entry to Enterprise', p. 202.

299. Palmer, *Faith in Conservation*, p. 49.

300. I. Young, *Inclusion and Democracy*, Oxford University Press, 2000, pp. 56, 63, 74, 75. Atherton, *Marginalization*, pp. 113–4.

301. Palmer, *Faith in Conservation*, p. 55.

302. Palmer, *Faith in Conservation*, p. 54, quoting Walter Fust.

303. G. Davie, *Religion in Modern Europe*, p. 156, and 'Pilgrimage and Place', pp. 157–62.

304. Palmer, *Faith in Conservation*, p. 61.

305. Long, *Divine Economy*, p. 177.

306. A. Hira and J. Ferrie, 'Fair Trade: Three Key Challenges for Reaching the Mainstream', in *Journal of Business Ethics* 63, 2006, p. 107.

307. G. Moore, 'The Fair Trade Movement: Parameters, Issues and Future Research', in *Journal of Business Ethics* 53, 2004, p. 73.

308. M. Northcott, 'The World Trade Organization, Fair Trade and the Body Politics of St Paul', in Atherton and Skinner, *Through the Eye of a Needle*, p. 183.

309. Moore, 'The Fair Trade Movement', p. 75.

310. Long, *Divine Economy*, p. 228f.

311. Atherton, *Christianity and the Market*, p. 142.
312. Atherton, *Social Christianity: A Reader*, p. 19.
313. Moore, 'The Fair Trade Movement', pp. 73–4.
314. Moore, 'The Fair Trade Movement', p. 81.
315. Hira and Ferrie, 'Fair Trade', p. 114.
316. Hira and Ferrie, 'Fair Trade', p. 114.
317. Hira and Ferrie, 'Fair Trade', p. 116.
318. Moore, 'The Fair Trade Movement', pp. 73, 74.
319. Hira and Ferrie, 'Fair Trade', p. 115.
320. J. K. Galbraith, *A History of Economics: The Past as the Present*, 1989, pp. 26, 26–7.
321. Marshall, *Mind, Heart and Soul*, p. 39.
322. Marshall, *Mind, Heart and Soul*, p. 36.
323. Marshall, *Mind, Heart and Soul*, p. 37.
324. Marshall, *Mind, Heart and Soul*, p. 44.
325. Marshall, *Mind, Heart and Soul*, p. 36.
326. Marshall, *Mind, Heart and Soul*, p. 44.
327. Atherton, *Marginalization*, pp. 169–72.
328. Long, *Divine Economy*. P. Goodchild, *Capitalism and Religion: The Price of Piety*, Routledge, 2002.
329. *Faiths and Finance*, Manchester, p. 15.
330. R. H. Preston, *Religion and the Ambiguities of Capitalism*, SCM Press, 1991, Appendix 1. 'Usury and a Christian Ethic of Finance'. R. Wilson, *Economics, Ethics and Religion: Jewish, Christian and Muslim Economic Thought*, Macmillan, 1997. S. L. Buckley, *Teachings on Usury in Judaism, Christianity and Islam*, The Edward Mellen Press, 2000. M. U. Chapra, *Towards a Just Monetary System*, The Islamic Foundation, 1985.
331. Atherton, *Marginalization*, p. 171. Final quote, E. Gellner, *Postmodernism, Reason and Religion*, 1992.
332. For a list of such financial instruments, and definitions, see Z. Hussain in Atherton and Skinner, *Through the Eye of a Needle*, pp. 113–14. *Faiths and Finance*, pp. 21–2.
333. Atherton, *Marginalization*, pp. 170–1, quoting Buckley.
334. Hussain in Atherton and Skinner, *Through the Eye of a Needle*, p. 112.
335. *Faiths and Finance*, pp. 24, 24–5.
336. *Faiths and Finance*, p. 25.
337. *Faiths and Finance*, p. 27.
338. *Faiths and Finance*, p. 28.
339. *Faiths and Finance*, p. 30.
340. *Faiths and Finance*, p. 30.
341. *Faiths and Finance*, pp. 32–3.
342. Hira and Ferrie, 'Fair Trade', p. 116.

Part 3 Introduction

1. C. Cowley, *The Value of Money*.
2. P. Jay, *Road to Riches*, p. 111.

Chapter 8 Faith-Based Contributions to Post-scarcity Anthropology

3. Layard, *Happiness*, p. 72.

4. Hardt and Negri, *Empire*, p. 413.

5. Palmer, *Faith in Conservation*. Marshall, *Mind, Heart and Soul*.

6. In Soulen and Woodhead, *God and Human Dignity*.

7. In R. Ruston, *Human Rights and the Image of God*, SCM Press, 2004.

8. D. Browning, 'Human Dignity, Human Complexity, and Human Goods', in Soulen and Woodhead, *God and Human Dignity*, pp. 229–316.

9. E. Graham, 'The "End" of the Human or the End of the "Human"? Human Dignity in Technological Perspective', in Soulen and Woodhead, *God and Human Dignity*, pp. 264, 278.

10. Wilkinson, *The Impact of Inequality*, p. 248.

11. E. Graham in Soulen and Woodhead, *God and Human Dignity*, p. 281.

12. D. Browning in Soulen and Woodhead, *God and Human Dignity*, p. 300.

13. Browning in Soulen and Woodhead, *God and Human Dignity*, p. 301.

14. Browning in Soulen and Woodhead, *God and Human Dignity*, pp. 301–2.

15. Browning in Soulen and Woodhead, *God and Human Dignity*, pp. 306–7.

16. Browning in Soulen and Woodhead, *God and Human Dignity*, p. 309.

17. Browning in Soulen and Woodhead, *God and Human Dignity*, pp. 310–11.

18. Browning in Soulen and Woodhead, *God and Human Dignity*, pp. 311–12.

19. Browning in Soulen and Woodhead, *God and Human Dignity*, p. 313.

20. C. Baker and H. Skinner, *Faith in Action. The dynamic connection between spiritual and religious capital*, William Temple Foundation, 2006, p. 20.

21. Palmer, *Faith in Conservation*.

22. L. Woodhead, 'Apophatic Theology', in Soulen and Woodhead, *God and Human Dignity*.

23. D. Martin, *On Secularization*, pp. 176–7.

24. Palmer, *Faith in Conservation*, p. 50.

25. Soulen and Woodhead, *God and Human Dignity*, 'The Self in the Psalms and the Image of God', p. 27.

26. Soulen and Woodhead, *God and Human Dignity*, pp. 3–4.

27. Soulen and Woodhead, *God and Human Dignity*, p. 5.

28. Soulen and Woodhead, *God and Human Dignity*, pp. 3, 6.

29. Soulen and Woodhead, *God and Human Dignity*, p. 6.

30. Soulen and Woodhead, *God and Human Dignity*, pp. 6, 7.

31. Soulen and Woodhead, *God and Human Dignity*, pp. 7–8.

32. Soulen and Woodhead, *God and Human Dignity*, p. 27.

33. Browning in Soulen and Woodhead, *God and Human Dignity*, pp. 313–14.

34. Browning in Soulen and Woodhead, *God and Human Dignity*, p. 314.

35. Browning in Soulen and Woodhead, *God and Human Dignity*, p. 314.

36. Browning in Soulen and Woodhead, *God and Human Dignity*, p. 315.

37. L. Robbins, *The Nature and Significance of Economic Science*, 1934, quoted in P. Donaldson, *Economics of the Real World*, Penguin, 1973, p. 22.

38. Browning in Soulen and Woodhead, *God and Human Dignity*, p. 315.

39. Browning in Soulen and Woodhead, *God and Human Dignity*, p. 316.

40. Browning in Soulen and Woodhead, *God and Human Dignity*, p. 316.

41. Greenwood and Burgess, *Power*, p. 25, referring to J. D. Zizioulas, *Being as*

Communion: Studies in Personhood and the Church, 1985.

42. F. D. Maurice, *The Life of Frederick Denison Maurice*, Vol. 2, p. 32.
43. Greenwood and Burgess, *Power*, p. 25.
44. Greenwood and Burgess, *Power*, p. 25.
45. V. Ramachandra, 'Who can say what and to/for whom? Postcolonial theory and Christian theology', in Yates, *Mission and the Next Christendom*, pp. 140, 139, 140.
46. Atherton and Skinner, *Through the Eye of a Needle*, p. 91. D. Allchin, *Participation in God: a Forgotten Thread in Anglican Tradition*, Darton, Longman & Todd, 1988.
47. Graham in Soulen and Woodhead, *God and Human Dignity*, p. 280.
48. Woodhead in Soulen and Woodhead, *God and Human Dignity*, p. 235.
49. Woodhead in Soulen and Woodhead, *God and Human Dignity*, p. 237.
50. H. S. Reinders, 'Human Dignity in the Absence of Agency', in Soulen and Woodhead, *God and Human Dignity*, pp. 121, 139.
51. Woodhead in Soulen and Woodhead, *God and Human Dignity*, p. 246.
52. Browning in Soulen and Woodhead, *God and Human Dignity*, p. 316.
53. C. Baker, *The Hybrid Church in the City*, p. 75.
54. V. Ramachandra in Yates, *Mission and the Next Christendom*, pp. 139–140.
55. Haidt, *The Happiness Hypothesis*, chapters 8, 9, 10.
56. Browning in Soulen and Woodhead, *God and Human Dignity*, p. 314.
57. R. K. Soulen, 'Cruising toward Bethlehem: Human Dignity and the New Eugenics', in Soulen and Woodhead, *God and Human Dignity*, p. 117.
58. R. Ruston, *Human Rights and the Image of God*, SCM Press, 2004, Part 2.
59. On St Irenaeus, Woodhead in Soulen and Woodhead, *God and Human Dignity*, p. 238; Baker, *The Hybrid Church in the City*, p. 75 on interim ethics, and especially in M. Brown, *After the Market: Economics, Moral Agreement and the Churches' Mission*, Peter Lang, 2004, pp. 206–7.
60. Browning in Soulen and Woodhead, *God and Human Dignity*, p. 313.
61. On parallel hermeneutics, L. S. Mudge, 'Covenanting for a Renewing of Our Minds: A Way Together for the Abrahamic Faiths', in J. de Santa Ana, *Beyond Idealism*, p. 177f.

Chapter 9 Personalist Ethics and the Common Good

62. M. Burleigh, *Sacred Causes: Religion and Politics from the European Dictators to Al Qaeda*, HarperCollins, 2006.
63. Layard, *Happiness*, chapter 7 'Can we pursue a common good?'
64. Morisy, *Journeying Out*. Himmelfarb, *The De-moralization of Society*.
65. J. Atherton, *Christianity and the Market*, SPCK, 1992.
66. Cowley, *The Value of Money*, p. 55.
67. Cowley, *The Value of Money*, p. 57.
68. Cowley, *The Value of Money*, p. 58.
69. Cowley, *The Value of Money*, p. 59 – and Janssens' eight dimensions.
70. Cowley, *The Value of Money*, p. 59.
71. Cowley, *The Value of Money*, p. 59.
72. Cowley, *The Value of Money*, p. 60.
73. Cowley, *The Value of Money*, p. 61.

74. Cowley, *The Value of Money*, p. 61. See I. M. Young, *Justice and the Politics of Difference*, 1990.

75. Haidt, *The Happiness Hypothesis*, pp. 166–7.

76. Cowley, *The Value of Money*, p. 66.

77. Cowley, *The Value of Money*, p. 59.

78. See Palmer, *Faith in Conservation*.

79. Cowley, *The Value of Money*, p. 67.

80. Cowley, *The Value of Money*, pp. 154–5.

81. Cowley, *The Value of Money*, p. 177.

82. Cowley, *The Value of Money*, p. 177, quoting A. MacIntyre, *After Virtue*, 1981, and p. 180, quoting A. MacIntyre, 'How can a Virtue Become Socially Disruptive', 1988.

83. Himmelfarb, *The De-moralization of Society*, p. 78.

84. Himmelfarb, *The De-moralization of Society*, p. 164.

85. Himmelfarb, *The De-moralization of Society*, p. 176. B. Potter (later B. Webb) 'The Jewish Community', 1891.

86. Himmelfarb, *The De-moralization of Society*, p. 179, quoting B. Webb.

87. Himmelfarb, *The De-moralization of Society*, p. 187.

88. Baker, *The Hybrid Church in the City*, pp. 42–3, quoting Amin, 'Ethnicity and the Multicultural City', 2002.

89. Morisy, *Journeying Out*, pp. 168, 169. Reference to D. Hay, *Religious Experience Today*, 1990.

90. Morisy, *Journeying Out*, p. 170.

91. *Prosperity with a Purpose: Exploring the Ethics of Affluence*, CTBI, 2005, p. 15.

92. P. Riordan SJ, *A Politics of the Common Good*, Institute of Public Administration, Dublin, 1996. D. Hollenbach SJ, *The Common Good and Christian Ethics*, Cambridge University Press, 2002.

93. Cowley, *The Value of Money*, p. 72.

94. Cowley, *The Value of Money*, p. 72.

95. Cowley, *The Value of Money*, pp. 73–4.

96. Cowley, *The Value of Money*, p. 74, referring to G. Grisez, *The Way of the Lord Jesus, Vol. 1. Christian Moral Principles*, 1983.

97. Cowley, *The Value of Money*, p. 75.

98. Cowley, *The Value of Money*, p. 75, referring to N. Rigali 'Christian Morality and Universal Morality', 1994.

99. Cowley, *The Value of Money*, p. 75.

100. Cowley, *The Value of Money*, p. 76.

101. Cowley, *The Value of Money*, p. 76.

102. Cowley, *The Value of Money*, pp. 77–8.

103. Cowley, *The Value of Money*, p. 78, reference to C. Taylor, 'Irreducibly Social Goods', 1995.

104. Cowley, *The Value of Money*, p. 78, quoting Quadragesimo Anno, 1931.

105. M. and R. Friedman, *Free to Choose*, Penguin, 1980. A. Sen, *Development as Freedom*, Oxford University Press, 2001. F. Hayek, *The Road to Serfdom*, Routledge & Kegan Paul, 1996.

106. Cowley, *The Value of Money*, p. 81.

107. Atherton in Atherton and Skinner, *Through the Eye of a Needle*, p. 93.

108. Cowley, *The Value of Money*, p. 82.

109. Cowley, *The Value of Money*, p. 82.

110. Cowley, *The Value of Money*, p. 84, quoting *Gaudium et Spes*.

111. Cowley, *The Value of Money*, p. 87.

Chapter 10 Collaborative Working

112. Atherton and Skinner, *Through the Eye of a Needle*, p. 260.

113. Atherton and Skinner, *Through the Eye of a Needle*, p. 262.

114. A two-year research programme, *Promoting Greater Human Wellbeing: Interacting the Happiness Hypothesis and Religion*, funded by the AHRC/ESRC.

115. M. L. Stackhouse, *Public Theology and Political Economy: Christian Stewardship in Modern Society*, Eerdmans, 1987, pp. xii–xiii.

116. F. Iremonger, *William Temple, His Life and Letters*, Oxford University Press, 1949, p. 387.

117. H. Küng, *A Global Ethic for Global Politics and Economics*, SCM Press, 1997, p. 92.

118. R. H. Preston, *Confusions in Christian Social Ethics: Problems for Geneva and Rome*, SCM Press, 1994, pp. 115–23.

119. de Santa Ana, *Beyond Idealism*, p. ix.

120. Mudge in de Santa Ana, *Beyond Idealism*, p. 164.

121. Mudge in de Santa Ana, *Beyond Idealism*, pp. 173–4.

122. Mudge in de Santa Ana, *Beyond Idealism*, p. 177.

123. Mudge in de Santa Ana, *Beyond Idealism*, p. 177.

124. Mudge in de Santa Ana, *Beyond Idealism*, p. 178, quoting W. Schweiker, 'Religious Convictions and the Intellectual's Responsibility', 2003.

125. Kamergrauzis, *The Persistence of Christian Realism*, pp. 221–2, referring to MacIntyre 'Epistemological Crisis, Dramatic Narrative and the Philosophy of Science', 1989, and *Whose Justice? Which Rationality?*, 1988. Also see the use of MacIntyre in reformulating tradition, in M. Brown, *After the Market*, chapter 3, 'A Framework drawn from MacIntyre'.

126. Mudge in de Santa Ana, *Beyond Idealism*, p. 178.

127. D. Forrester, *Christian Justice and Public Policy*, Cambridge University Press, 1997, pp. 3, 201.

128. Mudge in de Santa Ana, *Beyond Idealism*, pp. 180–1, referring to H. Arendt, *The Human Condition*, 1978.

129. On thick and thin, Mudge in de Santa Ana, *Beyond Idealism*, p. 202, referring to M. Walzer, *Thick and Thin: Moral Argument at Home and Abroad*, 1994.

130. Mudge in de Santa Ana, *Beyond Idealism*, p. 183.

131. See J. Reader, *Beyond All Reason: The Limits of Post-Modern Theology*, Aureus, 1997, 'Habermas and the unfinished Project of the Enlightenment', pp. 52–5, referring to J. Habermas, *The Theory of Communicative Action: Vol. 2. The Critique of Functionalist Reason*, 1987, pp. 153ff.

132. Mudge in de Santa Ana, *Beyond Idealism*, pp. 183–8.

133. Mudge in de Santa Ana, *Beyond Idealism*, p. 187.

134. Mudge in de Santa Ana, *Beyond Idealism*, p. 187.

135. Mudge in de Santa Ana, *Beyond Idealism*, p. 188.

136. Mudge in de Santa Ana, *Beyond Idealism*, pp. 188–93.

Notes

137. Mudge in de Santa Ana, *Beyond Idealism*, p. 188.
138. Mudge in de Santa Ana, *Beyond Idealism*, p. 192.
139. Mudge in de Santa Ana, *Beyond Idealism*, pp. 193–8.
140. Mudge in de Santa Ana, *Beyond Idealism*, p. 140, quoting W. Brueggemann, 'Law as Response To Thou', 2001.
141. Mudge in de Santa Ana, *Beyond Idealism*, pp. 197–8.
142. Mudge in de Santa Ana, *Beyond Idealism*, p. 202, referring to J. Rawls, *A Theory of Justice*, Harvard University Press, 1971.
143. *Faiths and Finance: A Place for Faith-Based Economics*, Manchester, 2006, pp. 34–40.
144. Quoted in C-H. Grenholm and N. Kamergrauzis (eds), *Sustainable Development and Global Ethics*, University of Uppsala, 2007, pp. 9–10.
145. Palmer, *Faith in Conservation*, p. xv.
146. Palmer, *Faith in Conservation*, pp. 67, 68.
147. Palmer, *Faith in Conservation*, 'Islam', pp. 101, 102.
148. Palmer, *Faith in Conservation*, 'Buddhism', p. 79.
149. Palmer, *Faith in Conservation*, 'Islam', p. 99.
150. Palmer, *Faith in Conservation*, 'Buddhism', p. 77.
151. Forrester, *Christian Justice and Public Policy*.
152. Palmer, *Faith in Conservation*, 'Islam', p. 104.
153. P. F. Knitter and C. Muzaffar (eds), *Subverting Greed: Religious Perspectives on the Global Economy*, Orbis, 2003, p. xi (Foreword, D. Ikeda).
154. P. Knitter in Knitter and Muzaffar, *Subverting Greed*, p. 7.
155. Knitter in Knitter and Muzaffar, *Subverting Greed*, p. 11.
156. Knitter in Knitter and Muzaffar, *Subverting Greed*, p. 14.
157. P. Sedgwick, 'The Vocation of the Christian in the World of Work', in Atherton and Skinner, *Through the Eye of a Needle*, p. 217.
158. Swami Agnivesh, 'Religious Conscience and the Global Economy: An Eastern Perspective on Sociospiritual Activism', in Knitter and Muzaffar, *Subverting Greed*, p. 38.
159. Z. Qin, 'A Confucian View of the Global Economy', in Knitter and Muzaffar, *Subverting Greed*, p. 84.
160. Swami Agnivesh in Knitter and Muzaffar, *Subverting Greed*, p. 44.
161. On Oxford, see J. C. Bennett, 'Breakthrough in Ecumenical Social Ethics. The Legacy of the Oxford Conference on Church, Community, and State (1937)', *The Ecumenical Review*, Vol. 40, No. 2, April 1988, p. 144.
162. Swami Agnivesh in Knitter and Muzaffar, *Subverting Greed*, pp. 54–5.
163. Swami Agnivesh in Knitter and Muzaffar, *Subverting Greed*, p. 40.
164. Grenholm in Grenholm and Kamergrauzis, *Sustainable Development*, p. 14.
165. Grenholm in Grenholm and Kamergrauzis, *Sustainable Development*, p. 14.
166. N. Dower, 'The Challenge of Global Ethics: Is a Global Ethic either Possible or Desirable?', in Grenholm and Kamergrauzis, *Sustainable Development*, p. 79.
167. Grenholm in Grenholm and Kamergrauzis, *Sustainable Development*, p. 14.
168. Grenholm in Grenholm and Kamergrauzis, *Sustainable Development*, p. 15.
169. Grenholm in Grenholm and Kamergrauzis, *Sustainable Development*, p. 16.
170. Grenholm in Grenholm and Kamergrauzis, *Sustainable Development*, pp. 95–110.

Chapter 11 Of Typologies and Traditions

171. On practical theology, see D. Forrester, *Truthful Action: Explorations in Practical Theology*, T & T Clark, 2000, p. 127; on performative theology, see E. Graham, *Transforming Practice: Pastoral Theology in an Age of Uncertainty*, Mowbrays, 1996, p. 7.

172. G. R. Dunstan, *The Artifice of Ethics*, SCM Press, 1974.

173. H. R. Niebuhr, *Christ and Culture*, Harper & Row, 1951; E. Troeltsch, *The Social Teachings of the Christian Churches*, Allen & Unwin, 1931.

174. Atherton and Skinner, *Through the Eye of a Needle*, p. 256.

175. S. Platten, 'Editorial: Living Practical Divinity?', in *Crucible*, October–December, 2006, pp. 1–5.

176. Atherton in Atherton and Skinner, *Through the Eye of a Needle*, p. 258.

177. J. Bhagwati, *In Defence of Globalization*, p. 3.

178. Baker, *The Hybrid Church in the City*, p. 35, referring to L. Sandercock, *Towards Cosmopolis: Planning for Multicultural Cities*, 1998.

179. I have used this before, in my *Faith in the Nation: A Christian Vision for Britain*, SPCK, 1988, p. 28. The actual reference continues to elude me.

180. M. Brown in Atherton and Skinner, *Through the Eye of a Needle*, chapter 3.

181. Graham in Soulen and Woodhead, *God and Human Dignity*, p. 276.

182. A. Sen, *On Ethics and Economics*, pp. 2–7.

183. Baker, *The Hybrid Church in the City*, p. 26, referring to *The Satanic Verses*, 1991, and to L. Sandercock's *Cosmopolis II: Mongrel Cities in the 21st Century*, 2003, in Baker, *The Hybrid Church in the City*, p. 32f.

184. J. Reader, *Blurred Encounters: A Reasoned Practice of Faith*, Aureus Publishing, 2005.

185. Putnam, *Better Together*, p. 141.

186. R. H. Preston, *Religion and the Persistence of Capitalism*, SCM Press, 1979.

187. E. Hobsbawm, *Age of Extremes: The Short Twentieth Century 1914–1991*, Michael Joseph, 1994.

188. M. Weber, *The Protestant Ethic and the Spirit of Capitalism*, Unwin University Books, 1930. R. H. Tawney, *Religion and the Rise of Capitalism*, Penguin, 1966 edition. V. A. Demant, *Religion and the Decline of Capitalism*, Faber & Faber, 1952.

189. M. Weber, *The Religion of China*, and *The Religion of India*.

190. R. H. Preston, *Religion and the Persistence of Capitalism*, p. 17.

191. S. J. Guscott, *Humphrey Chetham 1580–1653. Fortune, Politics and Mercantile Culture in Seventeenth-Century England*, The Chetham Society, 2003, p. 167, n.1.

192. Guscott, *Humphrey Chetham*, p. 168.

193. Guscott, *Humphrey Chetham*, pp. 261–9.

194. U. Duchrow, *Global Economy. A Confessional Issue for the Churches?*, WCC Publications, 1987.

195. R. H. Tawney, *Religion and the Rise of Capitalism*, p. 280.

196. R. H. Preston, *Religion and the Persistence of Capitalism*, pp. 7–8, quoting D. MacRae's review of Weber, 1977.

197. R. H. Tawney, *Religion and the Rise of Capitalism*, p. 188.

198. *R. H. Tawney's Commonplace Book*, Cambridge University Press, 1972, pp. 43–4.

199. R. H. Preston, *Religion and the Persistence of Capitalism*, pp. 14, 16.

200. R. H. Preston, *Religion and the Persistence of Capitalism*, p. 16.

201. D. Munby, *The Idea of a Secular Society*, 1963. My wife remembers him and his family in Aberdeen, at St Mary's Episcopal Church, before his move to Oxford, and his untimely death in Istanbul. He made an important contribution to the dialogue between economics and Christianity – see his *Christianity and Economic Problems*, 1956.

202. See M. Reeves (ed.), *Christian Thinking and Social Order: Conviction Politics from the 1930s to the Present Day*, Cassell, 1999, p. 215.

203. R. H. Preston, *Religion and the Ambiguities of Capitalism*, SCM Press, 1991.

204. I. Steedman in *Faiths and Finance*, pp. 25–33; in *Through the Eye of a Needle*, pp. 67–81.

205. R. H. Preston, *Church and Society in the Late Twentieth Century: The Economic and Political Task*, SCM Press, 1983, pp. 143, 155.

Chapter 12 Faithful Economics

206. J. Atherton, *Marginalization*, chapter 6.

207. J. H. Henderson and J. Pisciotta (eds), *Faithful Economics: The Moral Worlds of a Neutral Science*, Baylor University Press, 2005. Tanner, *Economy of Grace*.

208. D. Meeks, *God the Economist: The Doctrine of God and Political Economy*, Fortress, 1989. R. T. Peters, *In Search of the Good Life: The Ethics of Globalization*, Continuum, 2004. C. D. Moe-Lobeda, *Healing a Broken World: Globalization and God*, Fortress Press, 2002.

209. Sen, *On Ethics and Economics*, pp. 2–7.

210. See Waterman, *Revolution, Economics and Religion*.

211. Waterman, *Revolution, Economics and Religion*, pp. 11–12.

212. Henderson, 'The Christian Perspective and Economic Scholarship', in Henderson and Pisciotta, *Faithful Economics*, pp. 1–2.

213. Long's concept to describe the mainstream liberal tradition of Christian social ethics, in *Divine Economy*, p. 7.

214. Cowley, *The Value of Money*, pp. 11–12.

215. F. Chesney, 'Economics and Technology', in J. Dean and A. Waterman (eds), *Religion and Economics: Normative Social Theory*, Kluwer Academic Publishers, 1999, p. 154.

216. M. Friedman, *Essays in Positive Economics*, University of Chicago Press, 1953, p. 7, in *Studies in Ethics and Economics 8*, Uppsala University Press, 2001, pp. 11–12.

217. L. Robbins, *An Essay on the Nature and Significance of Economic Science*, Macmillan, 1935, p. 148 (3rd edition, 1984); and in P. Donaldson, *Economics of the Real World*, Penguin, 1973, p. 22.

218. Henderson in Henderson and Pisciotta, *Faithful Economics*, p. 3, quoting M. Friedman, *Essays in Positive Economics*, 1953.

219. Henderson in Henderson and Pisciotta, *Faithful Economics*, p. 3.

220. Henderson in Henderson and Pisciotta, *Faithful Economics*, p. 12.

221. Henderson in Henderson and Pisciotta, *Faithful Economics*, p. 3, quoting A. Smith, *The Theory of Moral Sentiments*, 1975.

222. Henderson in Henderson and Pisciotta, *Faithful Economics*, p. 3, quoting A. Sen, *On Ethics and Economics*, 1987.

223. P. Riordan SJ, 'Common Good or Selfish Greed?' in *Through the Eye of a Needle*; G. J. Hughes SJ, 'Christianity and Self-Interest', in M. H. Taylor (ed.), *Christians and the Future of Social Democracy*, G. W. & A. Hesketh, 1982.

224. Offer, *The Challenge of Affluence*, pp. 3, 188–90.

225. Henderson in Henderson and Pisciotta, *Faithful Economics*, p. 4.

226. Henderson in Henderson and Pisciotta, *Faithful Economics*, p. 4, and referring to F. Machlup, in R. Heilbroner (ed.), *Economic Means and Social Ends: Essays in Political Economics*, 1969.

227. Long, *Divine Economy*, p. 270: 'theologians must mention the priority of their language over that of the economists'.

228. Atherton in Atherton and Skinner, *Through the Eye of a Needle*, p. 261.

229. In J. Bhagwati, *In Defence of Globalization*, p. 221 – on ethical globalization. On Special and Differential Treatment, see H. Skinner, 'Trading Life and Death', in *Crucible*, January–March 2005, p. 6.

230. J. Stiglitz, 'The Ethical Economist', in *Foreign Affairs*, November–December, 2005.

231. Himmelfarb, *The De-Moralisation of Society*, p. 164.

232. *Faith in England's Northwest: Economic Impact Assessment*, 2005.

233. Henderson in Henderson and Pisciotta, *Faithful Economics*, p. 12.

234. Atherton, *Marginalization*, p. 148, from A. Smith, *Wealth of Nations*, 1, VIII, 36.

235. P. Knitter and C. Muzaffar, *Subverting Greed*, 'Igbo and African Religious Perspectives', Ifi Amadiume, pp. 15–37.

236. Atherton, *Marginalization*, p. 155, in A.-C. Jarl, *Women and Economic Justice*, 2000.

237. D. R. Loy, 'Pave the Planet or Wear Shoes?', in Knitter and Muzaffar, *Subverting Greed*, p. 66.

238. Henderson in Henderson and Pisciotta, *Faithful Economics*, quoting G. Marsden, *The Outrageous Idea of Christian Scholarship*, 1997, p. 4.

239. D. Forrester, *Christian Justice and Public Policy*, pp. 3, 201, in Atherton, *Public Theology for Changing Times*, p. 4.

240. Henderson in Henderson and Pisciotta, *Faithful Economics*, quoting Marsden, p. 4.

241. Pisciotta in Henderson and Pisciotta, *Faithful Economics*, p. 143, on A. Yuengert.

242. D. P. Gushee, 'The Economic Ethics of Jesus', in Henderson and Pisciotta, *Faithful Economics*, chapter 5.

243. Henderson in Henderson and Pisciotta, *Faithful Economics*, pp. 13–14.

244. Tanner, *Economy of Grace*.

245. Tanner, *Economy of Grace*, pp. 12–15, 17–24.

246. Tanner, *Economy of Grace*, pp. 5–8.

247. R. Niebuhr, *Man's Nature and His Communities*, Bles, 1966, pp. 90–6.

248. For example, J. P. Wogaman, *Economics and Ethics: A Christian Enquiry*, SCM Press, 1986, 'The Priority of Grace over Works', pp. 34–5.

249. Tanner, *Economy of Grace*, p. 14.

250. Tanner, *Economy of Grace*, p. 89. E. R. Wickham, *Church and People in an*

Industrial City, Lutterworth Press, 1957, 'hooks and eyes', pp. 235–8.

251. H. E. Daly and J. B. Cobb, *For the Common Good: Redirecting the Economy toward Community, the Environment, and a Sustainable Future*, Merlin Press, 1989, chapters 8 and 9. R. T. Peters, *In Search of the Good Life*, 'Globalization as Localization', pp. 105f.

252. Tanner, *Economy of Grace*, pp. 88, 89.

253. Tanner, *Economy of Grace*, p. xi.

254. See D. Meeks, *God the Economist: The Doctrine of God and Political Economy*, 1989.

255. Tanner, *Economy of Grace*, pp. 24, 26–7.

256. Tanner, *Economy of Grace*, p. 27.

257. Tanner, *Economy of Grace*, pp. 68–9.

258. Tanner, *Economy of Grace*, p. 85.

259. Henderson, in Henderson and Pisciotta, *Faithful Economics*, p. 11.

260. Tanner, *Economy of Grace*, pp. 87–142.

261. Tanner, *Economy of Grace*, p. 89.

262. Tanner, *Economy of Grace*, p. 92.

263. Tanner, *Economy of Grace*, p. 92.

264. Tanner, *Economy of Grace*, p. 93.

265. Tanner, *Economy of Grace*, p. 96.

266. Tanner, *Economy of Grace*, pp. 121, 123.

267. Tanner, *Economy of Grace*, p. 114.

268. Wolf, *Why Globalization Works*, p. 303.

269. I. Steedman in *Through the Eye of a Needle*, 'Competition and Co-operation', pp. 76–8.

270. Tanner, *Economy of Grace*, p. 106.

271. Tanner, *Economy of Grace*, pp. 108, 106.

272. Tanner, *Economy of Grace*, p. 113.

273. Tanner, *Economy of Grace*, p. 101

274. In D. Hicks, *Inequality and Christian Ethics*, 2000, p. 62, quoting J. Speth in *New Perspectives Quarterly*, 1996.

275. Tanner, *Economy of Grace*, pp. 103, 104.

276. Tanner, *Economy of Grace*, p. 129.

277. Tanner, *Economy of Grace*, p. 131.

278. Atherton, *Marginalization*, p. 157.

279. Tanner, *Economy of Grace*, p. 139.

280. Tanner, *Economy of Grace*, p. 134.

281. Wilkinson, *The Impact of Inequality*, p. 248.

282. James, *Affluenza*, p. 330.

283. R. H. Tawney (Winter, J. M., ed.), *The American Labour Movement and Other Essays*, Harvester Press, 1979, p. 112.

284. Dunn, *Setting the People Free*, p. 127.

285. Dunn, *Setting the People Free*, pp. 127, 158, 164, 187.

286. Dunn, *Setting the People Free*, pp. 177–8. Layard, *Happiness*, p. 70. Halpern, *Social Capital*, p. 173.

287. Dunn, *Setting the People Free*, p. 185.

288. J. R. Atherton, *R. H. Tawney as a Christian Social Moralist*, unpublished PhD, Manchester, 1979, pp. 334–5.

289. Dunn, *Setting the People Free*, p. 188.
290. Tanner, *Economy of Grace*, p. 142.

Chapter 13 Religion and the Transfiguration of Capitalism

291. D. Lee, *Transfiguration*, Continuum, 2004, p. 1.
292. Lee, *Transfiguration*, p. 134.
293. Graham in Soulen and Woodhead, *God and Human Dignity*, quoting D. Kelsey, 'Human Being' in *Christian Theology*, ed. P. Hodgson and R. King, 1998, p. 277.
294. Lee, *Transfiguration*, p. 130.
295. Lee, *Transfiguration*, p. 96.
296. Martin, *On Secularization*, pp. 11, 12.
297. Woodhead in Soulen and Woodhead, *God and Human Dignity*, p. 237.
298. Lee, *Transfiguration*, p. 97.
299. W. Storrar, 'Democracy and Mission', in W. Storrar and P. Donald (eds), *God in Society: Doing Social Theology in Scotland Today*, St Andrew Press, 2003, p. 19.
300. D. Clark, *Breaking the Mould of Christendom*, p. 57, quoting R. Titmuss in I. Martin (ed.), *Community Education*, 1987. See R. M. Titmuss, *The Gift Relationship*, Allen & Unwin, 1971.
301. Hardt and Negri, *Empire*, p. 185.
302. Hardt and Negri, *Empire*, p. 218.
303. Hardt and Negri, *Empire*, p. 284.
304. Hardt and Negri, *Empire*, pp. 206, 207.
305. Hardt and Negri, *Empire*, p. 239.
306. Hardt and Negri, *Empire*, p. 319.
307. Hardt and Negri, *Empire*, p. 275.
308. Hardt and Negri, *Empire*, pp. 358, 359.
309. Hardt and Negri, *Empire*, p. 388.
310. Hardt and Negri, *Empire*, p. 413.
311. Mudge in de Santa Ana, *Beyond Idealism*, p. 193.

Select Bibliography

Alkire, S., *Valuing Freedoms: Sen's Capability Approach and Poverty Reduction*, Oxford University Press, 2002.

Allchin, D., *Participation in God: a Forgotten Thread in Anglican Tradition*, Darton, Longman & Todd, 1988.

Arrighi, G., *The Long Twentieth Century: Money, Power and the Origins Of Our Times*, Verso, 1994.

Atherton, J. R., *R. H. Tawney as a Christian Social Moralist*, unpublished PhD, University of Manchester, 1979.

—— *Faith in the Nation: A Christian Vision for Britain*, SPCK, 1988.

—— *Christianity and the Market: Christian Social Thought for our Times*, SPCK, 1992.

—— *Social Christianity: A Reader*, SPCK , 1994.

—— 'Church and Society in the North West, 1760–1997', in C. Ford, M. Powell and T. Wyke (eds), *The Church in Cottonopolis, Essays to Mark the 150th Anniversary of the Diocese of Manchester*, The Lancashire and Cheshire Antiquarian Society, 1997.

—— *Public Theology for Changing Times: Christian Social Thought for our times*, SPCK, 2000.

—— *Marginalization*, SCM Press, 2003.

—— 'The Happiness Hypothesis: Reflections on the Religion and Capitalism Debate', *Crucible*, January–March 2007.

—— and Skinner, H. (eds), *Through the Eye of a Needle: Theological Conversations over Political Economy*, Epworth, 2007.

Backstrom, P., *Christian Socialism and Co-operation in Victorian England*, Croom Helm, 1974.

Baker, C. R., *The Hybrid Church in the City. Third Space Thinking*, Ashgate 2007.

—— and Skinner, H., *Faith in Action: The Dynamic Connection between Spiritual and Religious Capital*, William Temple Foundation, Manchester, 2006.

Ballard, P. and Couture, P. (eds), *Globalization and Difference: Practical Theology in a World Context*, Cardiff Academic Press, 1999.

Becker, G. S., *The Economics of Discrimination*, University of Chicago Press, 1971.

—— *The Economic Approach to Human Behavior*, University of Chicago Press, 1976.

Bennett, J. C., 'Breakthrough in Ecumenical Social Ethics. The Legacy of the Oxford Conference on Church, Community, and State (1937)', in *The Ecumenical Review*, Vol. 40, No. 2, April 1988, p. 144.

Berger, P. (ed.), *The Desecularization of the World: Resurgent Religion And World Politics*, Eerdmans, 1999.

Bhagwati, J., *In Defense of Globalization*, Oxford University Press, 2004.

Bobbitt, P., *The Shield of Achilles: War, Peace and the Course of History*, Allen Lane, 2002.

Bourdieu, P., 'Genesis and Structure of the Religious Field', in *Comparative Social Research*, Vol. 13, 1991, pp. 1–44.

—— *The Social Structures of the Economy*, Polity Press, 2005.

Braudel, F., *Civilization and Capitalism, 15th–18th Century, Volume 1: The Structures of Everyday Life; The Limits of the Possible*, Collins/Fontana Press, 1981.

—— *Civilization and Capitalism, 15th–18th Century, Volume 2: The Wheels of Commerce*, William Collins, 1982.

—— *A History of Civilizations*, Penguin, 1995.

—— *Civilization and Capitalism, 15th–18th Century, Volume 3: The Perspective of the World*, Phoenix Press, 2002.

Brown, M., *After the Market: Economics, Moral Agreement and the Churches' Mission*, Peter Lang, 2004.

—— and Ballard, P., *The Church and Economic Life: A Documentary Study: 1945 to the Present*, Epworth, 2006.

Browne, J., *Charles Darwin: The Power of Place*, Pimlico, 2003.

Bruce, S., *From Cathedrals to Cults: Religion in the Modern World*, Oxford University Press, 1996.

Buchan, J., *Capital of the Mind: How Edinburgh Changed the World*, John Murray, 2003.

Buckley, S. L., *Teachings on Usury in Judaism, Christianity and Islam*, The Edward Mellen Press, 2000.

Burleigh, M., *Sacred Causes: Religion and Politics from the European Dictators to Al Qaeda*, HarperCollins, 2006.

Butler, E., *Adam Smith – A Primer*, Institute of Economic Affairs, 2007.

Chapra, M. U., *Towards a Just Monetary System*, The Islamic Foundation, 1985.

Clark, D., *Breaking the Mould of Christendom: Kingdom Community, Diaconal Church and the Liberation of the Laity*, Epworth, 2005.

Clark, G., *A Farewell to Alms: A Brief Economic History of the World*, Princeton University Press, 2007.

Collier, P., *The Bottom Billion: Why the Poorest Countries are Failing and What can be Done About It*, Oxford University Press, 2007.

Cowley, C., *The Value of Money: Ethics and the World of Finance*, T & T Clark, 2006.

Daly, H. E. and Cobb, J. B., *For the Common Good: Redirecting the Economy toward Community, the Environment and a Sustainable Future*, Merlin Press, 1989.

Davie, G., *Religion in Britain since 1945*, Blackwell, 1994.

—— *Religion in Modern Europe: A Memory Mutates*, Oxford University Press, 2000.

—— *Europe: The Exceptional Case, Parameters of Faith in the Modern World*, Darton, Longman & Todd, 2002.

De Santa Ana, J. et al., *Beyond Idealism. A Way Ahead for Ecumenical Social Ethics*, Eerdmans, 2006.

Dean, J. and Waterman, A. (eds), *Religion and Economics: Normative Social Theory*, Kluwer Academic Publishers, 1999.

Deane, P. and Kuper, J. (eds), *A Lexicon of Economics*, Routledge, 1988.

Demant, V. A., *Religion and the Decline of Capitalism*, Faber & Faber, 1952.

Devine, T. M., *The Scottish Nation*, Penguin, 2000.

Diamond, J., *Guns, Germs and Steel: A Short History of Everybody for the Last 13,000 Years*, Random House, 1998.

Dilulio, J. J., *Godly Republic: A Centrist Blueprint for America's Faith-Based Future*, University of California Press, 2007.

Donaldson, P., *Economics of the Real World*, Penguin, 1973.

Duchrow, U., *Global Economy. A Confessional Issue for the Churches?*, WCC Publications, 1987.

Dunn, J., *Setting the People Free: The Story of Democracy*, Atlantic Books, 2005.

Dunstan, G. R., *The Artifice of Ethics*, SCM Press, 1974.

Easterlin, R. (ed.), *Happiness in Economics*, Edward Elgar, 2002.

Faith in England's Northwest: The contribution made by faith communities to civil society in the region, Northwest Regional Development Agency, 2003.

Faith in England's Northwest: Economic Impact Assessment, Northwest Regional Development Agency, 2005.

Faith in the City: A Call for Action by Church and Nation, Church House Publishing, 1985.

Faithful Cities: A Call for Celebration, Vision and Justice, Church House Publishing, Methodist Publishing House, 2006.

Faiths and Finance: A Place for Faith-Based Economics (A preliminary Statement from Muslims and Christians in Manchester), the Diocese of Manchester, 2006.

Ferguson, N., *The Cash Nexus: Money and Power the Modern World: 1700–2000*, Penguin, 2001.

—— *Empire: How Britain Made the Modern World*, Penguin, 2003.

—— *Colossus: The Rise and Fall of the American Empire*, Allen Lane, 2004.

Fogel, R. W., *The Escape from Hunger and Premature Death, 1700–2100: Europe, America and the Third World*, Cambridge University Press, 2004.

Forrester, D., *Christian Justice and Public Policy*, Cambridge University Press, 1997.

—— *Truthful Action: Explorations in Practical Theology*, T & T Clark, 2000.

—— *On Human Worth: A Christian Vindication of Equality*, SCM Press, 2001.

Francis, L. and Robbins, M., 'Prayer, Purpose in Life, Personality, and Social Attitudes among Non-Churchgoing 13 to 15 Year Olds in England and Wales', *Research in the Social Scientific Study of Religion*, Vol. 17, 2006, pp. 116–17.

—— Katz, Y., Yablon, Y. and Robbins, M., 'Religiosity, Personality and Happiness: A Study Among Israeli Male Undergraduates', *Journal of Happiness Studies*, Vol. 5, 2004, pp. 315–33.

Freeman, R. B. (ed.), *Inequality Around the World*, Palgrave, 2002.

Friedman, M. *Essays in Positive Economics*, University of Chicago Press, 1953.

—— and Friedman, R., *Free to Choose*, Penguin, 1980.

Fukuyama, F., *The End of History and the Last Man*, Penguin 1992.

—— *The Great Disruption: Human Nature and the Reconstitution of Social Order*, Touchstone, 2000.

Galbraith, K., *A History of Economics: The Past as the Present*, Penguin, 1989.

Gallagher, V., *The True Cost of Low Prices: The Violence of Globalization*, Orbis, 2006.

Gill, R., *Churchgoing and Christian Ethics*, Cambridge University Press, 1999.

Gillett, R. W., *The New Globalization: Reclaiming the Lost Ground of Our Christian Social Tradition*, Pilgrim Press, 2005.

Goodchild, P., *Capitalism and Religion: The Price of Piety*, Routledge, 2002.

—— *Theology of Money*, SCM Press, 2007.

Graham, E., *Transforming Practice: Pastoral Theology in an Age of Uncertainty*, Mowbrays, 1996.

—— and Reed, E., *The Future of Christian Social Ethics: Essays on the Work of Ronald H. Preston, 1913–2001*, T & T Clark, 2004.

Greenwood, R. and Burgess, H., *Power*, SPCK, 2005.

Grenholm, C-H. and Kamergrauzis, N. (eds), *Sustainable Development and Global Ethics*, Acta Universitatis Upsaliensis, 2007.

Guscott, S. J., *Humphrey Chetham 1580–1653: Fortune, Politics and Mercantile Culture in Seventeenth-Century England*, The Chetham Society, 2003.

Haidt, J., *The Happiness Hypothesis: Putting Ancient Wisdom and Philosophy to the Test of Modern Science*, Heinemann, 2006.

Halpern, D., *Social Capital*, Polity Press, 2005.

Hardt, M. and Negri, A., *Empire*, Harvard University Press, 2000.

—— *Multitude*, Penguin, 2006.

Hauerwas, S., *The Peaceable Kingdom: A Primer in Christian Ethics*, SCM Press, 1984.

Harvey, D., *The New Imperialism*, Oxford University Press, 2003.

Hastings, A., *A History of English Christianity 1920–1990*, SCM Press, 1991.

Hayek, F., *The Road to Serfdom*, Routledge & Kegan Paul, 1996 edition.

Henderson, J.W. and Pisciotta, J. (eds), *Faithful Economics, The Moral Worlds of a Neutral Science*, Baylor University Press, 2005.

Herbert, D., *Religion and Civil Society: Rethinking Public Religion in the Contemporary World*, Ashgate, 2003.

Heslam, P. (ed.), *Globalization and the Good*, SPCK, 2004.

Hicks, D., *Inequality and Christian Ethics*, Cambridge University Press, 2000.

Hilton, B., *The Age of Atonement: The Influence of Evangelicalism on Social and Economic Thought*, Clarendon Press, 1988.

Himmelfarb, G., *The De-moralization of Society: From Victorian Virtues to Modern Values*, IEA Health and Welfare Unit, 1995.

Hira, A. and Ferrie, J., 'Fair Trade: Three Key Challenges for Reaching the Mainstream', *Journal of Business Ethics*, Vol. 63, 2006, pp. 107–18.

Hobsbawm, E., *Age of Extremes: The Short Twentieth Century, 1914–1991*, Michael Joseph, 1994.

Hollenbach, D., *The Common Good and Christian Ethics*, Cambridge University Press, 2002.

Huntington, S. P., *The Clash of Civilizations and the Remaking of World Order*, Simon & Schuster, 1998.

—— *Who Are We? America's Great Debate*, Simon & Schuster, 2005.

Iremonger, F., *William Temple, His Life and Letters*, Oxford University Press, 1949.

James, O., *Affluenza: How to be Successful and Stay Sane*, Vermilion, 2007.

Jarl, A.-C., *In Justice: Woman and Global Economics*, Fortress Press, 2003.

Jay, P., *Road to Riches or the Wealth of Man*, Weidenfeld & Nicholson, 2000.

Jenkins, P., *The Next Christendom: The Coming of Global Christianity*, Oxford University Press, 2002.

Johns, H. and Ormerod, P., *Happiness, Economics and Public Policy*, Institute of

Economic Affairs, 2007.

Kamergrauzis, N., *The Persistence of Christian Realism: A Study of the Social Ethics of Ronald H. Preston*, University of Uppsala, 2001.

Keane, J., *Global Civil Society?*, Cambridge University Press, 2003.

Kennedy, P., *The Rise and Fall of the Great Powers: Economic Change and Military Conflict from 1500 to 2000*, Fontana Press, 1988.

—— *Preparing for the Twenty-First Century*, HarperCollins, 1993.

Kenny, A. and C., *Life, Liberty and the Pursuit of Utility: Happiness in Philosophical and Economic Thought*, Imprint Academic, 2006.

Kepel, G., *The Revenge of God: The Resurgence of Islam, Christianity and Judaism in the Modern World*, Polity Press, 1994.

Knitter, P. F. and Muzaffar, C. (eds), *Subverting Greed: Religious Perspectives on the Global Economy*, Orbis Books, 2003.

Küng, H., *A Global Ethic for Global Politics and Economics*, SCM Press, 1997.

Landes, D., *The Unbound Prometheus*, Cambridge University Press, 1969.

—— *The Wealth and Poverty of Nations: Why Some are so Rich and Some so Poor*, Little, Brown and Company, 1998.

Layard, R., *Happiness: Lessons from a New Science*, Allen Lane, 2005.

Lee, D., *Transfiguration*, Continuum, 2004.

Lewis, B., *The Middle East: 2000 Years of History from the Rise of Christianity to the Present Day*, Weidenfeld & Nicolson, 2000.

Livi-Bacci, M., *A Concise History of World Population*, Blackwell, 2001.

Long, D. S., *Divine Economy: Theology and the Market*, Routledge, 2000.

Macfarlane, A., *The Riddle of the Modern World: Of Liberty, Wealth and Equality*, Palgrave, 2000.

MacIntyre, A., *After Virtue: A Study in Moral Theory*, Duckworth, 1981.

Maslow, A. H., *Motivation and Personality*, Harper & Row, 1954.

Marshall, K. and Keough, L., *Mind, Heart and Soul in the Fight against Poverty*, The World Bank, 2004.

Martin, D., *On Secularization: Towards a Revised General Theory*, Ashgate, 2005.

Maurice, F. D., *The Life of Frederick Denison Maurice*, 2 volumes, MacMillan, 1884.

McGrath, A., *The Twilight of Atheism: The Rise and Fall of Disbelief in the Modern World*, Doubleday, 2004.

Meeks, D., *God the Economist: The Doctrine of God and Political Economy*, Fortress, 1989.

Merchant, R. and Gilbert, P., 'The Modern Workplace: Surfing the Wave or Surviving the Straightjacket?' *Crucible*, January–March, 2007.

Moe-Lobeda, C. D., *Healing a Broken World: Globalization and God*, Fortress Press, 2002.

Moore, G., 'The Fair Trade Movement: Parameters, Issues and Future Research', *Journal of Business Ethics*, Vol. 53, 2004, pp. 73–86.

Morisy, A., *Journeying Out: A New Approach to Christian Mission*, Continuum, 2004.

Munby, D., *Christianity and Economic Problems*, Macmillan, 1956.

—— *The Idea of a Secular Society*, Oxford University Press, 1963.

Niebuhr, H. R., *Christ and Culture*, Harper & Row, 1975.

Niebuhr, R., *Man's Nature and His Communities*, Bles, 1966.

Norman, E. R., *Victorian Christian Socialists*, Cambridge University Press, 1987.

Northcott, M., *An Angel Directs the Storm: Apocalyptic Religion and American Empire*, I. B. Tauris, 2004.

Novak, M., *The Spirit of Democratic Capitalism*, Simon & Schuster, 1982.

Nussbaum, M., *Women and Human Development: The Capabilities Approach*, 2000.

Offer, A., *The Challenge of Affluence: Self-Control and Well-Being in the United States and Britain since 1950*, Oxford University Press, 2006.

Ormerod, P. and Johns, H., 'Against Happiness', *Prospect*, April 2007.

Palmer, M. with Finlay, V., *Faith in Conservation: New Approaches to Religions and the Environment*, The World Bank, 2003.

Peters, R. T., *In Search of the Good Life: The Ethics of Globalization*, Continuum, 2004.

Pogge, T., 'An Egalitarian Law of Peoples', *Philosophy and Public Affairs*, Vol. 23, No. 3, 1994, pp. 195–224.

Polanyi, K., *The Great Transformation: The Political and Economic Origins of our Time*, Boston, Beacon Press, 1957 edition.

Preston, R. H., *Religion and the Persistence of Capitalism*, SCM Press, 1979.

—— *Church and Society in the Late Twentieth Century: The Economic and Political Task*, SCM Press, 1983.

—— *Religion and the Ambiguities of Capitalism*, SCM Press, 1991.

—— *Confusions in Christian Social Ethics: Problems for Geneva and Rome*, SCM Press, 1994.

Prosperity with a Purpose: Christians and the Ethics of Affluence, CTBI, 2005.

Prosperity with a Purpose: Exploring the Ethics of Affluence, CTBI, 2005.

Putnam, R. D., *Bowling Alone: The Collapse and Revival of American Community*, Simon & Schuster, 2000.

—— and Feldstein, L. M. with Cohen, D., *Better Together: Restoring the American Community*, Simon & Schuster, 2004.

Rack, H., *Reasonable Enthusiast: John Wesley and the Rise of Methodism*, Epworth Press, 1992.

Reader, J., *Local Theology: Church and Community in Dialogue*, SPCK, 1994.

—— *Beyond All Reason: The Limits of Post-Modern Theology*, Aureus, 1997.

—— *Blurred Encounters: A Reasoned Practice of Faith*, Aureus, 2005.

Reeves, M. (ed.), *Christian Thinking and Social Order: Conviction Politics from the 1930s to the Present Day*, Cassell, 1999.

Richardson, J. (ed.), *Handbook of Theory and Research for the Sociology of Education*, Greenwood Press, 1986.

Riordan, P., SJ, *A Politics of the Common Good*, Institute of Public Administration, Dublin, 1996.

Roberts, J. M., *The Penguin History of the World*, Penguin, 1980.

Robbins, L., *An Essay on the Nature and Significance of Economic Science*, Macmillan, 1935.

Ruston, R., *Human Rights and the Image of God*, SCM Press, 2004.

Sen, A., *On Ethics and Economics*, Blackwell, 1988.

—— *Development as Freedom*, Oxford University Press, 2001.

Skinner, H., 'Trading Life and Death: Reflections on Current Trade Negotiations', *Crucible*, January–March, 2005.

Smith, A., *An Inquiry into the Nature and Causes of the Wealth of Nations*, Oxford University Press, 1976.

—— *The Theory of Moral Sentiments*, Liberty Fund, 1984.

Soulen, R. K. and Woodhead, L. (eds), *God and Human Dignity*, Eerdmans, 2006.

Stackhouse, M. L., *Public Theology and Political Economy: Christian Stewardship in Modern Society*, Eerdmans, 1987.

Stiglitz, J., *Globalization and its Discontents*, Allen Lane, 2002.

—— *Making Globalization Work: The Next Steps to Global Justice*, Allen Lane, 2006.

Storrar, W. and Donald, P., *God in Society: Doing Social Theology in Scotland Today*, Saint Andrew Press, 2003.

Tacey, D., *The Spirituality Revolution – the emergence of contemporary spirituality*, HarperCollins, 2003.

Tanner, K., *Economy of Grace*, Fortress Press, 2005.

Tawney, R. H., *The Attack and Other Papers*, Allen & Unwin, 1953.

—— *Religion and the Rise of Capitalism*, Penguin, 1966 edition.

—— *R. H. Tawney's Commonplace Book*, Cambridge University Press, 1972.

—— (Winter, J. M., ed.), *The American Labour Movement and Other Essays*, Harvester Press, 1979.

Taylor, M. H. (ed.), *Christians and the Future of Social Democracy*, G. W. & A. Hesketh, 1982.

Temple, W., *Christianity and Social Order*, 1942, SPCK, 1976 edition.

Thorpe, R., Holt, R., Macpherson A., Puttaway, L., 'Using knowledge within small and medium-sized firms: a systematic review of evidence', *International Journal of Management Reviews*, Vol. 17, No.4, Dec. 2005, Blackwell Publishing.

Tillich, P., *On the Boundary*, Collins, 1967.

Titmuss, R. M., *The Gift Relationship*, Allen & Unwin, 1971.

Troeltsch, E., *The Social Teachings of the Christian Churches*, Allen & Unwin, 1931.

Ward, K., *Is Religion Dangerous?* Lion, 2006.

Waterman, A., *Revolution, Economics and Religion: Christian Political Economy, 1798–1833*, Cambridge University Press, 2004.

Weber, M. *The Religion of China*, Free Press, 1951.

—— *The Religion of India*, Free Press, 1958.

—— *The Protestant Ethic and the Spirit of Capitalism*, Unwin University Books, 1970.

Wickham, E. R., *Church and People in an Industrial City*, Lutterworth Press, 1957.

Wilde, W., *Crossing the River of Fire: Mark's Gospel and Global Capitalism*, Epworth, 2006.

Wilkinson, R. G., *The Impact of Inequality: How to Make Sick Societies Healthier*, Routledge, 2005.

Wilson, B., *Religion in Sociological Perspective*, Oxford University Press, 1982.

Wilson, R., *Economics, Ethics and Religion: Jewish, Christian and Muslim Economic Thought*, Macmillan, 1997.

Wogaman, J. P., *Economics and Ethics: A Christian Enquiry*, SCM Press, 1986.

Wolf, M., *Why Globalization Works: The Case for the Global Market Economy*, Yale University Press, 2004.

Woodhead, L., Davie, G. and Heelas, P. (eds), *Predicting Religion: Christian Secular and Alternative Futures*, Ashgate, 2003.

Transfiguring Capitalism

Transfiguring Capitalism

Yates, T. (ed.), *Mission and the Next Christendom*, Cliff College Publishing, 2005.
Young, I., *Inclusion and Democracy*, Oxford University Press, 2000.

Index

Index

Index

Index

Russia 31, 49, 71, 82, 118
Ruston, R. 23

Saddleback megachurch 169, 172–5, 250
Salvation Army 114
sanctions 87–92, 94, 98, 124, 132–3, 142, 160, 221
Sandercock, L. 248, 250
Sao Paulo 78
Saudi Arabia 82
  Bank 189
scarcity 113, 139–40, 142, 203
  absolute 148, 152, 199, 276
  post 203, 209, 211, 228, 256, 260, 271, 280, 285, 289
Schkade, D. 121
Schumpeter, J. 59, 261
Schweiker, W. 233
Scotland 15–16, 52, 285
Scott, Sir W. 16
Scottish Executive Closing Gaps Programme 153
Scotus, D. 117, 132
Seattle 47, 60
secularization thesis 70–1, 84, 98, 175
Sedgwick, P. x, 241
Selfish Capitalism 45, 52, 118, 123, 127, 139, 242, 254, 280
Seligman, M. 117, 120–2, 135–6
Sen, A. 37, 115, 121, 125, 132, 152, 154, 158–9, 205, 218, 226, 260, 262, 279
Senegal 158
Seoul 78–9
setpoint 213
Shajarian, M. 158
Shanghai 64, 127
Shari'ah 190, 192
Sheffield 174, 255, 268
  Closing Gaps Policy 153
Sheldon, K. 121
Shosan, S. 51
Sicily 78
Sierra Leone 78
Singapore 127
single parents 122
Skali, F. 157
Skinner, H. x
small/medium sized enterprises 87
Smith, A. 4, 16, 20, 34, 36, 47, 52, 57, 62, 66, 88, 116, 121, 134, 141, 201, 220, 235, 262, 265
social gospel 143

sociology 6, 16–17, 54, 60, 70, 90–1, 97, 100, 115, 201, 204, 217, 234–5, 246
  of religion 84
Solidarity 222, 225, 226–8, 233–5, 264, 289
solidaristic individualism 96
Solow, R. 92
soul 116, 136, 157, 166, 186, 238, 267
Soulen, R. 213
  and Woodhead, L. 206–9
South Africa 78
South East Asia 23, 33, 140
Spain 23, 25, 33, 77, 144
  empire of 78, 202, 214
Special and Differential Treatment 154, 180, 264
spectrum 111, 124, 126–7, 130, 138, 145–6, 232, 247–50
  principles of 155
  of resurgent religion 70
  ethics to religion 151
spiritual currency programme 169, 172
spirituality 46, 85, 101–2, 124–6, 135–6, 149, 158–9, 160, 177–8, 217, 220, 222, 277
Spurgeon, C. 26
St Clement 207
St Cuthbert's Way 2
St Francis 46, 201, 236, 288
St Hilda 199
St Ignatius Loyola 136
St Irenaeus 214
St Johns College Durham 181
St Mark 198–9
St Paul 152
Stalin, J. 29, 171
state 17, 20, 22–4, 29, 36, 38–9, 43, 71, 81, 97, 171, 226, 234, 253, 255
  market 23, 33, 45, 57–8, 118
  -nation 23, 45
statues 171–2
Steedman, I. x, 180, 190–2, 263, 256, 275,
Steuart, Sir J. 5
stewardship 230, 239,, 241
Stiglitz, J. 264, 274
stocks and shares 22, 43
Storrar, W. x
story 79, 85, 101, 126, 156, 162, 167, 170, 175, 177–8, 206–9, 220, 222, 232, 235–6, 238, 267, 269, 283–5, 287, 289
strategic essentialism 210, 212–13
stress 134